Data Protection
Ensuring Data
Availability

Data Protection
Ensuring Data
Availability

Preston de Guise

CRC Press
Taylor & Francis Group
Boca Raton London New York

CRC Press is an imprint of the
Taylor & Francis Group, an **informa** business
AN AUERBACH BOOK

CRC Press
Taylor & Francis Group
6000 Broken Sound Parkway NW, Suite 300
Boca Raton, FL 33487-2742

Printed on acid-free paper
Version Date: 20161123

International Standard Book Number-13: 978-1-4822-4415-1

Visit the Taylor & Francis Web site at
http://www.taylorandfrancis.com

and the CRC Press Web site at
http://www.crcpress.com

Printed and bound in Great Britain by
TJ International Ltd, Padstow, Cornwall

Dedication

For Daz

Contents

Preface

This is the fundamental truth about data protection: backup is dead.

Or rather, *backup and recovery*, as a stand-alone topic, no longer has relevance in IT. As a stand-alone topic, it's been killed off by seemingly exponential growth in storage and data, by the cloud, and by virtualization.

So what is data protection?

This book takes a holistic, business-based approach to data protection. It explains how data protection is a mix of proactive and reactive planning, technology, and activities that allow for data continuity. It shows how truly effective data protection comes from a holistic approach considering the entire data life cycle and all required SLAs. Data protection is neither RAID nor is it continuous availability, replication, snapshots, or backups—it is all of them, combined in a considered and measured approach to suit the criticality of the data and meet all the requirements of the business.

The book also discusses how businesses seeking to creatively leverage their IT investments and to drive through cost optimization are increasingly looking at data protection as a mechanism to achieve those goals. In addition to being a type of insurance policy, data protection is becoming an enabler for new processes around data movement, copy data management, and data processing.

This book arms readers with information critical for making decisions on how data can be protected against loss in the Cloud, on premises, or a mix of the two. It explains the changing face of recovery in a highly virtualized datacenter and techniques for dealing with big data. Moreover, it presents a model for where data recovery processes can be integrated with IT governance and management in order to achieve the right focus on recoverability across the business.

Acknowledgments

Every book is an amalgam of ideas and feedback, and that's before you start to consider all the long-term background learning that goes into the foundation concepts. There's also the inevitable lost time with friends and family that comes from investing so much of yourself into a long-term creative project. So inevitably there's a host of people who specifically need to be called out in gratitude and thanks for their help in bringing this book to completion.

First and foremost, I have to thank my partner, Daz Woolley, for always being there for me—not only while I've been working on the book, but also throughout my career. He's been my continuously available backup, and every other pun you can think of for data protection for nigh on 20 years.

My parents put me on an IT path when I was relatively young, and actively encouraged me in my interests as I was growing up, culminating in funding university for me, letting me concentrate on my study throughout my time there. Lynne and Peter, I can never repay what you did for me all those years ago.

The book wouldn't have happened without the suggestion, feedback, encouragement, and patience of my editor, John Wyzalek, and I remain grateful for his insights and support over the years.

Of course I need to thank colleagues from around the world who donated their time to review and provide feedback for all the content of the book: Berin Smithson, Brendan Sandes, Conrad Macina, Danny Elmarji, Deborah van Petegem, Geordie Korper, German Garcia, Jerry Vochteloo, Jim Ruskowsky, Michael Arnold, Michael Levit, Mike van der Steen, Nicolas Groh, Pawel Wozniak, Peta Olson, Peter Hill-Cottingham, Rajesh Goda, Russell Brown, Steve de Bode, Tony Leung, Vedad Sapcanin, and Warren PowerJones. They are all spiritual brothers and sisters who all share a passion for data protection, and I'm hoping I didn't forget to mention anyone!

There's another group of people that need to be called out in thanks: my customers. Over the years I've been graced with a plethora of customers from the smallest to the largest, in pretty much every industry vertical, and it's been their trust in my work and my recommendations, and their collaboration with me on data protection projects, that's given me the depth *and* breadth of experience, both technical and business, that served as the foundations of this work.

Finally of course, I have to thank you, the reader, for having the interest in and desire to learn more about data protection: for being willing to invest your time to read what I have to say on the topic. I truly hope that if you're not actually already passionate about data protection, I'll have imparted some of my passion to you by the time you finish the book.

Author

Preston de Guise has been working with data recovery products for his entire career—designing, implementing, and supporting solutions for governments, universities, and businesses ranging from SMEs to Fortune 500 companies. This broad exposure to industry verticals and business sizes has enabled Preston to understand not only the technical requirements of data recovery but the management and procedural aspects too.

1 Introduction

In 1799, French forces discovered the Rosetta Stone. It contained on a single piece of stone the same decree, written in ancient Egyptian hieroglyphics, Demotic, and Ancient Greek. Until the discovery of the Rosetta Stone, ancient Egyptian hieroglyphics had been a mystery. Guesses had been made as to their meanings, but that was all. The Rosetta Stone allowed scholars to build an accurate translation mechanism by offering comparative text in other, known languages. In doing so, they opened up for us a realm of understanding that might otherwise been forever lost.

Human history is replete with examples of what happens when data is *not* adequately protected. Speculation abounds as to what information was lost with the destruction of the Library of Alexandria (pegged as happening during one of several events between AD 48 and AD 642), yet it remains indisputable that a significant amount of knowledge was, indeed, lost.

More than ever before, we are now at a crossroads in human information history: we have the capability of ensuring information is preserved, generation-to-generation, without loss.

This is data protection.

All the storage in the world will not help ensure continuity of information if adequate steps are not taken to preserve it. In a perfect world, no one would ever need Redundant Array of Independent Disks (RAID) protection, no one would ever need to recover files, and no one would need to protect against loss of site. It is not a perfect world: mechanical failures happen, as does corruption, accidental deletion, site failures, and malicious acts. The simplest part of preserving information is to store it—the more complex task is to *protect* it.

When examined in a silo situation, those who work in data protection preserve information for banks, for airlines, for search engines, for telecommunications companies, for small businesses, and even for individual people, but at a collective level, data protection is the pursuit of *information preservation.*

Information preservation of course is not just some ephemeral goal based on the noble act of protecting data for future generations. There are immediate, tangible business benefits too. A study conducted in 2014 on behalf of a leading storage vendor surveyed 3300 IT decision makers across 24 countries and determined approximately US$1.7 trillion was lost in incidents relating to data protection, either in terms of actual data loss, or the downtime associated with it in just 12 months. The average surveyed business lost more than 2 TB of data, yet only 64% of respondents claimed that data protection was critical to the success of their organization.*

---

* EMC Global Data Protection Index, http://www.emc.com/about/news/press/2014/20141202-01.htm.

1

1.1   THE LAY OF THE LAND

Backup is dead.

If it seems odd to the reader of a book titled *Data Protection* that one of the earliest statements of the book is *Backup is dead*, imagine how much more surreal it is to write it as a consultant who has worked with backup technology almost exclusively for nigh-on 20 years.

Yet, this is the fundamental truth about data protection: backup is dead.

Or rather, *backup and recovery*, as a stand-alone topic, no longer has relevance in IT. As a stand-alone topic, it's been killed off by seemingly exponential growth in storage and data, by *the cloud*, and by virtualization. Each one of these alone represents a substantial assault on backup and recovery as a dedicated topic, but combined, it's insurmountable.

Originally, backup and recovery systems were a function of system administrators. Over time, those systems evolved and became a specific job function. A company could have potentially hundreds of system administrators spread across a large number of geographic locations, but it might have backup services centralized and controlled by a small number of administrators operating out of a single location.

By itself backup and recovery does not offer sufficient scope for *data protection* for the needs of the modern business. Regardless of whether those backups are done via daily fulls, weekly fulls with daily incrementals, grandfather–father–son mixes of fulls, differentials and incrementals, or even *incrementals forever* and synthetic fulls, growing data and shrinking windows in service-level agreements have fundamentally altered the way organizations consider and plan data recoverability.

It used to be that saying *data protection* to someone meant *backup and recovery*. Such is the state of the business IT environment now that data protection is a considerably broader topic.

1.2   WHAT ARE YOU DOING HERE?

You've been looking forward to your holiday for months. You spent a year saving for it, then finally purchased the round-the-world ticket, organized the accommodation, booked dozens of hotels in the United States, the United Kingdom, France, China, Japan, and Australia. You've spent seemingly countless evenings working out things to do in each city you'll be visiting and budgeting how much you can spend in each country.

Then, when you turn up at the airport, you're told that the airline doesn't have your booking. You've got a printout of your ticket, *showing* your flight details, but those seats have been allocated to someone else who has already checked in: the airline lost your data.

Of course, that doesn't happen—businesses have long known that they have to take steps to ensure the recoverability of data. Losing airline bookings, forgetting salary payments, corrupting driver's license details—none of these are acceptable. Short of the provision of the service itself, nothing is more important in IT than data protection.

Conventional backup techniques have been around for decades. The *towers of Hanoi* backup regime may no longer be directly relevant, but *full*, *incremental* and *differential* levels remain the staple of the backup and recovery world.

As the song says, though, *the times, they are a changin'*. New approaches to service provisioning, higher volumes of data than we've ever seen before, and the commoditization of IT have demonstrated *peak scaling* in conventional techniques.

Vendors and mega IT companies—especially those at the apex of social media—are furiously rewriting the definition of a *datacenter*. Companies now have a plethora of options for their data—in-house conventional, in-house (private) cloud, hybrid cloud, colocation centers, or public cloud. That data may be substantially beyond the capabilities of conventional tools to analyze as well, regardless of where it's hosted.

With all of these options, and considering the snowball effect of virtualization in the midrange space, the conventional approaches to backup and recovery no longer economically scale to meet all options—and even when they do, the next challenge is whether or not they're even compatible with *where* the data is hosted.*

This book doesn't pretend to have all the answers—that's not really possible when the questions are still being written and revised sometimes seemingly on a daily basis. Ten years ago, when midrange virtualization was still a relatively young topic, and *cloud* was something that rained on you, such an assumption might have been made, but no more.

It's often the case that real knowledge comes not from knowing the answer to every question, but from knowing which questions you *don't* know the answer to.

1.3 WHAT'S CHANGED IN THE DATACENTER?

When I first started in backup, in 1996, the local datacenter of the company I worked for had

- A collection of Unix hosts (primarily Solaris, HPUX, and Tru64, but with a smattering of AT&T Unix systems as well)
- A collection of Windows NT4 servers
- A couple of Tandem FT servers
- An IBM mainframe
- Several VMS clusters
- Novell NetWare servers

In addition to that, there was the standard collection of tape drives, network switches and hubs, and a few other bits and pieces. There were even one or two systems still using reel-to-reel tapes, and someone would carry them out of the datacenter each morning, threaded onto arms like some fantastically over the top set of technological bracelets.

Storage was all either internal or Direct Attach Storage (DAS). There were some storage options just starting to appear in the datacenter that, when coupled with Veritas Volume Manager™ (VxVM), would allow volumes to be migrated from

---

* While we're on the topic of *midrange*, it's these systems with their cheap compute and storage costs that have driven so much of the data explosion. Long gone are the days when "serious" applications and data were reserved for mainframes or supercomputers.

one host to another, so long as both hosts were plugged into the same storage. *That* was cutting-edge technology.

I remember fighting, tooth and nail, for 2 × 2 GB SCSI hard drives for a mirror in a new backup server I was going to build so that I could store backup metadata such as indices.

Somewhere along the lines, VMware for Linux appeared, allowing Unix system administrators to switch to a Linux desktop and still access Windows, rather than running highly problematic emulation software. Midrange virtualization was arguably the catalyst that changed everything in IT.

The modern datacenter looks very different. It may not be on-site, and it may not be owned by the business using it. Colocation ("colo") facilities offer physical hosting services; cloud providers offer service or platform provisioning where the *equipment* that the company runs business critical applications on may not even belong to the company. For some businesses, the on-premise server room for a business may now be tiny compared to what it was 10 years ago, acting as a mere tip of the iceberg for a much larger presence in a shared datacenter or public cloud facility. For other businesses, particularly those centered around the bourgeoning mobile and cloud platform, there may be *no* datacenter, with all of their resources provided by a cloud service provider. Yet, public cloud is not a fait accompli; many businesses adopting a cloud model for agility are keeping their cloud private, and their datacenters are growing as they add petabytes—or even in some cases, *exabytes* of data.

1.4   WHAT IS DATA PROTECTION?

Ask the question, *"What is data protection?"* to a group of IT workers across a variety of fields, and the answer will vary substantially:

- "Backup," says a junior backup administrator
- "Recoverable backups," says a seasoned backup administrator
- "RAID," says a junior storage administrator
- "Replication and snapshots," says a seasoned storage administrator
- "Clustering," says a system administrator
- "Automated data replication," says a database administrator

About the only guarantee on this topic is that every answer will be correct, yet every answer will be *incomplete**. The reason for this is simple: data protection is *not* an IT function—it's a business function. IT may enact specific functional aspects of data protection, but the core decisions and processes should come as a result of close, strategic alignment between IT and the business.

For the purposes of this book:

> Data protection is the mix of proactive and reactive planning, technology, and activities that allow for data continuity.

This is shown in Figure 1.1.

---

* It is also worth remembering that "data protection" can be an overloaded term in IT. For other IT workers, "data protection" can be an umbrella term for security-related activities.

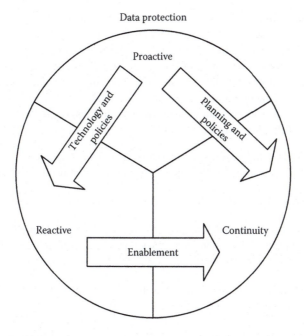

FIGURE 1.1 Data protection.

The proactive and reactive technologies are in themselves mostly straightforward:

- *Proactive*: Attempting to avoid data loss:
  - Backup
  - RAID
  - Snapshot
  - Replication
  - Continuous availability
- *Reactive*: Responding to data loss or situations that may lead to data loss:
  - Restoration and recovery
  - Rebuilding and reconstruction
  - Replication

Yet, none of these components can be reliably deployed without appropriate planning and policies. *Doing* is easy. Doing it *right* is another matter.

1.5 KEY CHALLENGES

1.5.1 RISE OF UNSTRUCTURED DATA

If you can recall data protection conversations businesses were having a decade or more ago, the key focus was more often than not the mission critical database systems requiring protection. While they present their own management and data protection challenges, databases were generally *easy* data protection sources because they represented that holy grail of data protection: structured data. Structured data keeps data all in one place, collated and condensed into predictable locations and stored in such a way as to allow for high-speed streaming or transfer of data.

Databases and the other various forms of structured data still exist within business, but unstructured data—file data, sensors, streams, and other disorganized information—has been growing rapidly for some time and shows no sign of slowing down. Unstructured data by its very nature is less predictable, less organized, less *known*, and as such more difficult to protect. An IDC whitepaper predicts the "digital universe":

> ... is doubling in size every two years, and by 2020 the digital universe – the data we create and copy annually – will reach 44 zetabytes, or 44 trillion gigabytes.*

IDC acknowledges that much of this "digital universe" is transient:

> Most of the digital universe is transient – unsaved Netflix or Hulu movie streams, or Xbox One gamer interactions, temporary routing information in networks, sensor signals discarded when no alarms go off, etc.†

This data transience is a boon for data storage since data storage itself is growing at a slower rate than the digital universe. IDC added:

> In 2013, the available storage capacity could hold just 33% of the digital universe. By 2020, it will be able to store less than 15%.‡

Estimates for the percentage of unstructured versus structured data (both now and in the future) vary from the very conservative 50% unstructured through to the highly worrying 80% or more.

Unstructured data has been making its mark in the traditional datacenter for some time and has led to the concept of *scale-out* network attached storage (NAS). NAS has been traditionally expanded by adding shelves or trays of disks until an array is at its maximum size, then deploying a new NAS to accommodate new systems. This worked for multi-terabyte storage, but as data growth continued created excessive management and data migration headaches—and of course the staffing cost associated with managing so many storage arrays continued to balloon. Scale-out NAS works on the principle of an ever-increasing number of nodes (physical storage appliances) attached to a single addressable storage system, with the filesystem(s) presented dynamically expanding (scaling out) as nodes are added. This allows for a company to meet unstructured data growth without seeing their storage administrator staffing costs skyrocket. Scale-out NAS allows businesses to have multiple *petabytes* of storage under the control of a single administrator.

Of course, scale-out NAS isn't the only solution to unstructured data, but it helps to demonstrate how businesses are already adapting their data storage solutions (and vendors, their offerings) to deal with this onslaught of potentially disorganized data.

---

* Vernon Turner, David Reinsel, John F. Gantz, Stephen Minton, The digital universe of opportunities: Rich data and the increasing value of the internet of things, IDC, April 2014, IDC_1672.
† Ibid.
‡ Ibid.

1.5.2 BIG DATA

Big data is often characterized by the "four Vs"—volume, variety, velocity, and veracity,* where

- *Volume* refers to the *amount* of data being dealt with
- *Velocity* refers to the speed at which data is coming in (or going past)
- *Variety* refers to the seemingly inexhaustible number of forms data may take now
- *Veracity* refers to the measure of reliability (of accuracy) of the data

All of these *on their own* present unique challenges to data protection planning within an organization—combined, they can represent a substantial headache to coherent, reliable, and cost-effective protection solutions. Big data requires big, bold data protection strategies and relies on a very meticulous data classification program, something we'll cover more in Chapter 2.

1.5.3 CLOUD

Stepping away from which particular model might be considered (private, public, hybrid, etc.), cloud computing is potentially the greatest disruptive factor to the traditional IT environment that we've ever seen, and it's being increasingly adopted. It represents the commodization of IT functions and deployment models through self-service portals and multitiered service catalogs. Except in perhaps the smallest of businesses, it won't *end* the IT department, but it will have a profound impact on the way IT departments run and present services to the core business in almost all organizations.

Using a simple web interface, a person untrained in IT can deploy core business IT systems such as email, customer relationship management (CRM), and database servers with minimum effort … but at what cost of data protection? This has led to the term *shadow IT*, which is as concerning in practice as it sounds.

> *Case in point*: In most modern countries, a mandatory requirement to driving a car is getting formal approval from a government body to be allowed to *drive* a car: getting a driver's license. Having a driver's license verifies someone has obtained sufficient knowledge of the road rules and demonstrated a practical ability to drive a car on a road. Shadow IT is akin to anyone being able to get in a car and drive without getting a driver's license. Sure, there is nothing *technically* stopping people from doing it, but the implications can be serious—and dangerous—if the person turns out to make the wrong decisions from a lack of formal training.

The industry abounds with stories of businesses who trusted in a single public cloud provider only to have their entire operations grind to a halt during cloud-wide disruptions, and when you're just one customer among hundreds or hundreds of *thousands*, that self-service model via predefined service catalog options might force a number of compromises on data recoverability or protection in return for

---

* Veracity is a relatively new addition to what was previously the 3Vs approach to explaining big data.

a cheaper deployment method. Many cloud providers provide data protection that is limited solely to protecting the base *infrastructure* only—the subscriber often remains blissfully unaware that their own data is largely unrecoverable for most situations until it is too late.

Yet still, cloud is here to stay, and both IT and business personnel must focus a high level of attention to the data protection considerations of its use or else risk the entire organization to ultimate data disaster scenarios. This is why IT departments in organizations must realign themselves to be able to *broker* cloud services; by doing so, they can vet the available cloud services, picking or designing the ones that match business requirements, ensuring they're safe and compatible with Service Level Agreements (SLAs) and/or Service Level Objectives (SLOs). Returning to our driver's license analogy: by taking control of the cloud experience, IT departments have the opportunity to ensure if someone jumps into a car without a license they put neither themselves nor others at risk.

1.5.4 Virtualization

What was once the domain of mainframe systems only, virtualization is now a cornerstone in the IT environment for almost all businesses. It allows for high-density application and business functions through optimized use of compute, storage, and memory and introduces enhanced management functions as a result of entire hosts being nothing more than moveable data. Virtualization is expanding to encompass storage, networks, and almost everything else in the datacenter, and each item in turn raises new considerations for the data protection administrators within a business. In a little more than a decade, we've seen the rise of virtual servers, virtual storage, virtual networking, and even the *virtual datacenter*. Seemingly everything in IT now can be software defined. This provides new opportunities for highly customized control, but equally presents new challenges for ensuring we don't forget about data protection along our *software-defined* journey.

1.5.5 The Law

Digital data retention was once a very informal thing. Some businesses would approach it from a reasonably formal perspective of mapping old-style record retention requirements, others would retain what they could and not worry about the rest, and others would deliberately delete data as soon as possible, regardless of whether or not an impartial observer might consider it to be morally correct. It was entirely possible to be told any of the following within an IT department:

- We keep everything because it's just safer that way.
- We only keep email for mid-level executives and higher for more than 12 months.
- We get told to delete all email older than 6 months for "space" reasons.
- We have no idea what retention we have to apply to data.
- The business has no idea what retention we have to apply to data.
- The business hasn't told us how long we have to keep data for, and if we don't ask, we can't be blamed.

Numerous scandals and major financial crashes have seen this lasses-faire approach to electronic data retention largely disappear. While smaller organizations may sometimes be ignorant of their data retention requirements, larger organizations, enterprises, and businesses operating in a financial or legal sphere will now be intimately aware of what sort of data they need to retain and how long they need to retain it for. This is a major realignment from the datacenters of old and has introduced new constraints on how data protection strategies need to be developed, what sort of data protection storage can be used, and how rigorous businesses need to be about ensuring data is not prematurely removed.

1.5.6 CRIME

Just like the rest of IT, criminal use of IT has continued to evolve. Where once we were worried about viruses causing system crashes, worms deleting data, or denial of service attacks flooding external connectivity, we're now in an era where criminal organizations and individuals seek to inflict maximum damage or extort as much money as they can. The attack-de-jour that keeps IT managers and board members awake of a night time now is cryptographic—viruses that don't *delete* data, but instead *encrypt* it. *Ransomware* packages in the hands of criminals can create significant financial impact on businesses: "pay up or never see your data again." A single cryptographic attack within a business can result in it losing hundreds of gigabytes or more of data unless steep ransoms are paid—tens or hundreds of thousands of dollars are now being regularly paid out by businesses desperate to get their data back. We are also seeing a rise in *hactivism* and similar attacks. This is where a business is specifically targeted in a meticulously planned (or at least executed) way. There have been multiple examples already of businesses where hackers, having penetrated the network, delete backups and other forms of data protection *first*, before moving on to delete or encrypt data on original systems. (This new type of threat is already driving an evolution in data protection practices which we will cover later.)

1.6 A BRIEF HISTORY OF DATA PROTECTION

It's worth starting this book by looking back at how data protection has evolved over the decades. We start with Figure 1.2.

As computer use grew, it became apparent that it was necessary to protect the data that was being stored on them. The starting point for the most part was a

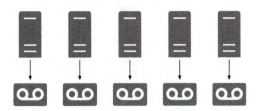

FIGURE 1.2 Completely decentralized backup strategy.

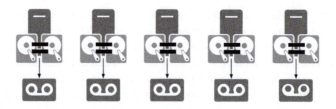

FIGURE 1.3   RAID added a new layer of data protection for business.

completely decentralized backup strategy where tape drives would be attached to each server deployed. Backups would be run nightly (sometimes less frequently), and there would be a modicum of protection available in the event of a system failure. Over time though as disk capacities increased while prices (slowly) decreased, the amount of data stored on servers grew. Likewise, the criticality of the data to the business increased, and the *tolerance* within the business to a sustained outage due to hardware failure fell. This resulted in adding RAID to server storage to allow systems to continue to operate even if a disk failed, such as that shown in Figure 1.3.

With RAID we could achieve higher levels of availability, protection, and hardware failure tolerance, but through it all we still needed backup.

As the number of servers within a business grew, the practicality of deploying tape drives on every single server for backup fell sharply. Tapes might have been comparatively cheap compared to disk, but since the amount of data on a server was traditionally tiny compared to the capacity of tapes, every tape that was sent off-site would usually be half empty—or more. Media wastage was common.

The next phase was to start centralizing backup operations, shown in Figure 1.4.

By shifting to a client/server architecture, backup protection storage—at this point still tape—could be centralized at a single host in the environment and more productive use could be made of the tape media. Tapes could be filled more regularly, and

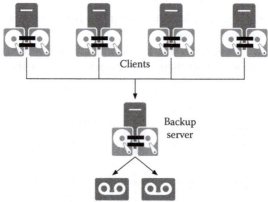

FIGURE 1.4   Centralized backup topology.

because a backup server wasn't doing business production activities, it could start to do additional data protection activities, such as duplicating backups for higher levels of redundancy during recovery.

Particularly in the midrange systems market this drove the adoption of tape libraries to further consolidate resources—rather than individual drives that required tapes to be manually changed, increasingly larger units could be deployed with multiple tape drives and slots for tens, hundreds, or even (over time) thousands of tapes all within the reach of a robotic arm.

Another consolidation was starting to happen in the datacenter around the same time though—centralized *storage*. This allowed for more efficient use of disk, easier management, and more RAID levels. It also allowed the individual servers accessing the data to have data management decoupled—the central storage server would take care of that. This ended up in a layout similar to that shown in Figure 1.5.

The advent of centralized storage systems increased online and storage-related protection activities. Whereas the previous focus had simply been around RAID to protect against individual drive failure, new options were needed both from the centralization of the storage and continually shrinking outage tolerances. Thus, snapshots and replication entered the datacenter—shown in high level in Figure 1.6.

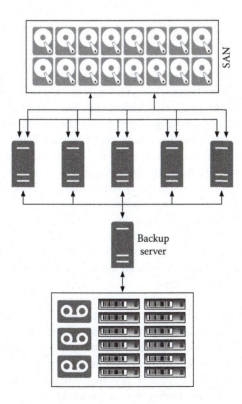

FIGURE 1.5   Centralized storage *and* centralized backups.

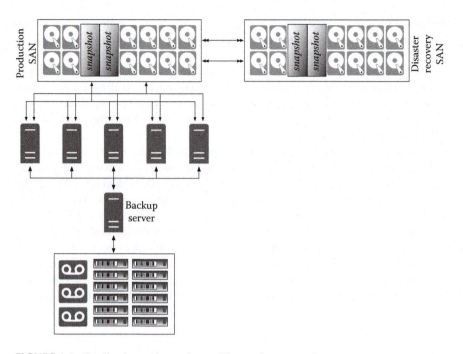

FIGURE 1.6   Replication and snapshots adding to data protection.

The volume of data in the datacenter was continuing to explode, and centralized backup servers were becoming increasingly unable to handle the load. Scaling occurred by introducing secondary backup servers—"media servers" or "storage nodes," dedicated to data movement and under the direction of a backup server that may or may not still actually perform backups itself. Fiber channel networks in particular—originally developed for access to centralized storage systems—played a critical part in this by allowing multiple systems to access the same tape infrastructure (though often at the price of stability and reliability). Thus, the three-tier backup environment became commonplace, shown in Figure 1.7.

With the introduction of storage nodes or media servers, the three-tier backup environment also became a 3.5-tier backup environment as that same media throughput functionality often migrated into the backup client software as well, allowing the largest systems to also connect to shared tape infrastructure to reduce the network impact and speed up their backups.

As disk capacities increased and their prices started to fall more dramatically on a $/GB ratio, the inherent limitations of tape became increasingly apparent. While the performance of tape is excellent for streaming sustained loads, it comes at the cost of easy, random access, or efficient handling of gaps and pauses in a stream. Systems were growing to have millions or tens of millions of files, and the backup process in reading from these types of systems suffered inherent limitations. Thus, we evolved to the notion of staging storage for backup—"backup to disk to tape," shown in Figure 1.8.

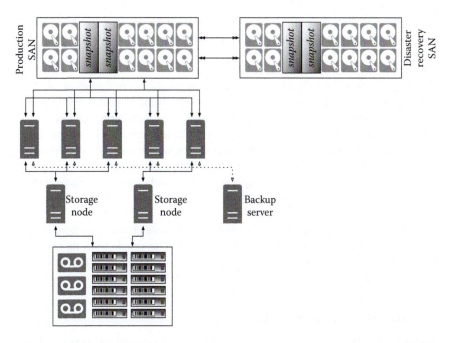

FIGURE 1.7 Three-tier backup environment.

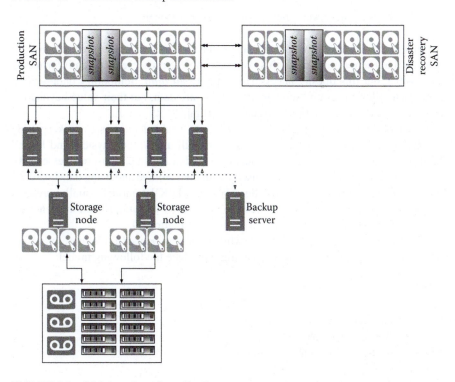

FIGURE 1.8 Disk-based staging of backups.

Still data protection continued to evolve. As will be discussed in their specific chapters, we've seen additional enhancements including

- Continuously available storage
- Continuous data protection—journalled, application-aware replication
- Purpose-built backup appliances—offering advanced protection options and reducing the overall backup storage footprint with deduplication
- Integrated data protection appliances—offering capability beyond just backup, integrating deeply with end point applications and storage systems
- Advanced snapshots at the storage and virtualization layers
- Elimination of tape from backup workloads entirely for some organizations
- Protection for data moved to or born in the cloud

There have been multiple points in the history of data protection where it's been declared innovation is over—or no longer required. The simple truth though is that data protection has been forced to grow and evolve as the volume and criticality of data has evolved.

1.7   THE MISERLY HOARDER

There's a common enough saying in the traditional backup and recovery discipline:

> It's always better to backup a little too much than not enough.

This is true of the broader topic of data protection, but newer technologies are proving that there *are* limits to this. We may want to preserve as much information as possible, but this doesn't necessarily apply to all *data*. Temporary data—cache print cache files, program "scratch" files, etc.—are data, but their value beyond the momentary executed function is arguably negligible.

Constantly increasing storage capacities have enabled businesses to keep truly staggering amounts of data online—yet, there will always be physical and logical limits to the amount of data it is practicable to hold or manage. Thus, businesses have to walk the fine line between being miserly with their storage and being data hoarders.

The Data, Information Knowledge, Wisdom(DIKW) model usually presents us with a good explanation of the need to be focused in data protection scenarios. A simple representation of this model is shown in Figure 1.9.

The DIKW model emphasizes that while data may be useful it's more of a *start* rather than *end* point. For instance, we might produce the following model:

- *Data*:
    - An item is red.
    - An item is round.
    - An item is edible.
- *Information*: The item is a tomato.
- *Knowledge*: Tomato is a fruit.
- *Wisdom*: Tomato doesn't go in fruit salad.

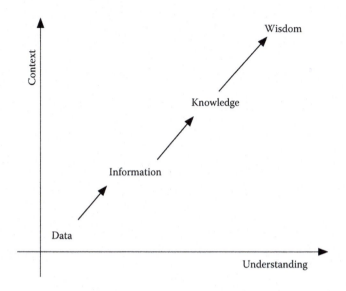

FIGURE 1.9 DIKW model.

Consider a grocery store: there's potentially a lot of data to track and protect when it comes to their supplies, but it's unlikely the store would specifically need to track the number of *red* items it has in stock or the number of *round* items it has in stock. It *might* track the number of *edible* things it has in stock, and it would definitely want to track the number of tomatoes it has in stock.

At the most primitive level, this is the line businesses must walk between being data hoarders and miserly with their data, and that same line must be walked for the protection of the data, too, and that will be the focus of Chapter 2.

2 Contextualizing Data Protection

2.1 INTRODUCTION

Data protection is an umbrella term that encompasses multiple information disciplines, including storage, backup and recovery, and systems and application administration, just to name a few.

As mentioned in the introduction, there are two distinct fields of activity within data protection: *proactive* and *reactive*. Proactive activities refer to such areas as

- *Storage*:
  - RAID (and other low-level protection methodologies)
  - Snapshots
  - Replication
  - Continuous data protection (CDP)
  - Continuous availability
- *Backup*:
  - Establishing backup and recovery systems
  - Maintaining systems and adding hosts for protection

On the other hand, reactive activities focus on

- *Repair*:
  - Reconstruction (automatic or manual) following storage failure
- *Recovery*:
  - Retrieval of information from backup systems
- *Restore*:
  - Reinstating integrity of recovered data (usually an activity relating to databases and other complex applications)*

In order to have a true data protection strategy, a business needs to focus holistically on both proactive and reactive activities, and these activities *must* be considered synergistically rather than individually. Without that approach, a business can develop storage strategies, and backup/recovery strategies, but these will be silo-like in nature: lacking in both efficiency and capability.

---

* While the terms *recover* and *restore* may seem synonymous, they are often perceived as being quite different, particularly in the realm of database administration. This allows database and application administrators to differentiate between the act of retrieving *crash-consistent* data (recovery) and the act of applying *application consistency* (restore) to that data. We'll cover terms such as crash-consistency and application-consistency in later chapters.

Merging storage and backup processes is often seen as being the *key* approach to developing an effective data protection strategy. While this is important, there's another step—a precursor step—many organizations pay insufficient attention to measurement.

One of the most central tenets of almost all processes, including project management, ITIL* and COBIT† (just to name a few), is the simple truism:

If you can't measure something, you can't improve it.

By *improve*, it's not just a case of random pot luck or educated guesses, but actual tangible results, such as being able to assert an anticipated percentage improvement in return for a particular investment in terms of cost and time—and then confirm whether or not it was achieved.

The same is true of data protection—but contrary to popular belief, that doesn't start with being able to measure your backup and/or recovery speeds, or the length of time it takes a RAID-6 system to rebuild after a drive failure. Those are important metrics, and metrics that are essential to understanding service-level offerings and capabilities within a business, but they're not the *starting* metrics; the starting point for the metrics actually derive from data classification.

Many businesses will go out of their way to avoid data classification, believing it to be too hard or too costly (or both). It's something regularly shied away from, its utility questioned, and its expense exaggerated. The negativity toward data classification invariably comes from a perception that at whatever time it's discussed there's already too much unclassified data in the business to ever allow the process to complete. As the amount of unclassified data in the business grows, this becomes a self-fulfilling prophecy. Like a proverbial ostrich with its head stuck in the sand, this approach simply means the business remains unaware of the holes and gaps in a data protection strategy that has been built on shaky foundations.

We will see in this chapter why data classification is imperative for the purposes of building a holistic and successful data protection strategy.

2.2 DATA CLASSIFICATION

Data classification, regardless of how formally it is done within an environment, provides the baseline metrics required for data protection and ultimately assists in identifying data by five fundamental questions about data—what, where, who, when, and how:

- *What* is the data?
- *Where* is the data?
- *Who* uses the data?
- *When* is the data used?
- *How* is the data used?

---

* Information Technology Infrastructure Library.
† Control Objectives for Information and related Technologies.

In a broader scope, data classification is used within information lifecycle management (ILM) to address other management aspects of data, including access restrictions and regulatory compliance relating to the data. Thus, a fully established data classification process operating as an ongoing exercise will yield substantial benefits to a business—both at the frontline and in relation to back-end processes. The value to the business extends far beyond that of making data protection more accurate.

2.2.1 What Is the Data?

The first metric—arguably the most important metric—is to know *what* you actually *need* to protect. If you can't measure and articulate that, you're designing blind. If you can't say *what* your data is, you can't in any meaningful way argue that it's being adequately protected, regardless of operational metrics such as the success rates of your backup/recoveries or the reliability of your storage systems.

> *Case in point*: You might be able to get 100% successful backups of 100% of your servers from a file-level agent, but if every one of those servers has a database on it, it is likely every single one of those backups is useless for the purposes of recovery.

For data protection to be effective, you need to not only understand what you're protecting, but what you're *not* protecting—and in both cases, this needs to be documented. While everyone understands the need to document what *is* backed up, documenting what *isn't* tends to be less understood. If we compare data protection to an insurance policy, we can immediately see why—insurance policies are *always* written with exclusions and disclaimers as to what is and isn't covered. It's just as important to know what events *aren't* covered by your home insurance policy as knowing what events are. Similarly, keeping accurate documentation as to what data *isn't* protected allows a business to gauge the level of risk it's exposed to *and* determine whether that's acceptable.

Except for particularly special environments, data isn't stagnant. The way the business uses it adapts over time, and the content can obviously change as well. This can happen in three distinct ways:

- *Seasonally*: The importance placed on data may depend on the time of the year. Educational facilities, for instance, will have maximized requirements for data protection on enrolment data for a period of months around the start of a new educational year. Financial organizations will require additional protection processes during end-of-month (EOM) and end-of-financial-year (EOFY) situations, and so on.
- *Evolutionarily*: Some data will grow and change with the business: standard financial records, filesystem data, etc.
- *Revolutionarily*: Few, if any, businesses work entirely in a vacuum, independent of the marketplace. Businesses may face revolutionary changes to the importance of their data as new competitors emerge, or existing

competitors introduce substantially new products. In such times, the company may be forced to adopt completely different business approaches, which in turn may leverage their data and information systems in substantially alternate ways. Additionally, companies leveraging research or exploration can face major new data requirements whenever these activities pay off. For example, a pharmaceutical company may bring a new drug onto the market or an exploration company may find and start working on mining a new gold deposit.

In short: What was unimportant last month or last year may be important in 3 months time—but if the data was lost or forgotten about because of its *perceived* irrelevance, it's likely no-one will notice that it's become important until too late.

An understanding of *what* the data is will immediately set some broad parameters on how the data will be protected. For instance, consider the following collections of data:

- *Business critical database*: Core business operations require this database to be up and available at all times.
- *Corporate fileserver*: Used by significant number of users for standard file storage.
- *Development database*: Used by the database/application administration team to develop new functionality for the business critical database systems.
- *Software installation repository*: Used to hold all the various installers, packages, and stand-alone binaries deployed by the company for the build of laptops, desktops, and servers.

Each of these systems will trigger completely different data protection strategies (Table 2.1).

TABLE 2.1
Sample Data Protection Strategies Based on What the Data Is

Collection	RAID	Snapshots	Replication	Backup
Business critical database	RAID10	Hourly, 24×7, expiring after 48 hours	Synchronous	Nightly full, half-hourly incremental log backups
Corporate fileserver	RAID6	Hourly from 7 am to 7 pm, retained for 1 week	Asynchronous	Weekly synthetic full, daily incremental from 6 pm snapshot
Development database	RAID5	None	None	Nightly full
Software installation repository	RAID5	Weekly	Asynchronous	Quarterly full

2.2.2 WHERE IS THE DATA?

In addition to needing to know *what* you need to protect, you equally need to know *where* it is. This serves two key purposes:

1. *Data placement*: You could have three arrays maintaining synchronous replicas of RAID-10 volumes, with each array asynchronously replicating to other arrays geographically dispersed around the world, knowing that if a single hard drive or a single array fails, there's no way you'll lose any data *as long as that data is stored on the arrays*. If you can't be certain that the data will be *on* the arrays, then you equally can't be certain that your data protection system works.
2. *Protection options*: Many businesses refer to different *tiers* of data protection (e.g., "gold," "silver," and "bronze"). Once data has been located, it is usually the case that various forms of data protection will fall into place based on the redundancy options associated with the storage.

Consider as well both cloud services and colocation/shared datacenter facilities: as such, asking *where is the data* is potentially a significantly more complex question than even 10 years ago. Discovering data locality is no longer a case of determining if it's on a server, storage array, or laptop, but covers a multitude of options, including

- Is it on centralized business-owned storage?
- Is it stored on desktops/laptops?
- Is it stored only on mobile devices? (Phones, tablets)
- Is it stored in a colocation facility?
- Is it stored in a cloud? If so
  - Public?
  - Private?
  - Hybrid?
  - Geographically, where in the world is the cloud?

If data is determined to be stored in a colocation facility or cloud, this raises additional questions that must be considered around the data protection services offered for those locations and can lead to alternate service-level agreements (SLAs) tiered on locality alone. For example, consider sample SLAs for recovery time objective (RTO) of data based on whether the data is stored traditionally, in a hybrid cloud or a fully public cloud (Table 2.2).

In such scenarios, for instance, it may be that no data protection activities are taken on bronze data in a public cloud, and this would require reseeding from a private source. Alternately, while a 1-hour RTO may be *desirable* for gold public data, the longer RTO may recognize the potential for longer outages where the business is just one customer among many, rather than being completely in control of its own datacenter. As such, the SLAs documented may not be representative of the ideal goals of the business, but of the hard limitations of the chosen location for the data, and becomes statistical information that feeds into the decision-making process on where data

TABLE 2.2

Sample RTO SLAs for Data Types Based on Locality of Data

	Traditional or Private Cloud	Hybrid Cloud	Public Cloud
Gold	1 hour	4 hours	8 hours
Silver	4 hours	8 hours	24 hours
Bronze	1 day	2 days	7 days

will be stored*. (One mistake made by some cloud adopters, for instance, is failing to reconcile internal business SLAs with those offered by the cloud services providers for the storage and systems their data and applications reside on.)

Seemingly a simple question, *where is the data* provides a wealth of information for data protection activities.

2.2.3 WHO USES THE DATA?

The importance of data, and therefore how it is to be protected, will often be measured against the user(s) accessing it. In some instances, this will be due to the number of users who access it, and in other instances, it will be due to the *roles* of the users accessing it.

This introduces a more difficult to quantify consideration that still has to be factored into the data protection equation, notably *perceived* versus *actual* importance by user role. For instance, in accounting or legal firms, it's not uncommon to see considerably more attention paid to data protection for partners with a financial stake in the organization than for standard employees within the business, regardless of what those employees do. While someone in IT may not necessarily see the difference between the sets of data accessed by the different user roles, the *business* does and therefore we can say that the *perceived* importance overrides the *actual* importance. (Or to be more accurate: the perceived importance *becomes* the actual importance.)

While this may not necessarily impact the actual data protection mechanisms invoked from a technical perspective, it may impact the SLAs and operational-level agreements (OLAs) established around that protection.

2.2.4 WHEN IS THE DATA USED?

Data protection activities are typically *secondary production* activities, with the actual work done by the business being *primary production* activities. A common mistake, even in the data protection industry, is to classify data protection as *nonproduction*. This is a fallacy: it's a secondary production activity or a production support activity. Regardless, its function is a production one.

---

* In other instances, businesses may require the same SLA for data tiers regardless of where the data lives. This still requires an understanding of data placement however, since it will alter the protection options deployed in the various possible locations of the data.

As *secondary* production activities, however, it's critical that data protection does not unduly interfere with the actual work the company needs to do. For smaller businesses and noncritical systems in larger enterprises, that simply means backups run outside of standard business hours. However, it can fundamentally change *how* the protection takes place for those businesses with 24×7 requirements.

Data may also have different use cycles—financial account databases, for instance, require extreme availability during the day for banking institutions, but may not become immediately available for backup purposes after end-of-business. Such systems may instead be required for use in batch processing systems, further reducing the window of availability presented to data protection administrators. An entire subset of data protection is devoted to 24×7 use cases, that being CDP.

2.2.5 How Is the Data Used?

As much as anything this refers to the activity profile of the data and covers a variety of questions including (but not limited to)

- Is it read-only, used only for referential purposes?
- If the data isn't read-only, how regularly is it updated?
  - Daily?
  - Weekly?
  - Monthly?
  - Even less frequently?
- Is the data *transient*? Transient data is that which passes from system to system, requiring protection only in one location (usually the original source).
- Is it immediately visible data?
  - To the public?
  - Internally only?
  - A mix?
- Is the data directly worked on, or is it *reference* data? Meaning
  - If the data is directly worked on
    - What is the criticality of the data to the business processes it relates to?
    - What is the criticality of those business processes to the business?
  - If the data *is* reference data:
    - How many systems and applications reference the data?
    - How critical are *those* systems and applications?
    - How would those systems function without the data being available?

While this is often considered from the perspective of how the data is to be stored, it also directly impacts the level and frequency of data protection required.

Consider, for instance, traditional backup and recovery strategies, which see backups run once every 24 hours. If data is likely to only change at most once or twice a day, then that 24-hour data protection approach may be sufficient. If it's likely to change *hundreds* of times a day, additional strategies involving storage snapshots, replication or CDP may also need to be taken into consideration.

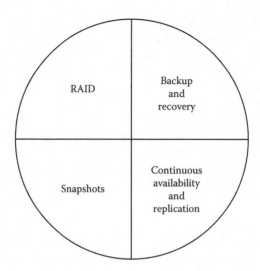

FIGURE 2.1   Information lifecycle protection strategies.

2.3   PROTECTION METHODOLOGY

While ILM does have an operational context to refer to data protection, I prefer to think of there being a sibling activity to ILM, that being information lifecycle protection (ILP).

In this sense, ILP is the recognition that data protection doesn't necessarily come from a single stream of activities or that protection mechanism remains the same for the entire lifespan of the information. As information ages, or as its access model changes, so too might the protection mechanisms applied for it. The four core activities or strategies within ILP are shown in Figure 2.1.

A *storage* strategy within an organization will consider RAID levels and snapshots, as well as replication, but won't necessarily consider backup and recovery. For mission critical 24 × 7 requirements, the storage strategy may even include continuous availability. Equally, a *backup and recovery* strategy within an organization will focus on that function, but not necessarily consider the storage. A true *data protection* strategy, on the other hand, will consider all four aspects together since they all play a role in ensuring data availability.

The importance of holistic developing data protection strategies rather than independent storage and backup/recovery strategies is simple: combined, they synergistically offer a better solution than either could in isolation.

2.4   PROTECTION VERSUS REGENERATION

When planning protection strategies, there's one other option to consider: whether the cost of protecting the data exceeds the cost of regenerating it. In this consideration, cost can refer to any of

- *Time*: How long it takes to be protected
- *Accuracy*: How accurate the regeneration is
- *Fiscal (Protection)*: Dollar price of protecting the data
- *Fiscal (Regeneration)*: Dollar cost of regenerating the data

For many types of conventional data and data sources, this isn't a discussion point—an airline booking system, for instance, can't possibly be recovered in the event of failure by asking customers to recreate their bookings, nor can medical records at a hospital be recreated by doctors and nurses re-entering details.

Decisions that can impact whether or not data will be protected or regenerated include

- *Original or copy?* Data that is original is more likely to require protection. Data that is a copy (e.g., a test/development copy of a production database) may not need the same level of data protection, if at all. (Transient data, merely being accessed from another source, will also likely fall into the "copy" category except for very rare circumstances.)
- *Organic or predictable?* Random data, such as that coming from end users, standard interactions, and normal use scenarios, is more likely to require data protection. Data that can be recreated by rerunning calculations against locked or read-only data and collecting the results may require less data protection.
- *Importance of specific content?* Data whose content itself is not immediately valuable (just the presence of it) may not necessarily need protecting. For example, random blocks of data used for performance testing, or corporate web-proxy data, may be considered sufficiently unimportant from a *specific* content perspective that they can be allowed to repopulate rather than be recovered.*

2.5 ORGANIZATIONAL CHANGE

It's no longer sufficient to merely have *backup policies* and *storage policies* when those policies are isolated from one another, either in their development or their operation. A variety of factors, including data growth, data use, and data locality, mean that it's absolutely critical for businesses to focus more on *data protection* policies that encompass all aspects of data protection—storage, replication, backup/recovery, and regeneration.

By necessity, this can lead to different organizational approaches. In the late 1990s, it became popular to separate enterprise backup administration into its own team to reflect the broader centralization that was taking place. Rather than having backup administrators for Unix, for Windows, and so on, there would be a single team of administrators providing backup services to all of IT and by extension, the

---

* Alternately if it were necessary to say repeat performance tests on new systems, keeping that random data in order to ensure test consistency might be entirely justifiable, but requiring a substantially lower tier data protection than, say, mission critical database data.

entire business. This entirely made sense, and businesses that followed that lead were almost invariably able to deliver far more efficient and cost-effective backup and recovery solutions than those who kept the backup strategies for each operating system or application siloed.

Centralized backup administration is still critical to a robust data protection policy, but it's no longer enough in and of itself. Instead, centralized backup administration must be combined with centralized storage administration so that fully dependable and appropriate data protection policies can be developed, implemented, and maintained.

Indeed, we're now seeing the emergency of a new breed of administrators within IT organizations, driven by hyper-convergence and the need for agility—the infrastructure administrator. These administrators need to have control over and input into the storage, virtualization and data protection processes, and a data protection solution that doesn't include infrastructure administration focus is likely to be insufficient.*

2.6 SUMMARY

Data protection is no longer as straightforward an activity as it was once considered. Data growth, changing locality, and increased reliance on 24×7 operations means that the more simplistic approaches for data protection developed in previous decades are now unaligned to business requirements.

Of course, that doesn't mean data protection is impossible—but just like any other evolving field, it now requires greater maturity and thought in order to successfully solve the problems faced by businesses.

Achieving adequate data requires a more centralized approach and a broader understanding of the classification of data within the organization. Without both of these aspects, a business is more likely to have isolated and inefficient policies covering *just* storage or *just* recovery.

Once the data is classified and understood, the next challenge becomes obvious: how to manage it in the context of data protection. This has significant overlap with the broader topic of ILM, and we'll refer to it as the *data lifecycle*, a topic to be discussed in detail in the following chapter.

---

* This of course doesn't reduce the need for application, database, and system administrators to be involved in the data protection process. In fact, we are seeing a new type of data protection evolve now where administrators and architects have control over the broad policies for backups and copies, as well as the protection storage, while application and database administrators are able to maintain control over day to day data protection operations.

3 Data Life Cycle

3.1 INTRODUCTION

Developing data protection policies in isolation and disconnected from any planning around data life cycle is a serious problem for any business to make. For example, a common criticism of backup and recovery in general is it's a "budget black hole"—that is, money is sunk into it without any return. Disregarding for the moment that the critical return from an adequately funded backup and recovery system is the insurance of being able to recover data when needed, there are two other key factors that lead to this erroneous attitude, namely:

- Unmanaged, unpredicted data growth
- Insufficient secondary use case scenarios of backup data

The second factor will be discussed later in the book, but the first often stems from a core failure to maintain an appropriate data life cycle.

Data life-cycle management is something that should be absolutely fundamental to the IT organization within any business, yet remains randomly or haphazardly implemented in most. For many organizations, data life-cycle "management" resembles a process similar to that shown in Figure 3.1.

Ideally, after we have first created then used data for its purpose and have no legal, operational, or functional requirement to keep it, deleting it makes sense: it removes the ongoing storage and protection requirements for that data. More often than not however, once data use is complete, it instead stagnates on primary storage, consuming space but not providing any benefit in return.

Ideally, data life-cycle management should follow a process similar to that shown in Figure 3.2.

While there is more background work going on than the diagram would suggest (particularly in relation to storage management and protection), the actual life cycle of the data is summed up in the diagram. Once data has been created, it will be used for a particular period of time (with the amount of time usually being specific to the function and content of the data), then once the primary usage cycle for the data has expired, the future of the data should be considered. This future should be one of only two functions:

1. The data is *deleted*.
2. The data is *archived*, meaning that it must be kept, but no longer needs to be actively worked on.

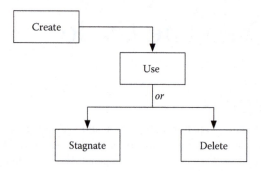

FIGURE 3.1   The data life-cycle "management" approach used in many organizations.

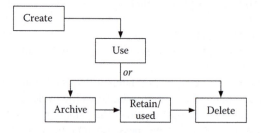

FIGURE 3.2   A true data life-cycle management approach.

While archiving often logically implies a migration of the data from a more expensive tier of storage to a less expensive tier, it also has an important life-cycle benefit: it puts the data under *management*.

In some IT departments, *delete* in particular is an indelicate word, but archive isn't far behind it. These IT departments are guilty of *data hoarding*—they mistakenly believe that it's cheaper (in terms of expenditure and time) to keep everything on primary storage than to actively reduce it.

Data hoarding is a serious problem well entrenched in many enterprises, and with the explosive growth of data within business, the problems faced by hoarders only continue to grow.

The common rule of thumb in the storage industry is that for every 1 TB of data you store, you'll need around 10 TB of capacity to protect it over its lifetime. That may not sound like a particularly odious task when your business is storing 2 or 3 TB, or maybe even 10 TB—but storage sizes are small now for many businesses. When a business has hundreds or thousands of terabytes of data (or even, as is starting to occur for very large businesses, *exabytes* of data), you can see the danger uncontrolled data growth poses to a business.

Quite simply: continuing down a path of not properly managing the data life cycle is only going to continue to cost businesses more. Eventually, all businesses must face and tackle data life-cycle management, and the longer it is avoided the more painful it becomes to initiate.

There are three particular ways that businesses can fail to understand and act on data life cycles:

1. Getting stuck in the "use" cycle for all data
2. Archiving but never deleting data
3. Deleting rather than archiving data

The first is penny-wise/pound-foolish, the second is true hoarding, and the third is usually quite reckless.

3.2 ARCHIVING AND DELETING

No matter how you look at it, primary storage in an enterprise isn't cheap. If you're using enterprise grade storage area networks (SAN) or network attached storage (NAS), the per-TB cost of adequately protected data storage is going to be higher than the expenditure on direct attach storage (DAS). That being said, the lack of adequate protection and management options on DAS makes it expensive in different ways.

Storing 20 TB of data at an enterprise level rarely if ever amounts to 20 TB of actual disk capacity used. Between filesystem overheads, RAID-type overheads, and free capacity to allow for growth, the actual occupied space could be significantly more—and that's before factoring in any snapshots or replication.

When you start counting all the costs, storage isn't actually all that cheap.

Consider the RAID requirements for 20 TB of data. Assuming this is business-critical and high-performance data, it may be stored on RAID-10 solid state storage (SSD). Using a series of mirrored 1 TB SSDs that are then striped together, 20 TB of storage presented to an operating system has immediately consumed 40 TB of storage space.

Since we've established such storage is business critical, it's reasonable to assume it's replicated to another two storage arrays—one local for immediate disaster recovery capabilities, and one remote for full business continuity capabilities. With replication to two locations, our 20 TB of presented storage has become 3 × 40 TB of storage space—120 TB.

Again, considering the storage is business critical, it's also reasonable to assume that multiple snapshots might be taken during the course of the day to allow for much smaller recovery windows than would be provided by a traditional backup system. While snapshot storage can be sourced from a shared data pool, for a business-critical system it's possible there'll be a dedicated snapshot pool—and in this case with replication to two locations, that dedicated snapshot pool needs to be maintained for all three copies of the data so that it's available regardless of where the active copy of the data resides at any given point. The business processes might require an additional 5 TB of storage space for snapshots, which again in this instance might be provisioned from RAID-10 storage—that's an additional 10 TB of storage space provisioned at each location to facilitate snapshots.

So far, our 20 TB of storage has consumed 40 TB of storage space for the primary copy, 40 TB of storage space for the secondary copy, and 40 TB of storage space for the remote copy *and* another 10 TB of storage space for each copy for provisioning snapshots: our 20 TB storage is consuming 150 TB of primary storage space.

Then, of course, you've got backup costs associated with it as well. Our first full backup will require a complete copy of the data, so that's another 20 TB of storage we need to consider for backups. However, that gets weekly fulls and daily incrementals, with a 2.5% daily change rate. Over the course of a week, the amount of data to be backed up will be

- Day 1, full: 20 TB
- Day 2, incremental: 500 GB
- Day 3, incremental: 500 GB
- Day 4, incremental: 500 GB
- Day 5, incremental: 500 GB
- Day 6, incremental: 500 GB
- Day 7, incremental: 500 GB

Assuming a 5-week retention period for those backups, the total data backed for 20 TB is 115 TB. Of course, that's not including monthly backups. Assuming no growth to the data at all, and retaining monthly backups for 7 years, that's another 1680 TB of storage.

All up, 20 TB of data might need as much as 1795 TB of backup capacity in a traditional backup model. That's for *one* copy. Assuming adequate redundancy options are in place as part of the backup regime, that number doubles—3590 TB of occupied space to protect 20 TB of data over 7 years. So far, our 20 TB of data has required 3740 TB of storage (150 TB primary, 3590 TB backup).

Calculations get a little more involved when advanced backup technologies such as deduplication come into play. Assuming a 10:1 deduplication ratio, the footprint for the protected data over the 5-week window might come down to somewhere in the order of 11.5 TB. However, that data either needs to be replicated to another deduplication device or it needs to be written out to tape for redundancy. If it goes to another deduplication device, it jumps to 23 TB across two physical devices; if it goes to tape, it jumps to 126.5 TB across the two storage technologies.*

Once monthly backups come into the equation, deduplication still works wonders, but it's not a silver bullet. Again assuming a 10:1 deduplication ratio over the course of the 7 years of storage, 179.5 TB of deduplication storage would be required—or 359 TB when replicated between deduplication devices.† Not all companies keep their long-term backups on deduplication storage though, and instead focus on replication for the short-term retention policies and tape-out for the longer-term retention policies. In that scenario, the footprints might be 23 TB of deduplicated storage for

---

* Writing data from a deduplicated source to tape almost invariably requires *rehydration*. Due to its sequential access nature, a read from deduplicated data dumped to *tape* is typically orders of magnitude slower than a standard tape recovery, as a much larger amount of data needs to be retrieved into a temporary storage area in order to then rehydrate the required data.

† It should be noted that long-term retention backups (i.e., monthlies as described) will usually yield less deduplication than short-term retention backups as we normally expect more content drift over such a lengthy period of time.

the short-term backups (including replication) plus another 3360 TB of tape storage (including secondary copies) for the long-term backups.

No matter how you look at it, the data protection costs for that 20 TB of data will stack up over time—both for the primary storage data protection and the data protection provided by backup and recovery systems.

Of course, so far that only covers the storage requirements of the data protection, it doesn't factor in the time taken such activities take. Restricting ourselves just to backup activities for the moment and assuming 300 MB/s for that backup, the full 20 TB would take approximately 18.5 hours to complete. At the same speed, the incrementals might complete as quickly as half an hour. Assuming those scenarios, over the course of a week, that 20 TB will generate 21.5 hours of backup activity; over the 5-week retention period, that scales to 107.5 hours of backup activity, and over the 7 years, it goes up to over 1600 hours of backup activity—almost 70 *days* of time devoted to protecting our 20 TB of data.

Even this isn't the end to potential cost considerations. Consider tape: 3360 TB of tape will require physical storage and transport costs. Assuming we can squeeze 4 TB onto every tape, and a tape is only sent off-site for storage when it is full, we're still left with moving, storing, and processing almost 850 tapes over the retention life span. If we're backing up to disk and replicating to disk at an off-site location, the bandwidth requirements for the backup replication have to be factored above and beyond standard production bandwidth requirements, and that link will impact the operational costs of the environment as well.

If that data is *continuously* in use, it's a fair price to pay. More than likely though, as is the case in many organizations, that data will be a mix of active and inactive data, with the weighting more toward inactive than active. Suddenly the effort involved in archiving infrequently used data seems quite trivial compared to the amount of capacity required for copies of data that is sitting stagnant on primary storage.

Contrary to popular opinion, before we look at archiving data, we should actually evaluate what can be deleted. After all, there's no point archiving totally irrelevant data. As to what data is relevant and what isn't, that will be a business-by-business decision. Some logical areas to consider include

- Temporary files that weren't automatically removed
- Installers for applications and operating systems that are no longer in use or have been superseded
- Personal correspondence and data that has crept into the system
- Unnecessary correspondence and data
- Out-of-date data

The notion of deleting stagnant, irrelevant data may seem controversial to some, but only due to the "storage is cheap" meme. By comparison, when companies spent considerable amounts of money on physical document management, with all the costs associated with physically occupied space, deleting was a standard business practice.

Legend has it that the Greek king Sisyphus was particularly crafty and managed to evade death several times through all manner of tricks. As a punishment, when

Sisyphus finally died, he was sent to Hades to be given the eternal punishment of rolling a boulder up and over a hill. The rock however was too heavy, and so each day Sisyphus would get the boulder almost to the top of the hill to have it tumble back down again.

In *The Odyssey*, Homer described the fate of Sisyphus thusly:

> And I saw Sisyphus at his endless task raising his prodigious stone with both his hands. With hands and feet he tried to roll it up to top of the hill, but always, just before he could roll it down on to the other side, its weight would be too much for him, and the pitiless stone would come thundering down again on the plain.

A business that doesn't delete irrelevant, stagnant data is doomed to share the same fate as Sisyphus. They task themselves daily with an impossible task—to keep all data generated by the company. It ignores the obvious truth that data sizes have exploded and will continue to grow. It also ignores the obvious truth that not all data needs to be remembered for all time. (Such a company *might* be a heavy investor in archive technology, but this is not guaranteed. Unlimited archive processes also go on to create new data management headaches for businesses.)

While such companies will try to continue to insist "storage is cheap," there's nothing cheap about paying to store data that you don't need. There's a basic, common logic to use here—what do you *personally* keep, and what do you personally throw away? Do you keep every letter you've ever received, every newspaper you've ever read, every book you've ever bought, every item of clothing you've ever worn, etc.? (Few people do, and those who do are recognized as obsessive–compulsive hoarders who need help, not more storage space.)

The answer for the vast majority of people is no: there's a useful life span of an item, and once that useful life span has elapsed, we have to make a decision on whether to keep it or not. The unpleasant truth is that saying "storage is cheap" is akin to closing your eyes and hoping a freight train barreling toward you is an optical illusion. In the end, it's just going to hurt.

That's not of course an argument that you must *only* delete and never archive. However, archive has to be tempered with deletion or else it becomes the stone, and the storage administrators suffer the fate of Sisyphus. Consider a sample enterprise archive arrangement whereby

- NAS is used for file serving
- Long-term inactive data is archived from NAS to single-instance WORM storage
- The single-instance WORM storage is replicated for redundancy and protection

Like it or not, there is a real, tangible cost to the storage of data at each of those steps. Undoubtedly, there is some data that must be kept on primary storage, and undoubtedly there's some data that legitimately must be kept, but can be moved to archive storage. Yet equally, siphoning off irrelevant data to archive storage— data that has no purpose, is no longer used, and has no legal/fiscal requirements for retention "just to keep it" will still cost money. Legally, businesses are also discovering—sometimes quite painfully—that keeping data they were entitled or permitted to delete can come back to haunt them. Just because data is "technically" expired does not mean it's excluded from legal discovery during litigation. Regardless of whether data *should* have been deleted or *could* have been automatically purged, if it's present, accessible, or recoverable, it can be sourced as part of legal discovery. Failing to delete data can also expose the clients of the company to all manners of risks and in doing so expose the company to litigation. In 2015, for instance, an online dating company suffered substantial data theft, exposing its users, *including those users* who had requested their profiles deleted.

Just as good storage isn't necessarily cheap (remember that there's a difference between *cost-effective* and *cheap*), effective and efficient archival systems that are wholly integrated into data access mechanisms also aren't cheap. Ideally, archived data should only require minimal data backup, but that means it must be replicated and highly protected. Why waste that storage by pushing irrelevant and unnecessary data on to it?

A common point of conversation you'll hear among long-term members of the backup community is *backup isn't archive*. Unfortunately, this gets discussed so regularly because for some businesses, that's *exactly* what backup becomes. In order to properly consider the recklessness of this, consider one important difference between backup operations and archive operations, namely:

A backup is about generating an *extra* copy of your data in case you lose the primary copy.

Backup should never delete, alter, or move the data being protected—it is and should always be the process of taking a new copy of that data. On the other hand:

An archive is about *moving* your primary data copy.

In short, archive should be about storage, and backup should be about protection. A good storage policy and a good data protection policy will both consider the other topics, but there's not a 1:1 mapping between the two.

Refusing to archive data can have one of two consequences:

1. The company continually expands its primary storage to always ensure that all data can be stored.
2. Users delete data to make room for new data.

It's very, very rare to find the decision *not* to archive coupled with unlimited primary storage budget—precisely because the decision not to archive is typically discussed as a financial one. Yet, the net result is a reckless approach to *relying* on the backup system as an extension to primary storage.

A university in Australia instituted filesystem quotas to limit data growth. Due to their interpretation of how academic freedom of expression and communication worked, they *didn't* institute email quotas.

At some point, an academic came up with the notion that when his home directory filled, he could create a zip file of everything in it, email it to himself, delete the contents and start afresh.

As a direct consequence, primary storage within the university suffered explosive, unplanned growth.

In the scenario described here, it was the email system, not the backup system, used as an adjunct to primary storage, but the net effect was remarkably similar—a system not designed to act as primary storage (email content) was enlisted to do so, all because archiving wasn't pursued for storage systems.

Choosing to treat a backup system as a safety net or blank check for data deletion is quite a reckless thing to do. It may seem "smart" since the backup system is designed to recover lost data, but it introduces a few vexing problems, namely:

- Requires intimate knowledge of the backup cycles
- Increases the recovery load on the backup environment
- Hides the real storage requirements, even resulting in supersaturated storage

Consider the first point—doing this requires intimate knowledge of the backup cycles. Consider a user who has heard that the quickest way to get more capacity is to delete some data, since "it can be recovered." However, if the data-generation cycle didn't match the data-backup cycle, it's entirely plausible that such data might *only* exist on daily and weekly backups, not the monthly backup retention period. Thus, if the user goes to recover it in 3–4 months when it's needed again, it may have been irretrievably lost.

Assuming the user *can* recover it, what's to say that the recovery of that data won't impact other backup and recovery operations that *technically* are more important? If it's just a single user doing it, the chances of impact are going to be reasonably low—but if it becomes a common enough practice within the organization, all those additional recovery requests are going to start impacting what we'd call the *true* backup and recovery operations.

If users and/or administrators are deleting *sometime-required* data at a whim, rather than seeing it archived, this has the potential to massively hide the measurement of how much storage is actually (not just currently, but *actually*) in use. On any given day, it may *seem* that there's plenty of storage available, but that can just be a mirage. This leads to supersaturated storage,* which in a worst-case scenario can resemble a storage structure similar to that shown in Figure 3.3.

As multiple deletes are done over time to restore primary storage capacity, the amount of data that is deleted but known to be required later builds to the point where it is no longer physically possible to have all of the required data residing on primary storage—even if at some point it becomes necessary. The difference between this and archiving of course is simple—in an archive situation that data is still properly accessible, albeit by a slower means, and its size is well known.

---

* If considering this simply from the perspective of storage management, the above might be termed as *overprovisioned*, but in this context, supersaturated is more appropriate. After all, *overprovisioned* implies a level of monitoring and management—neither of which applies to supersaturated storage.

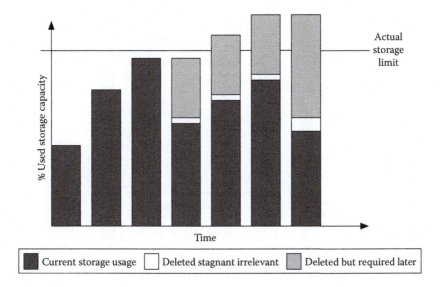

FIGURE 3.3   Supersaturated storage.

It's important to understand that archived data must *also* be protected. This will typically result in a high-level architecture such as that shown in Figure 3.4.

The most common objection raised by businesses to a formal archive architecture is the perceived cost of the infrastructure required and the necessity to still perform data protection against the archival storage. Both of these are real costs, but they're invariably developed on the false premise of equivalence to primary storage costs.

Consider that data is archived because it falls into two key categories, namely:

1. It is old and infrequently accessed (if at all).
2. It is required for compliance reasons and will not be accessed accept for a legal reason.

In both cases, this considerably changes the performance characteristics for the data stored in the archival layer. Businesses requiring a mix of enterprise flash and SAS storage for primary production data would be foolish to use the same speed storage for archive. Instead, bulk SATA or NL-SAS* will provide ample performance for data that is infrequently or indeed never accessed again. Further, while the primary production data might require more drive-expensive storage provisioning such as RAID-1, RAID 1 + 0, or, for bulk data, RAID-6, with drive counts optimized for access and rebuild times, archive data might be limited to RAID-6 but with larger drive counts to optimize storage capacity over rebuild times, on the basis

---

* Near-line SAS refers to serial attached SCSI storage that has drive mechanisms and rotational speed matching SATA drives instead.

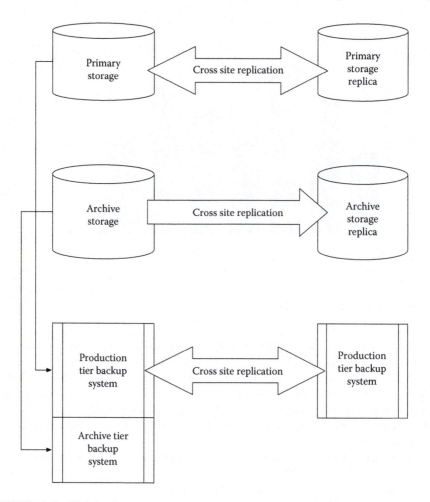

FIGURE 3.4   High-level architecture of data protection for primary and archival data.

that the performance impact of rebuild after a drive replacement is not relevant given substantially higher tolerances for longer access times.

Moving past LUN protection and drive performance, replication requirements for primary versus archive data will be considerably different. Storage arrays replicated between production and disaster recovery datacenters for *primary data* storage will focus on minimal replication lag between the two sites—achieved either via synchronous replication or low-lag asynchronous replication. Such replication will potentially need considerably higher bandwidth on cross-site links and demand a quality of service (QoS) guarantee so that data access performance (and therefore business functions) is not impeded. Such considerations may be substantially reduced for archival data. Replication is likely to take place asynchronously with potentially much larger lag times, with QoS policies *restricting* the available bandwidth rather than guaranteeing it.

Finally, backup and recovery requirements will be quite different for archived data rather than primary data. Backups for primary data will have strict SLAs for completion times, recovery point objectives, and recovery time objectives. Backups will need to be replicated and there may be requirements for those backup replicas to be stored off-site. For archives written with WORM*-type protection, businesses may choose to not backup archival data at all if it is replicated between two sites and the archive systems used have a high level of fault detection, self-protection, and self-healing capabilities, in addition to government-compatible retention locking. Even if archival data *is* backed up, it might be backed up only once per month rather than as part of a regular backup cycle and not replicated (particularly if the archive is WORM), given the backups can be reconstructed at any point simply by executing a new, fresh backup, as anything in the archive in month X will either still be in the archive in month $X + n$ or will no longer have been required for compliance purposes anyway.

While there will undoubtedly be data protection costs associated with archival storage, the net benefit achieved in reducing the storage, management, and data protection footprint on more expensive primary storage will typically see a return on investment within 1–2 years or during their next primary storage refresh cycle for most organizations.

3.3 SUMMARY

Storage isn't cheap or infinite, and time is always limited. While businesses can "get lucky" at times by not having data life-cycle policies, a truly enterprise class and dependable data protection schema should fully integrate with data life-cycle policies to deliver optimal protection at optimal cost for the business.

True hoarding is a recognized psychological condition. Just as we'd be concerned for Aunt Kim and Uncle Gary having a house stuffed full to the rafters with towers of newspapers in every space not occupied by appliances or bedding, we should be concerned with a business that accumulates all data without any consideration of expunging or archiving.

---

* Write once read many. Historically, this was seen as a tape function, but many storage arrays now feature compliance-level locking on writes to prevent overwrite or deletion and have secured acceptance from government regulatory bodies.

4 Elements of a Protection System

4.1 INTRODUCTION

It's a common misconception in IT that technology solves everything. If this were true, IT would be an entirely commoditized, cookie-cutter industry with no need for operational specialists or experts.

This is as equally true in data protection as anywhere else.

As shown in Figure 4.1, there are six distinct elements in a data protection system:

- People
- Processes and documentation
- Service-level agreements (SLAs)
- Testing
- Training
- Technology

In essence, technology comprises only one-sixth of the elements—and it is by far the simplest to deal with.

Arguably some of these topics might be considered to be subsets of one another; testing, after all, is something that by rights should be handled as part of a documented process, and training is something given to people. Yet when we collapse these into umbrella terms, it's common for individual requirements to be forgotten and harder to reconcile the different roles and functions that help to ensure these topics are dealt with. In a similar way to how ITIL differentiates between those who are *responsible* and those who are *accountable*, we deal with each of the components in the previous list individually to ensure their requirements are explicitly understood.

4.2 PEOPLE

There are three essential participants within data protection, regardless of how significantly it has been automated. These are

- Designers
- Operators
- End users

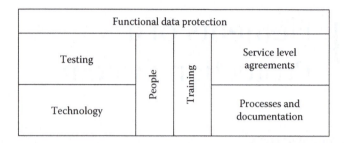

FIGURE 4.1   Elements of a protection system.

4.2.1 DESIGNERS

Ultimately, it makes little point what processes are put in place, what technologies are deployed, what SLAs are established, and what training is developed if the actual system as designed can't meet those requirements.

The designers or the architects of the data protection environment have the critical responsibility of ensuring that the system as architected and subsequently implemented meets the business requirements for protecting data. This of course includes both the *proactive* and *reactive* components.

More so than any other people involved in a data protection system, it will be the designers who will need to understand the business-level requirements of the system. The designers need to concentrate on a very broad set of considerations that include disaster recovery and its role in business continuity as much as individual system recoverability. This includes (but is certainly not limited to)

- Understanding what IT systems map to which business functions
- Understanding the dependencies between IT systems
- Understanding the criticality of the business functions
- Understanding the dependency between business functions
- Understanding the order in which IT systems should be recovered in the event of catastrophic loss

A protection system designed or implemented *without* these considerations is unlikely to meet the overall requirements of the business—except perhaps by sheer luck.

4.2.2 OPERATORS

Coming from a classic datacenter environment tends to encourage thinking of *operators* and *administrators* separately. This can still be the case in many businesses today, but the differentiation is increasingly a blurred one. Ultimately, both roles end up operating the environment, be it through maintenance, configuration, or business as usual functions.

So regardless of whether a person's job title includes *operator* or *administrator*, they're both tasked with making sure the systems, once put in place, run correctly, continue to function, and support growth.

While the system designers are responsible for making sure the data protection systems are *capable* of meeting the established SLAs, it's the job of the operators to ensure the systems *do* meet those SLAs. The designers focus on the theoretical, while the operators on the practical. (The most apt comparison is building a house: An architect will design the house and ensure the construction takes place as per the design. It's the people who take possession of the house afterward that have to live in it and make it a *home*.)

Similarly, once the designers have overseen the deployment of their solution, the challenge of making the environment livable for business comes down to the operators, and this necessitates a suite of activities including but not limited to

- Administration
- Operation
- Monitoring
- Reporting
- Maintenance and remediation
- Forecasting and trending

Most of those activities are understood well by the majority of those businesses. The lingering challenge within many organizations, however, is *forecasting and trending*. These are important for two entirely separate reasons:

- To predict ongoing conformance to SLAs or identify where they can no longer be met
- To provide detailed input into the *next* product cycle

Technology has a definite life cycle—it's planned, tested, installed, used, and then either phased out or upgraded. It's what happens next that can be wastefully challenging. If a business has not been collating data on the data protection systems and as a result has not been producing trending information and forecasts, then the *next* acquisition cycle can be potentially just as painful or more so than the previous one.

Anecdotally, it is usually the case that businesses that fail to adequately forecast their environmental growth and/or fail to adequately classify their data are the ones who are most likely to resent whatever investment they make into data protection. (One might suggest that appreciation of functional results can only be achieved when the goals are known and the targets are measurable.)

4.2.3   END USERS

Even end users have a place in a data protection system, albeit a role that is substantially removed from that of administrators or operators.

Common sense dictates that while users shouldn't have to be personally involved in data protection activities (and indeed should be able to assume that adequate steps are taken by the business to prevent data loss), they should also behave responsibly. In some organizations, users have taken advantage of data protection systems by deliberately deleting data to free up space, fully intending to request recovery of the deleted data at a later time.

Equally, users *should* be informed of situations where data protection doesn't take place, such as situations where data is refreshed from other sources as necessary, rather than being actively protected. (Test and quality assurance systems are quite typical of this.) This comes from having well-defined and documented SLAs that are mapped to business functions so they're clearly documented for and articulated to the end users in business-appropriate (rather than IT-focused) language.

Finally, users should understand how to make recovery requests—if they don't, it may be that they waste time recreating data that could otherwise be quickly retrieved from protection sources.

4.2.4 DATA PROTECTION TEAM

It's no longer the case that data protection options can be arranged in isolation. The traditional model that evolved from classic system administration teams saw backup, storage, and virtualization administrators all belonging to different units. Given is the plethora of data protection options that may need to be deployed in a modern business:

- *Backup administrators* need to understand storage and virtualization options in use.
- *Storage administrators* need to know how and where backup will supplement replication, snapshots, and redundant array of independent disk (RAID) and be closely aligned to virtualization for performance and protection reasons.
- *Virtualization administrators* need to know what protection, capacity, and performance options are available to them.

The best way to efficiently achieve this is to combine all three—backup, storage, and virtualization—into a single functioning team for the business. (We are already seeing businesses do this by establishing *infrastructure* administration teams, tasked with all of these.)

Increasing requirements around agility, driving the adoption of converged and hyperconverged infrastructure is making the move toward infrastructure administrators increasingly a question of *when*, not *if*, within the modern enterprise. Even if a business is large enough that combining their storage, backup, and virtualization administrators is seen as operationally impractical, the likelihood of there being at least *some* staff with oversight of administration at the infrastructure view is high.

4.3 TRAINING

Sadly in many organizations, training of staff in relation to data protection is inadequate, which can lead to significant challenges, such as

- Inefficient processes that do not maximize the capabilities of the technologies at hand
- Higher chance of human error via insufficient understanding of the products

Depending on who interacts with the protection systems (and in what way), a variety of training options are available to choose from. The first step will be to determine who requires certification-level training. Certainly for some staff that certification will be an important aspect of their training and development. This will particularly be the case for protection system designers and administrators. Past that, in-house-developed training courses or those offered by third-party suppliers, such as systems integrators and professional consultancy agencies, may offer more than sufficient knowledge transfer.

Of course, individual staff members need backups. Having only one person trained in any particular aspect of a protection system is a foolish concentration of knowledge that should be strongly discouraged, no matter how small the environment. Thus, at least two or more people should receive training wherever possible in the various data protection systems used within the organization. This fulfills several purposes, allowing for staff to

- Be on leave, sick, or otherwise away without compromising the business
- Move on without fear of essential knowledge being lost
- Peer review one another's planned or implemented changes

Companies tend to experience the most problems with enterprise data protection technologies when they don't allow staff to develop skills properly or refuse to accept that daily administration of such technology is part of the IT role. There is always a direct correlation between the level of customer staff involvement in the installation, configuring, testing, and training and the quality of the experience they have in using the products. That is, untrained employees are likely to have more issues and ultimately put the ability of the business to ensure data recovery at risk.

4.4 DOCUMENTATION AND PROCESSES

One could argue that *processes* and *documentation* are two separate items, but in terms of describing a system in its design and operation, they are invariably two sides of the same coin—processes that are not documented are of little benefit, and documentation either will exist to describe a process or should have been created *using* a process.

We can broadly break the requisite documentation for a data protection system into three categories:

- Design
- Implementation
- Operational

Andy Hertzfeld, in Mac Folklore, wrote a story about the development of the *round rect[angle]* function in QuickDraw. When Steve Jobs saw a demo of QuickDraw functionality, he asked for rectangles with rounded corners, which Bill Atkinson, the developer, objected to:

> Steve suddenly got more intense. "Rectangles with rounded corners are everywhere! Just look around this room!". And sure enough, there were lots of them, like the white-board and some of the desks and tables. Then he pointed out the window. "And look outside, there's even more, practically everywhere you look!". He even persuaded Bill to take a quick walk around the block with him, pointing out every rectangle with rounded corners that he could find.
>
> When Steve and Bill passed a no-parking sign with rounded corners, it did the trick. "OK, I give up," Bill pleaded.
>
> … Over the next few months, roundrects worked their way into various parts of the user interface, and soon became indispensable.
>
> Andy Hertzfeld, Mac Folklore
>
> http://www.folklore.org/StoryView.py?story=Round_Rects_Are_Everywhere.txt

Just like Bill Atkinson originally disagreeing with implementing round rectangles, only to discover how useful they were, it's quite regular to encounter such similar opposition to formal documentation within IT. It often gets short shrift in IT—yet we are often so demanding of it of others, both within IT and without. Someone who may studiously try to avoid writing any documentation about *how* they'd imple-mented a system would nevertheless rigorously complain if a critical component were left undocumented by the vendor. Equally, someone who insisted that up-to-date details about how a system has been implemented would vehemently reject the notion that the local bank staff will just try to "remember" their current bank balance after a paycheck has cleared, rather than it being recorded in the system.

4.4.1 Design

Design documentation reflects architectural information about an environment and, except in the smallest of environments, should be quite formal in its structure. This is also the documentation that will refer back to business goals and requirements most, since the design itself should be premised *on* those goals and requirements.

An adequately planned data protection environment will be developed from a series of business requirements, which are typically broken into two key categories:

- Functional requirements
- Nonfunctional requirements

If these requirements *have* been outlined, then they form the absolute core of the details that should be addressed in the design documentation. For instance, consider the functional and nonfunctional requirements outlined in Table 4.1.

The design documentation produced, in addition to outlining the *actual* design, must cite how the solution design meets originally stated requirements *and* just as critically where it doesn't.

TABLE 4.1

Functional and Nonfunctional Requirements

Type	Requirement	Criticality
Functional	A copy of all data generated in the system will be available at the secondary datacenter within 24 hours.	Mandatory
Functional	Data categorized as "Tier 1" must have an RPO of less than half an hour.	Mandatory
Functional	Data categorized as "Tier 1" must have an RTO of less than 10 minutes.	Mandatory
Functional	A real-time "dashboard" view showing any failed component in the system must be web accessible.	Nonmandatory if the system can integrate into <X>
Nonfunctional	The system shall be easy to use.	Mandatory
Nonfunctional	The system shall offer a variety of administrative interfaces.	Nonmandatory if evaluation deems available interface(s) acceptable

The design must be as complete as possible. Using the example of a backup and recovery system, for instance, simply stating schedules, policies, intended device configuration, and the data retention policy is insufficient—it must also outline the reports and monitoring options that will be configured, too.

4.4.2 Implementation

Once a data protection system has been designed, it has to be implemented, and documentation will be of critical importance to satisfy a service transition manager that there is sufficient explanation of the environment to enter an ongoing operational phase.

4.4.2.1 System Configuration Guide

From an individual project point of view, we often consider implementation documentation to refer to as "as-built" or "system configuration" guides. These outline (sometimes, seemingly in excruciating detail) exactly how the system is put together and exactly what the system looked like at the conclusion of the implementation. These form a *line in the sand*, so to speak. They clearly state what the system should look like and clearly outline (approved) deviations between what was designed and what was implemented.

As-built material typically falls into two categories, which for want of better terms we'd describe as *initial* and *ongoing*. The initial should be a static description of the environment at the conclusion of implementation, but since the system is likely to change over time, those changes should be reflected in updated implementation documents. Both such documents are necessary.

4.4.2.2   System Map

A system map can best be described as a network diagram/map showing systems connectivity, as well as system and application dependencies. In this case when we refer to *systems*, we refer to all components that make up the system, namely,

- Hosts
- Applications
- Networking connectivity
- Data storage

The dependencies tracked in a system map are best described as *operational* dependencies and reflect the interoperability of the environment and allow the mapping and prioritization of protection and recovery.

A system map should be a core component of the IT environment documentation for all organizations but in actuality mostly exists in the minds of IT staff and then only in segments—that is, different departments in IT will usually have different views of the system map.

As the size of the environment grows, the chances of a system map being an actual diagram decrease—just the same way as the chances of it being an actual comprehensive network diagram for the business IT environment decrease. In these scenarios, it's necessary to produce the system map as a table that accompanies the network diagram or diagrams.

A basic network diagram focusing just on the core production systems for a small business might resemble Figure 4.2. While this broadly shows the key components within an environment, it doesn't provide any details on how they relate to each other and how they map to business functions. For instance, there's nothing in Figure 4.2 that indicates that the intranet server hosts a web-based call management system that interfaces with the database server, using the authentication server to ensure only those users who are allowed to access the system can retrieve data. Thus, it's fair to say the standard network diagram is incomplete for the purposes of data protection.

Without this relationship information, there is no clear mechanism to determine the criticality of systems for protection or the recovery order in the event of a catastrophic datacenter failure. A common consequence of this is that even IT staff may not fully appreciate the recovery prioritization order or the level of protection required for individual system components. For example, most environments fully rely on centralized host resolution (e.g., Domain Name System (DNS))—yet a network diagram in itself will not explain the criticality of DNS for successful business operations.

By having a system map, not only can system and application dependencies be recorded visually, but they can also be referred to during data protection planning, design, and implementation activities and during disaster recovery and business continuity scenarios. A system map might extend the network diagram from Figure 4.2 as shown in Figure 4.3.

There is no standard or "best practices" approach to drawing a system map, and different organizations will utilize methods that are most appropriate to their

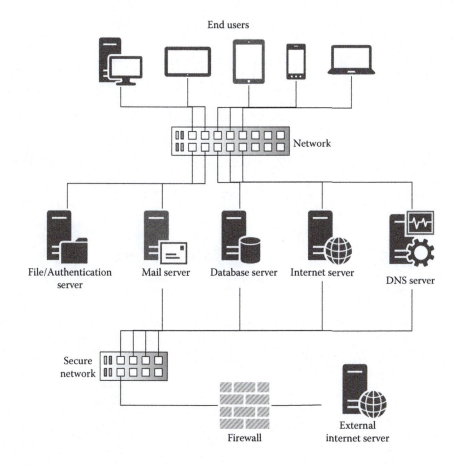

FIGURE 4.2   Basic network diagram.

requirements and logical size limits. In Figure 4.3, we have mapped dependencies as follows:

- Each piece of infrastructure is numbered.
- In addition to the infrastructure shown on the network diagram, we have introduced business functions. This is imperative: it ensures we identify not only individual systems, but the "net functions" that the business sells and relies on.
- Each system is labeled with its function and also its dependencies. For example, the figure shows that the file/authentication server (1) depends on the DNS server (5) for successful operation.

As the size of the infrastructure grows, the system map as a literal diagram can become unwieldy for successful maintenance—or reliable interpretation. At some point, it will usually become necessary to construct a system map as a table that

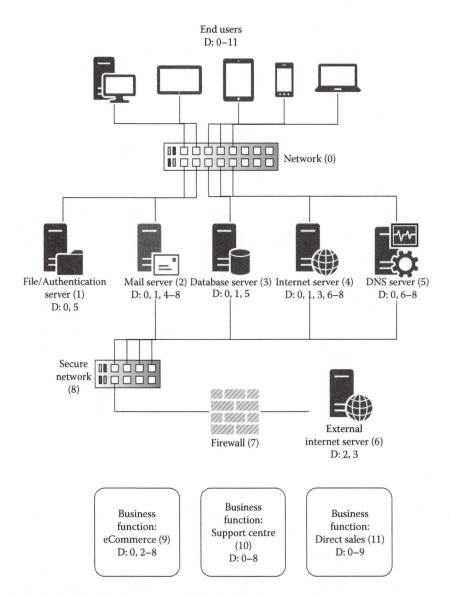

FIGURE 4.3   System map as an extended function of the network diagram.

accompanies the network diagram or diagrams. Such a table might resemble the one shown in Table 4.2.

Regardless of which mechanism is used to build the system map, the goal is to ensure that system, application, and business function dependencies can be quickly determined and noted. With this in place, the level of importance can be assigned to a system not just by the *perceived* user importance but by the number of systems that depends on it. This in turn may reveal the importance (particularly from a disaster recovery perspective) of systems not previously seen as high priority.

TABLE 4.2

System Dependency Map as a Table

System/Function	Depends on	Number of Dependencies
Internal network	None	10
DNS	Internal network External Internet server Firewall Secure network	8
File/authentication server	Internal network DNS server	5
Mail server	Internal network File/authentication server Internet server DNS server External Internet server Firewall Secure network	4
Database server	Internal network Authentication server DNS server	6
Internet server	Internal network Authentication server Database server DNS server External Internet server Firewall Secure network	1
End users	All	0
Business function: eCommerce	Internal network Database server Internet server DNS server External Internet server Firewall Secure network	1
Business function: support Center	Internal network File/authentication server Mail server Database server Internet server DNS server External internet server Firewall Secure network	0

(Continued)

TABLE 4.2 (*Continued*)
System Dependency Map as a Table

System/Function	Depends on	Number of Dependencies
Business function: direct sales	Internal network	0
	File/authentication server	
	Mail server	
	Database server	
	Internet server	
	DNS server	
	External Internet server	
	Firewall	
	Secure network	
	eCommerce function	

Based on Table 4.2, we can make the following observations—particularly when considering *production* systems:

- The higher the number of dependencies, the earlier a system is likely to require recovery.
- The smaller the number of dependencies, the more *visible* a system is likely to be to the company or end users.*

Some organizations feel system maps are only required for extreme circumstances, such as if all system administrators are unavailable *and* a disaster happens. It is believed in these situations that risk mitigation (e.g., having company policies prohibiting all system administration staff from traveling together) resolves this problem. However, system maps serve a far more important business need—they help to ensure that IT activities and systems are correctly aligned to business functions, activities, and products. Without a system map, many businesses end up in situations where the data protection goals of the IT environment don't align correctly to business needs.

4.5 TESTING

Without a doubt, testing is critical for adequate assurance of data protection capabilities. It is often said, for instance, that an untested backup is a failed recovery, yet it equally applies to all aspects of data protection, including RAID, snapshots, and replication.

4.5.1 TYPE TESTING

The statement *an untested backup is a failed recovery* may rankle some, and this is where the concept of *type testing* must come into consideration. Type testing is the means by which reasonable assurance can be provided of data recoverability without testing every single *instance* within an organization.

---

* Of course, there can be exceptions to this.

For instance, limiting ourselves to recoverability for the moment, consider that a heterogeneous enterprise backup and recovery system may be used to protect Solaris, Linux, Windows, AIX, HPUX, and VMware systems within an environment. A needlessly excessive test process would see comprehensive testing done on *every* Solaris server, on *every* Linux server, on *every* Windows server, and so on.

Type testing usually allows for sufficient assurance by identifying each unique *combination* of tests and randomizing the testing process against those combinations.

So, with a backup and recovery system, this would mean tests such as

- Filesystem backup for Solaris
- Filesystem recovery for Solaris
- Filesystem backup for Linux
- Filesystem recovery for Linux
- Filesystem backup for Windows
- Filesystem recovery for Windows
- Filesystem backup for AIX
- Filesystem recovery for AIX
- Filesystem backup for HPUX
- Filesystem recovery for HPUX
- Image-level backup for VMware
- Image-level recovery for VMware
- File-level recovery from image-level backup for VMware

In such scenarios, the tests are not repeated on every single instance of each platform, just one instance of each platform. In certain cases, there may be repeats—"platinum-level" systems—such as those deemed absolutely critical to the business or requiring satisfaction of particular legal/financial tests might each be tested, but overall the complete number of tests performed within the environment is significantly reduced. Type testing is most reliable in environments making use of "standard builds," or "standard operating environments" (SOEs), thereby providing a level of assurance that the base systems are designed and behave in an expected manner.

Of course, this applies to all aspects of data protection. Environments that make use of mirroring and replication will see similar type testing performed, such as

- Successful mount of replicated Windows filesystem
- Successful mount of replicated Solaris filesystem
- Successful read/write open of Oracle database on replicated Windows filesystem
- Successful read/write open of Oracle database on replicated Solaris filesystem

Further, testing will be integrated where data protection activities are integrated. Consider an environment where, for performance reasons, production filesystems are not directly backed up, but instead, replicated tertiary mirrors are split off, mounted on another host, and backed up from there. In such situations, type testing might include

- Filesystem backup from replicated Solaris split
- Filesystem backup from replicated Linux split
- Filesystem backup from replicated Windows split
- Successful recovery to production filesystem of data backed up from replicated Solaris split
- Successful recovery to production filesystem of data backed up from replicated Linux split
- Successful recovery to production filesystem of data backed up from replicated Windows split
- Successful read/write open of Oracle database recovered to production environment from backup of replicated Windows filesystem
- Successful read/write open of Oracle database recovered to production environment from backup of replicated Solaris filesystem

This further goes to show the importance of data protection to be approached from a holistic measure—it's not sufficient in such integrated environments that each component be tested individually, for the success of a system recovery (from the *business* perspective) can only be evaluated at the conclusion of *all* linked activities.

4.5.2 Informal versus Formal

Both informal and formal testing should be conducted. Informal testing is often considered a function of the original system implementation—that is, as technology is rolled out, those implementing it will periodically run snap tests to confirm that a particular aspect of the technology as deployed is working as intended. This could include

- Removing a hard drive in a newly created RAID-5 group, replacing it, and confirming the array rebuilds it successfully
- Confirming basic file backup/recovery to disk and tape options
- Confirming successful mount of a split, replicated filesystem on another host

During an implementation phase in particular, informal testing is typically seen as a basic "sanity" test on the system before moving on to conduct formal testing. Particularly given that formal testing typically involves multiple staff and therefore is more costly (both in terms of time and money) to perform, informal testing can in fact speed up implementation.

Beyond implementation, informal testing can be a means of conducting quick, random spot-checks, particularly for staff training or postrepair validation.

Unlike the more relaxed process of informal testing, formal testing is usually a time-intensive activity designed to meet legal or compliance requirements. Formal testing involves

- A test register
- A test procedure

- A documented evidence of completed tests
- A signed/notarized acceptance of each conducted test by two or more people
- A defect register

A business planning on undertaking formal testing will need to verify whether there are any regulatory requirements associated with that testing. For instance, some industries may have requirements that formal testing be conducted only by employees of the business and vetted by an external auditing agency. Other industries may be more relaxed and allow formal testing to be conducted by the company implementing the solution and so on. By verifying the regulatory requirements for formal testing ahead of conducting such tests, a business avoids both unpleasant repetition of activities *and* the risk of compliance-based fines.

4.5.2.1 Test Procedure

In formal testing, the test procedure outlines at minimum the following:

- The procedure version and publication date
- The author of the procedure
- The description of what the test is intended for
- The details of who (i.e., role) should conduct the test
- The test prerequisites
- The sequence of steps to perform test (or reference to exact documentation elsewhere)
- The expected results
- The defects and mitigations

4.5.2.2 Test Register

The test register is a document that outlines

- The formal tests that have been established for the environment
- The results of those tests each time they have been performed

When performing a formal test, at minimum the following should be recorded:

- The name and version of the test conducted
- The one who performed the test
- Actual results recorded
- Actions taken (e.g., if the results did not match the expected results)
- Whether the test was deemed successful or not
- Names and roles of those who performed/witnessed the test
- Signatures of those who performed/witnessed the test
- Defect register and risk mitigation statements

4.5.2.3 Test Schedule

It matters little how rigorously defined tests are if they are not performed. As such, the purpose of the test schedule is to outline the regularity to which each specific test should be conducted.

To ensure tests aren't forgotten, the test schedule should be automated. In its most primitive form, this may be something as simple as periodic evaluation of the test schedule and creation of suitable reminders and tasks for people to conduct the tests. For instance, a management team might review the test schedule quarterly, determine which tests need to be conducted during that time, and set calendar tasks and appointments as necessary for the appropriate staff and alerts for themselves to follow up with staff to ensure the tests have been performed and the results documented. More formal test management systems may handle that automation directly.

4.5.3   PERFORMANCE TESTING

Equally important as functional testing is performance testing. Whereas functional testing determines whether or not something can be done at all, performance testing establishes a baseline of how *long* something should take to complete.

Performance testing applies to all aspects of data protection and involves three separate activities:

- Baselines
- Standard testing
- Resampling

Baselines identify the expected amount of time activities should take in controlled situations. For example, on storage systems, baselines might be established for the rebuilding of RAID LUNs following drive replacements where

- The filesystems are inactive
- The filesystems are under moderate access load
- The filesystems are under substantial access load

Baselines relating to replication might include

- Length of time to perform first synchronization over a specific speed link
- Length of time to resynchronize over a specific speed link after 10% change during split
- Length of time to resynchronize over a specific speed link after a 30% change during split
- Length of time to resynchronize over a specific speed link after a 10% change during split while the source system is rebuilding its RAID system
- Length of time to resynchronize when the link is unused, 25% used, 50% used, or 90% used by other data if in a shared bandwidth arrangement

Baselines relating to backup systems might include

- Length of time to backup a 100 GB filesystem of no more than 100,000 files
- Length of time to backup a 100 GB filesystem of 1,000,000 files
- Length of time to backup a 500 GB database

- Amount of data that can be backed up in an 8 hour window
- Length of time to rescan 1 TB of backed up data without access to media indices

Equally, baselines for recoveries from the backup environment might include

- Amount of filesystem data for files between 5 KB and 1 GB that can be recovered in a 1 hour window over 1 Gbit and 10 Gbit network links
- Length of time to recover a 100 GB filesystem of no more than 100,000 files
- Length of time to recover a 100 GB filesystem of 1,000,000 files
- Length of time to recover a 500 GB database
- Length of time to recover a 100 GB database
- Length of time to recover 100 files from a virtual machine image-level backup
- Length of time to recover a virtual machine image-level backup as new virtual machine
- Length of time to recover a virtual machine image-level backup leveraging change block tracking for incremental restore when 1% of the virtual machine has changed since the backup

Ultimately, the number and type of baselines established for testing will vary based on the individual needs and size of each business. Optimum establishment of baselines should see tests repeated at least three times and their results averaged. Where performance is absolutely critical, it may even be necessary to run even more tests, discarding maximum and minimum results and averaging the others, though for practicality reasons this will be the exception rather than the rule. Some tests may even need to be baselined at different times of the day—for example, recovery performance of a critical system at 9 am, midday, 4 pm, and 1 am. Alternately, when load varies depending on the time of the month (particularly in relation to end-of-month processing), it may be necessary to gather baseline performance data from multiple days and times during a month.

Standard performance testing should be a mix of formal and informal testing, periodically confirming whether activities still complete within an acceptable degree of variance from the established baselines. Like standard functional tests, the formal performance tests should be scheduled and the results documented.

Where standard performance testing reveals that baselines are no longer accurate or in situations where there has been a substantial technology change or tangible data volume change, resampling will be run in order to determine new baselines. Optimally, the original baselines and new baselines established by resampling should be documented so that trending can be established throughout the lifecycle of the systems.

In an increasingly interconnected IT environment, performance testing is *at best* a decidedly complex challenge. Consider a wholly typical medium-size enterprise with

- Shared storage (a mix of storage area network [SAN] and network-attached storage [NAS])
- Mix of virtual (80%) and physical (20%) hosts
- Virtual hosts that can reside on any one of a number of physical servers

- Shared fiber-channel networking for both standard data and backup/recovery
- Shared IP networking for standard data and backup/recovery

At a high level, this may resemble the interrelationships shown in Figure 4.4.

In such a typical system, where networking, storage, processing, and memory are *all* shared, the performance of an individual component (e.g., a single virtual machine) is as much, if not more, dependent on the interplay of all the other components and the workloads they are experiencing at any given time as it is on its own operating system, applications, and usage profiles. A backup performance test conducted at 10 am on a Sunday may have no correlation whatsoever between a backup test conducted at 11 am on a Monday and so on. While many individual components may have the ability to set performance guarantees, getting these to all align across

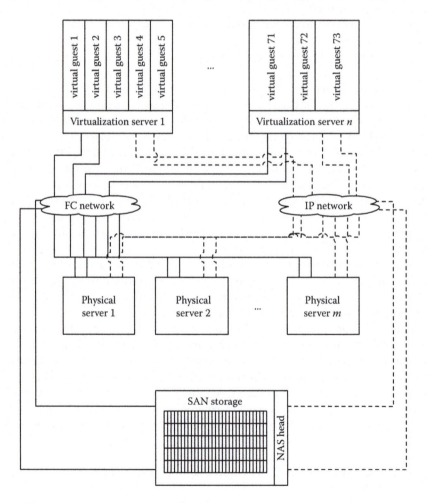

FIGURE 4.4 Systems interconnectedness.

potentially multiple levels of virtualization and resource sharing is as likely to be an art form as it is a science—particularly when required for *many* business systems concurrently.

There is no simple solution to planning adequate performance testing in such an environment—and there's certainly no *cheap* solution. Indeed, it would be impossible to accurately state the performance of an individual component from a single test. (Multiple tests at specific—or perhaps even randomized—times with the results averaged may even be merely a starting point.)

When approaching performance testing of the data protection environment, determining the initially required accuracy *and* measuring the overall loading of the environment become critical. Thus, it might be stated that the financial database server can be backed up at 130 MB/s, *when*

- The FC network is at no more than 20% utilization
- The IP network is at no more than 60% utilization
- The specific virtualization server hosting the database is at no more than 60% CPU load
- The specific virtualization server hosting the database is at no more than 50% memory utilization
- The SAN is recording less than 100,000 IOPS

Even this list is entirely simplistic for a truly accurate performance testing in an enterprise environment, but as such it still demonstrates the point: performance testing is a topic often bandied about in enterprise environments, but is no longer one that can be *casually* approached with any chance of reliability.

4.5.4 TEST RISKS

It's easy when first approaching testing to assume that testing is about mitigating risk in the environment. This of course is true. However, if conducted incorrectly, testing can *introduce* risk into the environment, and it's therefore important to plan tests in such a way as to minimize the impact they may have on the overall environment.

In an entirely optimum scenario, IT staff will have available to them a test environment that is isolated from but can mirror the production environment. For many organizations, this might sound like the perfect use case scenario for disaster recovery systems, but doing so introduces additional risks that must be managed. For instance, if destructive testing is taking place in the disaster recovery environment *and* a critical fault occurs within the production environment, what challenges and delays does this introduce into switching production operations over?

Equally, test scenarios that have the potential to impact actual production systems have to be evaluated seriously; removing a spinning drive from a production SAN, for instance, in order to confirm the system appropriately rebuilds RAID units is likely to succeed, but at the cost of a performance-impacting storage rebuild. Or it might introduce additional errors into the environment—the removed drive might be pulled out too far, too quickly, while still spinning down and become damaged. Or—since it's not an effective test of disk failure anyway*—it might work but bear no relation to a real failure scenario anyway.

For some tests, it's important to consider not the immediate risk, but the potential for cascading risk. For instance, if cross-site replication is being used for critical storage and the replication is deliberately broken in such a way as to force a new, full replication to take place, consider the following:

- The immediate risk is that production traffic making use of the cross-site link may be compromised by higher utilization for replication (particularly if quality of service is not used).
- If a failure occurs in the production storage during the testing, there's the potential that the outage will be longer, requiring restoration from backup, given the online, remote replica has not completed rebuilding.

Even standard recovery testing can pose challenges—periodic testing of the recoverability of data (particularly critical data) is important, but the risk needs to be understood that human error might result in the recovery overwriting in-use data or going to the wrong location and filling a filesystem or, in secure environments, traversing an unencrypted network link and being exposed to third-party snooping.

The potential risks in testing—particularly when the test environment is not 100% isolated from the production environment—are many, and the acceptable risk level will be largely needed to be decided by individual companies in response to the financial and regulatory implications of that testing.

4.5.5 WHAT IS A TEST?

Before we finish the topic of testing, we should briefly consider what *constitutes* a test. For instance, consider a business that has decided a complete filesystem recovery will be conducted at least monthly, on a random day for one randomly chosen Tier 1 system in the organization. If we come to the third week of the month and the test has not yet been conducted *but* a full filesystem recovery is performed for a Tier 1 system due to a production issue, *does that qualify as a test*?

This is a surprisingly difficult question for most organizations to answer, and there's no real single answer: in a business where there are no formal legal requirements for testing, it's entirely possible this *can* be designated a successful test execution. For those organizations bound by strict corporate compliance requirements, authorities (and therefore corporate legal counsel) may not agree. This is something that should be explored carefully and well documented in any business where reasonably formal testing processes are required.

4.6 SERVICE LEVEL AGREEMENTS

The SLAs are crucial to understanding the nature of the data protection and data recovery options that will be required within the environment.

---

* Unless there's a known risk that people will randomly remove active and working drives from enclosures.

TABLE 4.3

Sample Recovery Point and Recovery Time Agreements

System	RPO	RTO
Corporate NAS	1 hour	8 hours
Production financial database	2 hours	1 hour
Archive server	1 day	5 days
Standard server	1 day	8 hours
Production email	1 day	4 hours

From a backup and recovery perspective, we often consider SLAs around two key factors:

- *Recovery time objective (RTO)*—How long it takes to recover data
- *Recovery point objective (RPO)*—How much data can be "lost" in time

Table 4.3 gives several examples of possible RTO and PRO SLAs for a backup and recovery environment.

One thing that usually becomes immediately obvious from a review of RPOs and RTOs within an environment is that traditional once-a-day backup models don't always provide sufficient recovery capabilities.

This helps to highlight that data protection in the modern organization can't be met through the activities of traditional backup and recovery alone. In fact, the more urgent the RPOs and RTOs, the more likely it will be that a data protection design will need to meet these *without* resorting to traditional recovery mechanisms. (Consider, for instance, the corporate NAS example in Table 4.3, which is cited as having an RPO of 1 hour and an RTO of 8 hours. Clearly, in this scenario, if the maximum amount of data that can be lost, expressed in time, is just 1 hour, then a traditional backup that is performed just once every 24 hours is not suitable.)

It should of course also be noted where stated service levels are agreements (SLAs) or objectives (SLOs). Typically an SLO is a desired outcome, but not mandatory, whereas an SLA is typically seen as being a mandatory outcome.

4.7 TECHNOLOGY

Once everything else in a data protection system has been considered, we're left with the easiest components: the technology. It goes without saying that some of the technology deployed may be complex, and the implementation, maintenance, and ongoing operation of that technology requires specialist training. Yet, even taking those factors into consideration, the technology is the easiest aspect of the entire system.

There are two key considerations for technology selection in a data protection system: the technology must be fit for purpose and the technology must be adaptable to purpose.

In the first instance—the preferred instance—the technology being used is immediately applicable to the requirements at hand. In the shortest sense, this would imply that the technology being used meets *all* the functional requirements of the business and most, if not all, of the nonfunctional requirements as well.

Yet that is not always going to be the case—unless bespoke technology has been commissioned *and* the needs of the business are static, the technology deployed for data protection (like any other solution within the business) is unlikely to meet *all* functional requirements, let alone all nonfunctional requirements. This brings us to perhaps one of the most important aspects of any technology use for data protection in an enterprise environment: it must be a *framework* technology. That is, in addition to providing its base functionality, it should be extendable, and those capabilities should be well documented.* In many scenarios, this would imply at *least* one of the following:

1. There should be comprehensive command line utilities associated with the system.
2. There should be a complete administrative and operational API available for at least one or more common programming languages freely available.
3. The system should integrate all administrative and operational functions with industry standard management utilities.†
4. If *completely* GUI based, the system should offer its own automation options and *all* functions of the GUI should be susceptible to automation.

Since the requirements of most businesses change over time, it can be readily argued that this extensibility and adaptability of enterprise technical solutions via scripting, programming, or other automation methods is *equally* as critical as whether the technology can perform the initial requirements on deployment.

4.8 SUMMARY

Except in perhaps the most esoteric of business requirements, it's usually the case that the simplest component of a data protection solution is actually the technology to be used. It's the other components—SLAs, processes and documentation, people, training, and testing—that will typically be the deciding factors in whether or not a solution is going to work. There's almost always some data protection technology that will tick more functional boxes for a business than other technology, but just because its functions logically map to business requirements will not in any way be the sole reason for whether it works or not for a business.

Correctly determining the *right* data protection components and systems for a business is a process that has to start from above—there must be oversight, clear architectural direction, and strong guiding principles to the implementation of such solutions. These will be covered in more detail in Chapter 5.

---

* Indeed, the increasing pervasiveness of DevOps, REST APIs and the need for cloud-like business agility demonstrate exactly why framework technologies are so essential—and superior—to monolithic technologies in a modern business environment.
† This is often a double-edged sword. Integration with SNMP-based products, for instance, may allow monitoring and basic management functions to be performed from a third-party enterprise technology management system, but it's unlikely the third-party system will be able to manage *all* aspects of the product. In these scenarios, it's preferable that such extensibility is not the *only* form offered.

5 IT Governance and Data Protection

5.1 INTRODUCTION

In his book *An Executive's Guide to IT Governance: Improving Systems Processes with Service Management, COBIT and ITIL* (Wiley, 2013), Robert Moeller says of IT governance:

> IT governance is concerned with the strategic alignment between the goals and objectives of the business and the utilization of its IT resources to effectively achieve the desired results.

Everything done in IT for a business should align with the strategic goals of the business and fall under the aegis of IT governance. Even those businesses that may not necessarily refer to their control processes relating to IT as *governance* will eventually institute governance-like controls if they want a well-integrated IT department. (Even test and development systems and processes should fall into IT governance, albeit with different constraints and requirements compared to production processes.)

IT governance of course is a large enough topic that it would be impossible to map all its topics and considerations into data protection activities in a single chapter. Instead, this chapter will focus on the high-level picture of integrating IT governance with data protection, namely:

- Architecture
- Service transition
- Change management

While there will be elements of data protection to consider in almost all aspects of IT governance, these three topics represent the key junctions where data protection must be more than merely considered: it must be a *critical* consideration.

5.2 ARCHITECTURE

Every solution developed by an organization, regardless of whether it uses locally created technology, purchased components or outsourced systems, must be developed with three central data protection tenets (Figure 5.1):

1. *Integrity*—internal protection against data loss or corruption
2. *Reliability*—protection against downtime
3. *Recoverability*—ability to recover data should it be lost

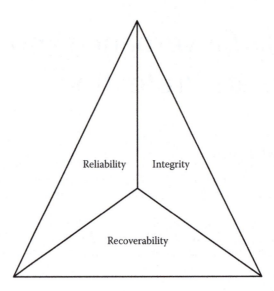

FIGURE 5.1   Key data protection considerations within solutions architecture.

It's vitally important to understand that these considerations don't just apply to *data protection* solutions within an organization: they must apply to *all* solutions within an organization. Consider the saying: "a chain is only as strong as its weakest link." This is our guiding principle to practical solutions architecture. If systems are designed or implemented with weak data protection principles, then the overall data protection strategy put in place within the organization will be similarly compromised.

5.2.1 INTEGRITY

A solution as a whole must provide a sufficient degree of data integrity in order to minimize data loss or corruption events. For storage systems, this might be as simple as adequate and effective RAID levels or replication capabilities. More advanced storage systems might feature self-healing functionality and routine data reliability checking options. For backup and recovery systems, this will refer to the ability to duplicate or clone backups, and the ability to detect write failure during a backup. For disk-based backup systems or appliances, this should overlap considerably with data integrity checking and self-healing functionality of primary storage arrays as well.

Data integrity confidence is just as much a function of primary production activities as it is of data protection activities. A database user should feel confident that the information he or she has input will be successfully stored. (This extends through the entire application stack for a business: while all-too-common a contrary experience, end users should have confidence the updates they've made to a word processing document or spreadsheet will be preserved across closing and reopening the files.)

Essentially, data integrity doesn't come from data storage and data protection systems alone, but from *all* systems. It's unlikely to be able to ever guarantee 100% there is no risk at all of data corruption or loss within an environment when it's comprised of hundreds or thousands of individual products, users, and functions. *However*, what can be guaranteed is if those systems don't take data integrity into consideration as a fundamental design requirement, the chances of data loss will increase substantially as the number of products or functions deployed into the environment is increased.

5.2.2 RELIABILITY

A solution should be designed to minimize the level of downtime users will experience, both planned and unplanned.

Planned downtime refers to any form of maintenance function that either blocks or substantially impedes the time for which the product is usable. For instance, a database that has to perform cleaning activities while the system is inaccessible to users is typically undesirable compared to a database that can simultaneously perform cleaning operations *and* allow user access. This also applies to data protection functions: If backup and recovery software, for instance, requires a long maintenance window that prevents core functions from executing (i.e., backup and recovery), the functional reliability of the product might potentially be seem to be impeded to the business.*

Unplanned downtime is more difficult to quantify by its very nature, but essentially refers to the *robustness* of the product. A critical application with an easy-to-trigger memory leak is going to be substantially more problematic for an organization, and in such circumstances will increase the risk of data loss. It is relatively straightforward (even if highly time-consuming) to vet new products being considered by an organization against both functional and nonfunctional requirements, but reliability still should be considered in evaluation. This might cover topics such as conducting stress-testing, asking vendors to provide information on the number of high-priority incidents flagged with recent releases of their software or to articulate their processes relating to the handing of such incidents and their standard patch cycles. Of course, some of this information may not be readily available. Even if a vendor doesn't publically release detailed information about the number of bug fixes, thorough reviews of recent release notes for products *can* provide a good comparative measure of product reliability, not only for individual releases but also for the upgrade processes between releases, etc.

Testimonials are often seen as a good means of determining product reliability, but in reality these can be of dubious utility, regardless of whether they're positive or negative. The more honest testimonials tend to be *warts and all* where both the good and bad features of a product or an experience are articulated. Searching the Internet for bad experiences with a product, for instance, will rarely tell the

---

* That is, regardless of the necessity of maintenance functions to overall product reliability, if as a result of those maintenance functions being executed the business is unable to, say, recover a critical database, the reliability of the product within the organization is reduced.

whole story, and the way in which a search is phrased may in itself entirely bias the returned search results. (This is, in fact, the heart of confirmation bias.) People writing negative testimonials, for instance, are less likely to include any potentially self-critical acknowledgment of business faults in the selection of the product, such as the following:

- Was the wrong product purchased? (i.e., was it fit for purpose?)
- Did the person who wrote the statement have appropriate training?
- Did the person who wrote the statement have some personal antagonism against the vendor or the product?

In short: testimonials can be a lazy and inaccurate way of trying to come to grips with the reliability of a product. Instead, a thorough review will start with product documentation, in particular release notes and upgrade instructions in order to develop a much more informed knowledge base from which to probe the reliability of the product.

5.2.3 RECOVERABILITY

It would be the height of foolishness to build a system or environment around the *hope* that recoveries were never required. As such, products and systems being considered, planned, or implemented must feature a minimum satisfactory level of data recoverability capabilities. The level of capabilities will entirely depend on the size of the organization and the level of use a product or system will have within that organization. For instance, within a small business with less than 20 staff, it may be entirely acceptable to deploy a backup and recovery system that doesn't offer granular-level recovery of individual email messages. In such environments, it may be necessary for the entire email system to be recovered to an alternate host and individual messages retrieved in the event of data loss. As the number of users and the amount of data stored within the email environment grows, however, the tolerance for nongranular recoveries will fall until granularity becomes an *essential* recoverability option.

Of course, recoverability options aren't useful unless they're *practical*. Using the same email example given earlier, switching to a backup product that supposedly offers granular-level recovery of email messages once the organization has, say, 100 employees may seem a sensible choice. If the process of retrieving individual messages is slower than a full restore to another host however, it may make little practical advantage in using it if the required storage is deemed cheap enough.

5.2.4 DATA PROTECTION ADVOCATE

The architecture of an environment, both the *design* and *planning* on the technical and business front, is crucial to the long-term viability of that environment. Just as there are specialist architectural roles in IT for networking, for messaging, for enterprise identification, and a plethora of other subjects, there is a clear need for specialist data protection architects: data protection *advocates* (DPA). These architects will be responsible for analyzing systems and solutions architecture with a primary focus on being able to address the three variables mentioned earlier, namely:

1. Does the system sufficiently ensure data integrity?
2. Is the system sufficiently reliable?
3. Is the system sufficiently recoverable?

More than this, the DPA also becomes the sort of person who thinks about all the areas within an enterprise where data is stored, regardless of whether it's an obvious or a nonobvious location.

The obvious locations are easy—they're the storage arrays (SAN or NAS), the individual servers, and the backup environments. The less and sometimes nonobvious locations relate to everywhere else in an environment, such as

- Network switches
- Fiber-channel switches
- PABX systems
- Encryption routers, either TCP/IP network or fiber channel

All of these "black box" appliances within an organization contain data, and sometimes *business-critical* data from a communications perspective. There is little benefit in having a backup environment that can rapidly *self-restore* if the environment uses encryption keys that are only stored on an appliance whose configuration and keys were never protected (or perhaps more ignominiously, only stored once in build documentation, and never updated). If this were the sum total of where data might be stored in unconventional locations, it would likely remain manageable by the individual architectural disciplines within IT—yet the modern data landscape is so incredibly complex by comparison that it requires specialist attention. The DPA must also consider such diverse data storage as end user laptops and desktops, mobile platforms (smart phones, tablets, and even emerging technologies such as smart watches), and the cloud—particularly hybrid and public.

Locally, the DPA should be the sort of architect who periodically walks the floor of the business and looks at every device, blinking light, or piece of technology and asks:

- What is this used for?
- What data does it accumulate?
- What happens to the data?
- What configuration does it have?
- Where is the configuration saved?
- What happens if it's no longer working?
- Who fixes it, and how?

- Has anyone tested fixing it?
  - If so, where are the results documented?
  - If not, when will it be done?
- What is its maintenance and support process?
- What department or functional manager is responsible for it?

The mistake made in many organizations is to believe this happens only within the computer room. That's merely the *controlled* area within the IT infrastructure of an organization—it's certainly not the *only* area. The DPA will need to visit every desk, every meeting room, every storeroom in the building or buildings occupied by the company and ask the questions mentioned earlier in case no one else has. A business without a DPA is a business with an *at best* incomplete data protection strategy.

When an organization has switched to public or hybrid cloud, the task of the DPA becomes more challenging, but even more important. In these situations, the DPA must be liaising with the cloud service providers to ensure everything stored in the cloud continues to meet required service-level agreements and press the cloud service providers for the requisite evidence. Usually when this is broached with organizations, at least one of the following objections will be rolled out:

- They don't provide specifics; we just have to rely on their stated SLAs.
- That information requires an account manager, and our service doesn't cover that.

Neither objection is acceptable. If an organization's data is held by a third party and that third party isn't sufficiently forthcoming about the data protection and recovery mechanisms and incidents it encounters, then it's *reckless* to use that organization. *Cheap* must never come at the expense of reliability, recoverability, or integrity. (This is sadly a common mistake—many businesses trust they'll have full recovery capabilities for cloud services, but a thorough review of the terms and conditions usually instead show the service provider only commits to infrastructure availability and recoverability—not data restoration for situations necessitated by a customer fault.)

5.3   SERVICE TRANSITION

While arguably service transition is just a specialist topic in change management (to be discussed next), it deserves being called out for special attention within data protection. Service transition is the *make or break* moment for a product or service within an organization. Within ITIL, service transition refers to the stage where services are either

- *Production enabled*—moved from the development or build part of its life cycle into full production use
- *Substantially modified*—beyond standard changes, such as when a central business management tool has entirely new modules implemented
- *Decommissioned*—when the service or product is removed from active use

In all areas, service data protection must be considered. Take, for example, the life cycle of just a single server, providing a single service, and focused *solely* on the backup and recovery considerations for that host:

1. Installation:
   a. Prior to purchase:
      i. The existing backup system should be considered in the context of the new system being purchased—that is, the existing backup infrastructure should be verified as having sufficient capacity to on-board the new system.
      ii. If the backup system needs to be expanded to accommodate the new system, the requisite components and features should be purchased at this phase
   b. Installation:
      i. New system is received and has the appropriate operating system install, patching and security options installed.
      ii. Backup software is installed on the host, and first backup is taken.
   c. Recovery testing (files):
      i. If this is the first install of this type of operating system, a complete disaster recovery test should be performed.
      ii. System has appropriate applications/software installed.
      iii. Backup is taken.
   d. Recovery testing (base applications):
      i. If this is the first install of this type of application, formal application recovery and disaster recovery testing should be performed and documented.
      ii. If this application has previously been backed up, formal checks should be executed to confirm that the setup meets backup operational requirements *or* if such checks cannot be done, formal recovery testing should take place.
2. Development cycle:
   a. Repeat:
      i. Daily development.
      ii. Daily backups, appropriate to the type of development occurring. These backups may be different than the backups the final system may receive in production (e.g., databases might be initially backed up cold rather than hot). Where there are differences, they should be noted.
   b. If the intended production backup mechanism is different to the development/test backup mechanism, the production backup mechanism must be implemented at the end of the development cycle, with suitable testing to confirm successful operations; only the production backup mechanism should be used from this time. If any expansion of the backup system was required, it should now be in place to support the new system.

    c. If this is a new system or application, then during the development phase at least one total disaster recovery test should take place to ensure applications and procedures under development are indeed recoverable.

3. Test cycle:
   a. End user testing with daily backups.
   b. Confirmation that all of the required recovery tests have been performed successfully, with their processes clearly (and correctly) documented. These might include
      i. Cold, offline backups
      ii. Standard hot backups
      iii. Disaster recovery tests
   c. An authorized manager should sign off against any decision not to conduct tests, with a valid reason given.

4. Production operations:
   a. Following successful completion of steps (1) through (3), and having met the primary development and business objectives, a system can be service transitioned into production.
   b. The production cycle is as follows:
      i. Daily use.
      ii. Daily backups.
      iii. Monthly/yearly/other periodic backups as required.
      iv. Periodic file, directory, and application recovery testing.
      v. Disaster recovery testing as required by company policies.
      vi. Data life-cycle operations as required.
      vii. After designated periods of time or the purchase of new backup technologies, monthly/yearly/archival backups should be migrated to new backup media or technologies, or processes put in place for the maintenance and testing of legacy media and technologies.
      viii. After designated periods of time, older media should be destroyed if necessary.

5. Post-production:
   a. System is decommissioned, with all applications shut down and no data access occurring.
   b. Final copies of the system are generated through cold, complete offline backups to minimize plug-in or OS compatibility requirements during any arbitrary future recovery.
   c. Documentation is generated for a recovery of the system from its final decommissioned backup and stored with the application, system, and infrastructure procedures. This documentation should include details of the backup software that needs to be used for recovery—in essence, this documentation should be written as if it were for a "green" site with no prior knowledge of the product that needs to bootstrap an implementation to recover the data.
   d. For business-critical systems in particular (or those with strong legal compliance restrictions), it may also be pertinent to generate additional

cold, offline backups with "common" tools such as native OS backup tools or open-source backup tools, so that very long-term recovery is not dependent on a single product.
    e. System is either redesigned for another purpose (potentially starting the process again) or retired.
    f. Processes should be enacted to maintain, test, and as necessary destroy the long-term retention backups independent of whether the original backup product remains the primary backup tool for the organization.

Bear in mind that the description mentioned earlier covers only *one* part of the data protection spectrum—yet it serves to demonstrate just how important it is for data protection activities to be considered within the service transition process.

5.4 CHANGE MANAGEMENT

Change management sits at the heart of any professional IT organization. There are two core groups who manage change within the business—the Change Advisory Board (CAB) and the Emergency Change Advisory Board (ECAB). The first deals with regular changes to IT infrastructure and systems, while the second (usually a subset of the first) meets as required to approve highly urgent and usually unanticipated changes that occur outside of the regular change process.

If data protection is to be seriously considered within an organization, an additional board needs to be considered, one that has at least one permanent member in each of the CAB and ECAB. This additional board is the Information Protection Advisory Council (IPAC).

The IPAC will be comprised of a variety of individuals and may include such roles as

- DPA—As described in the architectural component of this topic.
- *Key users*—The people in business groups who just *know* what is done. They're the long-term or go-to people within a department.
- *Technical owners*—While those who are accountable for a service should be involved in some level, it is the technical owners who are responsible for day-to-day successful operation, and as such they more appropriately sit on an IPAC.
- *HR/finance*—If the HR and finance departments are one-in-the-same, a single representative is usually sufficient; if they are separate, there should be a representative from each department.
- *Legal*—Somewhere, someone has to have an understanding of the legal ramifications of (a) choosing not to protect some data or (b) how long data should be kept for. This may not be a permanent role, but instead a floating role, which is invoked as required.
- *Business unit representatives*—Where key users and/or technical owners do not cover specific key business units, those business units should have a voice within the IPAC.

To avoid becoming unwieldy, the IPAC should be comprised of both permanent and floating members—the permanent members will represent the core, while the floating members will be appointed from key user groups, technical owners, and so on to *participate in* the group on an as-needed basis. Core members should have the authority and understanding of when and how to include interim/floating members in deliberations and decision-making processes.

The IPAC should meet independently of the change boards, and particularly for the standard change board, IPAC meetings should be scheduled such that members can evaluate proposed and upcoming changes on the basis of their potential impact to data protection capabilities within the organization. The IPAC should then determine who from the group should attend change board meetings to offer advice and guidance.

5.5   SUMMARY

IT governance is a topic large enough that an entire book could be dedicated to covering all the aspects of integrating data protection activities into it. Instead, this chapter has been deliberately brief, focusing on the key processes at a very high level instead. It should, however, be a spark for much larger conversations and collaborations within an organization, with the end goal being recognition (if not already present) of the importance of data protection in *all* aspects of systems design and management.

Our next chapter, Chapter 6, will serve as an in-depth example of the degree to which data protection processes should be built into activities already performed within an organization.

6 Monitoring and Reporting

6.1 OVERVIEW

There's a simple rule I recommend in data protection: if you don't know the state of a component or an activity, *assume it failed*. That means

- If you don't get told about the status of storage systems, assume drives are failing.
- If you don't know about the status of cross-site replication, assume it's down.
- If you don't know whether last night's backups completed without error last night, assume they all failed.

The list of potential failures could be an arm's length long and still nowhere near complete. This isn't to suggest you should be receiving constant alerts that every operation relating to data protection in an environment has finished and its failure/success status. However, all of the data protection activities in an environment *should* be monitored, and you *should* receive alerts whenever an error occurs that the relevant system can't automatically correct, and you *should* receive reports of all errors, system health checks, etc. If your systems aren't sufficiently monitored, you should always be assuming the worst.

Regardless of whether it's proactive protection or reactive recovery, data protection is a critical IT function for any business, and as a critical function, it requires the appropriate level of attention, which means it must be monitored, and there must be reporting. The growing number of devices and systems to be monitored and reported on within enterprises should not be seen as an impediment or reason to avoid these activities, but instead a driving factor *to* perform them. Indeed, there is a growing industry now around automated parsing and monitoring of events at the sorts of scale experienced by large multinational organizations; millions or hundreds of millions of log entries are filtered to hundreds of thousands of events that are parsed to dozens or hundreds of *incidents* that can be investigated and reviewed by an administration team within a single shift. The two alternatives to automated monitoring are both unpalatable: linear scaling of employee numbers based on the number of log entries generated by systems or blissfully ignoring something unless it triggers a failure somewhere down the track.

Monitoring and reporting are often two sides of the same coin. It is almost impossible to build reports without having harvested useful data in the monitoring phase, and those reports allow the business to determine potential new areas to monitor.

Monitoring and reporting of data protection within an organization must be a gestalt. While each individual component (backup/recovery, storage, replication, etc.) might have their own individual monitoring and reporting options, it's important the business be able to see their health and trends as a whole. The primary reason for this, of course, is that data protection isn't an individual activity—configuring a RAID storage system doesn't guarantee against data loss on its own. Configuring a backup and recovery system doesn't guarantee perfect data recoverability, either. In the modern enterprise, *cascading failure*, whereby two or more failures occur after one another, increasing risk of either downtime or data loss must be considered at all times in understanding the health of the data protection environment. For instance, many organizations will consider a lower-than-desirable backup success ratio acceptable as a one-off event. Trending and reporting within the backup and recovery system might indicate such one-off events are far too regular within the organization, but trending and reporting across the *entire* data protection suite might indicate a considerably higher danger level if, for instance, storage systems are encountering more drive swap-outs than normal at the same time regular backup failures are occurring. For some systems, failures are not only noted individually, but also cumulatively: a single backup failure for a system might be considered acceptable, but the same system failing its backup 3 days running may be considered unacceptable.

In short, an insular, silo-like approach to monitoring and reporting within individual components of data protection systems is the enemy of a healthy enterprise.

The ultimate strategy therefore of monitoring and reporting within data protection must be to have a *single source of truth*; a single platform that can reveal the entire health of the data protection environment. More so than health though, only by combining all aspects of data protection can a business understand its current risk levels, compliance levels, and operational costs. At a high level, we can envisage this *single source of truth* layer as per Figure 6.1.

The point of such a diagram is to emphasize the need to decouple the business visibility and reporting layer from the actual infrastructure and operations layer. It is common to see businesses focus too much on finding a single product that can achieve *all* of their data protection requirements; yet by the nature of the different functions, service level agreements (SLA) and operational aspects a single tool

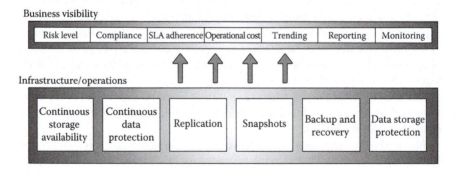

FIGURE 6.1   Monitoring and reporting as a single source of truth.

is unviable. Instead, the focus should be on the ability to integrate all of the *business visibility* of the discrete and individual data protection components into a single view.

6.2 MONITORING

Within data protection, monitoring is the real-time or semi-real-time capture and analysis of system events and data that gives the business a clear understanding of whether the environment is *reliable* (i.e., fit for purpose).

There are three key focuses of monitoring in data protection:

1. Health
2. Capacity
3. Performance

Ideally, all monitoring would be real time—that is, an event occurs, and it is immediately detected and analyzed by the business.* However, it's essential to be pragmatic—not all software and systems will offer the same broad levels of monitoring integration, and it's (largely) unreasonable to assume that every product an organization buys or leases will immediately and seamlessly integrate with whatever monitoring product is deployed.

Monitoring should therefore be able to aggregate real-time data collection and semi-real-time or business real-time data collection. Semi/business real-time data collection might cover scenarios such as

- Systems that do not support monitoring protocol X but do support monitoring protocol Y—Installing or configuring an interceptor/translator should be an acceptable alternative.
- Black box systems that perform logging only locally—If scriptable, remote login is capable, this should be investigated to still allow for the periodic extraction of logged data and inclusion in the overall monitoring system.
- Systems that provide valuable data both as automated logging and executable reports—If the executable reports generate summary information or other details not readily apparent from the automated logging, these reports should be periodically harvested if they can increase the quality of the monitoring.

Of course, monitoring encompasses other areas as well. Many businesses will typically need to monitor systems for security and compliance, for instance. Any monitoring or reporting system deployed for data protection should ideally be capable of integrating into umbrella systems that provide these capabilities and whatever other options are required by the business.

---

* Another approach is "business real-time": acknowledging that real-time monitoring may not always be required so long as the monitoring can be done frequently enough that it meets the business *needs*.

6.2.1 HEALTH

At the most basic level, monitoring for data protection health could be seen as monitoring of failures. That might include highlighting

- Storage components that have failed
- Data replication functions that have failed
- Backup and recovery failures

While this is a good starting point, it's not sufficient for truly effective monitoring of a data protection environment. Effective monitoring also has to consider data such as

- Mean time between failures (MTBF)
- Mean time to repair (MTTR)
- Predicted failures (e.g., system S.M.A.R.T.* status)
- Warnings

Both MTBF and MTTR offer very useful information in a data protection environment.

6.2.1.1 Drive Failures and Recovery Time

The classic use of MTBF and MTTR within data protection is of course RAID storage. While the reliability of storage systems has improved considerably over the years, they are not 100% immune to component failure.

RAID systems are a fundamental component of data protection—their entire purpose is to provide a mechanism to sustain continued access to data in the event of a component failure *and* be able to rebuild from that failure.

Consider two of the most common RAID levels:

1. RAID 1 (mirroring)—Whereby every block of data written to one device is written to another device. In the event of one device failing, the other device can still be read from (minimum two disks).
2. RAID 5 (parity)—Whereby data is written in stripes with a parity checksum written to one alternating drive in the stripe. In the event of a failure, the data can be reconstructed by the remaining data plus checksum information in each stripe (minimum three disks).

For any RAID level, we must consider that there is a cost (in time, and for that matter, energy) in reestablishing full protection after a failed component is replaced.

If a disk in a two-drive mirror fails, then the cost of reconstructing the mirror (MTTR) is in a worst-case scenario the cost of reading the entire contents of the first disk and writing that content to the replacement disk. Thus, however many blocks

---

* Self-Monitoring, Analysis and Reporting Technology.

there are, RAID reconstruction will take double that in operations—each block will trigger a read and a write.

If a disk in a three-drive RAID-5 unit fails, then the MTTR can be considerably higher than the MTTR in a two-drive RAID-1. Consider: Each stripe must be read and the data reconstructed based on the combination of available data and/or parity information, then the stripe must be adjusted in the RAID unit, either by writing the missing data/parity or rewriting the entire stripe.

Throughout the recovery time for storage, it's quite usual for the storage to still be online and being used—which of course impacts the recovery time even further. (Even if the storage is used *read only*, the remaining drives will be still required to facilitate data access *while* reconstructing, and such scenarios are rare regardless.) Such an impact is of course a two-way street; while it slows down the recovery time for the RAID unit, it equally slows down day-to-day usage of the system as well. Failures that occur during critical usage periods can therefore have a substantially higher impact on operations.

Combined knowledge of (average) MTBF results and the MTTR information can yield smarter operational decisions within a data protection environment, such as

- Understanding whether standard SLAs for data access continue to be met as the usage profile changes or the volume of data grows
- Understanding when data might be migrated between tiers or away from underperforming storage when there appears to be a higher risk of potential failure
- Predicting, based on prior recovery times, how long a recovery is likely to take in order to provide accurate performance degradation time frames to the business

6.2.1.2 Broader Uses of MTBF and MTTR

While usually considered from the perspective of disk drives and RAID units, the concept of MTBF and MTTR equally applies to other areas of data protection. Consider the different data protection scenarios outlined in Table 6.1.

Even if these aren't tracked *literally* in terms of MTTR and MTBF, it's pertinent to keep in mind that the core concepts of *time to recover* and *time between failures* are absolutely critical in the planning, implementation, and maintenance of a data protection system.

6.2.2 CAPACITY

While health is undoubtedly the most critical *immediate* concern for data protection monitoring, monitoring for capacity plays an important role as well.

This will likely have a significant overlap with general information life-cycle capacity monitoring, but there are particular areas that need to be focused on for data protection.

6.2.2.1 RAID/Data Storage

In a classic RAID environment where all LUNs and storage are 100% allocated on initial request, there is very little monitoring to be done within RAID or data storage

TABLE 6.1

Broader Uses of MTBF and MTTR

Data Protection Activity	MTTR	MTBF
Backup and recovery	Time taken to recover data once it is requested *or* once the recovery commences.[a]	How soon after data is backed up before a recovery is requested for it vs. the frequency at which the backup is performed.[b]
Snapshots	Time taken to roll back to a point in time or retrieve data from a snapshot.[c]	How regularly data needs to be retrieved from snapshots vs. the frequency at which the snapshots are taken.
Replication (usually cross-site)	Time taken to *either* bring the remote replica online for primary production access *or* replicate it back to repair a failed primary replica (will depend on the usage profile of the replica).	How regularly the site link fails (or perhaps more correctly—how *reliable* the site link is). The impact of the reliability of the replication link will depend considerably on the volume of data being generated and the way in which the replication system reestablishes synchronization after a failure.

[a] Both metrics are actually important, but the former usually requires a mix of manual and automatic processes and is thus more challenging to discover. The latter metric can usually be provided directly from the backup and recovery software.

[b] This is actually a highly important consideration when designing backup and recovery systems in order to ensure that data most regularly requested for recoveries can be retrieved as quickly as possible.

[c] The former applies to block and file-level snapshots, the latter more usually to file-level snapshots that are automatically made available to users.

for capacity as it affects data protection. That's not to say monitoring isn't required, but it falls to the broader topic of storage capacity tracking.

However, with storage systems offering increasingly advanced options relating to thin provisioning or just-in-time capacity expansion, the importance of tracking capacity and its impact on data protection *is* asserting itself.

At a most basic level, consider even home-office/small-office storage arrays from companies such as Drobo®. One of the unique selling points of the Drobo storage system is its ability to present a thinly provisioned filesystem constructed of multiple drive sizes and/or types while still providing data protection. A five-drive unit, for instance, might be initially populated with 5 × 2 TB drives. On the expectation that storage would *grow*, a filesystem can be presented to the end user/computer based on the *eventual* capacity of 5 × 4 TB hard drives.

Thus, the initial filesystem would be presented by around 10 TB of drives providing in the order of 7–8 TB of *protected* capacity while appearing to the operating system as being approximately 18 TB.

Obviously in this scenario, it's not possible to copy, say, 12 TB of data to the initial filesystem that's provided by just 5 × 2 TB drives. The Drobo system is designed to *monitor* and report where capacity growth is preventing adequate data protection, and thus highlight the need to replace individual drives with larger ones in order to allow for continued data growth at the requested levels of redundancy.

This is the nature of thinly provisioned storage with data protection—not only is the actual storage presented to the end user thinly provisioned, but so too is the data redundancy, hence the need to monitor such systems carefully.

Monitoring in such a scenario can and should certainly be tied to general capacity modeling/monitoring. It's no good, for instance, to know that there is sufficient room for 20% data growth if broader capacity models predict there'll be a 40% spike in data over the 3 weeks and the purchasing cycle for additional storage is 6 weeks.

6.2.2.2 Snapshots

The first implementations of snapshots within IT were closer to tertiary mirrors in RAID-1 environments where the third mirror was snapped off to allow access to a quiesced copy of the data. (Indeed, in the early days, it was more likely to be the case that it was only a dual-drive mirror and it was the secondary mirror being temporarily removed.)

Such "snapshots" presented significant performance overhead. For instance, reattaching a previously detached mirror meant recopying the *entire* contents to resynchronize the mirrors.

This slow rebuild time leads to the use of bitmaps to more rapidly reattach mirrors. The bitmap would be used to track "dirty" regions on the detached mirror; in essence, whenever a write occurred to the *actual* mirror (the one still mounted for production use), the bitmap would be updated to indicate which blocks had been written to. When the detached mirror disk was subsequently reattached, the bitmap would be referred to and only those regions marked as *dirty* would be copied back across. (Presuming, of course, the detached mirror had been used *read only*, of course.)

Most snapshots now tend to be *incomplete* copies. While many storage systems provide options for snapshots that are exact 1:1 duplicates of the original LUN, the more common scenario usually involves a variation of *copy on first write* technology. (This will be explained in more detail in Chapter 10.)

Snapshots are not preprovisioned with storage; even a low-end enterprise storage system may support hundreds of snapshots of an individual LUN, and thousands of snapshots in total. Typically, the storage administrators will allocate a percentage of the storage array for use as a snapshot pool, and for the purposes of data protection, this pool capacity and utilization needs to be monitored carefully. The pool utilization will be mostly dependent on the workload of the original filesystems while snapshots are active; a single LUN for which there exists a snapshot could cause the consumption of a considerable amount of snapshot pool storage if it undergoes an unanticipated volume of updates.

6.2.2.3 Replication

Replication capacity considerations fall into two main categories:

1. Target capacity
2. Link bandwidth

Link bandwidth refers to whether the connection between the source and destination replication target is sufficient to allow the throughput of the data that must be sent. The speed of the link should have been considered long before replication is turned on, as it will directly affect considerations such as whether or not replication occurs synchronously or asynchronously. (Other factors, such as physical distance and latency, will also come into play here.)

For data protection scenarios, used link bandwidth must be continuously monitored and compared to data growth and (for asynchronous scenarios) data *backlog*— how far "behind" updates the replication target is from the source. More advanced replication technologies may employ compression and other bandwidth-saving techniques, yet the efficacy of such techniques is likely to be dependent on the type of data being replicated and the frequency at which it is updated.

Additionally, replication isn't always a 1:1 ratio. A business may deploy a 100 TB SAN in their primary site, but only deploy a 50 TB SAN in the disaster recovery site, with the intention to only replicate primary production data. However, it's easy to envisage scenarios in such a configuration where the data designated as "primary production" grows to exceed the capacity of the replication target. Alternately, replication can be many-to-one—a single replication target might receive data from multiple replication sources. If one or more of those replication sources grows in capacity, the cascading effect can equally be disastrous. What's more, in scenarios where there are multiple sources replicating to a single target, it's more likely than not to involve geographically disperse source systems, making capacity monitoring all the more important. This scenario in itself demonstrates the need for a global view approach to capacity monitoring; storage administrators at individual sites may very well be monitoring and managing data growth for their individual systems entirely reasonably, but the cumulative effect on the capacity requirements on the replication target needs to be considered *in light* of the capacity growth on the individual systems, not apart from them.

6.2.2.4   Backup and Recovery

The backup capacity requirement in a traditional storage model is relatively easy to understand. Let's consider a production environment that has 10 TB of data requiring backup and assume there's a 7% incremental change, day on day. Taking a fairly classic model approach, we'll assume the following backup cycles:

- Weekly full backups retained for 5 weeks
- Daily incremental backups retained for 5 weeks
- Monthly full backups retained for 7 years

For the daily/weekly backup cycle of 5 weeks, the storage requirements will be

- 5 [weeks] × 10 TB (fulls) = 50 TB
- 5 [weeks] × 6 [days] × (7% of 10 TB) = 5 × 6 × 0.7 TB = 21 TB

For the monthly full backups retained for 7 years, the storage requirements will be

- 7 [years] × 12 [months] × 10 TB = 840 TB

(Of course, this all assumes zero growth, which is fairly rare within a data environment.)

From these calculations, we see that a traditional backup model for 10 TB could result in storage requirements of 911 TB. Even if we shrink the requirements by dropping weekly fulls and moving to a monthly full backup cycle, the storage requirements stay reasonably high:

- (Average) 30 [days] × (7% of 10 TB) = 21 TB
- 7 [years] × 12 [months] × 10 TB = 840 TB

This gives a reduced total of approximately 861 TB—yet the ratios remain significantly high. Assuming even the better scenario of just doing monthly fulls, the ratio stands at 1:86.1—for every 1 TB of production data used, we're using 86.1 TB for the backups of that data over the life span of the data.

We'll cover storage requirements for data later, particularly in light of the impact deduplication is having on this footprint problem; in the meantime, the examples mentioned earlier serve well to demonstrate the profound requirement for backup capacity monitoring within an environment. Increasing the data backup requirements by a single terabyte can have significant flow-on effects to backup storage utilization, and traditionally this has been an area that businesses have paid little attention to. Tape in particular made this a hidden problem—a box of tapes here, a box of tapes there, and before they knew it businesses had *thousands* or *tens of thousands* of tapes in vaulted storage with backups on them that *may* never be recovered from.

Backup system capacity monitoring falls into two essential categories:

1. Knowing the "on-boarding" capacity of the backup environment: In its current configuration, what is the capacity it offers for taking *new* systems in, and what is the capacity impact of doing so?
2. Feeding into reporting, what does the capacity utilization growth of the backup system say about the long-term growth of the environment—that is, when will expansion be required?

Capacity does also need to be monitored for recovery situations as well, but this will be largely dependent on the products used for backup/recovery and the recovery scenarios the business requires. For example:

- Some deduplication products, for instance, may require particular recoveries to be staged *through* the appliance.
- If image-level backups are being taken of virtual machines but file-level recovery is not supported, it implies recovering an entire virtual machine, even if only a single file needs to be recovered from within that virtual machine.
- Database or application administrators may insist that backups be generated as dump files to disk and backed up as part of a normal filesystem

backup operation. In a recovery scenario, it may be necessary to provide recovery capacity not only for the destination database, but also the dump file to restore from.*

Recovery capacity requirements demonstrate the need for reasonably tight integration between production and backup/recovery systems capacity monitoring. It is not unheard of recoveries to be delayed or even canceled when there's insufficient storage space for the recovery to be facilitated.

6.2.3 PERFORMANCE

Having already dealt with monitoring for health and capacity, performance monitoring is actually the simplest variable to consider, given that performance of a data protection environment is affected and governed most by

- The health of the components—Failing components or components in recovery mode will have different performance characteristics from normal.
- Capacity—Growth in capacity will have a direct impact on the performance of the data protection activities.

In this, performance monitoring is actually the most straightforward:

- RAID and data storage—how long it takes to rebuild
- Backup—speed of backups versus backup windows
- Recoveries—speed of recoveries versus the recovery SLAs required
- Snapshots—whether or not snapshots adversely affect (or are adversely affected by) production storage load, and vice versa
- Replication—speed at which data is either replicated from the source to the target or in the event of a significant failure from the target back to the source

6.3 REPORTING

6.3.1 REPORTING AS MONITORING AGGREGATION

In the simplest scenario, reporting represents the aggregated data collected by the various monitoring systems in the environment. Reports based purely on data collected by monitoring may focus on "dashboard" functionality—for example, the status of backup operations may be shown color coded like traffic lights—red, amber, or green depending on whether there are serious issues, warnings, or entirely successful operations, respectively. This would allow an administrator to view the

---

* In this case, you'll note I've used the words *recover* and *restore*. Typically in database circles, a recovery refers to retrieving the files and data from the backup storage, and a *restoration* refers to either rebuilding the database from those recovered files or reinstating database consistency using those recovered files.

health of backup operations at a glance and only require drill down to investigate serious issues or warnings.

Aggregation of monitoring allows for at-a-glance views of overall data protection health, such as

- Were there storage drive failures during the month?
- What capacity of the snapshot storage pool was used each day during the quarter?
- Did replication fall behind at any point during the week?
- What was the percentage of successful backups each day?
- Did any recoveries fail?

Once data protection monitoring is being aggregated into these simple reports, the business can start looking at trending.

6.3.2 REPORTING FOR TRENDING AND PREDICTIVE PLANNING

Reporting on trends is a crucial step in understanding how an environment is changing. A backup system, for instance, may be deployed on the expectation that data is only growing at 9% year on year, but month-by-month monitoring of backup utilization may quickly demonstrate an *actual* growth rate of 15% or more.

Equally, trending may determine that the bandwidth allocated for replication will be exhausted in 6 months based on data growth, not 18 as originally budgeted for when the link was installed.

Referring again to the DIKW model presented in the introduction (Figure 1.2), we can say

- Base data is collected by monitoring.
- Information is the collation of the individual units of data into a picture of system health, capacity, or performance.
- Aggregated monitoring information presented as reports provides the business *knowledge*, be it in the form of dashboards, traditional reports, or drill-down details.
- Wisdom comes from using all the accumulated data, information, and knowledge to provide trends on utilization and predictions on system exhaustion.

Predictive planning comes from applying situational understanding from trending information or smoothing out details in order to see trends past individual spikes or troughs. For instance, consider the sample backup utilization details shown in Table 6.2.

If the final 12 months utilization from Table 6.2 were to be graphed, it would likely resemble that shown in Figure 6.2.

In such a format, this reveals the spike of backup utilization around end-of-financial year (assuming it's an Australian company), but the spike itself makes understanding overall utilization trending a little more difficult.

TABLE 6.2
Backup Utilization over Time, Raw Data

Months	Backup Utilization (TB)
Aug	19.1
Sep	11.1
Oct	9.8
Nov	10.2
Dec	10.4
Jan	10.5
Feb	11.2
Mar	11
Apr	11.5
May	12.4
June	17.4
July	18.4
Aug	19.6
Sep	11.4
Oct	12.3
Nov	12.9
Dec	13.5

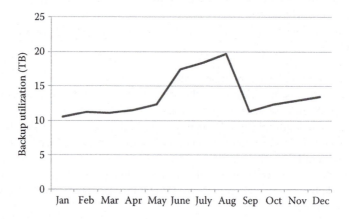

FIGURE 6.2   Raw backup utilization graph.

Switching to a 3-month rolling average, we'd have a set of data such as that shown in Table 6.3.

When graphed, the data from Table 6.3 would resemble that shown in Figure 6.3.

Even with a slightly smoothed graph, there's little substantive information to be gleaned in terms of trending—but switching to a 6-month rolling average introduces better clarity, and this can be seen in Table 6.4 and Figure 6.4.

TABLE 6.3
Backup Utilization with 3-Month Rolling Average

Month	Backup Utilization (TB)	3-Month Rolling Average (TB)
Aug	19.1	
Sep	11.1	
Oct	9.8	
Nov	10.2	
Dec	10.4	
Jan	10.5	10.4
Feb	11.2	10.7
Mar	11	10.9
Apr	11.5	11.2
May	12.4	11.6
June	17.4	13.8
July	18.4	16.1
Aug	19.6	18.5
Sep	11.4	16.5
Oct	12.3	14.4
Nov	12.9	12.2
Dec	13.5	12.9

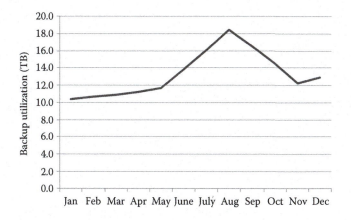

FIGURE 6.3 Backup utilization with 3-month rolling average.

With a 6-month rolling average being graphed, we can glean a better understanding of the overall backup capacity utilization trend. These are the sorts of differences between reporting based on the raw data and reporting on trends that are important to data protection planning within an environment. Both sets of information (in this case, the raw data and most particularly the 6-month rolling average) are of significant use—the raw data when graphed most succinctly points out the need for

TABLE 6.4

Backup Utilization with 6-Month Rolling Average

Months	Backup Utilization (TB)	6-Month Rolling Average (TB)
Aug	19.1	
Sep	11.1	
Oct	9.8	
Nov	10.2	
Dec	10.4	
Jan	10.5	11.9
Feb	11.2	10.5
Mar	11	10.5
Apr	11.5	10.8
May	12.4	11.2
June	17.4	12.3
July	18.4	13.7
Aug	19.6	15.1
Sep	11.4	15.1
Oct	12.3	15.3
Nov	12.9	15.3
Dec	13.5	14.7

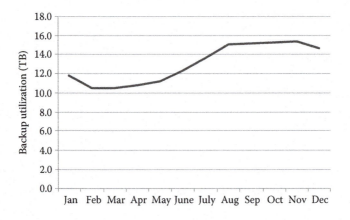

FIGURE 6.4   Backup utilization with a 6-month rolling average.

the backup environment to be able to cope with a potentially significant spike in capacity requirements during the June–Aug time frame. The 6-month rolling average (particularly if we envisage it being extended to a 2- or even 3-year time frame) gives a reliable trend, largely unaffected by spikes observed in any specific months, of the growth of backup capacity utilization within the environment.

The larger the business, the more likely it is that there'll actually be a need for full-time employees (FTEs) to concentrate on reporting and monitoring analysis; except in the largest of organizations it's likely this will be tasks that are shared between data protection and broader data life-cycle processes, but regardless, it is a required function. (Intelligently designed monitoring and reporting systems that can provide visibility over the entire data protection environment are also likely to reduce FTE requirements and deliver more reliable results.)

6.3.3 AUTOMATED REPORTING

It's a well-known fact within the backup and recovery realm that a backup that is not automated is not done. Or rather, while it may be sporadically performed, it hardly represents a reliable process deserving of the appellation of *system*.

One might argue the same for reports—while there will always be situations where it is necessary to manually run a report (either as an out-of-band execution of a standard report or an entirely new report), wherever possible reports should be developed to be executed and distributed automatically.

However, a report that isn't read may as well not be executed, so automated reports don't solve the perennial problem of being *used*, they just make it easier for people to use them.

As such, once the system reaches the point where there is monitoring in place, reports generated from aggregated monitoring data, and reports based on trends and predictive analysis, it becomes a *process* problem to ensure that the reports are actually dealt with.

As covered in Chapter 4—the technology is the easy part. The human and process aspects are the more challenging. Yet a business has to be prepared to tackle these problems if it is to have any chance of reliably understanding the state or direction of its data protection environment.

6.4 MONITORING AND REPORTING SLA COMPLIANCE

Throughout the book, we discuss SLAs. Chapter 19 in particular will discuss SLAs in the broader context of data protection service catalogs. When SLAs are established, it's important that monitoring and reporting systems be capable of (or can be extended to) actually tracking and providing details of SLA compliance. For instance, it may be established that as part of backup SLAs, no system can fail more than three consecutive backups. In order to ensure those SLAs are met, it will be necessary not only to have an appropriately designed backup system, but it will also be necessary to report consecutive failures of backups within the environment— such as providing a dashboard view for backup administrators showing hosts that have failed 1, 2, or 3 consecutive backups. While arguably this information can be assembled from individual backup completion reports, a single panel showing critical information related directly to SLA compliance becomes increasingly critical as the size and the complexity of the environment grows.

6.5   SUMMARY

There's an old philosophical thought exercise:

> If a tree falls in a forest and nobody is there to hear it, does it make a sound?

In a nutshell the question is about perceived versus actual reality. This is perhaps the heart of the requirement around monitoring and reporting—if something fails but its failure is not recorded, not noted, not *noticed*, then how do we know it has failed? An environment is only as reliable as its components, and if we're not actively aware of the health of the individual components, we can't truly be aware of the health of the environment itself.

Monitoring and reporting within a data protection environment shouldn't be seen solely as a means of tracking and reporting failures or issues. While those functions are critical, monitoring and reporting make charge-back processes simple *and* accurate. Similarly, they enable the management and administrators of the environment to justify resources, budget, and attainment of key performance indicators. In compliance-dominated businesses, these details actually become *essential* to allowing the business to pass mandatory external audits of its infrastructure. Individually inspecting a month's worth of backup results, for instance, to calculate the average success rate experienced in the business can be done, of course, but it will be a time-consuming process potentially subject to human error. Statistics automatically published by monitoring systems every day providing the same formatted information make the auditing process simple and the justification of the data protection environment substantially easier.

Arguably you could well state that a data protection environment that doesn't include comprehensive monitoring and reporting is merely a loose assemblage of components. Indeed, far too much focus is given in most businesses toward the notion of a single unified management interface that can administer *every* layer of data protection from backup through snapshots and replication all the way through to continuous storage availability and continuous data protection. While such interfaces are likely to evolve as a result of hyperconverged infrastructure, a real data protection *environment* can be created *already* by focusing instead on a unified and integrated approach to monitoring and reporting. Having both layers available will undoubtedly further hone data protection integration, but the unified monitoring and reporting layer will *always* remain critical.

7 Business Continuity

7.1 INTRODUCTION

The first mistake usually made in IT relating to business continuity, particularly among the more technical or more junior staff, is an assumption that the terms "disaster recovery" and "business continuity" are synonymous. In simple terms, this would be akin to believing that a regular schedule for changing the oil in a car is the same as complete servicing plan for it.

Business continuity is in actual fact *not* an IT function at all. Or rather, it's not a function that's driven by IT. Any business that *makes* it an IT-driven function has made a critical mistake. The purpose of business continuity, as its name suggests, revolves around keeping the business running, or in the event of a significant disruption, allowing the business to recommence operations. Without a doubt, IT will play a function in this for all except the most esoteric of businesses. Yet, IT can't be the driving consideration (even if the business is an IT company). The focus must always be the actual functions provided by the business to its consumers: its customers and clients both external and internal.*

While business continuity does have a much broader scope, our focus in this chapter will be constrained only to those topics overlapping with data protection.

7.2 BUSINESS VERSUS IT FUNCTIONS

One of the most essential activities in working on business continuity is to conduct all planning around *business functions* rather than *IT functions*. Business continuity in and of itself is not concerned with *email* or *DNS* or *intranets*, but instead with the services and functions the business offers to perform revenue generation. Business continuity therefore concerns itself wholly with those business functions. These will inevitably vary from business to business in detail and priority, but a few common functions for many businesses might include such areas as

- Billing
- Customer order fulfillment
- Stock control
- Payroll

While the continuity plan for any business function will very likely include IT-related disaster recovery plans, even for seemingly entirely IT-centric business

---

* Think of our system maps and system dependency tables outlined in Chapter 4, for instance. The final diagram and table both made clear mention of the *business functions* as well as any supporting IT functions.

functions, the IT disaster recovery plan will rarely be the *only* part of the business continuity plan.

In the same way that IT disaster recovery plans should be built around reliance on or importance of individual components via system dependency maps and tables, business continuity plans will also need to be built around the criticality of individual business functions being protected. This will typically result in business functions being broken down into categories such as the following:

- *Business (or mission) critical*—The business will fail if the function is not performed.
- *Critical*—The business will incur substantial costs if unable to perform the function or may be at risk of failure if multiple critical functions fail.
- *Essential*—The function is important to the business but an outage can be sustained without *risk* to the business.
- *Nonessential*—The interruption to the function does not cost or impair the ability of the business to operate.

Such classification of business functions will be in itself a business process, and the IT department will typically *at most* provide input as a standard business unit to such a classification process.

7.3   RISK VERSUS COST

When evaluating risk versus cost decisions for business continuity, the business should be prepared to evaluate three potentially different approaches, namely:

1. *Continuity*—where business processes must continue to run with as little (or no) interruption or alteration as possible (i.e., continuous availability)
2. *Restoration*—where an interruption is acknowledged, with deadlines established for the restoration of services
3. *Triage*—where an interruption is acknowledged, with plans for *work-arounds* to be put in place before restoration can be achieved at a later point

While such approaches *might* be determined on a company-wide scale, it will more usually be the case that they'll be determined on a business-function-by-business-function basis and will be related directly to the criticality of the business function, as discussed in the previous section. Consider an airport, for instance:

- Air traffic control systems will require *continuity.*
- *Restoration* plans and systems might be deemed sufficient for shared network and computing systems for individual airline help desks.
- A failure in the scheduling systems for airport parking allocation and shuttle busses might be handled through procedural *triage* until such time as a solution is determined.

While continuity and restoration approaches to handling failures will typically also include some form of triage, the difference will be that business functions will be severely impeded *without* primary restoration or ongoing operations, whereas lower priority systems might be kept running without risk or substantial business impact on an ongoing basis via triage alone.

No business, regardless of size, financial backing, employee knowledge, or geographic distribution, can entirely eliminate risk from their IT environment. For instance, with the human race effectively planet bound, even the most risk-averse company in the world is unlikely to develop strategies for dealing with scenarios such as

- Planet-killer asteroid hitting Earth
- Runaway nanotechnology experiment destroying all matter
- Rogue state destroying the moon and showering the world with debris

Business continuity therefore is *always* a risk-versus-cost elimination process. While a planet-killer asteroid striking the Earth would represent a considerable business disruption, the cost of developing and implementing a strategy to overcome such a scenario would likely *not* be considered as something that should be invested in.

Extreme examples may sound silly, but they do serve to highlight the decision-making and planning process that goes into business continuity. A business will evaluate particular failure models or event scenarios and determine

- The risk of it happening
- The risk to the business if it happens
- The cost of protecting against and recovering from the event
- The cost of *not* recovering from the event

After these have been determined, the business can more reasonably assess an approach to each potential scenario. It is here we start to see where business continuity strategies and considerations exceed those for disaster recovery. The IT approach or focus on a site loss will invariably deal with the infrastructure aspects of recovery—getting desktops and laptops available, enabling network infrastructure, getting servers and storage up and running, and restoration of data and activation of applications. For the business, this will be just a subset of the considerations. Other areas of focus will include plans for the number of staff that need to have access to the alternate site (and how many would be directed to work from home), physical security arrangements, general facilities management, and so on. In short: business continuity isn't specific to IT systems failures and, in addition to any specific considerations relating directly to IT systems failures, will encompass broader risks such as

- Human resource risks
- Competitive risks
- Environmental risks
- Legal and regulatory risks

Therefore from the perspective of the IT department, a disaster recovery plan might be titled "Restarting Production Systems at the Disaster Recovery Site," but this might be called by any of a number of business continuity plans including

- Physical destruction of primary datacenter
- Systems search and seizure in primary (colocation) datacenter
- Natural disaster
- Ongoing city grid power outage

While undoubtedly the IT disaster recovery plan relating to the restart of production systems at the disaster recovery site will play a valuable part in each of these scenarios, it won't be the only part. Other aspects considered by the business continuity plan might include

- Staff relocation processes
- Activation of crisis management teams
- Activation of fiduciary or compliance countdowns (a business, for instance, might have regulatory requirements stating it can only run without a DR site for 48 hours before it has to report to a government body)
- Changed business metrics (a plan, for instance, might work on the basis of only providing 75% of standard business responsiveness)

While IT staff may have to change their work location in such a situation and senior IT may form part of the crisis management teams, the core business will be responsible for countdowns, changed metrics, and ownership of the crisis management process.

7.4 PLANNING DATA PROTECTION STRATEGIES AND SERVICE LEVEL OBJECTIVES

An important aspect to the IT considerations in business continuity is to have a thorough understanding of (and agreement with the business over) the impact of a disaster recovery or business continuity situation on data protection requirements.

Consider, for instance, a scenario where a business has an NAS array at their production site with a series of volumes. In addition to standard snapshots taken periodically for rapid data protection, the business also replicates *all* volumes to another NAS array at their disaster recovery site so that if the primary site or primary array is lost, the data is still immediately accessible. This might resemble something along the lines of Figure 7.1.

In such a scenario, the business may seek to gain greater use out of the mirrored NAS by performing backups from *this* data, thereby practically eliminating any performance impact on active/in-use data at the production site, and such a configuration might resemble that shown in Figure 7.2.

This immediately makes the mirrored NAS considerably more useful to the business. Whereas before it had effectively been sitting "idle" other than to receive mirrored data in anticipation of a disaster that may not occur, it has now been

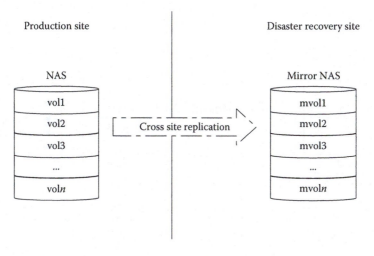

FIGURE 7.1   NAS in production site mirrored to NAS in disaster recovery site.

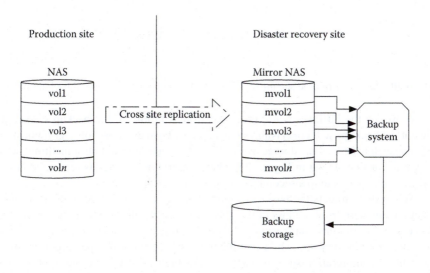

FIGURE 7.2   NAS in prod site mirrored to NAS in DR site with backups at DR.

incorporated more deeply into the business data protection environment by serving as the source for backups of NAS hosted data.

It is here that the *risk* versus *cost* component of business continuity and disaster recovery comes into play again. At this point, *in isolation to the components shown,* the business is arguably protected from the following scenarios:

- Loss of data at production site
- Loss of NAS array at production site
- Loss of production site

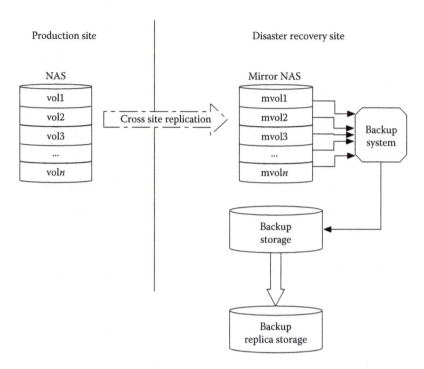

FIGURE 7.3   NAS in prod site mirrored to NAS in DR site with replicated backups at DR.

However, the business is *not* protected from a failure in the backup storage as historical backups will conceivably be lost. So the business must consider replication strategies for the backup storage as well. The first option might be something along the lines of that shown in Figure 7.3, where the backup storage is replicated at the disaster recovery site to a secondary copy of the backup storage.

While this protects the business against loss of backup storage, it does not protect the business from the loss of the disaster recovery site. At that point, there's no access to the backups that have been taken. To protect the business against a loss of the disaster recovery site while still theoretically allowing for data recovery from backup, a configuration such as that shown in Figure 7.4 will be required. In this configuration, the backup data is replicated across to the production site after it has been written at the disaster recovery site. (Or alternately, a third site entirely.)

In here, a business might think that it has resolved all data protection problems relating to the NAS data, but there's still another potential scenario to be considered, that being the loss of the production site *and* the failure of the backup storage. To counter this, a business would need a solution such as that shown in Figure 7.5.

The end state configuration shown in Figure 7.5 will not of course be a guaranteed state for any business with production and disaster recovery sites. Much of the determination of what data protection service-level objectives (SLOs) will exist in a disaster recovery situation will depend on the external and internal requirements of the business. A mid-size company with little to no legal compliance considerations may

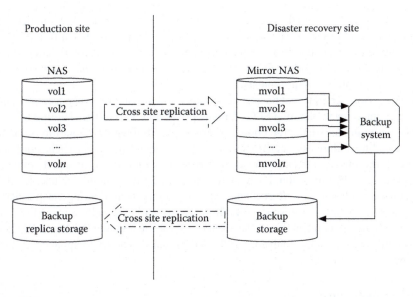

FIGURE 7.4   NAS in prod site mirrored to NAS in DR site with backups at DR replicated to prod site.

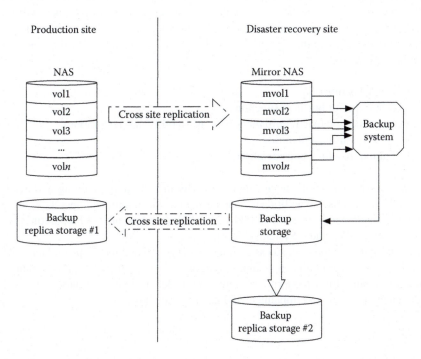

FIGURE 7.5   NAS in prod site mirrored to NAS in DR site with backups at DR replicated to prod site *and* a secondary copy at DR.

feel entirely at ease with the configuration shown in Figure 7.3 or 7.4. A smaller company again might feel no need to go beyond the configuration shown in Figure 7.2. A multinational finance firm however may find that only the configuration shown in Figure 7.5 meets both their internal recovery requirements *and* their externally imposed compliance requirements.

The lesson herein is that business continuity and disaster recovery scenarios must be accounted for in planning SLOs for data protection. Part of the planning for business continuity and data protection is a series of "… but what if?" questions relating to cascading failures or scenarios, with solutions determined for each, until such time as the business decides any further risk mitigation is unwarranted compared to the cost of the protection. Each contingency determined should include details of the enacted solution *as well as* changes to various targets and timings such as RPOs and RTOs—again with respect to both internally and externally imposed requirements. (This might mean that in the event of a total site loss, the RTOs and RPOs for standard recoveries are doubled, but the RPOs and RTOs for compliance-required recoveries are maintained.)

7.5   SUMMARY

The scope of business continuity planning is considerably beyond that of data protection systems. While data protection systems and policies can play a substantial part in either continuous systems availability or service restoration, they will be a subsidiary aspect to the overall process. Organizations wishing to perform adequate business continuity planning will need to be aware of a variety of factors, including but not limited to

- Business functions
- Criticality of business functions
- Legal compliance requirements (for availability and restoration)
- Risk versus cost planning
- Human resource considerations

Businesses wishing to engage more formally in continuity planning will need to consult legal counsel in addition to considering moral and human imperatives as well as recognized standards such as ISO-22301 ("Societal security—Preparedness and Continuity Management Systems—Requirements").

As such, the scope of business continuity is well beyond the scope of data protection systems and could occupy an entire book (or series of books) in itself, but it is now impossible for a modern company to consider business continuity *without* an adequately planned and implemented data protection system.

8 Data Discovery

8.1 INTRODUCTION

Imagine for a moment receiving a completely sealed shipping container with no manifest or description of its contents and being told you have to protect it and its contents. With no understanding of the content, coming up with a protection scenario is going to be challenging. Do you assume it's just full of nonperishable goods? Do you assume it's full of fragile filigree? Do you assume it's full of highly explosive and sensitive bombs? Or perhaps you simply assume that it's in fact empty? Now imagine being presented with a dockyard *full* of shipping containers and not knowing *which* shipping container you're meant to protect—you're just told you have to protect *the* shipping container the company cares about. Any reasonable person would quite rightly believe this to be a task that can only ever be achieved in one of two ways based on the dearth of necessary information. The first is the easiest and cheapest, but also the least likely to succeed—pure chance. Just do an "OK" job and hope it yields sufficient results. The second is the "overkill" approach—imagine the content is everything that would be difficult to protect, imagine every possible "failure" scenario, then do everything necessary to achieve the goal. (This is in fact a good way to waste money *and* still comes with no guarantees.)

You can't protect what you don't know about. This is the core message of *Discovery*. If you don't take the time to discover the data and information within your environment, it's entirely possible that a significant amount of what you do for data protection is either a waste of time or a waste of money.

We've already touched on some aspects of discovery within the introduction to the book. Section 2.2 encouraged answering the following five core questions:

1. What is the data?
2. Where is the data?
3. Who uses the data?
4. When is the data used?
5. How is the data used?

Some of those topics will be partly revisited in this section for expansion, and we'll introduce some new considerations to the discovery process as well.

This chapter is not meant to be a comprehensive analysis of data discovery—that's a topic deserving of its own book. Instead, the focus will be on providing a sufficient overview to understand the importance of a rigorous data discovery process as a precursor to developing an adequately comprehensive data protection strategy.

8.2   WHAT WILL BE PROTECTED?

Consider a public library: most people who think of libraries think of rows upon rows of shelves filled with books, magazines, and periodicals, and these days, electronic media as well. Taking a few more moments of reflection though, we know that isn't the sum total of the library content. There'll be books, media, and other material that has been acquired but not yet cataloged and added to the system. Similarly, there will be content that has been temporarily "retired" due to space considerations and stored in archival areas. There'll also be books, media, and other material that *is* in the system but is currently sitting somewhere within the library being used by a patron. Of course, there'll also be books, media, and other material owned by the library but which is out on loan. This is *still* not *all* of the library—we also have to include the metadata: catalogs of content and loan information. Then we need to also consider the personnel, not to mention all the operational data, such as finances, purchase orders, employee pay records, planning, and so on. A public library is far more than just "books."

So while the rows and rows of bookshelves in the library form an important part of the content of the library from the end users' perspective, it's not by any means the *whole* content of the library.

This in essence demonstrates a common enough mistake made in IT wherein it's assumed the servers and storage systems in the datacenters of the company are the sum total (or near enough to) of all data that needs to be protected.

Even within the datacenters, this isn't likely to be the case. Talk to just a few people in the storage industry and you'll hear horror stories where even large organizations have had their operations knocked out (or transferred to secondary sites) due to a core switch being rebooted, but essential changes made months before were never committed beyond the active state and so were lost on reboot.

Datacenters never were solely used for servers and storage systems. This should reinforce the need for data protection advocates (DPAs)—people whose primary focus is not the management of the data but the protection of it, regardless of where it is or what it may be. These are the people who should be able to walk around a datacenter and point at every appliance and ask a multitude of questions such as

- What is this?
- Does it have any configuration?
- Does it have any data?
- What business functions rely on it working?
- What IT systems rely on it working?
- What happens if it fails?
- Is it protected?
- How is it protected?
- Who is responsible for the protection?
- Who vetted the protection plans?
- Is the protection tested?
- What is the disaster recovery plan?
- When was the disaster recovery plan last tested?

While the average organization will these days be far more likely to have good answers to all of these questions for any server or storage array in the datacenter, network switches (be they IP or fiber channel), PABX systems, environmental systems, and so on can still yield inconsistent responses—ironically because when we consider dependency maps, these systems are often highly critical for business function continuity.

Remember in all this there are three different aspects to data protection:

1. Protecting against loss of data
2. Recoverability of data if it is lost
3. Protecting against loss of *access* to data

While data loss is a serious problem, loss of access to data can be just as serious from a legislative or financial perspective. In most countries, banks and other financial organizations, for instance, have rigorous compliance obligations relating just to the availability of data, and regardless of those obligations, a company that can't access data required for transactions or customer interaction will be just as helpless as a company that has lost the data entirely. It is for this reason that protection needs to focus on *all* components of systems rather than just data. What would be worse for an organization? A single server failing requiring recovery or an outage caused by a core switch being rebooted with uncommitted configuration changes? While "worse" could be quantified, it's indisputable that *both* represent an outage and both represent data loss (configuration data after all is still data).

Just as it's foolish to imagine the only things in a datacenter requiring protection are the servers and storage, it's equally foolish to believe the only *data* requiring protection is to be found in datacenters. Even before *cloud* became a ubiquitous IT term, this was not the case: laptops, desktops, mobile phones, and other removable storage either owned by the company or by employees of the company are all potential sources of *unique* data within the organization.

Another challenge for businesses and their IT departments is posed by that double-edged sword, bring your own device (BYOD). BYOD policies have existed in a variety of businesses and forms for some time—for instance, in some countries businesses have offered novated leases on technology as well as vehicles, allowing staff to choose their own laptops outright and pay for it out of their gross/pretax earnings, with the machine belonging to the staff rather than the business. More recently, businesses have taken to encouraging users to provide their own cellular telephones and expensing the business portion of their usage rather than supplying a phone outright as part of the salary package. Similarly, many businesses now allow for users to make use of their own laptops at work, seeing every device purchased out of an employee's home budget as a potential saving.

Such savings are not without their own risks, however. Risks such as data security, application licensing, and network security are relatively well understood, but data protection is another of those risks that must be considered in such scenarios. If the device is *owned* by the user, how does the business enforce adequate protection of data on the device? Security policies might prohibit the use of local storage while connected to the network, but will be less effective when staff are disconnected, and users retaining administrative control over their own devices may very well disable any data protection mechanisms put in place. Alternatively, a blanket rule to include employee-funded devices into corporate data protection policies may leave a business exposed to copyright violations in this modern age of torrenting and pirating movies, TV, and music. Cumulatively, data protection, security, and licensing has made BYOD a Pandora's Box for many organizations, resulting in frequent and radical policy changes.

8.3   SHADES OF DATA

Traditionally, *dark* data is considered to be data that hasn't been classified or associated with an analytical tool or use. For example, log files that are generated but never processed might in the simplest way be considered a form of dark data.

A more comprehensive definition of dark data however expands to cover all the *unknown* data within an organization. This is the data generated by individual users on unconnected or uncataloged systems that may be sitting outside of standard storage management and protection systems. In this sense, it's not only data that is not classified or associated with analytical functions, but it's also data the business may fundamentally be unaware of.

Dealing with dark data requires three distinct disciplines within an organization: acceptance, anticipation, and discovery. Acceptance refers to an understanding that dark data *will* appear within the organization. At bare minimum, systems will be periodically deployed where data accumulates without monitoring and *some* users will find invariably ways around security policies that prohibit localized storage. Accepting that dark data can appear or accumulate within the organization allows the business and IT processes to *discuss* the issue with staff and develop policies for its discovery. Anticipation implies responsibility—someone (or, more correctly, some *role*) must have primary responsibility for thinking about where dark data might appear within an organization, both architecturally and operationally. The role most suited for this is the DPA, initially discussed in Chapter 5.

Following acceptance and anticipation, a business can properly discover dark data, a process that will include both manual and automated activities. The automated activities will come from the appliances and software tasked with searching, indexing, or analyzing content, and the manual processes will be where dark data is dealt with architecturally and operationally. Architecturally in examining new or revised systems, applications or business functions to determine all the areas where data might be created, and operationally in reviewing those systems, applications or business functions already *deployed* to determine what's being missed.

Once dark data has been discovered, it doesn't automatically transition to being *data*. At this point, you might consider it to be *gray* data. This is identified data outside of either storage, protection, or both management policies and requires decisions to be made on its type, function, and usefulness to the organization. In an ideal scenario, the vast amount of classification done here should be automated, but there will on occasion be a requirement for human intervention to determine the nature of the data. Such classification will be the same as discussed in Chapter 2, namely:

- What is the data?
- Where is the data?
- Who uses the data?
- When is the data used?
- How is the data used?

Part of the discovery process may very well alter the answers to some or all of those questions. Discovered data that has real business use might be moved to centralized, protected storage and its usage profile substantially increased. Regardless of where it is moved to, we should aim to ensure all discovered data is placed under *management*—protection, life cycle, and functional.

8.4 INDEXING

For the most part, indexing is more a function of information life cycle management (ILM) rather than information life cycle protection (ILP). However, as a function of the discovery process, data indexing within an organization does have the potential to substantially increase the accuracy of data protection activities. Indeed, indexing can provide several data protection benefits including

- *Locating data that needs to be protected*—During the initial discovery phase, indexing can help to show where data exists within the business, thereby reducing the amount of dark or gray data within the company.
- *Locating data that has been protected*—As unstructured data in particular grows within an organization, the chances of users *losing* data will also grow, but there's two types of *losing*. The conventional is accidental data deletion or corruption, but equally as vexing is users simply forgetting *where* they've saved data to. A comprehensive and accessible indexing system can reduce the data recovery requirements for an organization by allowing users to readily locate documents they've saved but subsequently lost sight of.
- *Tracking data that gets moved*—Not all data archival is performed via hierarchical storage management (HSM) techniques. Some companies, either as a result of budget, perceived cost, or even business function, prefer to literally *move* data during the archive process rather than leaving stubs behind for seamless access. Industrial or graphic design agencies might move entire projects off primary storage a certain length of time after work has been completed, recalling media if and only if a repeat run of the project is required. Educational organizations and medical companies equally may be required from a compliance perspective to maintain their data about students and patients, respectively, but see no need to keep it stubbed from primary to archive storage once a particular period of time has passed. Indexing becomes critical in this situation to allow accurate location of data once it's been moved.

Like archive, many businesses resist data indexing technologies out of a perceived up-front cost, failing to understand the cumulative impact of reducing the accessibility and discoverability of their data. If data is not *known* about within an organization, it can't in any way be considered to be adequately protected (or for that matter, managed). Indexing is therefore not an overhead cost, but an essential part of the prerequisite discovery process for building a comprehensive data protection solution.

More often than not, choosing to avoid indexing (or the discovery of dark data) because there's "too much" is an exercise in kicking the can down the road. If it's "too much" effort now when the business has, say, 500 TB of data, it's not going to be any easier when the business grows to 510 TB, 550 TB, 600 TB, or so on. Just as data sizes rarely shrink over time, delaying management activities about data doesn't make future activities any easier.

8.5   CLOSING REMARKS

Data discovery is by itself a large and complex topic that exists almost entirely within the realm of ILM. Its connection to ILP is simple yet profound: any data protection solution developed without discovery will be blinkered and focused solely on what individual *people* within the organization *think* about data location and criticality. This is likely to be accurate only in very small or very focused businesses, and that accuracy will decrease rapidly as the business grows or its data becomes more distributed. Alternatively, a business will spend increasingly larger sums of money on data protection "hoping" they have an effective solution but really have no way of proving it. This almost inevitably leads to the business resenting data protection costs, when the real problem is a root data management one.

Some would argue that data discovery is unimportant for data protection in well-architected environments, but this assumes systems will grow in an ordered and expected way at all times. Such assumptions are at best an ill-considered luxury and may in fact recklessly endanger data that becomes critical to the functioning of the business at a later point in time. So long as systems grow and business needs are susceptible to either internal or external change, the need for data discovery as a precursor activity for data protection will remain constant.

9 Continuous Availability and Replication

9.1 INTRODUCTION

9.1.1 WHAT'S A FEW NINES BETWEEN FRIENDS?

Since almost the inception of the computer industry—at least its adoption in business—an ever-increasing goal has been high availability. The more a system is available, the more the business functions that *rely* on that system can operate. As the criticality of those business functions increases, so does system availability become increasingly crucial for business operations. Further, with the globalization of commerce, more businesses find themselves having to provide 24 × 7 × 365 operations in order to remain competitive.

System availability is typically measured as a percentage, and so for many businesses the most *desirable* availability is 100%. Depending on the size, location, geographic dispersal, and profitability of the business—and the nature of the IT systems—100% availability may be unachievable, and so the next best thing is "high nines" availability.

If you consider the figures in Table 9.1, you can see the differences between several common availability percentages.

While a business might be content with 98% or even 95% availability for non-production systems, it's typical that the lowest acceptable availability level for a production system is around the 99% mark. (Most enterprises tend to aim for somewhere around 99.99% or 99.999% availability unless regulated otherwise. It is worth noting that some of the major public cloud providers end up struggling to deliver even 99% availability over a yearly period.)

Establishing percentage availability targets is not as simple as picking a number. The business also needs to determine what the availability is measured against.

In the first instance, a business needs to understand whether the availability is being measured against the *total* time in the sample time period or against the *planned availability* time in the sample time period. Depending on the business, compliance requirements, or system type, businesses might use availability periods such as

- All times
- 00:00:01 to 23:59:59 Monday to Friday
- All days except 8 am to 8 pm on the first Sunday of every month

In each instance, scheduled downtime should *not* be factored into the availability statistics. Thus, a system that is available all day every day for Monday to Friday

TABLE 9.1

System Availability as Percentages and Hours/Minutes/Seconds

	Unavailable Time (Hours:Minutes:Seconds)	
Percentage	During a 30-Day Period	During a Year
99	07:12:00	15:36:00
99.9	00:43:12	08:45:36
99.99	00:04:19	00:52:33
99.999	00:00:25	00:05:155
99.9999	00:00:02	00:00:31

but is unavailable most weekends would still achieve 100% availability based on the second availability target cited in the previous list. This is not by any means a "cop-out," but a deliberate focus only on the availability *needs* of the business when determining achieved availability statistics.

It's also important to consider the difference between *availability* and *uptime*. A common enough mistake in IT is to assume a 1:1 mapping between system availability and system uptime. In fact, the relationship will more resemble that shown in Figure 9.1.

While it is true that a system that is not *up* cannot be *available*, the same is not true in reverse. An intelligent business measures system availability not by whether or not it is up, but by whether or not it is *operational*. This does make recording system availability more interesting since uptime is a quantitative measurement while operational status is more usually a qualitative measurement. In order to make operational status a quantitative measurement, a business needs to understand what key attributes define operational status and undertaking sampling of those as well.

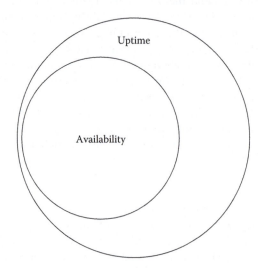

FIGURE 9.1   Example relationship between system availability and system uptime.

TABLE 9.2

Sample Response Times for Common User Tasks

Activity	Response Time		
	Available	Degraded	Unavailable
Load webpage	≤2 s	3–9 s	10 s+
Login completes	≤3 s	4–15 s	16 s+
List ≤7 days timesheet entries	≤5 s	6–20 s	21 s+
Load new timesheet entry form	≤3 s	4–10 s	11 s+
Lookup project code in timesheet entry	≤5 s	6–10 s	11 s+
Save timesheet entries	≤6 s	7–10 s	11 s+

For instance, consider a basic system such as employee timesheet service. Like any system, *uptime* will be easy to measure—it will be the amount of time the entire system is running. After planning with key users and business teams, the business might decide on several key indicators representing whether the system is *available*, *degraded,* or *unavailable* based on the potential for impact to user productivity. Example indicators are shown in Table 9.2.

Accounting for different usage profiles, different access locations and different usage periods make measuring availability even more challenging. The timesheet example used in Table 9.2, for instance, might have different response times required for Fridays if timesheets are due at the end of the business week and/or the final business day of the month if timesheets must be reconciled by then. If a business has staff in a dozen different offices, there might equally need to be allowances for variations in response times based on the link speed between each office and the central timesheet server location. Finally, finance teams using timesheets for processing salaries and project management teams using timesheets for client billing could have entirely different response time requirements (or at least, response times measured against other functions) to an end user wishing to update his or her timesheets.

9.1.2 DATA PROTECTION AND AVAILABILITY

There is not a 1:1 relationship between data protection and systems availability, but it *can* make an impact on systems availability beyond simple *up* and *down* status. For instance, returning to our timesheet example, we can say that

1. A system might be considered *unavailable* due to reasons beyond the scope of a data protection system (e.g., the network between the timesheet server and the end users is down).
2. A system might *become* unavailable in the event that its active data protection processes are insufficient for the required levels of availability or those processes fail (e.g., a clustered system without any equivalent protection for the storage it utilizes).

3. A system might be considered *unavailable* due to requiring the intervention of the data protection system (e.g., a recovery).
4. A system might be considered *unavailable* due to the *impact* of data protection activities (e.g., the system uses a copy-on-write snapshot scheme and over the course of the day performance degrades due to low-speed disks being used as the snapshot pool).

So while data protection alone cannot *guarantee* systems availability, the presence or absence of data protection can substantially contribute to the level of availability offered. (Indeed, as systems become more virtualized and therefore individual hosts themselves simply become data, we will only see that the relationship between data protection and systems availability continues to more closely align.)

9.2 CONTINUOUS AVAILABILITY

Many businesses have now evolved to a point where either based on a worldwide presence or due to government compliance requirements they have to keep systems available continuously, and active data protection techniques can play a significant factor in ensuring such a high level of availability.

9.2.1 CLUSTERING

Consider Figure 9.2, which shows a typical clustered application—in this case, a database.

In such a configuration, two or more cluster nodes will be configured to present a virtual clustered application or database. Users and user applications do not reference the individual cluster nodes, but instead reference a virtual clustered database. (From an IP networking point of view, this usually results in IP addresses and hostnames for the cluster nodes *and* the virtual clustered database. Additional IP addresses might be used for dedicated private heartbeat links between the physical cluster nodes.)

With the rise of centralized storage systems, a typical cluster will see the physical cluster nodes connecting to a fiber-channel network (or fabric), which will also have a SAN attached. Storage arrays usually employ a multitude of availability and protection features, such as

- Redundant power supplies and cooling
- Redundant storage processor units
- Redundant data paths between storage processor units and disk trays
- RAID protection to guard against disk failure
- Hot spare disks allowing RAID system rebuilds to start immediately after a disk failure
- Multiple fabric paths to the SAN

Similarly, in a high availability environment, cluster nodes will use a form of dynamic multipathing to allow multiple connections into the SAN fabric, protecting against the failure of a single cable or perhaps even a single host bus adapter (HBA).

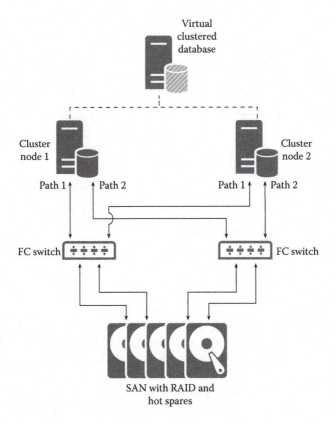

FIGURE 9.2 Traditional clustered application configuration.

Clusters can be configured in either an active/active arrangement or an active/ passive arrangement. (3+ node clusters will use some combination thereof—e.g., active/active/passive.) In the event of a cluster node failing, service continuity can be ensured by having the other cluster node take over the operational functions.

Clustering had been the de facto standard for some time within IT for providing *high availability*. Yet such a configuration does not provide full guarantee of continuous availability—there are still single points of failure within the configuration, most notably the SAN itself. While a SAN will offer an extremely high degree of reliability, a single SAN (or NAS) is still a single point of failure and therefore an inhibitor to continuous availability. Any engineered clustering solution employing a single point of failure will be unable to meet a continuous availability target.

9.2.2 Continuous Availability as a Virtualization Function

As they matured, virtualization environments supplanted many (but not all) of the common use cases for clusters. With multiple logically separated hosts/operating systems running on a single physical server, and the ability to transition a virtual host

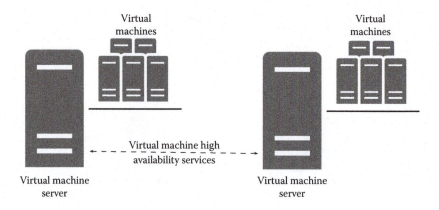

FIGURE 9.3   High availability via virtualization.

from one physical server to another, clustering use cases to do with hardware failure or load balancing became less pressing.

Figure 9.3 shows a very basic view of high availability via virtualization.

In a virtual environment with multiple virtual machine servers (or *hypervisors*) operating in a clustered resource pool, a virtual machine experiencing performance issues might be moved from one physical host to another without any form of interruption to the users of that system. In a modern virtualization environment, this allows entire virtual machine hypervisors to be taken offline for maintenance or replacement without service interruption to the individual applications or hosts running on it.

While continuous availability and site failover mechanisms for virtual machines have reduced the use of clustering technology in many organizations, they don't entirely eliminate the requirements. If corruption occurs within a virtual machine image held at the primary site and the image at the disaster recovery site is being kept in sync, then the corruption will become part of the failover image being maintained. With private application and operating system regions, and a shared database, a true cluster is likely to be more resilient to at least *some* forms of corruption.

Businesses in need of more comprehensive continuous availability will then combine clustering with synchronized virtual machine images, allowing for greater resilience to a wide range of failure scenarios. Virtual machine/affinity preferences can be used here to prohibit both virtual machines in a cluster from running on the same hypervisor on either site, thereby providing suitable protection against ad hoc hardware failure or maintenance.

At this level, it's reasonably common to find the hypervisors doing the work when it comes to keeping virtual machine images in sync. As an update occurs to a virtual machine on one hypervisor, that hypervisor will send the updates across to the hypervisor maintaining the replica to apply. As the number of virtual machines with this level of availability increases, so too does the load on hypervisors, reducing their available capacity for running virtual machines. Further, since this typically takes place over TCP/IP, the protection mechanism can directly impact performance service levels available to the virtual machines for network connectivity to client applications or end users unless management and end-user networks have been sufficiently separated. To ameliorate this, tighter integration between hypervisors and the storage they leverage is becoming more frequent. With such integration, hypervisors can direct virtual machine image synchronization down to the storage layer, leveraging both the compute cycles and (often) dedicated storage networks to isolate or at least drastically reduce the impact of the synchronization traffic/workload from the virtual machines and their business functions being protected.

9.2.3 Continuous Availability as a Storage Function

While clustering and virtual machine high availability can both provide a reasonable degree of protection against downtime, both availability mechanisms will be dependent on the level of availability that can be offered by the storage systems in use.

Even though enterprise storage arrays often offer very high availability capability, this may not always be sufficient for regulatory requirements or mission critical systems for the largest of enterprises.

In such situations, it becomes necessary to employ overlay virtualization systems for storage, integrating two or more storage arrays (perhaps even from different vendors). Such integration allows a volume or unit of storage to be defined at the storage virtualization layer by the storage administrator,* and mirroring of data written to the virtual volume handled between the arrays that comprise the system.

Such a system might resemble that shown in Figure 9.4.

Storage virtualization systems offering effective continuous data availability should not be confused with synchronous replication (which will be covered in a later topic in this chapter). While synchronous replication mirrors many of the features of continuously available virtualized storage, there is usually an assumption of an (even brief) outage in the event of the primary storage target experiencing a failure. Storage virtualization in this scenario *completely* masks such a failure from the hosts and applications accessing the system.

In such a virtualized storage environment the LUNs presented from each array will themselves typically have a degree of data protection configured. An example of this is shown in Figure 9.5. In this example, each physical array has presented a five-disk RAID-5 LUN (4 + 1) to the storage virtualization system. The storage virtualization system in turn mirrors writes between these two volumes, presenting a classic mirrored volume to the accessing hosts and applications of the storage.

The level of data protection offered by such a configuration is quite high and allows a business to expose a highly fault-tolerant storage system to mission critical applications. Just as importantly, it allows for high availability to be achieved *while* maintenance windows are still provided to the individual components. One of the storage arrays in the virtual storage system could be fully shut down for core component upgrades or datacenter power upgrades, without interrupting

---

* Or even by an automated process for self-service environments.

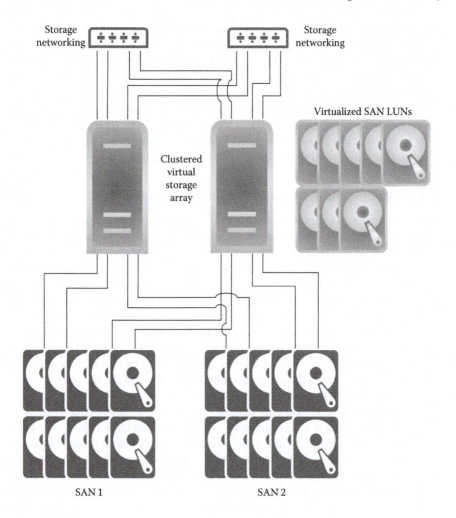

FIGURE 9.4   High level view of storage virtualization.

system availability.* This is why the individual physical LUNs presented by the independent storage arrays will have their own data protection configured—it allows data protection functionality to continue even in the event of a storage array outage our maintenance.

9.2.4   A COMBINED APPROACH TO CONTINUOUS AVAILABILITY

Realistically, neither clustering, virtual machine continuous availability, nor storage continuous availability is sufficient to provide continuous availability for the most mission critical enterprise systems. In such environments where there is extreme

---

* Though clearly this would cause an issue in the event of a failure in the remaining array, which may introduce enough risk for some businesses to require *three-way* virtualization of storage systems.

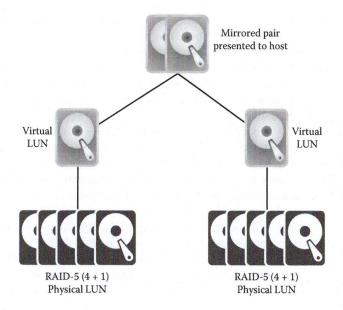

Mirrored pair
presented to host

Virtual
LUN

Virtual
LUN

RAID-5 (4 + 1)
Physical LUN

RAID-5 (4 + 1)
Physical LUN

FIGURE 9.5   Virtual storage LUN composition.

compliance, regulatory, or fiscal requirements, the only way to provide a high guarantee of continuous availability is to combine *all* the individual continuous availability mechanisms. In such environments, it is not uncommon to see active/active
clustered virtual machines residing on clustered hypervisor environments utilizing
LUNs presented by continuously available virtual storage infrastructure. All of these
of course also rely on fault-tolerant TCP/IP and storage networks.

9.3   REPLICATION

Replication exists at a service level below continuous availability, but offers many
shared characteristics. Replicated data storage systems are extremely important as
providing the first level of data recoverability and availability in the event of an
actual outage in high availability systems. Replication can be used to supplement
continuous availability: a mission critical system might reside on continuously available storage systems in one datacenter, with content replicated to another array, or
even another continuously available storage system in another datacenter for service
continuity in the event of a site loss.

Depending on the functionality of the storage system under consideration, replication might have a variety of uses beyond simple data protection and might be
available for original LUNs as well as their snapshots.

Consider, for instance, a business that wants to offload as much as possible the
IO impact of traditional backup activities on mission critical data sets. One very
common approach in this configuration is to take a point in time snapshot of a replication *target* and back up that snapshot. In such a configuration, the chances of

performance degradation on the primary copy of the data are substantially reduced during backup activities. (Furthermore, such backups are immediately off-site, providing a higher level of protection against site failures.*)

Other businesses might choose to make use of replication target volumes for testing major changes to their production environment—in such situations, the replication might be temporarily suspended and the replication target made read/write for local operations and testing.

In any situation where a replication target is broken or suspended, modern replication offerings will typically include some form of "fast reattach" capability to reduce the amount of IO involved in getting a replication source and target back in synch. (This might even be used in certain situations where the source volume in a replication pair suffers damage and needs to be reconstructed.)

The lazy approach to reattaching a replication pair is to simply copy all of the blocks in the source LUN across to the target LUN. For small replication pairs, this may even be acceptable, particularly for systems that do not have extremely high availability requirements or extremely small performance impact tolerances. For larger replication pairs or any environment where the resynchronization is either time- or bandwidth-sensitive, such an approach will not be viewed as efficient or acceptable.

One way of speeding up the replication resynchronization is to maintain a dirty bitmap or write-intent bitmap region. In such a configuration, each block or a set of blocks on a LUN correlates to a single element in the bitmap. In the event of a replication process being suspended, each time an update is written to the active LUN, the bitmap regions associated with the blocks changed on the primary LUN are also updated. When it becomes time to resynchronize the pairs, the bitmap region is used as a quick reference to determine which blocks on the source LUN have to be copied to the target LUN, rather than blindly copying everything.

In Figure 9.6, we see an example pairing where the replication is still occurring between the source and target LUN.

If the replication system supports fast resynchronization, then when the replication is broken or suspended, a bitmap region for the source LUN will be created. As blocks are updated on the source LUN, the bitmap region is updated to reflect the blocks that have changed. Note that the bitmap region *does not* need to actually contain the data that has been updated, just a space-efficient map of the data that has changed. This is shown in Figure 9.7.

When the replication is reestablished between the source and the target LUN, it is no longer necessary to copy the entire contents of the source LUN back across to the target LUN in order to have a consistent copy; instead, the bitmap region is referred to and only the blocks that changed on the source LUN after the creation of the bitmap region/replication break need to be copied across, as shown in Figure 9.8.

Even if the target LUN is made read/write during the replication suspension, bitmap regions can still be used to achieve fast resynchronization. In such situations, a bitmap region might be maintained not only by the source LUN, but also

---

* Though this in itself is not often sufficient reason to avoid making a secondary copy of the backup.

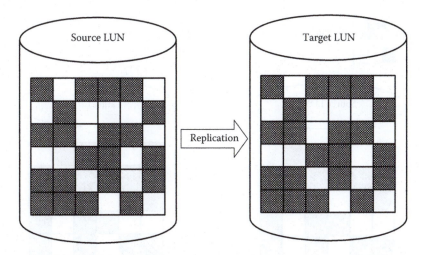

FIGURE 9.6 Sample replication pair.

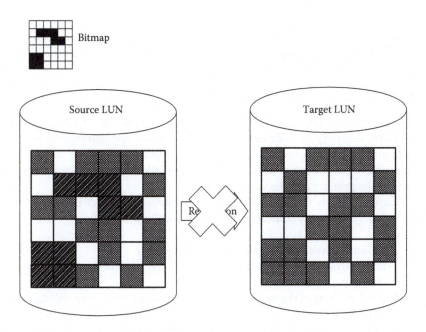

FIGURE 9.7 Active bitmap region to keep track of changes to the source LUN when replication is broken.

the target LUN. The source LUN bitmap will work as described earlier, and the target LUN bitmap will also be updated to indicate any blocks that are changed on it. Replication resynchronization is achieved by merging the two bitmap regions and replicating *all* "changed" blocks from source to target, regardless of whether the block was changed on the source or the target LUN.

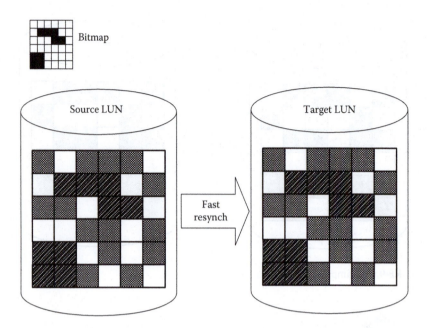

FIGURE 9.8   Fast resynchronization of only changed blocks between replication pairs.

9.3.1 SYNCHRONOUS REPLICATION

Synchronous replication, typically available only within the datacenter, across campus, or over relatively short distances (e.g., within a metropolitan region), is a form of data protection whereby writes written to one storage system are automatically written to another storage system. This effectively allows for zero lag between the content of the primary and the secondary volume.

To ensure there is no lag between the two source and target LUNs, the write process in a synchronous replication pair will typically work as follows:

1. Host sends a write instruction to the primary array.
2. Primary array sends the write instruction to the secondary array and concurrently performs the write.
3. Secondary array performs its write and sends back a write acknowledgment to the primary array.
4. Source array sends a write acknowledgment to the host.

This sequence is shown in Figure 9.9.

What is critical in this configuration is that the primary array used by the host *does not* send a write acknowledgment until such time as it has received a write acknowledgment from the secondary array. (The only way the write can be acknowledged to the host without it being acknowledged by the secondary array is when the replication pair is broken—either by the replication system or a storage administrator—or has failed.)

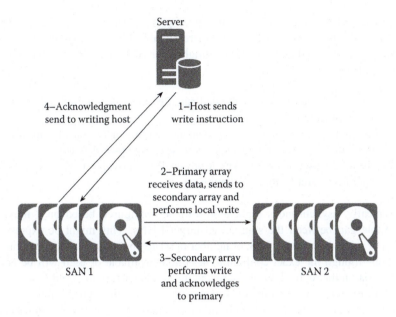

Server

4–Acknowledgment
send to writing host

1–Host sends
write instruction

2–Primary array
receives data, sends to
secondary array and
performs local write

3–Secondary array
performs write
and acknowledges
to primary

SAN 1   SAN 2

FIGURE 9.9   Synchronized replication data flow.

Synchronous replication allows businesses to keep a consistent copy of one or more mission critical LUNs at an alternate location or in an alternate array, but this will impose limits on the maximum bandwidth between sites based on any or all of the following:

1. IO requirements (specifically write IO requirements) of the accessing application(s)
2. Speed of light*
3. Cost of bandwidth
4. Reliability of bandwidth

Further, the more likely a business is to consider synchronous replication, the more critical the performance characteristics of that replication will be. (That is, it is less likely for a business to consider synchronous replication for environments that have anything less than high-performance access requirements.)

9.3.2 ASYNCHRONOUS REPLICATION

Asynchronous replication is the process whereby a pair of LUNs is kept synchronized, but there is no guarantee that the content of the target LUN exactly matches

---

* As the distance between two sites/arrays grows, so does the limit on the fastest response time that can be achieved between those locations. For example, it is approximately 2727 km from Melbourne to Perth. This means that there will be a delay of at least 9 ms in transmitting data from Melbourne to Perth assuming a clear link operating at the speed of light.

the content of the source LUN at any given point in time. Asynchronous replication allows a business to achieve a still reasonably high level of synchronization between a source and target LUN and might be used for any or all of the following considerations:

1. Budget does not allow for the dedicated bandwidth required for synchronous replication.
2. Compliance or regulatory requirements require a reasonably up-to-date copy but do not impose the need for a perfectly up-to-date copy.
3. Distance between sites makes it physically impossible to achieve a fully synchronous replication configuration.

Typically, asynchronous replication will be configured based on a maximum allowable gap between the source and target LUNs. This might be expressed in terms of seconds, minutes, MB, or number of write operations or some combination thereof—though the exact configuration options available or used will be entirely dependent on the replication software and the storage arrays involved.

More recently, some forms of asynchronous replication will be integrated into various application layers, allowing point-in-time consistency replication between arrays, and we would typically consider such integration to be representative of continuous data protection (CDP). In such a situation, the time gap between the source and target LUNs will correlate to application-consistent pauses gaps in the data stream. (For example, a LUN hosting a database might have application aware delays of 5 minutes between the data in such a way that the database can be started/recovered against the data on the target LUN as required with only 5 minutes of data loss. Data may actually be kept up-to date in a *crash*-consistent manner for much shorter windows (e.g., 30 seconds or less), with less frequent application consistent recovery points in the data flow.)

Figure 9.10 shows a high level view of the write process in an asynchronous replication pair. When a write operation occurs with an asynchronous replication pair, the sequence is usually as follows:

1. The host sends a write instruction to the source (primary) LUN it is accessing.
2. The primary array writes the data and sends a write acknowledgment immediately back to the source host.
3. The primary array then seeds the details of the write to a replication journal. This will be an actual copy of the data that was written to the source LUN.[*]

---

[*] An actual copy of the data is written rather than a pointer to the blocks on the source LUN for both performance and data consistency considerations. If the replication process simply includes pointers back to the source LUN, the replication process will then trigger additional reads against the source LUN, which may be undesirable and make performance optimization difficult. Regarding consistency, if we only use pointers, blocks queued for replication may be modified out of sequence prior to being replicated, corrupting the target LUN.

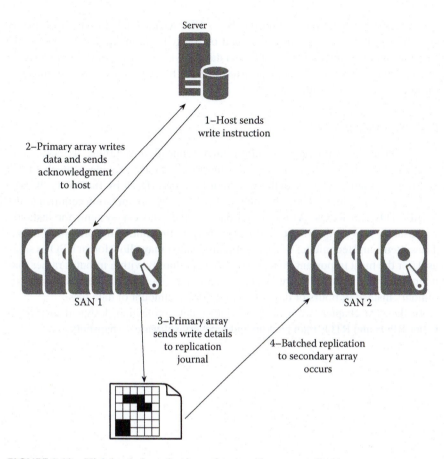

FIGURE 9.10   High level view of writes using asynchronous replication.

4. At a suitable time (based on workload, filled buffers, etc.), the replication system will send the batched blocks in the replication journal across to the target array to be written.

A key consideration when designing and configuring asynchronous replication will be the capacity of the replication journal. If this journal fills, it can trigger a fault condition. The source LUN may stop accepting writes, or (depending on the arrays, replication software, and/or configuration) the replication is suspended but requires a complete reseeding. Such an event becomes one to be avoided as much as possible and will usually trigger intervention by a storage administrator.

Where asynchronous replication is combined with CDP, the journal concept will be extended to include not only the batched replication details, but also an understanding of application-consistent periods in the data stream—effectively checkpoints that can either be rolled back to. (Consider, for instance, the difference between standard asynchronous replication and CDP for a SQL database. Asynchronous replication might see a requirement to have the replica database never more than

5 minutes behind the production database. CDP would include the capability of ensuring appropriate *commits* are issued or tracked within the database to make sure the content written to the replication database is similarly committed, ensuring the replica database can be easily started without further recovery requirements in the event of a failover situation.)

9.4 SUMMARY

Both continuous availability solutions and replication solutions (regardless of whether they are synchronous or asynchronous) usually provide a much higher and more granular form of data protection than be offered by traditional backup and recovery products. These become critical for any organization requiring very small RTOs and RPOs. A traditional backup and recovery system, for instance, will usually provide an RPO of 24 hours—back to the time of the previous backup. The systems and techniques discussed in this chapter may allow for an RPO as small as 0 (for the most important systems) or more commonly within minutes rather than hours or days. Similarly, the recovery time might be measured in seconds, minutes, or hours instead of hours or days depending on the amount of data loss.

In the next chapter, we'll discuss another data protection designed to provide better RPOs and RTOs than backup and recovery software—snapshots.

10 Snapshots

10.1 INTRODUCTION

Snapshots have become a reasonably ubiquitous feature within data protection services, regardless of whether they occur at the operating system, hypervisor, or storage layer.

There are a variety of snapshot techniques but most are bound by the reliance they place (be it permanent or short term) on the presence of the storage they are protecting. In this, they offer less robust protection against hardware failure than full replication but offer potentially better RPOs and RTOs than backup and recovery software (depending on the nature of a failure experienced by a business) while still providing reasonably space-efficient point in time copies.

Contrary to some beliefs, snapshots are not the be-all and end-all of data protection: a data protection "solution" entirely built on snapshots is not a solution at all except in perhaps the most niche of scenarios. However, it can be equally argued that a data protection "solution" that doesn't use snapshots *anywhere* may very well be suboptimal in what it offers to a business.

There are a variety of snapshot techniques that can be used in data protection, and this chapter will discuss the various techniques and their applicability.

10.2 SNAPSHOT TECHNIQUES

10.2.1 COPY ON FIRST WRITE

The copy on first write (COFW) snapshot technique is designed to minimize the amount of storage capacity required to take a snapshot of a filesystem. When a COFW snapshot is taken, the snapshot image does not actually contain any data, but instead a series of pointers back to the original data, as shown in Figure 10.1.

The snapshot is presented as being a separate filesystem to the filesystem it is protecting, effectively seen as an independent entity even though the actual data is shared between the source and the snapshot. If an attempt is made to access data on the snapshot, the read is redirected back to the equivalent region on the source filesystem. (We should note that COFW snapshots can equally apply to block storage, i.e., at a layer below filesystems. For the purposes of simpliicty we are focusing on a filesystem example.)

Keeping in mind the goal of a snapshot is to present a point in time copy of data, and that the source data should continue to be available for whatever operation is required (and specifically, for *writing*), COFW snapshots earn their name whenever an attempt is made to write data to the original filesystem.

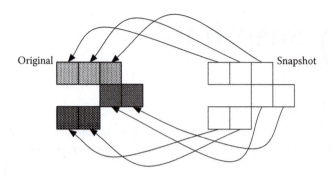

FIGURE 10.1   Copy on first write snapshot after initialization.

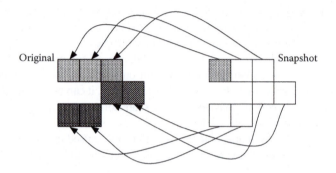

FIGURE 10.2   COFW write process—block is copied to snapshot region.

Considering the snapshot depicted in Figure 10.1 again, let us step through the process that occurs when an attempt is made to write new data to the first block in the filesystem. This will resemble the following sequence:

1. The accessing host attempts to write to the block of data protected by a COFW snapshot.
2. The snapshot intercepts the write and first copies the original content of the block across to the equivalent empty block in the snapshot map (Figure 10.2).
3. With the data copied across to the snapshot, the pointer for that block is removed (Figure 10.3).
4. The new data is then written to the block on the original filesystem, updating its content (Figure 10.4).

While COFW is a highly space-efficient snapshot technique, you may have already noticed the performance side-effects, that being every time an attempt is made to write to the original filesystem, an additional read and write is triggered to copy the original data to the snapshot region. With this in mind, it's usually recommended that COFW snapshots only be performed against filesystems that will have only a very small number of changes while the snapshot is active.

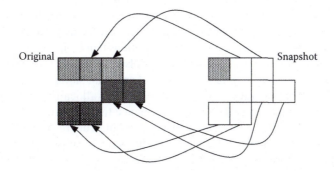

FIGURE 10.3 Pointer for first block on snapshot back to source filesystem is removed.

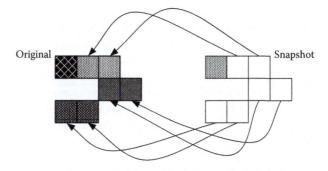

FIGURE 10.4 New data is written to source filesystem, overwriting original block.

Equally, this creates the requirement that the storage pool used for snapshots has high enough IO performance as to minimize the impact of the additional write operations; performing snapshots of filesystems running on 15,000 RPM or even 10,000 RPM disk drives (let alone flash) to storage pools serviced by 7,200 RPM or 5,400 RPM drives can result in serious performance degradations even with minimal write loads on the source filesystem. (This was in fact a common problem encountered by businesses as snapshots became more ubiquitous and before the performance implications were more broadly understood.)

Beyond performance considerations, the *sizing* of the snapshot storage pool plays an important factor in the reliability of COFW snapshots. If the storage pool that provides space for the snapshots fills, this will result *at least* in corruption within the snapshot(s), and possibly even the suspension of writes to the primary filesystem, depending on how the snapshot system is architected.

To get around the dual risks of performance impacts and snapshot storage capacity, differing storage systems may offer options such as:

- Multiple snapshot storage pools differentiated by capacity and/or performance profiles
- Dedicated snapshot storage for individual volumes

It should be noted for both approaches that these only *isolate* the impact caused should one of the above scenarios occur rather than completely eliminating the potential for it to occur. Nevertheless, both options can be highly useful in a data protection configuration. Snapshot storage pools based on performance characteristics allows a business to limit the amount of snapshot storage space allocated to each performance tier (rather than the alternative of allocating all snapshot storage space from the highest required performance tier). Equally, when a business has particular volumes of storage that have a very high degree of criticality and/or performance requirements, dedicated snapshot storage substantially reduces the risk of disruption from other snapshot storage areas, even on the same storage system.

10.2.2 Copy on First Access

Copy on first access (COFA) is a snapshot process typically associated with generating clones of data, typically at the volume/LUN level. These initially look quite similar to a COFW snapshots, in that the snapshot copy starts as a set of pointers back to the original content that was snapshot. This is illustrated in Figure 10.5.

The snapshot starts as a series of pointers, but since the goal is to generate a copy of the original data rather than a space-efficient set of referential links, the snapshot changes considerably as both it and the original data is accessed.

Typically for this type of snapshot, as soon as data is accessed on the original volume, regardless of whether it is for a write *or* a read, the original data is copied across to the snapshot volume.

Figure 10.6 shows how, similarly to the COFW style snapshot, as data is *accessed* on the original volume, it triggers a copy operation across to the snapshot storage.

This in itself would not guarantee the generation of a complete copy of the original data to the snapshot/clone data—after all, only a fraction of the entity being snapshot might be accessed over the lifetime of the snapshot—and it's here we have to start considering the snapshot as also being a clone operation. To ensure the "snapshot"

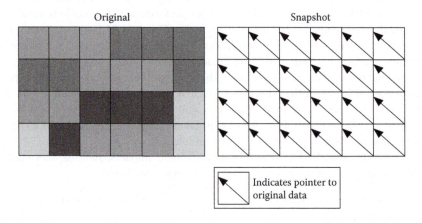

FIGURE 10.5 COFA snapshot in initial state.

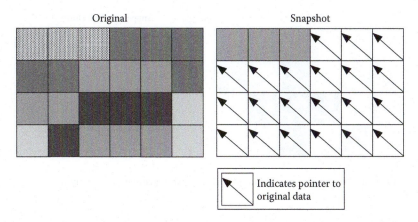

FIGURE 10.6 COFA snapshot with source data modified triggering a copy of the original data.

eventually becomes a fully independent copy, a background copy operation will be initiated from the source to the target. As such a copy operation may impact the access performance for the source copy, the copy usually comes with an option to limit the number or percentage of IOs that can be executed for the copy operation versus standard access operations.

To optimize the copy process, COFA is used at this point to push any accessed data to the front of the copy queue, thereby avoiding the need to read it again at a later point. Figure 10.7 shows us how the COFA snapshot differs from a COFW snapshot over time. For the purposes of our illustration, assume the background copy operation of data from the original to the snapshot occurs left to write, top to bottom. In Figure 10.7, we can see that the remaining data in the first row has been copied by the background process from the original to the snapshot storage even though it

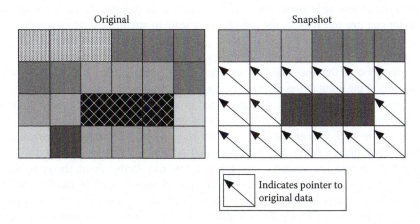

FIGURE 10.7 COFA snapshot showing a mix of background copying and on-access copying of data.

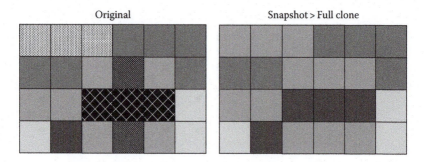

FIGURE 10.8   End-state situation of a COFA snapshot leading to full volume clone.

has not been changed on the original. However, three blocks on the third row *have* been changed, and so these updates have been bumped ahead of the background copy queue.

Figure 10.8 shows us the "final" state situation of a COFA snapshot using a background copy operation; the entire content of the original volume has now been copied across to the snapshot storage, thereby occupying the same amount of space as the original storage and giving a *completely independent* copy of the original data. This copy was accessible immediately upon creation, without needing to wait for full data copy/synchronization by mixing snapshot pointer technology, copy on first access, *and* a background copy process.

10.2.3   Redirect on Write

Virtualization hypervisors such as those developed by VMware also make use of snapshot technology. This enables virtual machines to be protected prior to potentially destructive changes, substantially reducing the likelihood of data loss. (For instance, an administrator might snapshot a virtual machine before performing an operating system upgrade within it. If for some reason the upgrade fails, the administrator can just roll back to the pre-snapshot state to attempt the operation again at a later point in time.)

The snapshot technique used in hypervisors tends to differ from traditional storage snapshots in that the original data (the virtual machine files) effectively become read only at the point of the snapshot being initiated. As writes are performed against the virtual machine, these writes are stored in a snapshot data file located with the virtual machine. An example of this can be seen in Figure 10.9.

In Figure 10.9, we can see that after the snapshot was initiated, two new blocks of data had been written. Since the original content is effectively treated as read only, these blocks are written to an alternate data file. At this point, the system will need to start maintaining a bitmap associating "changed" original blocks with the position in the snapshot data, since the content in the snapshot data file is currently the logically "correct" copy. Thus, redirect-on-write (RoW) also implies redirected reads to access any data that has changed since the snapshot was initiated (while that snapshot is active).

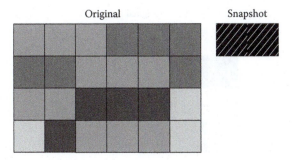

FIGURE 10.9 Redirect-on-write snapshot with updates written after snapshot initiation.

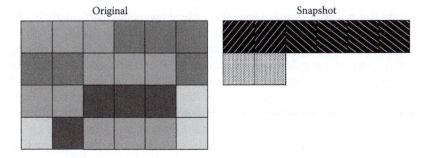

FIGURE 10.10 Redirect-on-write snapshots with additional updates.

A distinct advantage of RoW snapshots is they allow for a single consolidated read of the original data for copy operations (such as in backup situations).

As the original content continues to be used while the snapshot exists, the snapshot will grow in size—with any updates to the original content being redirected to the snapshot data file, as shown in Figure 10.10.

While filesystem snapshots are often executed on the basis of later being entirely dropped without having been accessed, or perhaps mounted independently to copy required data back, virtual machine snapshots are as often as not performed with the expectation that the snapshot state will be merged back into the original storage state.

In the event of snapshot being released without state merger, the release process from this form of snapshot is fast—the original data was not changed, so there's little more to do than simply delete the snapshot data file(s). If we consider the state shown in Figure 10.10 for instance, we can see the original content is exactly as it was at the start of the snapshot process, and dropping the snapshot simply requires the deletion of the snapshot data and turning off any write-redirect process that had previously been enabled.

In the event the snapshot is to be *kept*, it becomes necessary to merge the updates stored in the snapshot file with the original data, which will result in an end-state position such as that shown in Figure 10.11.

As the snapshot merger features ongoing IO operations to the current state of the entity *and* increased IO operations to copy the content of the snapshot data across into the original data source, these snapshot mergers can cause a performance hit on

Original

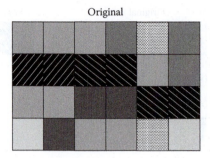

FIGURE 10.11   Content of "original" data post snapshot merger.

the entity that had been snapshot under heavy load operations, particularly if a large number of writes/updates occurred during the lifetime of the snapshot.

It's worth noting RoW is not exclusive to hypervisors; some storage systems make use of it to provide snapshot functionality as well. As mentioned for hypervisors, merging the original content and a RoW snapshot together can create a high burst of write activity, and if not managed correctly this can cause IO interruptions for systems sitting on top of RoW. One technique to avoid this write-load during snapshot merger is to simply avoid doing a merger at all; instead, a pointer system (or some variant thereof) for the "correct" blocks can be maintained. Snapshot merger simply creates a new map to the storage system based on the correct combination of the original blocks and the snapshot blocks. However, this is not without its limitations: this can result in maintaining the snapshot(s) within the same storage pool as the original LUNs or volumes being snapped. For example, a 5 TB storage pool may be configured with 4 TB of active space and 1 TB of snapshot space, all sharing the same disks. Other snapshot methodologies such as CoFW and CoFA can better split the original storage pool and the snapshot storage pool into entirely separate collections of LUNs/volumes, thereby allowing primary volume capacity and snapshot volume capacity to be managed independently of one another.

10.3   CRASH-CONSISTENT VERSUS APPLICATION-CONSISTENT SNAPSHOTS

Consider again the redirect on write snapshot: as mentioned at the time, this is most typically used in virtualization environments, and is particularly useful in a situation where one wishes to take a backup of a virtual machine. Since the original content does not change during the backup process, it can be safely copied into the backup storage environment for later recovery in the event of a failure. (Chapter 14 will cover additional aspects of this.)

When we think of snapshots, we have to consider whether they are *crash consistent* or *application consistent*. Crash consistent implies a state upon restoration that might closely resemble a system that has unexpectedly crashed and rebooted. When a snapshot is taken of a virtual machine, there are likely to be open files within the virtual machine, not to mention active communication states between the virtual machine and the broader IT infrastructure. If the virtual machine is restored from this snapshot, it will to all intents and purposes appear to the operating system within the virtual machine that it has unexpectedly restarted.

Application-consistent snapshots are a slightly different matter, however. They imply the hypervisor snapshot system interacting to a higher degree with virtualization software running within the virtual machine to suitably quiesce (at the start of the snapshot process) whatever databases may be running within the system. While the virtual machine might still, following recovery, behave as if it had unexpectedly crashed, the application/database running *within* the virtual machine would have been prepared for the "crash" state in such a way that it can be reliably restarted and used immediately, rather than requiring a separate database restore.

In effect, this crash- versus application-consistent snapshot question is one that applies to each type of snapshot technology, since a multitude of different applications or systems might be running and making use of storage that is snapshot. Virtualization systems may be the most obvious, but they are not unique in this scenario. Particularly, as 10 Gbit networking becomes ubiquitous within a datacenter, we are increasingly seeing many businesses placing application and database workloads (not to mention virtualization workloads themselves) on standard NAS storage. How these application layers and hypervisor layers react to a sudden reversion of a snapshot in the event of a major failure can define the difference between a successful data protection strategy and a waste of money.

This effectively harkens back to the Data Classification discussion in Section 2.2 focusing on five core questions:

1. What is the data?
2. Where is the data?
3. Who uses the data?
4. When is the data used?
5. How is the data used?

While NAS systems in particular represent easily configurable mass shared storage for a large number of users and/or systems within an IT infrastructure, the fact they provide snapshots is not sufficient demonstration of an adequate data protection strategy if insufficient consideration is made regarding the accessibility of data residing on filesystems following a snapshot rollback/restoration activity.

This also often differentiates "workgroup" laissez-faire approach to data protections and truly enterprise understanding of the complexity of data protection. All too often new entrants to the data protection market might blithely claim that it is perfectly acceptable to perform crash-consistent backups of virtual machines running database software, using supposed "logic" such as the following:

- It *should* work:
  - So long as the database isn't *too* busy
  - And *if* the storage system responds fast enough
  - And *if* the hypervisor isn't too busy doing other activities
- And *if...*

Data protection promises premised on "if," "maybe," and "hopefully" are not *promises* at all—and can place business data in considerable danger. Data protection architects in particular within an organization must be mindful as to whether any deployed snapshot technology merely offers crash-consistent snapshots or application-consistent snapshots—and inevitably, if they're application-consistent snapshots, what applications are supported and whether there are any caveats around that support.

10.4   READ-ONLY VERSUS READ/WRITE SNAPSHOTS

Another consideration relating to snapshots are the utility of them beyond providing a reasonably high level of granularity for recovery time and recovery point objective, particularly dealing with individual file loss.

The level of utility that can be achieved with snapshots largely depends on whether the snapshots are made available read only or whether they are made available read/write. By its nature, a RoW snapshot is a read/write snapshot: the writes are *made* to the snapshot region. However, neither COFA nor COFW snapshots necessarily have to be provisioned as read/write.

As mentioned in RoW snapshots, an advantage of permitting read/write access to a snapshot is that a potentially destructive activity can be undertaken, and if it fails, we can roll back to a pre-snapshot state and avoid a prolonged outage or data loss situation. Along these lines, read/write snapshots of filesystems hosting databases might be used by database administrators to test major upgrades to the database software *against* production data, but without putting the "real" production data at risk (i.e., the test is made against a reasonably up-to-date replica of the production data, rather than a manual copy of the data *or* just a collection of test data).

While RoW is explicitly designed for this technique, it is equally arguable that the primary operational purpose of both a COFW and COFA snapshot is to provide a "pristine," unalterable copy of the data as of the time the snapshot was executed. While logically a COFA snapshot, once background cloning completes, could allow for an administrator to easily access the snapshot data for writing as well as reading, no such capability is inherent in the COFW snapshot previously described. Further, in such situations, allowing users to *modify* that data is counter-intuitive: for certain, this may allow destructive testing of particular scenarios to take place, but for the duration of that testing the system doesn't have a copy of the data that can be used for restoration purposes—and this is almost always the *primary* purpose of the snapshot.

The solution for read/write snapshots is almost always provided by snapshot technology itself. If we consider a COFW or COFA snapshot, we can effectively create a read/write instance of the snapshot by employing a RoW snapshot against it (or something similar). In this scenario the original snapshot data is left preserved, but a virtual copy of the data is made available to the required processes or personnel via the RoW snapshot technique.

Figure 10.12 shows a combination of COFW and RoW being used to effectively generate an (indirect) read/write snapshot of the original volume.

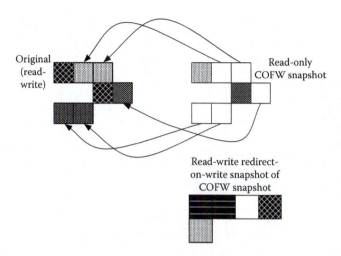

FIGURE 10.12 Read/write snapshot of a COFW snapshot.

Such a combination of snapshot techniques achieves both the original data protection consideration of the snapshot *and* provides additional utility to the business by allowing potentially destructive testing to be performed against a copy of the original data.

10.5 INTEGRATION POINTS IN DATA PROTECTION

A single snapshot by itself provides a single point in time of data protection, but snapshots become particularly more useful when we consider the speed at which they can be generated and how space efficient they are (depending on how active the original entity being snapshot is).

This allows storage administrators (particularly when we focus on NAS environments) to offer considerably tighter and more business compatible SLAs regarding RPO and RTO than a traditional backup strategy. If a business requires no more than an hour of data loss from the filesystems presented by a NAS server, this might be achieved by taking hourly snapshots, as shown in Figure 10.13.

Many NAS vendors feature client operating-system integration points with their snapshot technology that allows individual end-users to perform self-service recoveries. By this, users are able to execute read-only mounts through operating system hooks (e.g., integration into Microsoft Windows Explorer) of prior snapshots of a filesystem and simply copy the files they wish to retrieve from the snapshot. This allows for easy retrieval of data without requiring a formal recovery process to be initiated, and is often seen as a major time saving advantage over traditional daily backup processes.

While this provides a high level of granularity for recovery and allows a business to meet tight RPO objectives, we must keep in mind the potential performance impact it can create. For instance, consider a very simple example just covering 2 hours of COFW snapshots. Figure 10.14 shows a state where the snapshot for the

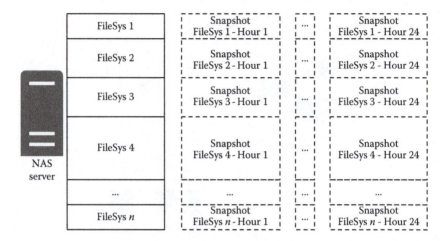

FIGURE 10.13   Achieving 1 hour RPO via hourly snapshots.

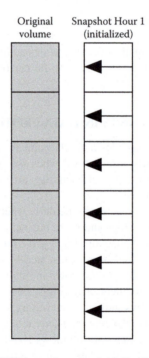

FIGURE 10.14   First hour COFW snapshot after initialization.

first hour has just been initialized, and Figure 10.15 shows the state after an update has been executed against the original data.

Assuming that was the only update done to the original volume during the first hour, at the start of the second hour we initialize another snapshot, as shown in Figure 10.16.

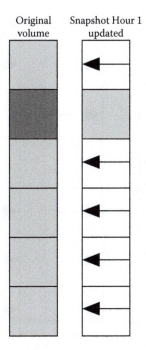

FIGURE 10.15 First hour COFW snapshot after update performed on original volume.

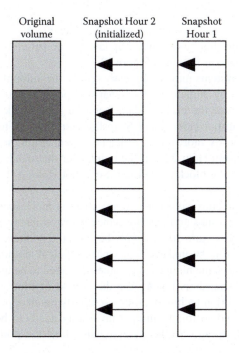

FIGURE 10.16 Second hour COFW initialized.

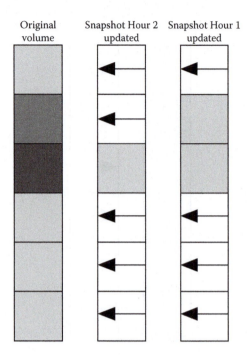

FIGURE 10.17   First and second hour COFW after update performed to block on the original volume.

At this point, consider a situation where another block in the original volume gets updated. Before this block can be updated, it potentially has to be copied to *two* snapshot volumes, as shown in Figure 10.17.

Some snapshot systems may intelligently reduce the amount of storage required for such a situation by adjusting *where* snapshot pointers direct to. For instance, in Figure 10.17 we see the original data from the third block (from the top) was copied to both Snapshot Hour 2 and Snapshot Hour 1 prior to being updated on the original volume. A more space efficient system might see that data instead *just* copied to Snapshot Hour 2, with the pointer for that block in Snapshot Hour 1 adjusted to point to the block copied into Snapshot Hour 2. This is demonstrated in Figure 10.18.

While this architecture shown in Figure 10.18 is more space efficient, it does not necessarily yield a substantial performance improvement over the multiple-copy scenario described in Figure 10.17, simply because the pointers themselves are still bits of data that need to be updated—the space-efficient method minimizes actual data copying, but the same number of pointers still need to be updated.

While multiple snapshots taken over the course of time are undoubtedly an excellent data protection technique, they eventually create a performance drag on the original data, and so this technique invariably needs to be balanced against both the potential storage overheads associated *and* the potential performance impact.

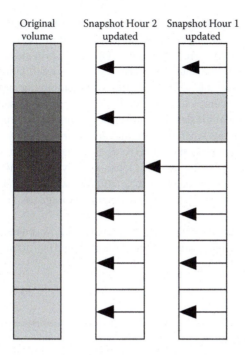

FIGURE 10.18   Space-efficient multiple COFW updates.

10.6   SUMMARY

Snapshots frequently offer a very efficient mechanism of achieving low recovery time objectives. In certain disaster recovery situations, a volume or virtual machine that has been snapshot can be "rolled back" considerably faster than, say, complete restoration from a traditional backup. Equally in many circumstances a snapshot can be quickly accessed to retrieve data from it rather than executing a more formal recovery process from a traditional backup system.

Also, as the amount of data to be protected grows, snapshots allow for point-in-time copies to be generated very quickly with potentially very little in the way of storage requirements (compared to the original data set), thus allowing a business to meet reasonably short recovery point objectives.

Snapshots do not come without their risks or limitations, however. While many storage systems theoretically support thousands or even hundreds of thousands of snapshots operating simultaneously, the performance impact from this many snapshots can make the entire exercise pointless—well-protected storage that has become unresponsive due to excessive snapshot updates is not useful to any business. Similarly, a large number of snapshots will see snapshot storage requirements continue to grow in a way that may not offer the most space-efficient form of data protection for an environment. Finally, for the majority of snapshot techniques, we must keep in mind that the original data is effectively being used to protect itself. Both COFW and RoW, for example, can be used to protect against a large number of potential failure scenarios, but *both* become effectively useless against, say, the underlying storage suffering a catastrophic disk failure beyond the ability of the LUN's RAID system to correct. Equally, COFA only provides protection against a catastrophic failure in the source storage system after full cloning has been completed, and is as vulnerable to such failures while cloning is in progress as COFW snapshots are. The incomplete nature of the copy is not an issue when we want to recover from individual file deletion or even some forms of corruption, but it doesn't protect against situations where the original data is irretrievably destroyed at a layer below the filesystem, and so should serve as a constant caution against focusing all of the data protection resources into snapshots only. An infinite number of snapshots provides zero data protection in a situation where they reside on the same array as the original storage, require the original storage to exist, and that original storage is lost.

In Chapter 18, we will evaluate in greater detail how a data protection strategy may require multiple mechanisms (snapshots included) to offer a truly comprehensive protection architecture.

11 Backup and Recovery

11.1 INTRODUCTION

There was a time where "data protection" was practically synonymous with "backup and recovery."* Still critical in a holistic data protection environment, recovery from backups is increasingly being seen as an action of last resort, particularly for mission-critical applications and systems. Like all data protection mechanisms, the usefulness of backup and recovery systems is directly tied to the level of service-level agreement (SLA) they can be used to meet. While previous chapters have talked about continuous availability, replication, and snapshots, all of which offer RPOs of zero through to minutes or at most, hours, backup and recovery systems are more likely to offer RPOs of potentially a day or more. However, while these other systems are mainly deployed for short-term retention purposes (measured in periods of "none," and seconds to days), backup and recovery services both short-term retention (in some environments as short as a day) and longer retention periods that may be measured in months, years, or even decades.

In the introduction, it was suggested that there are two broad types of data protection—proactive and reactive. While continuously available systems, replication, and, to a degree, snapshots are about proactively preventing data from being lost in the first place, backup and recovery systems are squarely aimed at getting data *back* after it's been lost. While undoubtedly a backup *is* proactive, it's usually done solely to position an organization to *react* to a data loss situation.

For the average business, a backup and recovery system represents the most pervasive data protection option that will be deployed. Replication, snapshots, and continuous availability are typically focused on mission-critical or business-essential systems (or compliance regulated systems), while backup and recovery systems might interact with as much as 100% of the systems in an environment.

Many businesses make the mistake of assuming that because they've purchased and deployed enterprise backup software that they have a *recovery system*. Yet, as touched on earlier, data protection isn't solely about technology, it's about people, processes, documentation, and training. Software may allow a company to make the journey, but its installation is only the first step toward a backup and recovery *system*.

Before we go too far with backup, we have to stop to consider what a backup actually *is*. We will use the following definition:

> A backup is a copy of data that can be used to recover or otherwise reconstruct the data as required.

Note the key word there is *copy*, which differentiates backup completely from an archive. The process of archiving refers to *moving* an instance of data from one location to another. Backup revolves around making one or more additional copies of the

---

* With RAID perhaps the notable exception.

data so that we can get the data back if necessary—further proof of its purpose as a *reactive* form of data protection.

11.2 BACKUP AND RECOVERY CONCEPTS

Backup and recovery has evolved substantially since it was first thought of in IT. As technologies, infrastructure approaches, and data localities have changed, so too has backup and recovery needed to evolve. Fundamental to understanding how backup and recovery fits into a data protection strategy is an understanding of the key concepts within backup and recovery.

11.2.1 Host Nomenclature

When describing a backup environment, the following terms are used to describe the hosts within it:

Server: The backup server or *master* server, which is responsible for the scheduling of backups, coordination of recoveries, management of media, processing of indices, and being the repository of the backup configuration and/or service catalogs.

Client: Any host protected by the backup server. This will usually include many or even all of the machines that would be referred to as *servers* in normal infrastructure classifications such as fileservers, mail servers, database servers, and so on.

Media server or storage node: A host that exists between the client and the server to offload some of the processing, but still under the control and direction of the backup server. It may perform backup and recovery operations solely for itself *or* for a variety of clients.

Additionally, we should consider two more host types that have become increasingly prevalent in backup and recovery systems:

Purpose-built backup appliance (*PBBA*): A "black box" appliance directly targeted at providing backup storage. This will have some array-like characteristics, but also other options that are highly suited to backup, such as deduplication or back-end tape-out functionality. While many arrays can be used for backup purposes, PBBAs will be systems that are designed from the ground up for backup and recovery workloads, not primary data storage or access.

Integrated data protection appliance: This will be a PBBA with additional features that allow it to operate more effectively within a data protection environment, extending backup and recovery functionality beyond traditional enterprise systems. Such a system might offer plugins that allow databases to directly interact with it or include primary storage area network (SAN)/ network attached storage (NAS) interoperability for tighter snapshot integration. As this is a relatively new extension to the PBBA, we should expect to see more functions evolve over time into these enhanced appliances.

11.2.2 BACKUP TOPOLOGY

The backup environment topology refers to the layout of the servers and the clients (as per the nomenclature discussed in the previous section). There are three effective topologies available today—centralized, decentralized, and hybrid.

11.2.2.1 Decentralized Topology

A decentralized backup environment is one where each host backs up its own data to backup devices that are directly attached to it. If a commercial backup product is involved, then typically each host within the environment is its own "master server," being entirely self-contained and separate from the rest of the environment for backup. This is a backup model more commonly found in small businesses that have grown from 1 or 2 servers to maybe 10 to 20 at most. In these environments, backups are usually considered as an afterthought following system purchase, resulting in the perceived need for stand-alone backup storage for each system. A decentralized backup system might resemble that shown in Figure 11.1.

While smaller IT environments may see decentralized backups as having the benefit of reducing the number of dependencies each host has for recovery, their disadvantages quickly stack up, and they are unable to scale as the number of hosts and applications within an environment increases. Key disadvantages of a decentralized backup environment include the following:

Cost—Unless backup and recovery software being used is free, it will invariably be the case that a single server license and multiple client licenses will be cheaper than a multitude of stand-alone server licenses. (Similarly, centralizing whatever protection storage is used will inevitably create cost optimizations.)

Storage inefficiency—Attaching dedicated backup storage to each host will result in backup storage inefficiency. Consider, for instance, if tape is used as the backup medium: the backup of five servers concurrently will require the use of at least five tapes, when in actual fact under a centralized model all five servers might comfortably fit onto a single tape.

Reporting—Any reporting will be on a per-host basis, making it very difficult for a business to readily understand its data protection status.

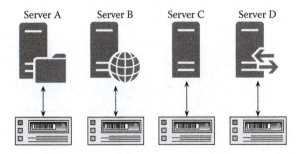

FIGURE 11.1 Decentralized backup environment.

Configuration complexity—While a single product protecting a single server may sound less complex to configure than an enterprise backup product, this only lasts until configuration changes across many servers have to be implemented. With enterprise backup software, changing the backup time for, say, 20 hosts could be as simple as changing one field in one resource. For a decentralized backup environment, this would involve in accessing the backup configuration on 20 hosts one after the other and making the same change. This will not only be time consuming, but will also introduce greater risk of configuration mismatches.

Media handling—As the amount of media increases within an environment, the handling and storing costs (both human and physical) will also increase.

Virtualization—Such a topology does not lend itself well to working in virtualized environments, particularly if any form of removable media is to be used.

11.2.2.2 Centralized Topology

A centralized backup approach, such as that shown in Figure 11.2, reduces infrastructure requirements, configuration requirements, operational management, and costs by having multiple hosts backup via a dedicated backup server.* While the example centralized backup solution shown in Figure 11.2 shows clients and the server communicating over a TCP/IP network, there are a variety of mechanisms where centralization can be achieved, and, most importantly, the *control* flow is typically separated from the actual data flow. This allows for distribution of backup data to multiple locations based on network bandwidth, firewalls, physical location, and so on, while still being centrally controlled.

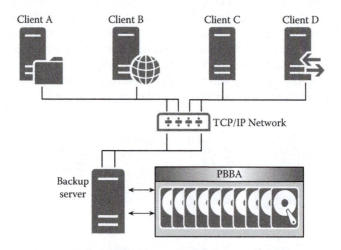

FIGURE 11.2   Centralized backup environment.

---

* We will cover how storage nodes/media servers fit into this arrangement later.

Some of the advantages of centralized backups include

Infrastructure efficiency—In an enterprise environment, backup storage requirements can quickly grow to outpace the capacity of the systems they are protecting as the number of historical copies are kept. Centralizing backup storage into fewer locations (or even a single one) allows for greater storage efficiencies. Larger storage pools allow for better deduplication rates, reducing storage footprints while still protecting the same amount of backups (and often more). If removable media is required, its management becomes easier and costs will be well lower than linear based on capacity increases.

Workforce consolidation—Regardless of whether administrators for a backup environment are dedicated solely to that or to a mix of data protection and other infrastructure, a centralized approach to backup allows for more efficient staffing and greater levels of knowledge among the staff responsible for backup and recovery systems.

More flexible recovery models—With centralized systems, more recoveries can be facilitated from online media (disk or tape), allowing a broader spread of employees to participate in the recovery process. Thus, instead of being an activity only performed by a backup administrator, recoveries could more readily be executed by system and virtualization administrators, application administrators, help desk staff, or even end users. With cloud-based approaches to IT requiring greater attention to "self-service" models, flexible recoveries are becoming increasingly important. (In a large-scale disaster recovery operation, eliminating bottleneck of a single employee performing all recoveries is a critical design requirement.) Additionally, centralized backup services typically increase the ease at which data from one host may be recovered to another.

Ease of configuration—Since all configuration is controlled from a single source, it becomes easier for data protection administrators to adjust and review that configuration, and configuration changes become more efficient at scale by reducing the amount of effort required to alter the backup characteristics of larger numbers of hosts.

Reporting—A single centralized system can give more advanced reports and statistics on data growth over the entire environment with less need for manual collation or merger of reports generated from a multitude of individual, decentralized systems.

11.2.2.3 Hybrid Topology

Mission-critical applications can introduce a challenge in enterprise backup and recovery. Businesses want the application backups to be integrated into a centralized system, but equally recognize the importance of keeping control of the backup process within the applications and/or separate enterprise job scheduling systems that can accommodate arbitrary job dependency processing.

The "classic" solution to this dichotomy has been to provision additional storage for application administrators so that they can control their application backups and write them to system storage (directly attached or mapped from a SAN/NAS), with those backups then swept up by standard filesystem backup agents. Such a model is easy, but not cheap—the storage provisioned is usually expensive primary tier storage similar to the performance characteristics of the databases, and administrators will usually request sufficient storage to hold multiple full backups of their applications. (If not given this space, database administrators (DBAs) may instead compress their backups on disk, either during or after the backup. If compressed during the backup, this will slow the backup process down, and if compressed *after* this may compromise system performance. Additionally, large compressed files may cause flow-on challenges within the backup environment, particularly if deduplication storage systems are used.)

This is usually due to the lack of integration between the application backups and the system backups—application administrators will want at least a few of the most recent backups online and accessible to meet tight RPO/RTO SLAs rather than having to resort to a two-stage recovery where application backup files are first retrieved from the backup storage and then recovered into the application. Thus, a 1 TB database might require up to 10 TB of similar storage attached to the database server for fast recovery from online backups.

The evolution of PBBAs into integrated data protection appliances (IDPAs) has allowed for an efficient hybridization of the centralized and decentralized models while still allowing both the data protection administrators *and* the application administrators to retain control.* A high-level view of a hybrid model is shown in Figure 11.3.

In such a model, the data protection storage becomes a centralization locus. The backup and recovery system should still be a largely centralized environment (with even the application and database servers performing filesystem and

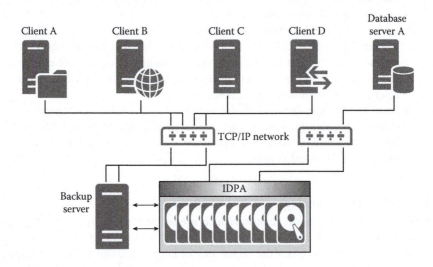

FIGURE 11.3 Hybrid backup topology.

---

* While both tape and PBBAs will in theory integrate into a hybrid model, the integration points are typically inefficient compared to those points offered by an IDPA.

OS layer backups to the system), which allows for continued efficient management of much of the data protection strategy for the environment. In addition, the key application and/or database servers can work closely with an integrated backup appliance via plugins to their native backup and recovery tools, directly controlling and administering the backup process while sharing data protection storage with the rest of the backup and recovery environment. This can substantially reduce storage costs for mission-critical systems by eliminating backup logical unit numbers (LUNs) directly attached to the application and database servers while still ensuring the applications receive the highly granular backup controls required by the business.

While a fully centralized backup and recovery topology would usually be preferable over the hybrid topology from the viewpoint of the data protection administrators and architects, the topology must ultimately support the needs of the business. With mission-critical applications requiring particular focus and data protection control, the hybrid model achieves a good compromise while ensuring the business can still achieve efficiencies and cost control in data protection storage.

11.2.3 BACKUP LEVELS

Each time a backup is performed, data is transferred from the client storage to the data protection storage. Exactly how much data is transferred is first and foremost determined by the backup *level*. While a backup will also have some type of content selection associated with it (e.g., "all local filesystems" or "database named PROD"), the level will determine how much of the selected data set is backed up as part of any operation.

11.2.3.1 Full Backups

Full backups transfer all of the selected data set from the source to the data protection storage, regardless of how recently it has been backed up. Particularly if tape is used, full backups undoubtedly provide the simplest recovery mechanism for businesses, as a recovery operation is a single consolidated read from the backup storage, without need to use multiple sources generated at different dates or times.

A key requirement of a full backup is that the backup window needs to be large enough to accommodate a complete read of all data on a system for every backup. While this may be acceptable to smaller organizations, it will likely represent a burdensome requirement for many larger enterprises or businesses where data growth is occurring. Indeed, since data growth has continued at a rapid pace for most businesses while backup windows have *shrunk*, it is becoming increasingly common to see businesses try to reduce the number of full backups they need to do.

Advantages of full backups are usually as follows:

- Recovery from a full backup involves a single consolidated read from one backup "set."
- Full backups typically do not have dependencies on one another. That is, the loss of a full backup taken on day 1 will not impact the recoverability of a full backup taken on day 2.

Disadvantages however include the following:

- Without mitigating activities such as snapshots or source-side deduplication, the backup window is the largest for all types of backup levels.
- Without deduplication (source or target), a full backup will use the maximum amount of media possible for the data set per backup—and will have the most cost.

It should be noted that backup products that perform true source-side deduplication, where only unique, never-before-seen data is sent from the client to the server, may have the luxury of performing full backups daily without the client-side impact typically associated with daily full backups. By utilizing local databases of previously encountered data segments and integrating with operating system tracking for changed files, a source-side deduplication product can scan and process the changed content on a host far faster than a traditional full backup. We will cover such options in Chapter 13.

11.2.3.2   Incremental-Level Backups

An incremental-level backup targets only those files or items that have changed since the last backup (regardless of what level it was).* This often results in considerably smaller backups and can usually be accommodated within a much smaller backup window—though the amount of data backed up may not always have a 1:1 relationship with the elapsed time.

At a filesystem level, incremental backups look for files that have changed or been added since the last backup. However, they do not apply just to filesystem backups: databases, complex applications, virtual machines, and so on all leverage some form of incremental backup technology. A 50 TB database, for instance, may have only a 2%–5% change rate during the course of a day, and in the same spirit as filesystem backups, incremental database backups will allow these changes to be captured and backed up, then integrated with a prior full backup for restoration purposes if required.

Introducing incrementals into a backup strategy will often result in a backup configuration such as that shown in Tables 11.1 and 11.2.[†]

TABLE 11.1
Weekly Full Backups with Daily Incrementals

Monday	Tuesday	Wednesday	Thursday	Friday	Saturday	Sunday
Incremental	Incremental	Incremental	Incremental	Incremental	Full	Incremental

---

* Some backup products refer to incremental backups as *differential incremental*—i.e., an incremental that consists of the *differences* since the last backup.
[†] Of course, the first backup performed for a particular data set will always be a full one, regardless of any schedule.

TABLE 11.2

Monthly Full Backups with Daily Incrementals

Saturday	Sunday	Monday	Tuesday	Wednesday	Thursday	Friday
1st—full	2nd—incr	3rd—incr	4th—incr	5th—incr	6th—incr	7th—incr
8th—incr	9th—incr	10th—incr	11th—incr	12th—incr	13th—incr	14th—incr
15th—incr	16th—incr	17th—incr	18th—incr	19th—incr	20th—incr	21st—incr
22nd—incr	23rd—incr	24th—incr	25th—incr	26th—incr	27th—incr	28th—incr
29th—incr	30th—incr	31st—incr				

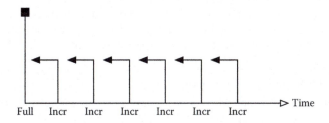

FIGURE 11.4 Backup change chart.

Figure 11.4 shows a "change chart" for different backup levels and their relationship can be depicted. In this case, a weekly full with daily incrementals is shown.

In Figure 11.4, the full backup is seen as a vertical line stretching the height of the diagram. The horizontal axis represents time—the days on which the backups are executed. Each incremental backup is shown pointing *back* to the backup taken on the day before it, which indicates it only processes the data that has changed since the last backup.

Some companies still subscribe to a 5 × 9-operations-style backup methodology where backups are not executed on the weekend—the rationale being that users are not typically making modifications to systems. This is almost invariably a false economy, and even more so unaligned to an increasingly 7 × 24 environment. Systems may automatically patch on weekends, and backups should definitely be taken before and after these. Mobile users are more likely than ever before to be checking and sending emails on the weekend, and even if no users *are* accessing a system over a weekend, backups can still be used to provide recoverability in the event of corruption or data deletion by rogue processes or applications. This leads us to an essential rule of backup and recovery:

> It is always better to backup a little more than is needed than not enough.

The advantages of incremental backups include the following:

- Less backup media is used per backup job as only content that has changed since the last backup is copied. By implication, a backup regime combining full and incremental backups will use considerably less media than a backup regime where only full backups are performed over the same period of time.

- The backup window can be considerably shorter than a full backup. In the (now reasonably) rare event of an outage being needed as part of the backup process, this equally can reduce the length of the outage window.

The disadvantages of incremental backups include the following:

- Recoveries from a mixed full and incremental regime can require more media changes depending on how many incremental backups have been done since the last full backup (when removable media such as tape is used).
- Complete recoveries have dependencies—that is, a complete system recovery cannot be done without the full backups and all incremental backups between the full and the failure. If any of these backups are lost or otherwise fail to be read from, the recovery cannot be 100% completed.*

11.2.3.3   Differential-Level Backups

A differential backup is one where a series of changes are backed up, possibly covering several days worth of changes. This "rolls up" multiple changes into a single backup job.† Arguably differential-level backups are now less frequently used—while they are particularly effective when tape is the primary backup target as a means of reducing the amount of media required for a recovery while still allowing for faster backups, their usefulness in environments that focus on backup to disk is quite limited.

While a differential backup effectively means the same thing for any standard filesystem backup, the meaning can vary quite considerably when differential backups are applied to databases and applications. A database vendor, for instance, might declare a differential backup to be one where all transaction logs since the last backup are backed up and then deleted. Another database vendor might consider a differential backup to be a backup of the appropriate data *and* the transaction logs. In short, when considering differential backups for anything other than a filesystem, read the documentation provided by both the database/application vendor *and* the backup vendor to understand how such a backup will execute and *what* will be backed up.

There are actually two types of differential backups that products might use: simple and multilevel. We will provide an overview of both.

A simple differential backup merely backs up all the changes that have occurred since the most recent full, regardless of what backups have occurred in between. Consider, for instance, a weekly backup regime such as that shown in Table 11.3.

---

* It should be noted that some so-called "enterprise" backup products do not perform adequate dependency checking, and can actually delete full backups—by design—that incrementals still rely on for complete system recoverability.
† Some backup products will refer to differential backups as *cumulative incrementals*—i.e., an "incremental" that is the accumulation of all changes since the last full backup.

TABLE 11.3

Sample Weekly Backup Regime Mixing Full, Incremental, and Differential

Saturday	Sunday	Monday	Tuesday	Wednesday	Thursday	Friday
Full	Incremental	Incremental	Incremental	Differential	Incremental	Incremental

In the backup regime under consideration, a full backup is performed on the Saturday, with incrementals performed Sunday–Tuesday. A differential backup is performed on Wednesday, with incremental backups subsequently performed on Thursday and Friday. We can show this in a backup change graph as per Figure 11.5.

In Figure 11.5, we can see that while the first three incrementals simply capture the changes that have occurred since the previous day, the differential invoked on the fifth day will instead backup all changes that have occurred since the full backup. The incremental backup subsequently performed on the sixth day will only backup content that has changed since the differential on the fifth day.

Sometimes, differentials would be used to replace incremental backups entirely. Thus, at any given day, the only backups required for recovery of a system would be the full backup and the most recent differential. This would resemble a configuration such as that shown in Figure 11.6.

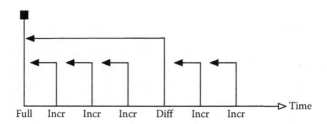

FIGURE 11.5 Backup change diagram for simple differential level.

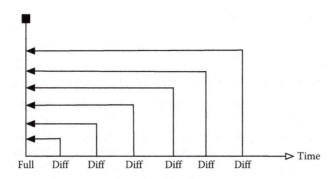

FIGURE 11.6 Backup change diagram for a "differentials only" backup regime.

In such a configuration, our backups would work as follows:

- The full backup captures all content.
- The first differential backup captures all content that has changed since the full.
- The second differential backup captures all content that has changed since the full.
- The third differential backup captures all content that has changed since the full.
- *And so on.*

Historically, differential backups were usually integrated into monthly backup cycles—where a full backup is performed only once a month. Such a backup configuration might resemble that shown in Table 11.4.

Such configurations had two key goals:

1. Ensure daily backups take as little time as possible.
2. Minimize the number of backup sets/media required for system recovery.

To perform a complete system recovery from such a backup configuration, the full backup, the most recent differential backup, and any incremental backups performed since that differential would be required for recovery. For instance, to recover the system on the 27th, *after* its backup, you would need to use

- The full backup taken on the first
- The differential backup taken on the 22nd
- The incremental backups taken on the 23rd through to the 27th inclusive

In addition to simple differential backup levels, some backup products may offer multilevel differentials, allowing additional options. Multilevel differential backups inherit their methodology from old UNIX tools such as "dump" and "restore." Using such methodology, rather than a single "diff" or "differential" backup level, the backup levels available become

- Full
- Incremental
- Differential levels 1…9

TABLE 11.4

Monthly Backup Regime with Fulls, Incrementals, and Differentials

Saturday	Sunday	Monday	Tuesday	Wednesday	Thursday	Friday
1st—full	2nd—incr	3rd—incr	4th—incr	5th—incr	6th—incr	7th—incr
8th—diff	9th—incr	10th—incr	11th—incr	12th—incr	13th—incr	14th—incr
15th—diff	16th—incr	17th—incr	18th—incr	19th—incr	20th—incr	21st—incr
22nd—diff	23rd—incr	24th—incr	25th—incr	26th—incr	27th—incr	28th—incr
29th—diff	30th—incr	31st—incr				

TABLE 11.5
Multilevel Weekly Differential Backup Configuration

Saturday	Sunday	Monday	Tuesday	Wednesday	Thursday	Friday
Full	Incremental	Diff level 5	Incremental	Diff level 7	Incremental	Diff level 3

In this approach, any differential-level x backs up all files that have changed since the last full or last lower/equal numbered differential level (whichever was more recent).

Table 11.5 gives a simple example of a multilevel differential backup configuration for a single week.

In the configuration outlined in Table 11.5, the backups would work as follows:

- A full backup is performed on Saturday.
- An incremental is performed on Sunday, backing up all content that has changed since the Saturday full.
- A differential level 5 is performed on Monday, backing up all content that has changed since the Saturday full.
- An incremental is performed on Tuesday, backing up all content that has changed since the Monday differential level 5.
- A differential level 7 is performed on Wednesday, backing up all content that has changed since the Monday differential level 5.
- An incremental backup is performed on Thursday, backing up all files and content that has changed since the Wednesday differential level 7.
- A differential level 3 is performed on Friday, backing up all content that has changed since the Saturday full.

A backup change diagram for this configuration is shown in Figure 11.7.

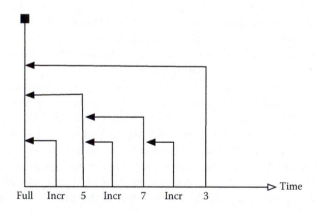

FIGURE 11.7   Backup change diagram for multilevel differential backups.

TABLE 11.6

Multilevel Differential Backup Strategy Spread over a Quarter

Saturday	Sunday	Monday	Tuesday	Wednesday	Thursday	Friday
Month 1						
1st—full	2nd—incr	3rd—incr	4th—incr	5th—incr	6th—incr	7th—incr
8th—5	9th—incr	10th—incr	11th—incr	12th—incr	13th—incr	14th—incr
15th—5	16th—incr	17th—incr	18th—incr	19th—incr	20th—incr	21st—incr
22nd—5	23rd—incr	24th—incr	25th—incr	26th—incr	27th—incr	28th—incr
29th—5	30th—incr	31st—incr				
Month 2						
			1st—incr	2nd—incr	3rd—incr	4th—incr
5th—3	6th—incr	7th—incr	8th—incr	9th—incr	10th—incr	11th—incr
12th—5	13th—incr	14th—incr	15th—incr	16th—incr	17th—incr	18th—incr
19th—5	20th—incr	21st—incr	22nd—incr	23rd—incr	24th—incr	25th—incr
26th—5	27th—incr	28th—incr	29th—incr	30th—incr		
Month 3						
					1st—incr	2nd—incr
3rd—3	4th—incr	5th—incr	6th—incr	7th—incr	8th—incr	9th—incr
10th—5	11th—incr	12th—incr	13th—incr	14th—incr	15th—incr	16th—incr
17th—5	18th—incr	19th—incr	20th—incr	21st—incr	22nd—incr	23rd—incr
24th—5	25th—incr	26th—incr	27th—incr	28th—incr	29th—incr	30th—incr
31st—5						
Month 4						
	1st—incr	2nd—incr	3rd—incr	4th—incr	5th—incr	6th—incr
7th—full	...					

Mainly when tape was a primary backup target, multilevel differential backups were seen as quite useful for stretching out the amount of time between full backups (particularly for larger filesystems with a very low change rate) while still attempting to minimize the number of backup sets required to facilitate a complete system recovery. For instance, a multilevel differential backup strategy might be considered for an ad hoc archive fileserver where full backups are only performed quarterly. Such a strategy might resemble that shown in Table 11.6.

In such a configuration, a full backup is taken on the first Saturday of the quarter. Incremental backups are done on all weekdays other than Saturdays. On all remaining Saturdays in the month, a level 5 backup is taken. This ensures that on any given day during the first month the only backup sets required for complete system recovery are the full, the most recent level 5 (assuming one has been done), and the incrementals done in that given week. On the first Saturday of the second month in the quarter, a level 3 backup is performed. This backs up all content that has changed since the full done at the start of the quarter. Incrementals still occur for all days other than Saturdays, and the remaining Saturdays in the second month all revert to level 5 backups. Thus, at most a complete system recovery in the second month will only be required:

- The full backup
- The level 3 backup
- The most recent level 5 backup
- Any incremental backups that have been performed since the level 5

The third month of the quarter is a repeat of the second month for scheduling. It is only on the first Saturday of the *next* quarter (month 4) that we see a new full backup being taken.

The advantages of differentials are as follows:

- Reduces the number of backup sets that need to be referred to for complete recovery (typically not relevant unless backing up to tape).
- In a tape environment, differentials can *reduce* the risk that a failed tape will prevent complete recoverability (if content has remained static on multiple days, it will appear in multiple differential backups).

The disadvantages of differentials are as follows:

- For filesystem backups in particular, their utility when performing backup to disk is limited and may result in unnecessary media consumption (particularly when backing up to disk that does not deduplicate)
- Variably interpreted by database/application vendors
- Systems where the change rate is large and the content that changes each day may generate very large differential backups by the end of a backup regime

Multiple-level differentials are decreasing substantially in use (and even availability) as businesses are increasingly shifting toward disk as a primary backup target. The advantages offered by differentials are mitigated when backups are available at disk speed access levels.

11.2.3.4   Synthetic Full Backups

A common problem in data protection is the amount of time it takes to perform a full backup, not to mention the potential impact to the client from performing a complete read of all its data.

Synthetic full backups approach takes the processing of a full backup away from the client and performs the work wholly within the backup infrastructure. This is achieved by synthesizing a new full backup from a previous full backup and all the incrementals that have been done since that point in time. This would resemble the backup change diagram shown in Figure 11.8.

In Figure 11.8, we show the synthetic full backup as being constructed (via dotted line sequences) from the full and incremental backups previously taken. Note that

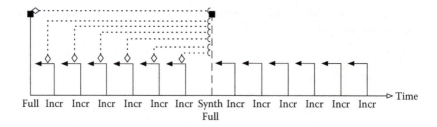

FIGURE 11.8   Backup change diagram showing synthetic fulls.

ideally a new incremental backup will be taken immediately before the full backup synthesis takes place so that the most recent changes to a system are included in and protected by the synthetic full backup.

Many backup products offering synthetic full backups will provide guidance as to whether the synthetic fulls can be carried on indefinitely or whether they should be periodically supplemented with standard full backups—users of synthetic fulls should be certain to follow this guidance to avoid recoverability issues.

The advantages of synthetic full backups include the following:

- Eliminates or at least substantially reduces the need to perform multiple full backups over the life span of the system
- Allows for recovery from a recent full regardless of how long it has been since an actual full backup has been performed
- Useful for backing up remote offices over slow links to a central location (providing the first full backup can be performed centrally *or* a trickle* first full backup can be performed)

The disadvantages of synthetic full backups include the following:

- Usually very limited support for databases and complex applications.
- Not supported by all backup products.
- Some backup products will require periodic standard full backups after a certain number of synthetic full backups have been completed.
- While synthetic full backups might be executed to provide backups for remote offices over slow links, they do not address the potential recovery slowness that occurs over such a link.

11.2.3.5 Virtual Synthetic Fulls

This is a relatively new backup concept and refers to the capabilities offered by highly IDPAs, particularly those using deduplication functionality. In this scenario, the

---

* A "trickle" full backup is where the complete data is slowly copied over a longer cycle than would normally be acceptable for a full backup. This might be as simple as the first full backup taking a week or more to complete (depending on bandwidth), or it might be through a "rolling full," whereby the first full is completed over a series of phased full backups of subsets of the data.

creation of a synthetic full is actually *offloaded* to the data protection storage—the backup server will instruct the protection storage to assemble a new full backup by combining previous backups executed and stored on the system, but will not actually do the data movement itself. Particularly when deduplication storage is used, this allows for high-speed construction of synthetic full backups without needing to *rehydrate* the data during the process.*

Virtual synthetic fulls offer all the advantages of standard synthetic full backups, but with the added advantages of avoiding data rehydration and offloading the data processing from the backup servers or media servers/storage nodes. The disadvantages of virtual synthetic fulls remain the same as the disadvantages for standard synthetic fulls.

11.2.3.6 Manual Backups

Although not technically a backup level, it's often worth differentiating whether a backup product supports manual backups. These are ad hoc backups initiated by an administrator or end user rather than scheduled from within the backup software.

Manual backups offer an additional level of protection and allow for user extension to the backup product, catering for applications and scenarios the backup vendor was either unable to anticipate or willing to support directly. If manual backups are supported, they should be used carefully since they represent a resource utilization the backup server/services cannot anticipate. For instance, while a backup server might be sized to provide backup and recovery services for, say, 2000 clients, this might be load balanced in such a way that no more than 200 clients are being backed up at any given time. If individual administrators execute too many manual backups concurrently while planned backup jobs are already being executed, this could result in resource exhaustion in the backup server.

The following are the advantages of manual backups:

- Allows for ad hoc backups to be run on as required, without scheduling
- Allows for extension of the backup system beyond the design of the original backup vendor

The following are the disadvantages of manual backups:

- If misused, may result in resource contention or even exhaustion on the backup server
- May create administrative overheads or maintenance delays if used regularly

11.2.3.7 Skipping Backups

While preventing a backup from running is also not really a backup level, it does play an important part in enterprise backup regimes. This allows administrators to deliberately prevent backups from running at predetermined times/dates. The purpose

---

* Data rehydration will be covered in more detail in Chapter 13.

of such a feature is to avoid a scenario where backups have to be turned off and on manually. For instance, consider a business that wants

- Daily incremental/weekly full backups kept for 6 weeks
- Monthly full backups kept for 13 months

In such a scenario, it wouldn't necessarily make sense to run a full backup in the "daily" sequence on the same day (or even in the same week) as the full backup in the "monthly" sequence. Sensible backup scheduling will allow the daily sequence full to be skipped while the monthly backup full executes, without manual administrative intervention. Being able to facilitate backup skipping is actually an important feature in a backup product—without it, there is increased risk of human error and a requirement for manual intervention.

There are typically two specific approaches to "skip" backup operations:

1. The skip option defined as a level, so that it can be inserted into the backup schedule as appropriate
2. The skip option defined as a window during which backups cannot run (either globally or on a per backup-set basis)

The advantages of skip backup levels/windows include the following:

- Allows backup schedules to be completely automated, requiring less manual administrator intervention
- Allows nonregular backup downtimes to be scheduled in advance

The disadvantages of skip backup levels/windows include the following:

- The use of skip levels/windows should be documented and understood to prevent risk of data loss in the event of backups not running and a subsequent failure occurring.

Another potential challenge created by skip levels is when they need to be manually defined for each date versus perpetually recurring options. For instance, while some products might support definitions such as "skip last Friday every month," more ad hoc skip requirements (e.g., skipping each Easter Sunday) or backup skipping for products that don't support perpetual options can result in administrators bulk-setting these levels for 1 or more years in advance. If these aren't revisited regularly and updated, these may result in unexpected backup behavior.

11.2.3.8   Full Once, Incrementals Forever

While more an overall backup function, this is intimately tied to backup levels and warrants consideration at this point. Defined as a time-saving function, a single full backup is generated during the first backup, but following that all backups are incremental. This is different to synthetic full backups in that no full backup synthesis ever occurs. Instead, products featuring this technology will typically perform some form of media consolidation, whereby expired backups (either in terms of number of versions of data or the time since the backup) are expunged. For tape, this necessitates copying off current/required backups once the percentage of expired backups has reached a particular threshold. For instance, a product might be configured to keep 10 versions of a file. Once the number of files on a tape that are version 11 or higher reaches, say, 35%, the files on the tape that are still current/active are migrated to another tape so that the tape can be recycled.

In a tape-only environment, this can represent a staggering number of units of media being required for full system recovery. For instance—consider a 1 TB file-server—some files on the fileserver may rarely if ever change. If we assume there are enough servers overall within an environment that 1 tape per day is used to perform backups, there will be 365 tapes after a year. Even assuming a relatively high change rate (allowing for 11+ versions to be achieved on 65% of the files), it may be that only a 5:1 media reduction occurs over the course of a year. Therefore, at the end of a year, up to 73 tapes might be required for a complete fileserver restoration.

Particularly in tape-only environments, these backup strategies typically bet on never needing to perform total system restoration, with another data protection or high availability system to perform that function. Consider, for instance, the previous example of 73 tapes (after media consolidation) being required for a complete filesystem restoration. If we assume 3 minutes of load/unload time added to the recovery for each piece of media and another 5 minutes of tape seek time added to the recovery for each piece of media, such a recovery strategy might require an additional 9.7 hours of media handling operations *outside of actual data reading.*

The advantages of an incrementals forever strategy include the following:

- After the first full backup, the backup window will be substantially smaller for all future backups.
- If a deployed backup product doesn't support synthetic full backups, but supports this model, it may allow for a smaller backup window indefinitely, albeit at a price.

The disadvantages of an incrementals forever strategy include the following:

- Even if the model supports databases, database administrators may be extremely reluctant to embrace it, requiring a two-phased backup approach.
- Complete system or complete filesystem recoveries may need to make use of a large number of backup volumes.
- Allowing for media aggregation without disrupting regular backup and recovery operations will require many additional backup devices, and this will continue to increase as the amount of data being protected by the system increases.
- Physical wear and tear on media and devices during larger-scale recoveries may be excessive.

11.2.4   DATA AVAILABILITY

Depending on the type of backup performed, the availability of the data to end users may be affected—or rather, the level of data availability required by the organization will make a profound impact on the type of backup operations that can be performed.

11.2.4.1   Offline Backups

An offline backup is where the data or system that is backed up is unavailable for other uses for the duration of the backup. In database circles, these types of backups are referred to as cold backups.

As is implied by its name, this results in an outage on the data and application(s) using that data and will take as long as the backup takes to complete. This presents obvious disadvantages for 24/7 businesses that cannot be denied. However, in applications or businesses where 24 × 7 availability is not required, there are some advantages to offline backups, most typically where there are no dedicated IT staff to perform more complex recoveries that may arise from other forms of backup.

Such backups can be cheaper, too. For some enterprise products, database backups will be a licensed feature*: businesses may enact a policy whereby hot/online backups are performed for production databases, but development and test databases requiring backup are instead shutdown.

Offline backups may actually cause performance problems *outside* of the backup window. Many modern enterprise applications, particularly databases, use sophisticated caching techniques to reduce the number of IO operations required, with SAP and Oracle being two such applications. As soon as an application is shut down, any cache it may have been maintaining is typically lost. Indeed, some vendors will strongly recommend against frequent restarts of their applications for cache performance reasons.

The advantages of offline backups include the following:

- Recovery is typically trivial.
- For even complex environments, recoveries can be performed by staff who might otherwise not be application or system administrators when following well-tested instructions.
- When combined with snapshots, volume replication, and/or clustering, this technique might allow for simpler backups with minimal application downtime by performing the backup against a temporarily shut down and static copy or node.

---

* For many enterprise backup products, capacity-based licensing is increasingly supplanting feature-based licensing. This allows for more adaptive deployment models where a business is entitled to use most, if not all available functionality of a product, but pays for licenses based on (approximately) the amount of data being protected. Capacity licensing might be calculated on front-end capacity (the size of a full backup of the protected environment) or back-end capacity (the total capacity of all backups that can be stored under the license). Front-end capacity licensing is usually more desirable.

The disadvantages of offline backups include the following:

- Without snapshots or other expensive techniques, applications that rely on data are unavailable for the duration of the backup.
- Care has to be taken to ensure that all components of the data are unused during backup. (For example, if data resides on multiple filesystems, there must be no changes to *any* of those filesystems during backup for the purposes of consistency.)
- For databases in particular, incremental offline backups are usually not supported—that is, an offline backup will force a new full backup. If the database is only a few gigabytes in size, this may be OK—however, it quickly becomes impractical as the size of the database increases.
- Over time, this model is unlikely to work as the amount of data to be backed up and the business systems availability requirements increase.

11.2.4.2   Online Backups

In an online backup, the data or systems being backed up remain completely available for the duration of the backup. Database administrators will know this form of backup as a *hot* backup.

Online backups can create an impact on the applications or systems they are protecting—the systems will remain available to the users, but will have a performance hit as a result of needing to service regular user functions as well as backup reads. Whether this is noticed by end users will depend on the design of the system, the design of the backup system, the performance characteristics of the system, the amount of processing being performed by the system during backup, and the amount of data to be backed up.

For databases, this performance hit is usually caused by the requirement to do greater levels of transactional logging during backup. Transactional logging is used in circumstances where a possibly inconsistent backup is taken of a database file, but another file generated (and backed up *after* the database file has been fully backed up) can be used to restore consistency by replaying writes.

Regular filesystem backups (say, of an operating system disk, user accounts) can be taken in two ways. Feature-rich operating systems with tight backup integration points may offer the ability to perform filesystem snapshots, presenting the snapshots as quiesced point-in-time copies to the backup application. Other operating systems may offer no such integration, and the backup becomes a risk-based approach: the backup is run at a time when the system is used least frequently. Files that are changed during backup are (ideally) reported on by the backup application and appropriate steps can be performed to ensure the data is still protected.*

Some applications, filesystems, or operating systems may implement exclusive file locking for data being accessed, which can result in files being missed entirely during the backup process, and administrators should understand what options there

---

* In such a situation, the most common form of file that changes during a backup will be log files and temporary files. Most system, application, and backup administrators will accept changes occurring during backup to these files, particularly if they can still recover *some* of the file content.

are to avoid this situation—for example, such systems may get around the problem by offering a read-only point-in-time snapshot of the filesystem or data to the backup application, as discussed earlier.

Equally requiring understanding are those applications and operating systems that *don't* implement exclusive file locking. While technically these may allow entire databases to be read and backed up while they are open and being actively used, without appropriate consistency restoration processes, the data backed is likely useless for the purposes of recovery.

As even the most basic of systems become required for 24/7 availability, online backups have been becoming the *only* option for many companies. Such organizations can no longer afford to shut an application down for hours for a backup if it means an end customer will refuse to wait or a vital business process is paused for the duration.*

The unfortunate relationship between offline and online backups is that while an offline backup possibly represents a significant interruption to service delivery, it represents an extremely streamlined recovery. In particular, depending on the database or application being backed up, online database backups designed for no interruptions to users may require a longer or more complex recovery procedure. (Conversely, it should be noted that granular recovery options from database/application backups usually require the backup to have been done as an online operation.)

The following are the advantages of online backups:

- No outage to end users or customers during the backup process.
- Complex granular recovery for applications and databases typically require an online/hot backup having been done.

The following are the disadvantages of online backups:

- May be more complex to configure and administer.
- For databases, a trained administrator may be more likely to be required as recoveries will not be simple filesystem restores.

11.2.4.3   Snapshot Backups

Alluded to previously, a snapshot backup is a point-in-time backup that allows immediate recovery of a system to the exact time that the backup was initiated. The difference between this and a regular backup is that the snapshot provides the same point-in-time backup for *all* files, regardless of what time the files are backed up, whereas a conventional hot/online backup will allow the backup of different files at varying times. For example, a backup might see files copied with the following time frames:

- C:\Data\File1.dat—backed up at 22:30
- C:\Data\File2.dat—backed up at 22:32
- C:\Data\File3.dat—backed up at 22:45

---

* Reporting "the system is currently unavailable" to a customer is now accepted as an informal way of saying "please buy this product or service from one of our competitors."

The difference between a snapshot backup and a regular online/hot backup is whether or not the files can change during the backup process. In a regular hot/online backup, there is nothing to prevent "File2.dat" from changing during the backup of "File1.dat," or "File1.dat" from changing after it has been backed up but before the backup of the other files have been completed. Indeed, there is nothing potentially stopping "File1.dat" from changing *while* it is being backed up.

In a snapshot backup however, the filesystem instance being backed up is a read only and cannot be updated by any processes. This means that *multifile* consistency (indeed, entire filesystem or system consistency) is guaranteed. None of the files in the example will change during the backup process.

The advantages of snapshot backups include the following:

- Allows the easy acquisition of point-in-time copies of the system for backup purposes.
- Can allow for faster recoveries—mount the snapshot and copy the required files (for individual file recovery) or roll the snapshot back to perform a complete filesystem recovery.
- Depending on the snapshot technology, consider the following:
    - Multiple snapshots can be performed over a short period of time, allowing systems to meet SLAs for minimal data loss that may be otherwise unachievable using standard daily backups.
    - Snapshots might be able to be mounted on alternate hosts, further reducing the load on the client during the backup process.

The disadvantages of snapshot backups include the following:

- Typically require additional volume management software or intelligent disk arrays.
- Require additional disk space (though rarely equal to the disk space being protected, thanks to modern snapshot functionality).
- Snapshot storage has to be the same speed as original disks to minimize the performance impact.
- Coordinating snapshots across multiple hosts (e.g., for clustered services or multihost database/application servers) can be tricky.

11.2.5 Data Selection Types

Backup products fall into two main categories—inclusive or exclusive backups. This refers to how data is selected for backup by the backup agent. Ultimately, remembering the rule that it is always better to backup a little more than not enough, exclusive backup selection models should *always* be favored over inclusive selection models.

11.2.5.1 Inclusive Backups

An inclusive backup is one where a list is populated by the administrator of the data or filesystems that require backup and *only* those items that are explicitly listed will be included in the backup process. For traditional filesystem backups, this might refer to a simple list of the attached filesystems:

- Unix/Linux:
  - /
  - /boot
  - /var
  - /home
- Windows:
  - C:\
  - D:\
  - E:\

Some organizations prefer this type of backup system under the belief that it provides them greater control regarding what data gets backed up. This is a misguided belief founded on false economies: time and time again across almost every company that uses the system this policy incurs data loss.

Most commonly, organizations using this model declare reasoning such as "we won't backup the operating system because it can be reinstalled and the settings reapplied." In most cases, this is not properly thought through. Take an average UNIX environment, for instance. The sequence might include

- Reinstalling the operating system
- Customizing groups and users who can access the system or reintegrate the host into a global authentication system
- Making amendments to such items as the mail delivery system to suit the organization
- Recreating any printers
- Reinstalling any third-party system administration tools that reside on the operating system area
- Performing any additional security hardening required
- Installing any security certificates, joining corporate domain services, etc.

Depending on the use of the system, the level of customization may be more or less than this list, but there will invariably be some activities that are required on the host after the base operating system has been installed. This level of customization usually exceeds a "short" period of time, even for a well-documented system. Windows systems are not exempt and will have their own issues that sometimes overlap the list mentioned earlier. For example, some backup products perform special backups of key Windows components such as the registry; rather than backing up those base files that comprise the Windows registry hives, it is necessary to export them properly first. These files may therefore not be backed up as part of a "C:\" backup at all, requiring additional special options enabled. A common mistake with inclusive backup policies is to forget about these special components and therefore be unable to perform host disaster recoveries.

As soon as the amount of time taken to customize a machine postrecovery exceeds a very short period of time (e.g., 10 minutes) and has nonautomated processes, any perceived advantages of not backing up the operating system are lost.

Consider a situation where the operating system of the machine might represent, say, 4 GB. As the operating system region changes very infrequently, the incremental backups on such a system will have almost no impact on media requirements. It would be reasonable to assume that such an operating system region will have less than 100 MB of changes per day, excepting times where large vendor patches are issued. Plotting a 6-week daily retention backup period, with fulls once per week, we could assume this would require 6 × 4 GB for full backups and 36 × 100 MB for incremental backups. This equates to approximately 28 GB (rounded) of additional backup capacity required over a 6-week cycle. If that same system has 200 GB of production data storage requiring backups, with a 5% change rate, the data component of the backup over the same schedule will be 1.52 TB in size. Particularly when considering the growing likelihood of backing up to deduplication storage, the capacity savings of failing to backup operating system and application regions are negligible when compared to the time taken to manually recreate settings (and the risk of forgetting one or more settings).

What this example should show is that in the best case, inclusive backups represent a false economy. Saving a few dollars here and there on backup storage capacity might improve the bottom line negligibly when no recoveries are needed, but such savings will quickly be forgotten by the business when systems cannot be accessed by even a handful of users.

Inclusive backups, however, represent a considerably worse threat than these—the potential for data loss due to human error. Inclusive backups typically end up in situations where data is stored on filesystems other than what is being backed up or an explicit list of files and filesystems to backup will miss a particular file that is required for easy (or worse, *successful*) recovery. A common mistake in inclusive backups is where an administrator adds a new filesystem to a host and then fails to update the backup criteria for the machine.

Inclusive backups invite human error: A company once had an SAP system whose nightly cold backups had been manually managed via inclusive backups. That is, each filesystem to be backed up was explicitly listed. During a review, it was determined that they had added an additional 2 × 30 GB filesystems containing SAP database files to the host without including those filesystems in the backup regime. This error was picked up several *weeks* after the filesystems were added. Although no failure had occurred in that time, the potential for failure was high—the production operations of the *entire* company had been geared around a total dependency on SAP; thus, the complete loss of the SAP system would have resulted in significant productivity outages or perhaps even the failure of the company. Even after being corrected, this left the company exposed to a window of retention where their systems could not be recovered—a likely compliance issue.

What was worse in this situation was the backup product being used normally worked via an *exclusive* file selection model but had been deliberately circumvented to be used as an inclusive backup model.

Inclusive backup policies and products should be strongly discouraged. Further, products that *only* offer inclusive backup strategies should be discarded from any consideration when evaluating enterprise backup software due to data loss potential *built into* the product.

The following is an advantage of inclusive backups:

- None. There are no features of an inclusive backup system that cannot be provided by an appropriately managed exclusive backup system.

The following are the disadvantages of inclusive backups:

- Require manual intervention into the backup configuration any time the host or application configuration changes, making it entirely unable to scale.
- Data loss can occur, resulting in anything from additional work being required, to job loss or even the collapse of a company dependent on a critical application or system whose backups were wholly inadequate.

11.2.5.2 Exclusive Backups

These are the exact opposite of inclusive backups. Rather than explicitly specifying what should be backed up, only what should *not* be backed up is explicitly defined. The automated selection of what is to be backed up is normally achieved through specifying a special "global" backup selection parameter, such as "All" or "ALL_LOCAL_DRIVES" for "All filesystems." While the parameter will inevitably vary depending on the backup product, the net result is the same—rather than manually specifying individual filesystems to be backed up and adjusting settings whenever more filesystems are added, the one parameter will act as a catch-all.

An exclusive backup product will automatically protect all filesystems attached to a client. Usually this is restricted to filesystems that are "locally" attached to the system—that is, network attached filesystems are not normally included. (As SAN storage is seen as locally attached storage to any applications, they would normally be included automatically by exclusive backup strategies.) If necessary, network attached filesystems could be explicitly added to the backup policy.

Exclusive backup systems are designed using the axiom "better to backup more than not enough" and should be favored at all times over inclusive backup systems. In this sense, exclusive backup products have been clearly designed to maximize data protection, whereas inclusive backup products have been designed to save a few dollars (while introducing massive risk of data loss). A key benefit that exclusive backup systems grant is the reduction in risk for human error when filesystems are added or otherwise changed. The backup system should automatically detect any new filesystems on hosts configured for exclusive backups in the environment and automatically protect them as part of the next backup.*

---

* You will note most of the discussion around inclusive versus exclusive backups center on filesystem backups. The ability to detect and automatically protect specific databases will be tied almost exclusively to the APIs offered by database vendors.

Users of backup software that works on an inclusive model will usually object to exclusive backups on the grounds of "there are things I just don't want to backup." If referring to operating system or application configuration, this can usually be discounted immediately as incorrect. In other examples, there may legitimately be a requirement to avoid some content. An organization might, for instance, want to perform file server backups but skip any MP3 file in a user home directory because of the risk of copyright violation. In such cases, exclusive backups offer a better mechanism than inclusive backups: rather than having to specify everything *other* than the multimedia files to be backed up, as one would have to do in an inclusive system, the exclusive system will allow for specific actions (such as skipping files or directories) to be configured against specific subdirectory locations or known file names/extensions.

The following are the advantages of exclusive backups:

- Maximizes the potential for the backup environment to provide recoverability of data and systems.
- Reduces the risk of human error or forgetfulness resulting in data loss.

The following are the disadvantages of exclusive backups:

- May require analysis of systems to confirm what, if anything, can safely be excluded from the backup. (It should be noted that this would be considered by many to be a standard system administration function regardless.)

11.2.6 Backup Retention Strategies

The way in which a backup product handles the retention of backups directly affects how recoveries work and for how long recoveries can be performed. Because we have stated from the outset that the purpose of a backup is to allow recoveries to be performed if and when required, retention strategies have a direct impact on the quality of the backup product.

There are two broad categories for types of retention strategies within backups: the simple model and the dependency-based model. Although it is the more complex one, the dependency model is the most appropriate to present first, since an appreciation of what it provides goes to demonstrate just how poor and inappropriate the simple model is in a backup environment.

11.2.6.1 Dependency-Based Retention

This model takes the approach that a specified retention period creates dependencies among the individual backups taken for true data protection. For example, consider a 6-week retention period. This implies that after a backup is 42 days old, it is no longer required, and we can show the retention periods in relation to the backups in a dependency diagram such as that shown in Figure 11.9.

Dependency-based backup retention models are designed on the principle that one individual backup may provide recoverability for the files and data contained

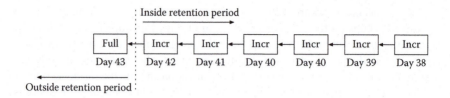

FIGURE 11.9 Backup dependency diagram.

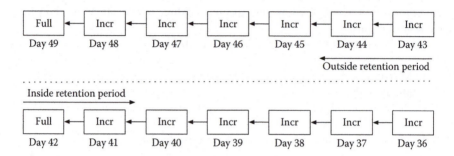

FIGURE 11.10 Two dependency chains.

specifically within that backup, but complete restoration of a filesystem or data will potentially require other backups that *depend* on the backup. Figure 11.9 shows a full backup that is outside the 6-week retention period. The incremental that was taken immediately following the full backup *depends* on the full backup in order to offer complete restoration capabilities. The incremental taken after the *first* incremental requires the first incremental (which in turn requires the full backup) in order to provide complete restoration capabilities.

In such models, even if a backup is *outside* its stated retention policy, it will not become eligible for removal until such time as all backups that *depend on it* for system restoration are equally outside of *their* retention policy. This will usually happen when additional full* backups are generated, breaking dependency chains. An example of this is shown in Figure 11.10.

Thus, we typically consider, in a dependency-based backup retention model, it is not the case that individual backups become eligible for removal, but rather, entire backup *chains* become eligible for removal once all their links (i.e., individual backups) have exceeded their retention.

Another way to think of this form of retention is that it offers "complete recovery protection"—the backup product is designed to not only allow any individual backup instance to be recovered from but on the basis that the worst-case scenario (complete

---

* Complex dependency chains with partial content removal can be built using differential backup models, but an examination of these is not necessary to understand dependency chains.

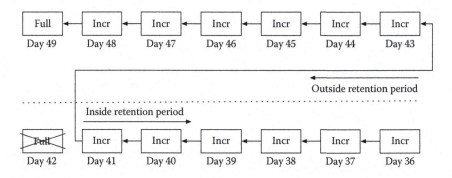

FIGURE 11.11   Extended dependency chain caused by a failed full backup.

system restoration) also needs to be achievable right through to the complete configured retention time. If backups must be preserved for legal or auditing reasons, it may mean that dependency-based retention models are the only legally acceptable option in an environment.

Although full backups are *always* important, they become even more important in a dependency-based retention system as they start new dependency chains and allow older ones to become eligible for removal. If a full backup—or for that matter, any backup that would otherwise terminate a dependency chain—fails to execute successfully, then the existing dependency chain must continue to grow. This might in turn result in a dependency chain such as shown in Figure 11.11. In short, if a full backup fails to execute, the backup product must extend the life span of the previous full and intervening incremental backups to force the integrity of the backup period set by the administrator. Note that in this instance we're referring only to a failed full or a full backup that did not run—rather than a backup that successfully ran but was subsequently erased or the media on which it resided failed.

The advantages of dependency-based retention include the following:

- Backups that are outside their retention time are only removed when the system is certain there are no backups still within the retention period that depend on them for complete system recovery.
- Complete system recovery (barring user intervention or media failure) is guaranteed for the entire retention period specified for the backups.

The disadvantage of dependency-based retention include the following:

- May require more backup media than a simple retention model.

11.2.6.2   Simple Retention Model

This is (unfortunately) still a common enough model of how backup retention is handled in some products. In this situation, the retention time specified for backups is viewed only on the basis of recovery from an individual backup.

TABLE 11.7

Removable Backups in a Simple Retention Model

Day 48	Day 47	Day 46	Day 45	Day 44	Day 43	Day 42	Day 41	Day 40	Day 39	Day 38	Day 37
Incr	*Incr*	*Incr*	*Incr*	*Incr*	*Full*	Incr	Incr	Incr	Incr	Incr	Incr

Take, for instance, the 6-week retention time we've been using in our examples so far. This equates to 42 days of backups. Viewing the backups via the retention window allows us to see what happens to backups that move outside their retention time. In the model shown in Table 11.7, all italicized backups would be immediately considered as available for removal.

This is a retention strategy based solely on false economies. If the full system backup from day 43 is expunged, it means the system as a whole cannot be recovered for a full 6 weeks' worth of backups. Instead, only 5 weeks' (assuming all full backups succeed) worth of backups can be recovered using the full system recover model. Although the incremental backups from days 37 to 42 could still be used to recover individual files, the entire filesystem they provide backups for could not be successfully recovered. This approach in essence hedges its bets on only needing to perform a complete filesystem recovery for the most recent full backups. However, there is a plethora of recovery scenarios that this fails to address.

One of the most common and illogical manifestations of this model is the encouragement for a user to see a separation between the full backup that occurs periodically and the incremental backup that occurs nearly every day. For example, in these types of backup products, users may refer to their "weekly backups" and "daily backups" as being two distinctly different sets. This for the most part tricks the users into believing there is no relationship between, say, a weekly full backup and the daily incrementals. When evaluated from a complete system protection perspective, such an idea is farcical.

When considering complete data protection requirements, backup products that use this type of retention model should be avoided wherever possible in corporate environments, unless longer retention models are used and management-signed acceptance of the system restoration risks involved is provided.

The following is an advantage of simplistic backup retention:

- None. The perceived media saving is irrelevant when compared to the risk of not being able to recover systems.

The following are disadvantages of simplistic backup retention:

- Does not guarantee full system recovery for the entire retention period specified by the backup administrator.
- Often encourages an artificial separation between full and incremental backups at the cost of system recoverability.

11.2.7 MANUAL BACKUPS REVISITED

Previously when outlining the various backup levels that might be offered by backup products, we discussed the notion of a manual or ad hoc backup. For the most part, backup products that calculate retention dependency will avoid factoring manual backups into the dependency chain at all—that is, the dependency chain is typically built on scheduled backups only due to the likelihood of manual backups being for only a subset of a normal, automated backup.

If planning to work with manual backups, be sure to consider the impact this may have on dependencies within the backup system. This should be documented or if not readily discoverable by asking the vendor.

11.3 RECOVERY STRATEGIES

There are several broad categories in which backup products will offer the means to accomplish recoveries. Not all products will support each strategy, so if looking for a new product, it will be necessary to determine which strategies are required the most and confirm from backup and recovery vendors which strategies are supported by their products.

11.3.1 RECOVERY TYPES

Recovery *type* refers to how the backup product facilitates recoveries—how files and data that have been backed up may be selected for recovery or recovered without selection. Although multiple types are presented here, there are three that should be considered mandatory for a backup product:

1. *Last filesystem view recovery*—This presents a view of the filesystem as it was as of the last backup.
2. *Point-in-time recovery*—Although last filesystem view is arguably the most common recovery that administrators and users will require, for many companies a substantial portion of recoveries will need to be of data that was backed up *prior* to the most recent backup. This option allows a user to step back through previous versions or views of the filesystem, allowing not only the selection of *what* to recover but *when*.
3. *Nonindex recovery*—Being able to perform a recovery from an index of files backed up is an obvious requirement, but less obvious is the need to be able to still perform a recovery even if that index has been lost. This allows for emergency recoveries to be initiated immediately rather than having to recover an index first *before* starting the actual recovery.

11.3.1.1 Aggregated Filesystem View

The aggregated filesystem view is almost the logical opposite of the last filesystem recovery view. Not only does the aggregated filesystem view show the filesystem contents as of the last backup, it includes into the view all files from backups between the most recent full backup and the last run backup.

To understand an aggregated filesystem view, let's imagine a backup schedule where the full backup happens on a Friday evening and incremental backups are run Saturday through Thursday evenings. Now consider the following scenario:

- Full backup occurs on Friday.
- On Sunday, the directory "/Users/pmdg/Archives/Oldest" is deleted by a scheduled job.
- On Monday, the file "/Users/pmdg/Desktop/expenses.xls" is created.
- On Tuesday, the file "/Users/pmdg/Desktop/expenses.xls" is deleted.
- On Tuesday, the file "/Users/pmdg/Desktop/Letter.pages" is created.
- On Wednesday, the "/Users" directory is accidentally deleted and needs to be recovered.

If a recovery agent using an aggregated filesystem view is used to recover on Wednesday morning, it will show both the "/Users/pmdg/Archives/Oldest" directory and the "/Users/pmdg/Desktop/expenses.xls" file, even though neither of these existed as of the most recent backup performed.

Although this model may initially appear to provide a good recovery mechanism, its advantages are outweighed by its disadvantages.

The advantages of an aggregated filesystem view include the following:

- Presents all files backed up since the last full (typically). This reduces the need to alter the point in time the recovery is browsed for.
- Provides an easy mechanism to recover from successive days worth of accidental or malicious data deletion.

The disadvantages of an aggregated filesystem recovery view include the following:

- May cause a security or compliance incident. If a deletion was intentional due to security or legal considerations, the recovery operator will have no visibility over this needing to be repeated following the recovery or to exclude the file(s) from recovery.
- Depending on the amount of data deleted intentionally, this model can result in a situation where the recovery fills up the target filesystem as older, intentionally deleted data is restored.
- Results in "messy" filesystems at the end of the recovery process.
- Users may be confused by previous versions of files and directories appearing—this may even result in data loss situations by users or administrators deleting newer content accidentally in favor of older content.
- If between successive backups files and directories have been moved around, this may result in data duplication following a recovery.

11.3.1.2 Last Filesystem View

This recovery variant only shows the files and directory structure that was present as of the last backup. That is, it assumes that deletions performed *between* backups are actually intentional and the desire is to return the filesystem as close as possible to what it was at the time of the failure.

In our previous example, we considered the following scenario:

- Full backup occurs on Friday.
- On Sunday, the directory "/Users/pmdg/Archives/Oldest" is deleted by a scheduled job.
- On Monday, the file "/Users/pmdg/Desktop/expenses.xls" is created.
- On Tuesday, the file "/Users/pmdg/Desktop/expenses.xls" is deleted.
- On Tuesday, the file "/Users/pmdg/Desktop/Letter.pages" is created.
- On Wednesday, the "/Users" directory is accidentally deleted and needs to be recovered.

As discussed previously, the aggregated filesystem view would show those files that had been deleted prior to the Tuesday night backup on Wednesday morning, potentially allowing an operator to recover a logically inconsistent filesystem or even an overfull one.

For the last filesystem view, we literally only see the files/directories present on the filesystem as of the last backup. Assuming a Tuesday night backup from our previous example, we would not see "/Users/pmdg/Archives/Oldest" (deleted on Sunday) and "/Users/pmdg/Desktop/expenses.xls" (deleted on Tuesday).

The advantages of the last filesystem recovery view include the following:

- Shows the filesystem as of the last backup performed. This allows recovery operators to very quickly retrieve the system state as of the last backup.
- When attempting to return a filesystem to its most recent state, it provides the most logically consistent view.

The disadvantages of the last filesystem recovery view include the following:

- Effectively requires point-in-time recoveries (see the following texts) in order to recover data that was deleted *prior* to the most recent backup.
- May require multiple recoveries if data loss has been gradual.

While disadvantages are mentioned earlier, it should be noted that these are *entirely* outweighed by the utility and practicality of the advantages.

11.3.1.3   Point-in-Time Recoveries

Point-in-time recoveries extend the notion of a "last filesystem view" recovery model to show a view of the filesystem as of a backup taken at a specific point in time. Examples of the usefulness of this model include the following:

- Over a series of days, a user makes a significant number of changes to a document that will be too difficult to back out of; hence, referring to the most recent backup or backups will not be useful for recovery purposes— the user will require document recovery from one or more backups past.

- Taxation lawyers request a copy of the company banking database from the closure of the previous financial year.
- A user working on a document leaves their terminal session logged on with the application running while on vacation for a few days. Unfortunately, during this time, the application crashed, leaving the document automatically saved with 0 bytes on disk. When the user returns from vacation and discovers the document "empty," a recovery from several days prior is required.
- Database administrator requests a copy of the database from a month ago to be recovered onto another server to complete last month's reporting.

In all of these examples, the goal is not to recover the most recent data backed up, but data that was backed up at some point in the past.

Point-in-time recoveries prove the need for backup duplication. In a later topic, we'll discuss backup duplication, which refers to generating a "backup of the backup." Some organizations insist they do not need to perform backup duplication if they backup to a remote site (e.g., protection storage in the disaster recovery site attached via high-speed networking). Point-in-time recoveries clearly show this to be a false statement: in the event of a loss of the disaster recovery site, although the current production data is undamaged, all file history has (conceivably) been lost.

Point-in-time recoveries prove that snapshots are not backups. Some will try to insist that implementing snapshots into an environment means customers never need to run another backup. However, it is neither technically nor financially feasible for almost any business to retain a sufficient number of snapshots to provide point-in-time recovery capabilities over the entire expected life span of a backup. For instance, most financial data needs to be kept for at least 7 years. The performance implications and financial cost of sufficient storage to maintain 7 years' worth of regularly executed snapshots will be very large compared to a comprehensive data protection solution.

The advantages of point-in-time recoveries are as follows:

- They allow prior system or data states to be recovered at any point a backup was done within the retention period rather than the most recent backup only.
- They facilitate audits and legal/tax obligations in many companies through the recovery of older records.
- They allow previously executed processing (or missed processing) to be rerun by recovering older data to alternate systems for replay without impacting or overwriting current live production data.

A disadvantage of point-in-time recoveries is as follows:

- None—it is essential that a backup product support point-in-time recoveries.

11.3.1.4   Destructive Recoveries

Although a destructive recovery may sound like a contradiction in terms, what it refers to is completely replacing the contents of a filesystem, entire host, or database with that which is being recovered, thereby deleting files or data that were not present at the time of the backup.

There are two types of destructive recovery. The first is where, on a file-by-file basis, files or data that were not present at the time of the backup are deleted as the recovery progresses. The second type leverages restoration from block-level backups rather than file-level backups to overwrite the filesystem completely. (We'll discuss block-level backups at a later point.)

The advantages of destructive recoveries are as follows:

- If an external agent has introduced corruption to a system, a destructive recovery may be seen as an appropriate mechanism to bring the system back to a usable state.
- If a block-level backup has been performed due to filesystem density, this may allow a recovery to be performed orders of magnitude faster than a conventional file-by-file recovery.
- When combined with a point-in-time recovery, a destructive recovery may provide increased coherence in the recovered system by removing files from a more recent time to the recovery.

A disadvantage of destructive recoveries is as follows:

- As implied by its name, a destructive recovery could result in significant data loss if not used correctly.

11.3.1.5 Nonindexed Recovery

So far we've primarily discussed recoveries that are performed via a "browse" of the filesystem or data to be recovered. Across almost all backup products, the indices that must be maintained for a per-file view of the backup can grow to a very large size. Additionally, indices may become corrupt or get accidentally deleted. Further, in the event of a disaster, it may be necessary to initiate a data recovery immediately due to SLA reasons, even *before* the index is available. (Additionally, some backups might even be generated with the index information deliberately turned off—for example, a "closure" backup of a fileserver used explicitly for a project might not have indices generated if it is determined individual file recovery will never be required.)

Most backup products therefore offer the ability to perform a recovery of an entire backup without the need to refer to indices. (Although for the most part this will refer to per-filesystem backups, it may encompass a larger target depending on the circumstances or the product.) That is, everything that was stored as part of an individual backup is recovered, regardless of whether the backup can be browsed on a per-file basis.

Sometimes, administrators may even choose to perform such a recovery even when the indices are available. This is typically chosen when the most recent backup is a full, and the "cost" of selecting all the files in the index for recovery is high. This cost can be perceived as high when there are a very large number of files on a filesystem as the backup product may need to enumerate the file selection process if in an interactive mode. In index-based recoveries, the index must be searched for relevant entries and those entries must be "tagged" for recovery. This requires time, and a tangible data structure must be built and maintained in memory for holding the details of the files to be recovered. This may not seem terribly relevant if waiting less than 10 seconds for file selection to complete, but if millions of files (or more) need to be recovered, this may have a significant impact on the recovery time.

Depending on the backup product, nonindex recoveries can also be used where there is physical damage to the backup media (especially for tape), so as to get the backup product to retrieve "as much as possible" of the backup.

The advantages of nonindex recoveries include the following:

- Can allow for the recovery of data even if the backup product is itself experiencing data loss or corruption.
- Depending on the product, this may facilitate faster recoveries when there are large numbers (e.g., millions) of files to be recovered.
- Depending on the product, this may facilitate recovering data from faulty media, skipping past soft errors.

The disadvantages of nonindex recoveries include the following:

- May result in additional data being recovered than intended, if not filtered correctly.
- Typically does not "merge" multiple backups (e.g., a full and multiple incrementals) for a complete recovery; instead, each backup that requires recovery needs to be selected and recovered individually. (This may even result in the equivalent of an "aggregate view" recovery being performed.)

11.3.1.6 Incremental Recovery

This refers to a situation whereby the backup product incrementally executes the recoveries from the last full to the currently selected backup, including all intervening incremental backups, whether the data is required or not.

While this may appear to be no different from a "last filesystem view" recovery, where this differs is that it performs the recovery without any intelligent mapping to expected directory contents or data that may have changed. For instance, imagine a situation where in 7 days of backups, a 2 GB file has changed each day and is backed up each day. For a last filesystem recovery, point-in-time recovery or aggregated recovery, recovering the filesystem will result in only the most recent (or most appropriate for point-in-time recoveries) copy of the file being recovered. For an incremental recovery process, *each* version of the 2 GB file would be recovered, incrementally, starting at the full backup (or the first time it appeared on the filesystem, whichever was more recent). Each copy of the file would be recovered on top of the previous copy of the file until the required version had been recovered. Thus, when recovering a filesystem from a full backup 7 days ago with six incrementals, 14 GB of data would be recovered for a single 2 GB file.

There are no advantages to a backup product offering an incremental recovery strategy, and it should be avoided if present in a product or the product avoided entirely if it defaults to this model.

11.3.2 RECOVERY LOCALITY

We refer to recovery locality as where recoveries are initiated from, with respect to the backup server, and the host that owns the data being recovered. Depending on the product in use, there may be several locality options available, and this may in turn increase the level of services that can be offered.

11.3.2.1 Local Recovery

A local recovery is one where the client the data was backed up from initiates the recovery, regardless of its network location and where the data it requires may have been backed up to. This could be considered to be a "pull" recovery—the client "pulls" the files and data from backup storage.

This is the simplest form of recovery and allows for end users or system administrators of individual hosts to have control over the recovery process with minimum involvement from the backup administrators or operators (particularly when recovering from disk).

Note that to support a local recovery strategy properly within the environment—particularly if the end users are not privy to the entire backup system—it will be necessary to configure the hardware and storage capacity of the backup environment to have enough backups online for the majority of recovery requests and automatically notify backup administrators/operators of the need to locate and load offline media to facilitate the recovery if required. This option works best in backup to disk environments where media load times and media contention are not architectural concerns.

11.3.2.2 Server-Initiated Recovery

A server-initiated recovery is where the backup server can be used to start a recovery, with the data either being recovered locally to the backup server or pushed out to the client. For that reason, some products will refer to this recovery model as a "push" recovery.

This offers a convenient mechanism for some recoveries, and when it exists as just one among many recovery locality options, it should be seen as a benefit in a backup product. However, products that *only* offer server-initiated recoveries may not scale well for larger environments.

11.3.2.3 Directed Recovery

Directed or remote recoveries are where the administrator or user (if appropriately authorized) can initiate a recovery on one host and recover the data to another host, which in turn may not be the host that the data was originally backed up from. A directed recovery features three different types of clients, which may or may not be the same:

1. *Control client*—The host the recovery program/process is being run from
2. *Source client*—The host whose data is being recovered
3. *Destination client*—The host that will receive the recovered data.

(When a backup product supports directed recoveries, it will also typically support local recoveries in that the source, destination, and control clients can all be the same host.)

Directed recoveries allow for considerable flexibility in how recoveries are performed but do require additional security considerations to ensure that the facility isn't abused and data misappropriated. They are particularly useful as the scale of the environment grows—it allows recovery operations to be performed by help desk staff or other nonadministrator IT users, and it is actually a fundamental aspect in allowing the backup and recovery system to provide additional functionality into the environment. For instance, a directed recovery could allow a data scientist to recover a production database into a big data environment for processing via a directed recovery, without in any way impacting the performance of the original production database or the workflow of the production database administrators.

An additional form of directed recovery is a *cross-platform* directed recovery. This is where files or data backed up on one type of operating system (e.g., Linux) is recovered onto another operating system (e.g., Windows). Depending on the product and its security model, this may have limited functionality within an environment—while the data itself may be retrievable, access controls, ownership, and so on will not necessarily translate between operating system platforms, even if integrated authentication is used. (Indeed, this may be considered a security flaw in some organizations.)

11.4   CLIENT IMPACT

Backup products and techniques can also be differentiated based on the level of impact they have on the performance of the client being backed up, which for the purposes of this section we'll refer to as the owner-host—that is, the machine that "owns" the data being backed up. This allows us to separate data ownership from backup ownership since depending on the model used the machine that *owns* the data may not be the machine that *hosts* the data for the purposes of the backup.

11.4.1   SERVER-BASED BACKUPS

In backup parlance, "server-based backups" refer to backups where data is read directly from the owner-host. This is the most common form of backup used in organizations where agent-based backups are deployed. During the process, the owner-host client is responsible for reading its own data and transferring it to the backup server, to an intermediary server or directly to backup media if it has been instructed to do so. Backups of this kind have the strongest impact on the owner-host—in addition to whatever other processing requirements it has during the backup period, it must also read the data and transfer it to the appropriate host or media.

This is the traditional backup model for decentralized- and centralized-via-network backups. For many organizations, server-based backups will be entirely acceptable, though virtualization may require alternate backup techniques, as can environments requiring high-performance guarantees at all times and days.

Server-based backups typically create two additional types of load on an owner-host: (1) CPU and network bandwidth for transfer of data from the owner-host to the backup media/host, and (2) disk IO from reading the data. While server-based backups were the process du jour in largely physical environments, as much of the IT infrastructure of companies has moved toward virtualization, the performance impact of such a backup arrangement may not be acceptable. After all, virtualization is about shared access to hardware resources on the basis that each individual system hosted by a hypervisor will only use a small subset of the performance capabilities of the hypervisor. Server-based backups are designed to transfer data from A to B as fast as possible in order to meet SLAs—a hypervisor hosting, say, 10 virtual machines, may have its required workload increased by orders of magnitude if each individual virtual machine starts doing a full backup. (The chapter on virtualization will cover alternatives to this in more detail.)

The advantages of server-based backups are as follows:

- Simplest backup method—easy to understand. There's a 1:1 mapping between the host that owns the data and the host that transfers the data for backup, making the location of data for recovery simple.
- Typically, no extra installation or configuration steps are required other than a basic backup agent install and setup to run this type of backup.

The disadvantages of server-based backups are as follows:

- Backup directly impedes the performance of the host that owns the data.
- Any outage required for the backup directly impacts the availability of the data being protected.
- Particularly in virtualized environments, server-based backups may introduce a strain on the virtualization hypervisors beyond their limit and negatively impact the performance of a large number of hosts in the environment.

11.4.2 SERVERLESS BACKUPS

When discussing server-based backups, we introduced the term "owner-host," which referred to as the machine considered to own the data being backed up. For serverless backups, we must also introduce the term "data-provider," which refers to the machine that provides storage for data. In a directly attached storage environment, the owner-host and the data-provider will be the same. However, this is increasingly rare in enterprise environments. When virtualization, SAN and NAS are added to the picture, the data-provider may be an entirely different machine or device.

In a traditional backup environment, the owner-host is responsible for the backup of its data. This works for most situations but sometimes isn't appropriate, such as the following:

- Where the data-provider presents data to multiple operating systems, it may not be possible (or safe) for any one operating system to take responsibility of the data backups—particularly so for NAS systems.

- Where the owner-host has strict processing availability requirements, it may not be allowed to suffer reduced processing capacity to provide data to the backup process.
- The owner-host may not be able to provide sufficient performance for the backup process (regardless of its production workload), whereas the data-provider can.
- The network linked to the owner-host may not be sufficient for a high-speed backup.

We can therefore state that a serverless backup is one where the owner-host suffers minimal impact during the backup process. Note that we don't say such backups are guaranteed to eliminate *all* impact of the backup from the owner-host—in all but the most exceptionally high-performance architected environments, there will still be some impact to the owner-host either before, during, or after the backup.

Several techniques can be used to achieve serverless backups, including but not limited to the following:

- For NAS devices, the most efficient way of completing backups is via the network data management protocol (NDMP), an industry standard backup and data protection protocol for systems where conventional operating system agents cannot be installed.
- For SAN systems, a clone of a volume (or a snapshot of a clone volume—thereby allowing replication to continue to occur) might be mounted on another host for backup processing. Depending on the proximity of the backup media, this may also result in a LAN-free backup. Similar techniques can likewise be used for NAS systems, though NDMP should still be used for the backup process.
- When IDPAs are used within an environment, this may allow for even more advanced serverless backup techniques where, say, a database backup agent on the owner-host simply *starts* the backup, but then the transfer of data is handled directly between the primary storage and the IDPA. This effectively off-loads the entire workload from the data owner. In situations where deduplication and change block tracking are used, this can massively accelerate a backup process.

Depending on the storage technology, backup product, and applications in use, serverless backups may even deliver application-/database-consistent backups through use of journaling and/or continuous data protection techniques.

The advantages of serverless backups include the following:

- Offloads most of the impact of the backup process from the owner-host (to the point where remaining impact is deemed negligible), which is particularly critical in high-performance environments
- May deliver higher performance during the backup process
- Can also be used to achieve LAN-free backups

The disadvantages of serverless backups include the following:

- Usually more complicated than a traditional server-based backup approach.
- May require additional recovery steps or processing.
- If volumes are mounted on alternate hosts for backup purposes, it may require additional documentation in the environment to ensure administrators are aware of *where* they need to look in order to find the data for recovery purposes.
- May not integrate fully with all applications and/or databases used within an organization.

11.5 DATABASE BACKUPS

Our earlier discussions on online and offline backups already introduced the concept of hot and cold database backups, respectively. We'll now discuss a few of the additional considerations associated with database backups that businesses and administrators need to take into consideration.

11.5.1 COLD DATABASE BACKUPS

A cold backup is the most primitive database backup that can be performed. Prior to the backup, the database and its associated processes are shut down to ensure no updates take place. The backup system then performs a simple filesystem backup of the client (i.e., database server), which encompasses all the database files.

While this sounds simple enough, we must consider that the process will require some scripting to ensure the database is shut down prior to starting the backup and then restarted immediately following the backup completing. For maximum certainty of backup success, the backup product should shut down the database using a "prebackup" script and should also restart the database following completion. (In such configurations, it is not uncommon to have a monitoring process that can abort the backup if it takes too long so that users may access the system by a specified time.)

If the shutdown and startup sequences are not handled properly and the database is shut down after the backup starts or is restarted while the backup is still running, one of the following may occur:

- A useless backup may be generated: Where the filesystems in use don't support exclusive file locking, the backup may continue but the data being backed up will be inconsistent and not be useful for recovery purposes.
- The database may be corrupted, requiring recovery: Where filesystems in use perform exclusive file locking, it's entirely possible the backup may have open handles on database files when the database is started. This can result in creating inconsistencies between files as the database processes those files on startup. Typically, such inconsistencies can only be resolved through recovery.

The advantages of cold database backups include the following:

- Complete disaster recovery or total database recovery is very easy and does not normally require intervention from an application or database administrator.
- Results in minimum software and licensing investment and may be particularly cost effective for the backup of nonproduction databases where longer outages are deemed acceptable by the business.
- If a database does not support any other backup method without access to snapshot technology (either array or filesystem based), this may be the only way to achieve a backup.

The disadvantages of cold database backups include the following:

- Database is unavailable for the duration of the backup.
- For most databases, using cold backups does not allow for incremental recoveries or point-in-time recoveries of the database.
- If the startup and shutdown sequence for the database is handled incorrectly, it may result in unusable backups or database corruption.
- If the backup repeatedly overruns the required window and is aborted each time, recoverability and any compliance requirements will be impacted.
- Databases frequently perform data caching to improve performance over time. If the database is shut down every night for backups, the benefit of that caching is lost every day.
- Uses the maximum possible protection storage capacity/media as incremental cold backups are rare if ever supported by database vendors.

11.5.2   Hot Database Backups

A hot backup refers to keeping a database up and running while the backup is performed. As previously discussed, it's the equivalent of an online backup for filesystems. When a backup product supports a particular database, it usually means it has a module or plug-in agent that allows the database to be backed up while staying available to end users.

If a backup module or plug-in performs the hot backup, the process will typically be as follows:

- Regular filesystem backups occur for the client as per normal but skips over database data files.
- Backup server initiates a special database backup, using an alternate backup command on the database server.
- The command on the database server runs a hot backup, passing data back to the backup server for inclusion with standard backups to disk or tape.

The advantages of hot database backups include the following:

- Database remains online and accessible for duration of the backup.
- Recovery is typically straightforward, as it can be controlled via either the recovery utilities provided by the backup software or the recovery utilities provided by the database vendor. This may even allow recoveries to be performed without an application or database administrator being available if there are suitable "wizards" or automation processes built into the utilities.
- Usually facilitates granular recoveries—for example, for mail servers this may allow the recovery of individual mail items or user mail folders, and for databases this may allow granularity down to the individual table or row.

The disadvantages include the following:

- Depending on the backup product, this may require additional licensing.
- Initial configuration is usually more complex than cold backups—though the benefit usually outweighs such considerations.

An alternate scenario might be database plug-ins that interact with an IDPA, allowing hot backups directly to centralized protection storage while DBAs retain control of the backup process.

11.5.3 EXPORT DATABASE BACKUP

A database export is typically a series of plain-text commands that can be used to recreate the database content and permissions. For example, the following is a section of a database export from a PostgreSQL database:

```
CREATE TABLE anywebdb_saved_query (
id integer DEFAULT nextval('anywebdb_saved_queries'::regclass)
  NOT NULL,
name character varying(75) NOT NULL,
"object" character varying(175) NOT NULL,
username character varying(16) NOT NULL,
private character(1) NOT NULL,
query text NOT NULL,
max_results integer,
sort_field character varying(32),
order_by character(1)
);
ALTER TABLE public.anywebdb_saved_query OWNER TO pmdg;
```

Unless explicitly stated by the database vendor, you should note the database export may not actually be consistent if the database is being accessed or updated at the time of the export. Before using this backup option, it's important to confirm the database supports hot exports. If they aren't supported, cold backups or cold snapshot backups should be favored instead.

The following are advantages of database export backups:

- If exports are supported while the database is being accessed and there are no other hot backup methods available, this will present a better availability strategy than cold backups.
- This may allow a backup of a database on one operating system (e.g., Windows), with a restore on another platform (e.g., Linux).

The disadvantages of database export backups include the following:

- An export may take up even more disk space than the original database as an export contains more than just the content of the database but also the commands required to recreate the database structure. Compressing the export as it is generated may result in significant space savings, but at a cost of high CPU load during the backup, and impact protection media compression or deduplication efficiencies.
- Typically, the export does not contain the instructions to recreate the database itself, merely its internal structure and data. The complexity/time of this task needs to be factored when planning recovery times.
- The export should be scheduled carefully in the same way as cold backups to ensure the resulting export file is properly backed up.
- An export of the database may take longer than a simple copy of the files associated with the database depending on the amount of data in the database.
- Some database vendors have additional requirements to achieve exports where binary large objects are involved.
- The export may not recreate the metadata surrounding the database. For instance, user accounts and passwords might not be exported, requiring these to be manually established prior to any import operation.*

11.6 BACKUP INITIATION METHODS

There are two primary methods of backup initiation—server and client. While server-initiated backups are a goal for almost all enterprise backup systems, there are some situations where client-initiated backups may be required.

Server-initiated backups refer to the backup server software on the "master" server starting the backups for one or more hosts at a designated time. Almost all backup software contains backup scheduling capabilities that allow backups to be started at nominated times. The advantages of server-initiated backups cannot be overstated: they give the backup administrator control over the timings of backups, which directly affects the resources available to the backup server to provide those services. When a backup server initiates the backup process, it should have an accurate understanding of what resources will need to be allocated to allow the backup

---

* If the database exports assign table, column, row, or tuple ownership or access by user ID, this may make restoring security/authorization credentials extremely troublesome.

to complete and an understanding of what resources are *available* based on other activities executing at the time. Furthermore, centralized timing and scheduling of backups are critical in reducing administrative overhead in the backup environment.

Client-initiated backups refer to individual machines running their own backup processes as required—either manually or via automated jobs scheduled to start at particular times from the client side. Having jobs controlled and executed on a per-client basis is a nonscalable solution and will result in resource contention on most backup servers—not to mention making it almost impossible for backup administrators to schedule maintenance activities.

Almost all backup administrators will agree on one thing about backups:

> If you rely on users to start the backups, the backups won't run.

For this reason, client-initiated backups should mostly be considered to be a *utility* function only—something useful for situations where administrators need to perform ad hoc backups, but they should not generally be central to the backup process.

One mild exception to this is in multitenant environments with multiple network segments, virtual private networks (VPNs), and/or firewalls. These scenarios may create a situation where the client *must* connect in to the server rather than the server being able to reliably connect *out* to the client. In such a situation, scheduling will still be ideally performed by the backup server—but rather than immediately starting a backup job, the backup server would create a work order. A connecting client will check to see if it has any work orders assigned to it and initiate the required activities. An alternate approach to this is laptop backups where a backup agent automatically looks for the backup server whenever it is connected to a network and performs a backup if it is able to reach the server. Critical to this is ensuring the user does not need to participate in the backup initiation process.

An alternate methodology for backup initiation is if an organization has batch control processes requiring initiation via a dedicated job scheduling system. In these situations, the job scheduling system should integrate with the backup product sufficiently to trigger backup jobs rather than executing manual backups from individual clients. This can be particularly useful in database backup environments where there are strict conditions placed on when and how a backup is started, making it problematic, if not impossible, for the scheduling to happen solely under the direction of the backup software. For instance, business processes may require that the backup is taken immediately following the completion of overnight batch processing activities, but depending on the data involved, this may take anywhere between half an hour and three or four hours. Or it may be that the backup for a system can only be initiated after a set of several conditions have been met, each one with dependencies. Such complex scheduling operations are not normally part of the job control capabilities of a backup product and usually require consideration outside of pure data protection activities. When considering externally scheduled backup jobs, it's important to ensure the system workload and resource utilization is balanced in such a way as to allow these externally scheduled jobs to execute without causing instability in the overall data protection environment.

11.7   JOB CONCURRENCY

While there are some backup products (most notably in the workgroup/free arena and with niche workload targets) that process all backup jobs one after the other, one of the most common features for enterprise backup technology is the ability to run multiple jobs concurrently. (This may be referred to as "multiplexing," "multi streaming," "parallelism," or "concurrency," among other terms.)

While different products may offer the option to set additional concurrency limits within particular areas of their configuration, the three most common places you can find job concurrency within a backup configuration are

1. *Server concurrency*—The number of concurrent backup jobs the server will execute or allow to be executing
2. *Client concurrency*—The number of concurrent backup jobs an individual client can send
3. *Device concurrency*—The number of concurrent backup jobs that can be written to an individual backup device*

Depending on the backup product, server and client concurrency *may* refer to the total number of jobs *or* the total number of backup jobs.[†]

Figure 11.12 shows these three primary job concurrency options—client A is sending four jobs simultaneously to the backup server, client B is sending a single job, and client C is sending three jobs to the server. The server is accepting all eight jobs and sending five of the jobs concurrently to the PBBA, while another three jobs are going direct to a tape drive.

Note that this is not representative of what may be the *total* number of concurrent jobs that is configured at any individual point in the environment.

11.7.1   Server Concurrency

Most backup products will support a very high level of server concurrency. (It is not unusual, for instance, to see backup servers in enterprise environments designed to accept *thousands* of concurrent jobs.) Due to the scale-out nature of backup environments as a result of either storage nodes/media servers and/or jobs sent directly from clients to IDPAs, server concurrency these days refers more often as not to the number of jobs being *controlled* rather than *passed through* the backup server.

---

* Note that device concurrency may also be tied to media multiplexing when using tape. This will be covered in more detail in Section 17.1.2.3.

[†] Some products will allow recovery sessions to start regardless of the job concurrency limits—an acknowledgment of the primacy of recovery operations. Others will actually reserve a certain number or percentage of the number of concurrent jobs for recovery purposes to ensure recoveries can always be executed.

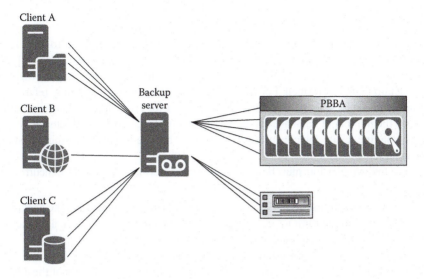

FIGURE 11.12   High-level overview of job concurrency options.

Server concurrency will be primarily dependent on the following three factors:

1. The number of concurrent jobs *all* backup devices in the environment can accept. If the server concurrency is set too low, backup devices may run suboptimally. Conversely, if server concurrency is set too high, the backup server may become overloaded (depending on its processing capabilities) or jobs may become queued for long periods of time waiting for available backup devices.
2. CPU speed and amount of memory available to the backup server. In addition to the CPU/memory requirements for handling the scheduling and execution of jobs and job reports, any data being transferred through the server will require CPU and memory resources as well.
3. Network bandwidth available to the server. Particularly in situations where the backup server is also receiving backup jobs for streaming to devices, the incoming network bandwidth for the backup server will directly impact the number of concurrent jobs it can handle.

In situations where storage nodes/media servers are in use, the same potential limits on concurrency for the backup server will apply to those individual hosts, with the exception that the device concurrency limitation cited earlier will be limited to the devices directly attached to or controlled by the storage node/media server.

11.7.2 Client Concurrency

Client job concurrency refers to an individual host being configured to send more than one stream of data to the backup environment at the same time. Typically, by "stream" we refer to filesystems, but this could be different depending on the type of backup being performed. For instance, for database backups this may refer to the number of databases simultaneously backed up or for even larger database environments the number of database data files backed up concurrently *per* database. As you may imagine, client job concurrency is used so that the backup of a single host can be completed sooner.

The following factors must be considered when determining client job concurrency*:

1. Other processing activities occurring, their priority compared to the backup job(s), and the limit to which the backup job(s) may impact those activities
2. CPU/RAM capabilities of the client
3. Underlying disk subsystem or filesystem performance
4. Whether the client is performing any encryption or compression of the data prior to sending it to the backup environment†
5. Whether another agent (e.g., antivirus software) is scanning the data the client sends to the backup environment
6. Network link between the client and the backup environment

To a lesser degree, client job concurrency will also be dependent on the speed of the backup devices, but it is rare in modern backup and recovery devices for device streaming performance to be *lower* than individual client streaming performance, and the other considerations on this will be covered in Section 17.1.2.3.

The performance of the underlying disk subsystem or the filesystem is a key factor in client performance that often takes people by surprise when evaluating job concurrency options for individual clients. When systems are being used for random file access, many design or layout issues (either at the operating system or at the system implementation level) may not be readily apparent—but during largely sustained sequential reads of the filesystems, previously unnoticed issues may be highlighted.

When clients are using direct attached storage, job concurrency should (at most) not be set higher than the number of physical disks providing storage to the client. Note that we say *at most*; if there are more filesystems defined than there are physical disks, then defining a higher level of job concurrency from the client than the number of disks will likely just result in drive thrashing as large sequential reads are

---

* An additional consideration in the modern datacenter is whether the client is a physical host or is virtualized—if it is virtualized, a plethora of other considerations will come into play. These will be discussed at length in Chapter 14.

† Traditionally client-side compression or encryption, performed via software, has been seen as very resource intensive. Some modern CPUs have incorporated special instruction sets and operational modes to speed up compression or encryption, and if backup software can leverage these instructions, it can result in minimizing the impact of these functions during backup operations.

executed simultaneously from two different locations on a drive (though flash and solid-state storage systems will eliminate this concern).

RAID systems do not immediately guarantee a higher level of job concurrency being acceptable for a client. Particularly in DAS/internal RAID structures, basic hardware or even software RAID controllers may yield suboptimal performance compared to SAN-level storage systems and offer no benefit compared to lower job concurrency levels—especially if in a degraded RAID state.

While SAN storage may ideally offer the best possible performance for client job concurrency, once shared storage systems are included in the backup environment, backup and storage administrators should work together closely to ensure that mass backup operations do not overload the performance capabilities of SAN (and even more so, NAS) storage. For instance, when evaluating optimum client job concurrency settings for clients using SAN storage, it's necessary to evaluate the IO load placed on SAN LUNs when *all* attached clients are backed up simultaneously and balance individual client job concurrency appropriately.

While it is important for a backup environment to be configured such that the network links between the clients and the backup targets are not underutilized, it's equally important to avoid swamping the network—especially if the network is being simultaneously used for production activities.* When evaluating job concurrency options for clients in relation to the network, administrators are well advised to keep in mind that TCP/IP communications streams include *more* than just the data being sent—each packet sent will include metadata identifying the stream itself and the packet's position in the data stream. If a single job from a client can saturate the client's network interface, adding a second stream is unlikely to make any performance improvement and may even reduce the performance by doubling the amount of packet metadata at the expense of the actual data.

11.7.3   DEVICE CONCURRENCY

The number of jobs a backup device can simultaneously handle will be largely dependent on the type of device it is and its own performance characteristics. Some high-end IDPAs are now capable of handling a thousand or more concurrent backup jobs, and since these write data to disk, this does not impact the recoverability of the data. Tape drives, on the other hand, should be optimized to have as few concurrent streams going to them as possible or else full recovery performance for larger backups may be impacted.

When using disk-based backup devices, the job concurrency should be set in accordance to the vendor's guidance on maximum simultaneous stream counts, or if simple disk/RAID systems are being used, this will need to be tuned per the performance characteristics of the devices. Considerations for tape-based backup devices will be discussed in more detail in Chapter 17.

---

* Both dedicated backup networks and source-based deduplication can be used to minimize the impact of distributed backups on production networks.

11.8   NETWORK DATA MANAGEMENT PROTOCOL

NDMP was developed to facilitate the backup of network appliances (typically NAS hosts). While these hosts include operating systems that may be *similar* to other operating systems supported by backup products, access to the operating system for installation of third-party software is usually prohibited by the NAS vendor to ensure maximized performance and stability.

NAS systems have taken over file serving functions in most enterprises due to their ease of use and configuration, in addition to their ability to integrate into enterprise authentication systems. In particular, they allow storage administrators to easily

- Add a new share
- Allow multiple hosts to concurrently read and write to a share
- Allow multiple operating system types to concurrently read/write a share

All of this typically occurs without any outage being required, even if the host has not previously accessed the NAS appliance. In comparison, adding a new host to a SAN will require zoning changes, potentially an outage to add fiber host bus adapters, and drive installation and SAN-level configuration to grant access to LUNs—as well as possibly additional host reboots to allow the newly presented LUNs to be visible. While such configuration complexity is deemed acceptable for servers, it is impractical and expensive for direct end user desktop/laptop access.

Returning to NAS systems, there's no such thing as a free lunch. The day-to-day management simplicity offered by NAS comes at a price, and this price is felt during backup and recovery operations. (With scale-out NAS now allowing organizations to grow a single logical filesystem to multiple petabytes or more in size, optimized NAS backups are a huge consideration for enterprises.)

To understand the importance of NDMP in an enterprise environment, first consider how a backup might be executed for NAS storage *without* NDMP. For this, refer to Figure 11.13.

Without NDMP, there is no direct way for the backup server to communicate with the NAS system, and therefore its data must be backed up through one or more of the hosts that have shares mapped from the NAS system. When it is time for a backup to be initiated, the data will stream as follows:

1. The data for a given share will be read from the NAS server across the TCP/IP network to one of the NAS clients or a specifically configured backup proxy.
2. The backup agent on the NAS client/proxy will read the data coming in from the NAS server as if it were a local filesystem.
3. The backup agent on the NAS client/proxy will then send the data back across the TCP/IP network to the designated backup target.
4. If the backup target is a network-connected PBBA or IDPA, the data will be subsequently streamed *back* across the TCP/IP network to the designated target (alternatively if going to tape, this might be sent directly from the client in question, but at the risk of introducing shoeshining and other tape-centric inefficiencies).

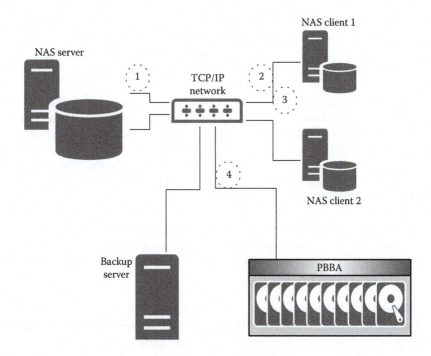

FIGURE 11.13 Overview of NAS backups without NDMP.

In such a configuration as outlined earlier, the same data must be transmitted three times. Even if the backup were going directly to a fiber-channel-connected device from the client, this would still be a minimum of two transmitting across the IP network. This form of backup may be acceptable for smaller workgroup environments with NAS shares in the order of at most a few hundred gigabytes and where there are no backup/recovery SLAs, but as NAS environments scale into the petabyte range, such backups are hideously resource intensive and disruptive. What's more, they're not even necessarily guaranteed to provide a comprehensive backup—if a NAS share is being accessed by multiple operating systems, such a backup will *only* protect access control lists/permissions associated with the operating system of the NAS host used to perform the backup. For example, if a Windows host was used for the backup/recovery using this mechanism but the share is accessed by Linux hosts as well, any Linux-specific access file permissions are extremely unlikely to be backed up or recovered as part of the operation.

NDMP neatly bypasses the backup configuration mentioned earlier by allowing the NAS server to stream its data directly to a designated NDMP-compatible device. Depending on the version of NDMP supported by the NAS system and the options available in the backup product, this may be any one of the following:

1. Tape drives/library directly connected and dedicated to the NAS system via SCSI or fiber channel

2. Tape library simultaneously connected to the NAS system and other backup hosts via fiber channel, allowing shared access to tape drives
3. Virtual tape library presented by a PBBA or IDPA
4. NDMP service on a backup server or storage node/media server

Since NDMP does not *natively* support backing up to anything other than a tape drive, the fourth option is the only way a backup environment can be configured to send NAS backups to anything other than physical or virtual tape. In such an environment, the NDMP service running on the backup server or storage node/media server *masquerades* as an NDMP target and then encapsulates the NDMP data into a standard backup stream. This then allows the backup product to exert more control over the NDMP data stream and introduces options such as

• Backup to a PBBA or IDPA in disk rather than VTL mode
• Multiplexing of the backup stream (not supported by NDMP natively)
• Mixing NDMP and non-NDMP backups onto the same backup volumes (not supported by NDMP natively)

Figure 11.14 demonstrates how an NDMP backup might look when writing in VTL mode to a PBBA. In this configuration, the NAS system has a fiber-channel connection to the VTL mode functionality within the PBBA. When the backup server instructs the NAS system to backup, the data is streamed directly over the fiber

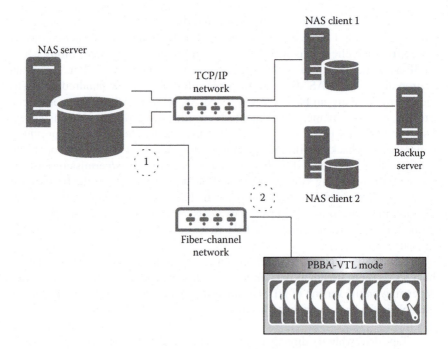

FIGURE 11.14   NAS backup via NDMP.

channel to emulated tape drives on the PBBA, bypassing the IP network entirely. (Further, the data is transmitted only once.)

As NAS systems continue to grow, their backups increasingly need strong architectural attention within a business to ensure data can be adequately protected within required time frames and will almost *always* require backup/recovery operations to be supplemental to primary protection methods such as snapshots and replication.

11.9 MISCELLANEOUS ENTERPRISE FEATURES

There is a collection of features that do not in themselves warrant entire categories but can be pooled together to form what we would still describe as enterprise features—that is, facilities that should be found in any enterprise backup and recovery product. In this section, we will give an overview of some of those features.

11.9.1 PRE- AND POSTPROCESSING

Pre- and postprocessing refers to the ability of the backup product to execute arbitrary scripts or commands on backup clients before and after the backup. Examples of where pre- and postprocessing might include any of the following:

- Prior to backup, a database is put into hot backup mode, and immediately following the backup, the database is brought out of hot backup mode.
- Prior to filesystem backup, a hot export is performed for a database.
- Prior to monthly backups, an application is shut down for a cold backup rather than its regular hot backup, and following the backup, the application is restarted.
- Following a successful backup completion on Friday nights, a client might be rebooted automatically to allow system updates to take effect.
- Prior to starting backups, a map might be built of a particular dense filesystem and the configuration for the client automatically adjusted to support massively concurrent backups of the dense filesystem in order to improve performance.

Pre- and postprocessing allows for a backup system to be extended considerably beyond the original design considerations from the vendor and ensures the product can be tightly integrated into the processes of a business. A few key considerations when evaluating pre- and postprocessing include the following:

- Is there a set timeout period for the commands or can the administrator define an arbitrary command timeout?
- Is it necessary to establish a command execution environment prior to running a pre- or postcommand?
- Are pre- and postprocessing commands done for each filesystem or unique backup set, or before and after all backups?
- For applications with more than one host, it is possible to schedule pre- and postprocessing across multiple clients using dependencies?
- Is security provided to prevent the execution of arbitrary commands?

- Does the backup agent run under a user account that will have the authority to execute the commands to be run? If not, can the user account be changed?
- What control options are there in the event of the pre- or postcommand failing?

11.9.2 ARBITRARY BACKUP COMMAND EXECUTION

Arbitrary backup command execution means being able to replace the native backup mechanism with a custom backup tool for particular machines so as to be able to process data that the backup vendor did not anticipate (or feel sufficient commercial need to support). For instance, companies have been known to use arbitrary backup command execution to perform hot backups for databases that do not have an agent or to simulate such a backup by detecting and reacting differently to database files.

Although it may be rare that companies would need to extend a backup product to this level, some backup products use arbitrary backup command execution as their mechanism for providing database and special application backup capabilities—that is, this is the facility they use to enable plug-ins or modules.

11.9.3 CLUSTER RECOGNITION

For a cluster to be effective, the end users of the cluster should not need to know or care which node in the cluster is currently being accessed. They certainly shouldn't be in a situation where they need to reconfigure their access manually when a cluster node failover occurs.

At the other end of the service spectrum, backup administrators equally should not need to keep track of cluster failover manually—the backup software itself should be able to do this, either automatically or as a result of an initial configuration where the cluster hosts are identified as such.

In any n node cluster providing y virtual services, a typical configuration might be

1. n client instances for the physical cluster nodes, used to backup their private data and OS configuration
2. y client instances, one per virtual cluster service, used to back up the shared/presented data and applications

For active/passive clusters, the goal of cluster recognition is to avoid situations where the recovery operator needs to know which node of the cluster was hosting the data backed up that now needs recovering. For active/active cluster configurations, the goal will be to avoid multiple backups of the cluster presented data, one per node.

11.9.4 CLIENT COLLECTIONS

At the most primitive, a "collection" of clients is a set of clients whose backups starts at the same time. This can be handled in two ways:

1. Each client has a start time/schedule associated with it and starts independently of all other clients.

2. The backup product provides a collection configuration resource that allows the logical grouping of similar clients to force a common start time (and possibly even a common backup schedule).

Various names exist for these collections, with "group," "policy," and "class" being the three common variants. When a backup product allows such groups, the administrative overhead becomes considerably simplified. For instance, assume 50 Windows clients normally get backed up at 21:35. If it is decided these machines should instead start their backups at the new time of 22:55, it is far more convenient to adjust the start time in a single group containing all 50 clients than it is to edit the configuration for all 50 clients.

11.9.5 BACKUP SEGREGATION

This refers to specifying what data can be sent to which collection of backup media. Such groupings of backup media are usually referred to as "pools." The following are some examples of backup segregation requirements:

- *Offsite versus onsite media*: Ensures that copies of backups generated to be sent offsite are not stored on the same media as copies that will remain onsite.
- *Data separation*: In some instances, it may be legally or contractually required to store backups for different divisions or companies on different media.
- *Backup retention periods*: Particularly when tape is used, backups of differing retention periods (e.g., 6 weeks for daily backups, 7 years for monthly) should be placed on different media so that media aging and recycling can occur as required.
- *Deduplicatability*: If using deduplication appliances, there may be some data within the environment that does not deduplicate (e.g., compressed or encrypted data). Backup segregation allows for sending this type of data directly to alternate backup media, thereby avoiding capacity impact on deduplication storage.

Primitive backup products will provide segregation solely on simple and unreliable mechanisms such as

- Which media is currently in a stand-alone device?
- What slot number backup media is placed into in a tape library?
- What label has been assigned to media?

In other words, the segregation in these instances is done by the backup administrator or operators as the media is provisioned. This becomes a manual process that does not scale well.

Automated data segregation however provides for splitting of backups to different media based on a variety of considerations such as

- Originating client collection
- Originating client

- Whether the backup is an original or a copy
- Intended retention period for the backup
- Backup level

By offering segregation based on these options, a backup product can provide automated data separation sufficient to meet the needs of most organizations and can scale with the backup requirements of the business.

11.9.6 GRANULAR BACKUP CONTROL

This refers to the alteration of the backup process for a particular host based on one or more criteria being met. One form has already been touched on in the context of data selection methods. Exclusive backup products work by automatically backing up everything on a host *except* for what has been excluded from the backup process. This in itself is a form of backup control. For instance, it may be necessary to configure granular backup control such that even though all filesystems are backed up on a particular host, any file with a ".mp3" extension is excluded.

There is, however, much more to granular backup control than merely excluding multimedia files. The following are examples of other types of granular backup control:

- Forcing software-based client-side encryption or compression for particular files or types of files
- Preventing database files from being backed up as part of the filesystem backup when they are protected by a database module
- Forcing the inclusion of additional filesystems that are not picked up as part of an automated probe of filesystems (e.g., a network filesystem presented by a host running an operating system not supported by the backup software)
- Suppression of error or warning messages about active files for system logs, etc., which don't need to be backed up or quiesced
- Forcing an exclusive lock to be taken out on a file being backed up so it can't be modified during the process

With fine-grained control of the backup process for individual hosts, the backup system can be modified to work with systems that the backup software designers had not necessarily anticipated.

11.9.7 BACKUP SCHEDULE OVERRIDES

All backup products will support scheduling of some sort—and we've already discussed the levels associated with scheduling. A common schedule, for instance, is "daily incrementals with full backups on Friday night."

To reduce administrative overheads however, it's important the backup product offers some mechanism to set overrides to the schedules that have been established. For instance, the schedule works well if *only* daily backups are performed. If monthly backups are performed as well, it will be necessary to override the daily schedule once per month to skip the Friday full, which will instead be performed by the monthly schedule. Equally, if a company is planning on a computer room shutdown for maintenance purposes, it would be desirable to be able to temporarily skip all the backups associated with machines in that computer room for the weekend only rather than manually disabling all the backups and then manually reenabling them at a later point.

Overrides are essential in order to maximize the automation of a backup environment and grow even more essential as the size of the environment grows.

11.9.8 SECURITY

There are two aspects to backup security that are not necessarily complementary:

1. To backup everything on a system, the backup software needs reasonably complete access to the system.
2. Due to this, if backup security is breached, the potential for data theft or destruction is severe.

With these in mind, it's imperative that organizations maintain tight, secure control over the backup environment and that the backup product supports this. Ideally, this will include having the backup software able to integrate with enterprise class authentication systems such as a centralized LDAP/Active Directory system. At bare minimum, the backup product must also be able to support defining

- Who can administer the backup server
- Who can interact with backup media and devices
- Who can recover data on a per-client basis

Additionally, the backup software should provide reports, logs, and details as required on activities performed within the backup environment.

A common security flaw introduced into many backup environments is allowing too many users access to the backup administration role. Like all other aspects of IT, security via obfuscation is not sufficient, and a security breach on the backup server should be seen as an extremely risky scenario for any organization. After all, if the security for the backup server has been breached, all data protected by the backup server is potentially compromised.

11.9.9 DUPLICATION AND MIGRATION

While this topic will be covered in more detail later, we can summarize for now that backup duplication is the method by which the IT environment (and by extension, the company) is protected from a failure occurring within any single backup. Ideally, all backups produced—at least all production backups produced—should have a duplicate copy so that in the event of the primary copy failing, another copy can be used to recover data required.

Backup migration, on the other hand, refers to moving a backup from one piece of media to another. Examples of where backup migration are used include the following:

- Moving backups written to disk across to tape or a cloud storage provider for long-term storage.
- Evacuating readable backups from failing media.
- Transferring long-term and archival backups from a decommissioned media type to a new media type.
- Media consolidation—If backup segregation by retention time was not performed, it may be necessary to move long retention backups to new media to allow media to be reclaimed when short retention backups have expired.
- Legal requirements—If ordered to destroy particular data, it may be necessary to migrate required data on the same media to alternate volumes prior to destroying the original. Alternately, it may be necessary to hand over copies of data to a departing customer or as part of a legal discovery process.

11.9.10 ALERTS

Running a graphical user interface (GUI) against a backup server and observing the current state is one thing, but not all organizations employ 24/7 staff, and even when they do, staff may not react fast enough to issues if there are other activities to be performed.

With this in mind, it's important that a backup product have alternate methods of alerting users, operators, or administrators of events that require attention rather than simply expecting someone to notice output in a GUI when the event happens.

Some within the industry get obsessed over whether a product supports a particular alerting method (e.g., SNMP, mobile phone SMS). However, thinking outside the square, as long as a backup product offers custom alerts (i.e., arbitrary command execution in response to a particular event), any form of required alert can be accommodated with a little scripting or data massaging. Therefore, if the preferred alerting mechanism for a company is not directly supported by a backup product, using custom alerts, it can still be integrated.

As businesses grow and acquire other businesses, it also becomes more likely that multiple backup products may end up being in use within an organization. If all the backup products support third-party alerting, it allows for a holistic view of the data protection environment to be built up, with reporting performed at a global level rather than per product.

11.9.11 COMMAND LINE INTERFACE

Although it might be said that a picture is worth a thousand words, a GUI is not necessarily worth a thousand command line options. GUIs fulfill a particular function—they simplify interaction with a computer program or operating system so as to make the system more accessible to users. This in itself is as admirable as it is required. Certainly in backup products, GUIs often allow users to get a better view of the "big picture" of the configuration of the backup server and allow for simpler control of the configuration, operation, and recoveries within the business. However, GUIs typically have limits such as the following:

- Cannot be easily automated
- Don't allow for much extensibility
- May be slower to display information across sub-LAN speed links
- Don't provide all the functionality of every single aspect of the backup system or replication every option of every function
- May not provide the same level of error/log messages as command line options
- May not sufficiently mask data and operational information for multitenant environments

Command line access to a backup product can also be instrumental in remote support, monitoring, backup, and recovery operations. Many backup administrators who do not use the command line for anything in the office may find themselves making use of the command line when connecting via VPN from home.

More importantly, by their very presence, command line interfaces support ongoing extensibility of a product. This promotes integration and long-term maintenance of the product and often allows a product that cannot natively perform a particular function to be extended with minimum scripting to provide it. As we move into environments that increasingly need to deal with multitenant situations, command line options (and also RESTful APIs) provide direct capabilities required by DevOps teams to integrate data protection processes into customer facing portals.

11.9.12 BACKUP CATALOGS

All backup systems need to provide a backup catalog. A catalog provides a mechanism to track backups that have previously been executed, allowing for rapid retrieval of data during a recovery operation. Without a backup catalog, an administrator would have to approach recoveries as follows:

- User wants to recover file(s) or data.
- Administrator or user must determine when the files were lost.
- Administrator must retrieve the media generated on or before that date.
- Administrator must read the media to search for the file(s) or data required.

Such a "solution" doesn't scale and violates the principle that we backup to recover. As such, catalogs facilitate rapid recoveries by allowing a process that resembles the following:

- User initiates a backup search for the required file(s) or data *or* browses the backup filesystem view to a particular date and time.
- User selects file(s)/data for recovery and initiates the recovery.

- Backup software automatically recovers the data if media is online or initiates a recall operation for media that is not online but required.

At bare minimum, the backup catalog should

- Track media in use by the system
- Track backups that are on each piece of media
- Track backup copies
- Prompt users/administrators for the required media when recoveries are initiated

Preferably a backup catalog should also contain features such as the following:

- For tape, sufficient indexing to allow fast-forwarding through media to the location of the backup rather than having to read through the entire tape
- For disk, sufficient indexing to know where in a backup file the data required for recovery can be located
- Searching for files and directories that users would like recovered but can't recall where they were located originally
- Media usage information—how often a piece of media has been labeled/rewritten, how many times it was mounted, when it was originally added, etc.
- Online, hot backup and maintenance of catalog data
- Automated and manual checking of catalog consistency
- Recovery of catalog data at a minimum granularity of per client or per volume and preferably on a per-backup basis
- Regeneration of catalog data by reading or scanning backup media

11.10   THE FUTURE OF BACKUP AND RECOVERY

As the amount of data businesses dealt with continues to grow, so too do the backup requirements for the business. There was a time once when it was sufficient to treat backup and recovery solely as an insurance policy within the business—it existed to facilitate data recovery should *bad things* happen. With increasing data growth, the investment required to adequately provide backup and recovery services also increases, and many businesses are looking at getting additional utility from their backup and recovery investment.

While the primary purpose for a backup and recovery system *must* still be data recovery, business processes can be extended to make use of the backup and recovery system beyond just a data recovery service.

Various businesses have had this utility approach to backups for some time. For instance, it has not been uncommon for years, if not decades, for development and test databases to be refreshed by recovering the production backups into the dev/test areas. This eliminates the need to place additional workload on the production database that would naturally occur in a direct production to development copy.

Big data is accelerating this utility approach to backups—drawing all the data required for data science activities and large-scale data analysis directly from their production sources can be time consuming, resource intensive, and impactful toward core business functions, yet the importance of interrogating and analyzing this data for future business decisions and new market insights is indisputable. By extending the old "recover prod into development" approach pioneered so many years ago, businesses can pull the required data from their backup system into the big data environments. Yet this is even only the beginning. If we consider the growing trend toward highly IDPAs, we can already see situations where data is not actually recovered out of the backup environment for processing but is instead read *directly from it* for analysis or accessed via read/write snapshots when testing is required but the cost in time of performing a recovery first is too much.

Beyond big data usage, backup and recovery systems can provide long-term visibility over protected content. Network search appliances may be able to provide a mechanism to rapidly find data and files that currently exist within an organization, but search capabilities included in backup software allows deep version searches across *all* protected content, no matter when it was backed up. This can serve more than just time-saving functions for users or administrators—it could also be used during a legal discovery process to rapidly respond to searches in a fraction of the time or effort, saving companies considerable amounts of time or money.

As we move into an IT era dominated by the impact of cloud and of cloud service delivery models and particularly the notion of a service catalog, backup systems when integrated into enterprise reporting and monitoring can play a vital role in determining not only what *is* being protected but what is *not* being protected. Similarly, since backup and recovery systems are deeply integrated into the IT infrastructure of many businesses to a degree matched usually only by actual networking infrastructure itself, the capture and analysis of backup activities and faults may very well provide a company with significant insight into the reliability and stability of its infrastructure.

This is an aspect of backup and recovery that is still being developed and will continue to change in line with data growth and the need for business agility. It is therefore vital that infrastructure architects and business analysts cease thinking of backup as something used *only* for recovery and to seriously evaluate how and where an investment into backup and recovery systems can be leveraged to save the company time and money.

As the introduction suggested, backup as a stand-alone topic is now dead within IT, and we are just starting to see the business benefits of a more integrated approach to data protection.

12 The Cloud

12.1 INTRODUCTION

Like its environmental namesake, cloud computing can be a somewhat nebulous topic, but there's no disputing it's becoming increasingly pervasive as businesses take advantage of a new utility approach to IT infrastructure (either purchased or leased). Cloud computing has seen a substantial shift toward OpEx models over previous CapEx models, allowing many organizations to take advantage of infrastructure they previously could never have afforded to purchase and deploy, let alone manage, before.

The U.S. National Institute of Standards and Technology (NIST) defines five essential characteristics of cloud computing*:

1. *On-demand self-service*—The consumer should be able to select compute options and have the system automatically provision those without any human intervention.
2. *Broad network access*—Provisioned services should be available from a wide variety of client platforms, both traditional and mobile.
3. *Resource pooling*—Infrastructure will be multi-tenanted and the location of the infrastructure will have no bearing on service delivery or features available.
4. *Rapid elasticity*—Infrastructure can grow (and shrink) on demand without consumer impact.
5. *Measured service*—Resource usage should be monitored, controlled, and reported in order for complete pricing transparency for both the users and the service provider.

Broadly, the three types of cloud models available are as follows:

1. *Public*—Cloud infrastructure is provided by a third party in a pure utility model, having hundreds, thousands, or more customers sharing access to multi-tenanted infrastructure.
2. *Private*—Cloud infrastructure is housed entirely within the business using it. This is deployed with the same guiding characteristics of cloud computing, but the business maintains complete control and privacy over its data and compute resources.
3. *Hybrid*—Private cloud that can *scale out* to make use of public cloud as required. This typically allows a business to make use of higher levels of

---

* "The NIST definition of cloud computing" (Peter Mell, Timothy Grance), September 2011. Special publication 800-145. Online at http://csrc.nist.gov/publications/nistpubs/800-145/SP800-145.pdf.

infrastructure than it could typically afford but still maintain a high degree of control over the placement of data and resources, their security, management, and protection.

(A pseudo-fourth type of cloud is referred to as "community" or "shared" cloud; this refers to trusted infrastructure shared by many businesses. While multi-tenanted, the actual infrastructure will typically be jointly owned by all the businesses cohabitating systems on the cloud service.)

The cloud model should not be confused with older data location models such as "on premises" (or "on prem") and "off premises" (or "off prem"). While it might be said that a *public* cloud definitely represents *off premises* data, the reverse might not necessarily be said of a *private* cloud. A business might choose to maintain a private cloud in a datacenter it does not actually own, thereby having a private, "off prem" cloud.

Regardless of the actual cloud model used, there are a variety of service models that might be offered or available to customers. These service models are typically defined as "X-as-a-Service," or *XaaS*, to use the common abbreviation. The three most accepted types of service models are as follows:

1. *Software as a Service (SaaS)*: This refers to a software package operating in multi-tenanted fashion, providing access to a potentially large number of businesses. Businesses such as *Salesforce* represent the high end of SaaS cloud computing.
2. *Infrastructure as a Service (IaaS)*: This allows the consumer to run (reasonably) arbitrary operating systems and applications on provisioned storage, compute, and networking infrastructure. From a pre-cloud mentality, this is a "virtual datacenter," with some limitations.
3. *Platform as a Service (PaaS)*: Typically PaaS sits on top of an IaaS environment, offering an extensible, high level programmable platform with specific functionality and allowing for subscriber extension without needing to manage virtual machines, operating systems, databases, etc., which are leveraged by the service. PaaS includes cloud-based big data analysis systems and frameworks for rapid cloud-based application development and/or deployment.

Of late, the *aaS* definition is being extended as cloud service models continue to grow and now includes additions such as the following:

- *IT as a Service (ITaaS)*: This is effectively a mix of outsourcing *and* IaaS, PaaS, or SaaS as required.
- *Storage as a Service (STaaS)*: This provides large-scale object-based access to storage for use in archive or other applications and may in turn be leveraged by other cloud providers for their SaaS, PaaS, BaaS, or AaaS offerings.
- *Backup as a Service (BaaS)*: Backup and recovery services provided via the cloud utility model.
- *Disaster Recovery as a Service (DRaaS)*: Typically sees service providers offering a replication target for a customer's own backup and

recovery environment. In the event of a major issue, the company can recover from the replica data. This may even be leveraged with the option for the DRaaS provider to provision a limited amount of compute and storage resources to the business in the event of a disaster so they can start some operations in the cloud.

- *Archive as a Service* (*AaaS*): Growing in popularity as a means of allowing businesses to forego tape entirely, archive as a service allows for large-scale storage of long-term archival or compliance data without needing to manage the storage.

With all these different models and services available, it is becoming increasingly obvious that a strong focus on data protection needs to be applied to cloud computing to avoid the risk of significant or even catastrophic data loss. This focus is also important to avoid *decreasing* the level of data protection available when moving workloads into the cloud when compared to what had been used within a traditional datacenter.

12.2 THE RISE OF SHADOW IT

The term "shadow IT" has been increasingly used to define scenarios where cloud-based IT resources are procured and organized *outside* of the IT department—by managers, pseudo-technical staff, or power users within other areas of the business. Shadow IT occurs when a group within the business require certain IT functions but are unable or unwilling to access them through conventional IT channels. Rather than waiting until the resources can be made available, they seek them through public cloud services. Thus, islands of IT the business may rely on that are outside of the watchful eye of IT departments spring up within the organization.

It can be argued that the existence of shadow IT within business points to a communication problem between the business and the IT department, and with the communication problem comes the inevitable problems of ensuring data integrity, recoverability, and availability.

Despite the potential short-term advantages presented by using shadow IT, managers within a business should be particularly cognizant of the risks posed by shadow IT: that business functions might be deployed on systems that do not meet business needs for recoverability, records retention, data availability, or data integrity. This does not mean cloud services should be avoided, but it does show the need for increased collaboration, maturity, and communication in IT service management regardless of where the service is being delivered from.

12.3 PUBLIC CLOUDS AND AVAILABILITY

12.3.1 What's a Few Nines between Friends (Redux)?

For years the enterprise IT industry has had a particular focus on "high nines" availability, referring to the percentage a system is operational. This was discussed in the introduction of Chapter 9 (Continuous Availability and Replication).

In the context of cloud, it's pertinent to briefly revisit high nines availability as a reminder that businesses must understand the advertised *and* achieved availability levels of cloud providers if they wish to move workloads out into a public or community cloud space.

While many public cloud providers will make strong promises relating to availability, those promises of availability do not always relate to protection—and may not even correlate to actual delivered availability. Others may simply make no promises whatsoever—which is hardly reassuring. Many public cloud providers fail to offer detailed information about their availability status, leading to the rise of third-party analysts or consultants who aggregate and present this information. For instance, CloudHarmony* (now owned by Gartner) states on its "About" page:

> CloudHarmony was founded in late 2009. At that time, we recognized a need for objective performance analysis to compare cloud services. Our intent is to be an impartial and reliable source for objective cloud performance analysis.

Businesses evaluating public cloud services do well to research availability of those services before becoming locked into agreements. While these figures undoubtedly reference up/accessible time, operational responsiveness of most cloud services will be almost always more determined by the link speed a business has between itself and a cloud service provider than the actual individual component responsiveness *within* the cloud.

As of July 4, 2015, the CloudHarmony aggregated 365-day availability statistics of Amazon, Microsoft Azure, and Google are shown in Table 12.1. These range between mere minutes and *days*.†

Unless a business has built a resilient load-balancing on-ramp to the cloud via a hybrid cloud offering with mirrored or highly available workloads, the outages shown in Table 12.1 for a business don't necessarily just represent *single system* outages but *entire datacenter* outages. That is, in each case it's entirely possible that an outage is not just a single workload but *all* workloads that have been moved into

TABLE 12.1

Example Downtimes on Three Noteworthy Public Cloud Providers

Provider	% Available	# Outages	Total Downtime
Amazon EC2	99.9984	17	1.35 hours
Amazon S3	99.9962	33	3.03 hours
Google cloud storage	99.9998	14	12.42 minutes
Google compute engine	99.9639	106	9.49 hours
Microsoft Azure object storage	99.9902	142	11.02 hours
Microsoft Azure virtual machines	99.9613	118	46.58 hours

* https://cloudharmony.com/about.
† Since this was written, CloudHarmony have reduced their review window to a maximum of a month.

that cloud service provider. Without careful planning and architectural mitigation, the decision to move workloads to public cloud has the potential to significantly, detrimentally impact a business.

12.3.2   DATA LOSS VERSUS ACCESSIBILITY LOSS

Particularly when we consider public cloud, data protection considerations will need to take into account both data *loss* scenarios and data *accessibility* loss scenarios.

Within the traditional infrastructure space, it's become standard practice for businesses with any operational dependency on their IT infrastructure to maintain at least two physically separate datacenters, with either datacenter capable of running *at least* the mission critical applications and functions.

The dual or multi-datacenter approach for many businesses has the primary purpose of disaster recovery and business continuity—in the event of a datacenter being unavailable, operations should be able to continue at the other datacenter. This accounts for a variety of faults, including

- Physical server failures
- Storage system failures
- Power failures
- Internet access failures
- Internal networking failures
- Physical site inaccessibility
- Physical site destruction

Such considerations should not immediately disappear for a business just because it no longer owns the infrastructure being used. Businesses must still look at the operational risk of losing access to a cloud service provider. While the rest of this chapter focuses on data loss, accessibility loss (particularly prolonged accessibility loss) can have just as negative an impact on a business as data loss itself.

Even the largest of public cloud service providers suffer outages. If mission critical workloads are placed in a public cloud, part of that placement must include a risk assessment not only of data loss but also of accessibility loss—and appropriate architectural and operational planning to keep the business functions going. This might be a reduced private infrastructure capability to deliver the service, emergency co-location service arrangements, or for truly mission critical systems, the same service replicated between and available from two or more public cloud providers serviced out of entirely different geographies. While some larger cloud providers may offer services that can span or failover between geographies, subscribers may be unable to leverage this if they have data sovereignty constraints. Further, all of the subscriber services are still within the same cloud provider and might still be susceptible to a truly global provider network or security issue.

This is nothing new, of course. Standard datacenter design practice will include much of the considerations that need to be dealt with in the public cloud model as well. A few rules normally considered for datacenter practice include the following:

- Datacenters should not rely on the same part of the power grid (or at least be serviced by different grid blocks).
- Datacenters should have redundant links from alternate network/Internet providers.
- There should be sufficient physical distance between datacenters to reduce the likelihood of the same disaster affecting both the primary and secondary datacenters.
- Datacenters should not be susceptible to the *same* physical disaster situations (e.g., don't have two physically isolated datacenters in basements if both regions they're in happen to be susceptible to flooding).

None of these considerations go away in public cloud, and while the aim will be to ensure SLAs with the service provider cover scenarios such as protection from physical destruction, a fault in a cloud service provider's networking that impacts its infrastructure regardless of geographic location is *not* unheard of.

In essence, this is dealt with by treating public cloud providers like conventional utility providers (power, water, networking), and making the same utility-like decisions to ensure the business is adequately protected from similar service losses.

12.3.3 OBJECTIVES AND AGREEMENTS

When evaluating contracts or stated availability/accessibility levels of public cloud providers, potential subscribers must be particularly mindful of noticing whether levels are stated as *agreements* or *objectives*. While legal definitions may change (or be challenged) between geographies, it's usually accepted in IT circles that a *service level agreement* (SLA) and a *service level objective* (SLO) have a critical difference.

We usually accept a service level *agreement* to be one that is backed by legal or financial incentives. That is, the notion of an agreement creates a contractual obligation of fulfillment, and if that fulfillment for some reason fails to take place, pecuniary penalties can be extracted by the party who has contracted the service. Depending on the severity of the failure, this may result in a refund, a credit, or perhaps even a fee-less termination of contract. In some contracts, it may even be associated with fines.

On the other hand, a service level *objective* is seen to be one where the supplier makes no binding commitment to achieve the stated levels of service. It has an *objective* to achieve the service levels, but it doesn't as such commit to meeting them and therefore doesn't agree to be held liable if it fails to do so.

A business that moves workloads (particularly production ones) from internal IT services with fixed SLAs to external IT services offering mere SLOs is effectively *gambling* its ability to offer the business functions reliant on those IT workloads (and dangerously so if those workloads are business critical or have externally imposed SLAs upon them). Just as Icarus fell after flying too close to the sun and having his wax-attached wings fall off, a business that *trusts* everything will be OK could find itself plummeting through the cloud with no means of arresting its fall.

In short, the difference between an SLA and an SLO is effectively the difference between a written contract and a handshake agreement, something that reflects upon the operational maturity of a business. A business that does not allow vendor or supplier service contracts to be based on unwritten handshake agreements should be extremely leery of relying on SLOs for business systems availability. The tendency for users of technology to skim over and blithely accept End User License Agreements (EULAs) and the accessibility of public cloud services to even non-IT staff make the risks of placing a business workload into an insufficiently protected environment much higher than we would like to see. That is, while an IT manager engaging a new service might have the terms and conditions for that service reviewed carefully, a developer or innovator in a department standing that service up as a "test" may not. Often these "test" services get transitioned to production when they become useful to the business. In such situations, it may be that due diligence on service levels has never been performed.

12.3.4 CASCADED PROVIDERS

Another availability factor that must be considered by a business when evaluating service providers is: *who are their service providers*? While some public cloud service providers will run their own infrastructure and datacenters, cloud-consolidation is a frequent occurrence within the services marketplace. For instance, a SaaS provider offering CRM systems may in fact host its CRM systems on the IaaS or PaaS offerings of another provider, irrespective of how large they are. (For instance, a small SaaS provider might choose to run on another public service providers' platform to avoid the cost of building infrastructure that may never be used. On the other hand, a large SaaS provider might recognize that the cost of running and maintaining the level of infrastructure required for the number of customers they have is too high and choose instead to utilize a service provider to limit infrastructure costs directly based on customer numbers and workloads.)

Thus, the reliability and availability of the services being engaged is not *just* measured against the primary service provider availability, but *also* the availability of *their* primary service provider and the level of resilience they have architected into their services. Unfortunately, there is no standard for the publication of this sort of usage data, and in fact many businesses consider it to be practically an *operational secret* so as to limit their exposure—a malicious hacker, for instance, knowing that a company uses a particular provider might use that provider as their primary vector of attack. In this sense, obfuscating service providers is no different to businesses not advertising the location of their business continuity site (even to the point of having no information on buildings, being rented through an agent, acquired through a management company etc.), though this can be cold comfort to subscribers needing to make an informed decision as to the reliability of the services they intent to engage.

12.4 DATA PROTECTION FOR BORN-IN-CLOUD DATA

Many of the most common major SaaS cloud providers might an almost customer-hostile approach to data protection. It is quite common, for instance, to see such providers take stringent steps to ensure data is kept available and is recoverable *for them*, but not include this in SLAs with their users. That is, their data protection strategies resolve entirely around service availability and preventing mass data loss situations, but they are not geared toward individual unit recovery.*

Some examples of recovery "services" offered by prominent SaaS providers include the following:

- Providing a "trash" can option for documents and emails; content is automatically expired and expunged after a certain time period and can usually be expunged on user demands. Once trashed content is expunged or expired, it cannot be recovered.
- Providing a "grace" period on account deletion; account contents are automatically expired and expunged after a certain time once an administrator has nominated them for deletion. Content cannot be recovered once it has been expunged/expired.
- Offering data recoverability at extremely high unit cost and extremely slow turnaround (amounts of $10,000 or more with 1–2 weeks resolution time have been observed).

None of these are truly effective or sufficient for data protection services for a business. In the first two instances, SaaS cloud providers might claim the "trash" or "grace" options are sufficient backup, but this is an absurd claim. More aptly stated, such providers are implicitly or otherwise informing their users, "if you delete it, you can never get it back." Equally, a recovery service that is so costly and so tardy on data that might be deemed business critical is clearly designed to discourage use.

Like SaaS, PaaS environments are usually far more focused on *service availability* than they are *data protection* for individual subscribers. Typically, subscribers will be faced with ensuring they keep a copy of their data or applications outside of the PaaS environment. In the case of big data systems, where content will be replicated into the cloud from a local source, the protection will often take place in the subscriber data-center via the local copy. For application frameworks, this may require building automation around options in the provider for exporting data and application definitions.

As such, it's important that businesses take control of the data protection process for *their* data that resides in the cloud. Several companies are now offering products for protecting data housed on SaaS and PaaS systems—"born in the cloud" data, so to speak. These products typically integrate with the tenant-wide administrator-level permissions assigned to a consumer either to allow an on-premises appliance/product to retrieve a copy of the data or to copy the data to a storage system defined in *another* cloud.

---

* Given such providers are offering software or specific applications as a service, they don't, after all, have any way of distinguishing the difference between a valid data deletion and an invalid one. But it's what they do *after* the data is deleted, which becomes important for data protection.

Conceptually, a SaaS provider and its customers might be represented as shown in Figure 12.1.

Any individual customer that wishes to construct an adequate and business-appropriate data protection solution to their SaaS data will be focused solely on *their* data; the solution deployed will only be applicable to their tenancy in the SaaS provider. Such a solution might resemble that shown in Figure 12.2.

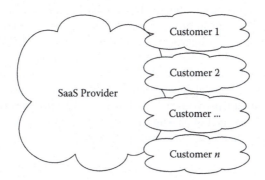

FIGURE 12.1 Conceptual representation of SaaS cloud provider and customers.

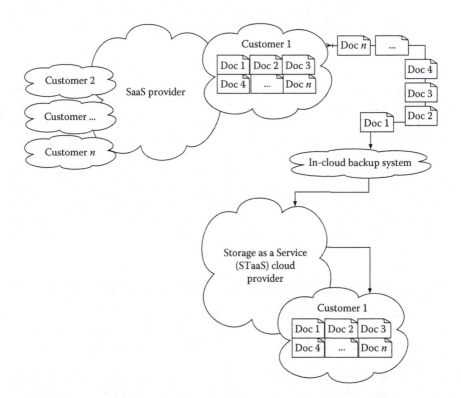

FIGURE 12.2 Logical representation of a "born in the cloud" backup solution.

Drilling down to a single client of the SaaS provider, *Customer 1* deploys an in-cloud backup system to provide reasonable and appropriate data protection against the data its users generate, above and beyond the basic "datacenter protection" offered by the SaaS provider. Assuming the SaaS offering is a document system (e.g., spreadsheets, word-processor documents, presentation files), the goal of such a system will be to provide backup of documents as they are changed by the users and the option to recover documents to a specific version over the number of revisions or days/months backup copies maintained by the backup service. The backup will be written to an alternate cloud provider—either the one hosting the in-cloud backup service itself or even a third-party cloud provider.

The net result of such a system is a far more holistic and business-centric approach to data protection for SaaS and PaaS data. Typically, such services will be charged on a flexible utility-based model per standard cloud systems—for example, a flat dollar cost per user per month, per year, or a combination of the per-user/per-period rate and a $/GB rate for the amount of backup data being generated.

This leverages data protection at two specific points:

1. Relying on data protection employed by the SaaS/PaaS provider for operational availability of the overall system being utilized
2. Relying on an external provider or service to protect the actual content/data in a suitably granular way that exists independently of the state of the service being subscribed to for compliance and retention purposes

While such a system increases the cost of utilizing cloud systems, it allows a business to adequately protect and ensure the recoverability of potentially mission critical data.

It is interesting to note that anecdotally, businesses looking to shift to a cloud-first SaaS model for deployment will leverage multiple SaaS providers, all with different levels of maturity when it comes to data protection. What is currently lacking is a common operating model or API for data backup and recovery. There is certainly scope for an industry-wide approach to developing a common framework for data backup and recovery operations for SaaS providers that could subsequently be leveraged by SaaS backup providers. If this seems fanciful, remember the storage and data protection industries worked together to develop the network data management protocol (NDMP) to allow easy backup and recovery operations for network attached storage (NAS) systems, regardless of vendor, that is, there is a precedent to such a level of industry cooperation.

12.5 DATA PROTECTION FOR IN-CLOUD INFRASTRUCTURE

When we move beyond SaaS and PaaS and return to IaaS, we enter more familiar territory. IaaS is essentially a cloud-based extension to the virtual datacenter, something most IT departments, CIOs and CFOs will by now be extremely familiar with.

There are two distinct approaches that can be taken with an IaaS cloud environment: service catalog or self-service. (A combination of the two might also be used depending on data criticality, costs, and retention requirements.)

12.5.1 SERVICE CATALOG APPROACH

The service catalog approach will leverage an IaaS provider's own data protection offerings. Depending on the provider, this may include features and options such as

- Virtual datacenter replication (allowing high availability and protection from a datacenter failure within the IaaS provider)
- Regular snapshots of virtual infrastructure (virtual machines and/or virtual data volumes)
- Traditional backup and recovery agents and/or policies for operating systems and databases/applications

Additionally, for snapshots and traditional backup/recovery options, a variety of retention time frames *may* be offered, such as

- Daily backups retained for 30 days
- Daily backups retained for 60 days
- Monthly backups retained for 12 months
- Monthly backups retained for 3 years
- Monthly backups retained for 7 years

Such retention will typically be charged on a cents-per-GB model, though for some providers the longevity of retention may impact the per-GB cost. (For instance, monthly backups retained for 12 months may cost less per GB than monthly backups retained for 7 years.)

Subscribers also need to anticipate that the data protection options offered by the service provider will cease at the moment the service ceases. While this may seem an entirely commonsense anticipation, it has the potential to create significant impact on an organization that must retain particular key data for compliance purposes (i.e., even if a subscriber no longer wishes to use the particular service, legal compliance reasons may require backups to be retained for longer, and thus the service kept active). Alternately, this can sometimes result in a "never delete" approach for IaaS subscribers—if a database is backed up every day for a month, but no content is ever deleted from the database, then arguably the backup from any single day represents a longer retention time. While logically this *may* be true, it may not satisfy either an external auditor or a regulatory body unless suitable, government-approved approaches that are demonstrable and documented are used to prevent arbitrary data deletion. Any subscriber choosing to go down this path should engage legal teams and independent auditors from the design stage through to post-implementation to ensure a completed solution will not earn the ire of a judicial authority or government body at a later point in time.

Another additional cost factor that may be introduced into data protection services by cloud providers (IaaS, BaaS, or even STaaS) relates to the deduplicatibility of the data being protected, or the daily change rate thereof. A service provider may for instance build its internal cost model for provisioning of backups to subscribers on the assumption that the daily growth in *unique* data is never more than say, 1%. When this is regularly exceeded (e.g., on average for more days in a month than not), an overhead fee may be automatically charged to the subscriber's account to allow the provider to compensate against unplanned storage or data protection costs. Thus, a subscriber must examine not only the base service catalog offerings, but also the exclusions and any cascading costs that they might incur based on the workload or data to be stored in the system. It also allows a service provider to discourage subscribers from say, deploying databases but choosing to generate compressed dumps of them rather than electing to have appropriate data protection agents deployed as a "cost-saving" mechanism.

The service catalog offerings for data protection will usually be on top of any base data protection enacted by the service provider to ensure service continuity, but the level chosen by the subscriber will directly affect and limit the recoverability of their environment. IaaS providers will explicitly excuse themselves from data loss situations not covered by the actual service catalog options chosen by the subscriber, and subscriber agreement to this will be contingent on service provisioning. For example, a smaller IaaS subscriber may choose only a low service level (say, daily backups) from the IaaS catalog. This could allow them to recover data or databases for a defined period of time (e.g., 30 days), but in the event of a datacenter failure for the IaaS provider, the low-SLA subscriber services would *not* be available for restart on a migrated datacenter. In such a situation, they would be dependent on the IaaS provider getting the original datacenter backup and running without data loss before their service could resume.

Particularly in light of the number of businesses planning to shift even *some* of their workloads to public cloud, it is not surprising that there is a burgeoning consultancy field to assist organizations:

- To understand the nuances and costs associated with cloud provider and service catalog selection
- To accurately identify and classify their data and workloads to determine cloud-readiness
- To understand the suitability of service catalog offerings for data protection to the business requirements and any gaps

12.5.2 SELF-SERVICE APPROACH

While the service catalog approach is usually simpler and requires less local IT resources for a business, it does open the business to several distinct risks, viz.:

- Service catalog options may be retrograde compared to existing on-premises capabilities.
- Longer-term retention is entirely dependent on retaining a contract with the service provider (effectively creating lock in with an IaaS provider).
- The subscriber will usually be exposed to the risk of total IaaS failure regardless of what individual data protection catalog options are chosen.

For these reasons and others relating to accountability and compliance, some businesses will choose to forego service catalog options offered by the IaaS provider(s)

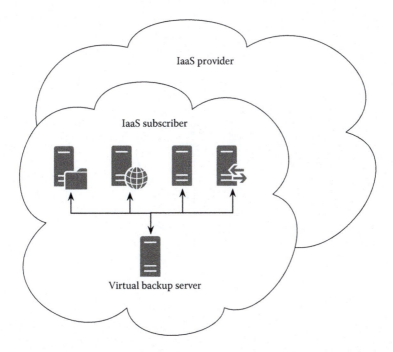

FIGURE 12.3 IaaS subscription with an in-service backup server.

they're subscribing to and build their own data protection environment directly into the cloud environment.

Such data protection schemes will need to be very carefully planned and provisioned to avoid obvious pitfalls relating to backup data placement. For instance, consider the scenario shown in Figure 12.3.

In such a configuration, an IaaS customer has deployed a virtualized backup server within their infrastructure subscription/virtual datacenter. This virtual backup server co-exists with the IaaS email, database, file, and generic servers. While this will provide localized backup/recovery services, thereby allowing recovery from individual file, email, or database loss, it still relies on the overall physical datacenter and infrastructure protection offered by the IaaS provider.

A more comprehensive approach to data protection for IaaS subscribers sees the backup infrastructure deployed into a secondary IaaS provider, such as that shown in Figure 12.4.

Such an in-cloud backup system will be highly dependent on the bandwidth available between the two service providers. This will not only include the bandwidth they can provide to individual subscribers from their Internet links, but also the subsequent Internet speed achievable between their two locations.

While such a consideration will be important for SaaS backup offerings as well, the volume of data to be considered in inter-IaaS backups can be considerably higher. To mitigate this, a source-based deduplication-centric backup system will be the most logical protection method to deploy—after the first backup, the amount of data that

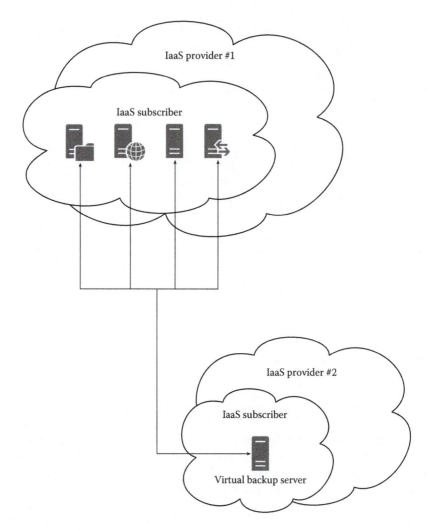

FIGURE 12.4 Data protection in an IaaS environment with protection against local service failure.

will need to be sent across the Internet should be substantially reduced.* It should be noted though that since most cloud providers also charge based on the amount of CPU and memory consumed by virtual machines running in their environment, deduplication within the cloud can be a double-edged sword: the cost and speed savings in the amount of data transferred between two cloud providers may be negated by the increased CPU and memory consumption to achieve the deduplication.

In situations where the link speed between two cloud service providers isn't sufficient, another approach that a business can take is to provision services in geographically different provisioning areas of a single provider. A worldwide provider,

---

* Depending on the type of data and its susceptibility to deduplication.

for instance, might allow a subscriber to "lock" services down to a particular location—East Coast USA, West Coast USA, France, and Australia. In such a situation, the intra-site bandwidth available will be more guaranteed than inter-provider links. In such a situation, provisioning primary services allowed to be located in say, US East Coast or US West Coast, and the backup service infrastructure locked to Australia may provide a level of protection and service separation acceptable to the business.

Like SaaS data protection processes, much of the consideration here has been on adequate backup and recovery systems, but we know there is more to data protection than just backup and recovery. Options such as replication, CDP, and snapshots will be entirely dependent on the level of access a business has to the infrastructure it is subscribing to, which in turn will depend on the technology the IaaS provider has utilized.

When a large amount of data is in a public cloud and requires data protection, data egress costs will require very careful consideration. A cloud service provider may not charge anything for data as it is coming into their services, but charge anywhere between a nominal fee and a high cost per GB for data *leaving* the service. Thus, an inter-cloud backup service needing to transfer hundreds of GB per day could incur significantly higher operational costs than say, traditional inter-datacenter backup replication costs. Companies should be particularly wary when evaluating data protection within or between public cloud providers that the cumulative costs of data transfer don't exceed or otherwise mitigate day-to-day operational cost advantages of "cheap" infrastructure.

12.6 PRIVATE AND HYBRID CLOUDS

We group private and hybrid clouds together for the simple reason that they both start *in the datacenter*. (For the purposes of our topic, that's regardless of whether it's a datacenter owned by the business, or a datacenter in which the business rents floor-space but has its own infrastructure installed therein.)

12.6.1 PRIVATE CLOUDS

When the term *private cloud* started to be used, it was often misunderstood as being a cunning marketing trick aimed at sticking a "cloud" badge on the same equipment businesses had previously been buying and selling it at an inflated price.

What has become increasingly obvious is that businesses are looking at the fundamental aspects of cloud (in particular aspects such as rapid elasticity, on-demand self-service, and accurate measurement of service provision) and expecting their IT departments adapt to be as flexible. This often requires IT departments to focus on *Converged Infrastructure* (CI). At its heart, CI helps to provide a highly virtualized datacenter that centralizes compute, storage, and network and features high levels of automation for provisioning and management thanks to a robust software overlay.

For the infrastructure groups within the IT department, CI will resemble something shown in Figure 12.5. All the traditional elements of IT infrastructure will be present—networking, storage, data protection, and compute. This will be tightly

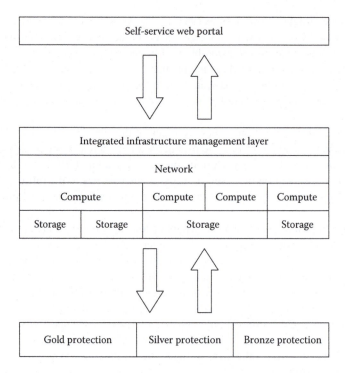

FIGURE 12.5 A logical view of a converged infrastructure.

woven together though by an integrated infrastructure management software layer. At the top—the tip of the iceberg, you might say—will be the self-service web portal that is presented to authorized end users within the business.

For the end users, however, the view will be quite different. Their experience of the infrastructure will be that of the web portal that allows them to provision services—something that may resemble that shown in Figure 12.6. Through one or more portal dialogs, they'll be prompted to select the type of infrastructure they require,* and also agree to the billing aspect (for private cloud this will usually equate to internal cross-charging).

For private cloud to work effectively within an organization, it needs to not only offer all the key cloud features users and the business is looking for, but it also needs to integrate with the process control elements of the business such as change management, service desk requests, and access control. This is typically where the infrastructure management layer will need to come into play or else the self-service web portal becomes nothing more than a simplified request layer. (In short, if a system isn't provisioned *automatically* within a predetermined period of time following the user request, it's a private cloud for marketing purposes only.)

---

* For the purposes of simplification, not all such options are shown in Figure 12.6. Some businesses for instance may also require users to select an option for required performance levels, and others may also require users to indicate how long the provisioned infrastructure will be required.

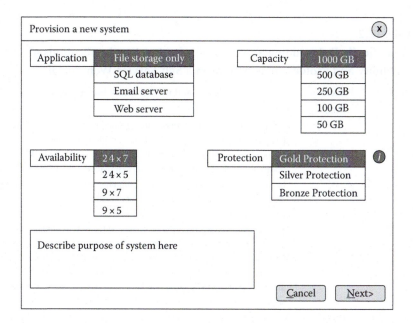

FIGURE 12.6 An end-user portal for self-service converged infrastructure.

An absolute advantage for businesses pursuing the private cloud datacenter is the automated provisioning of services *and* the requisite data protection models required. For instance, if we consider the provisioning dialog from Figure 12.6, there are actually two aspects of data protection cited:

1. *Protection*—gold, silver, or bronze
2. *Availability*—24 × 7, 24 × 5, 9 × 7, or 9 × 5

You'll note the protection levels cited align to what you'd expect to see as titles in service catalogs rather than comprehensive descriptions. A goal of cloud provisioning in general is to simplify the selection model and allow the subscriber to get on with what they *need* the components for. In this sense, IT and the business will have previously agreed on what each of *gold*, *silver*, and *bronze* protection models equate to.*

The options for availability equally provide guidance to the infrastructure requirements of the provisioned services, particularly when coupled with the protection options. Table 12.2 provides some examples of this. Provisioning portals that ask additional questions relating to system performance or encryption requirements would likely yield further automated policy granularity regarding overall data protection requirements.

An implication of such service provisioning for private cloud within organizations is a much tighter coupling of the two arms of data protection (proactive

---

* A full portal for self-provisioning would likely include "help" hyperlinks that lead to extended details about the service levels, exclusions, permitted outage times, etc.

TABLE 12.2

Automatically Determining Service and Infrastructure Implications of Availability and Protection Selections in a Self-Service Web-Portal

Availability	Protection	Service and Infrastructure Implications
24 × 7	Gold	*Mission critical.* It may require continuous replication of storage and virtual machines between two sites to allow immediate transition from one datacenter to the other without visible service interruption to subscribers. While traditional backups will be taken daily, application aware snapshots will be taken every half an hour with log shipping for applications, allowing for highly granular recoveries with very small RPOs and RTOs.
9 × 5	Gold	*Business function critical.* Requires continuous replication of storage and virtual machines between two sites to allow immediate transition from one datacenter to the other without visible interruption to subscribers *during business hours*, but with asynchronous replication and lag permitted out of hours. Application aware snapshots will be taken hourly during business hours, with the final snapshot of the day "rolled over" into the daily backup for system.
24 × 7	Bronze	*Noncritical yet important service.* This may be indicative of a service that the business wants to see operational at all times, but an outage can in theory be sustained. For instance, the front-facing web services (so long as they don't include eCommerce) may be designated 24 × 7 to reflect a global market. This would require clustered availability rather than continuous replication between sites, and standard daily backups would likely be more than sufficient to meet RPOs and RTOs.

and reactive). To achieve this, data protection options within the business have to be the following:

- *Policy driven*—Administrators will define broad policies instead of pin-point per-system configuration.
- *Integrated*—The higher the service level required, the greater the integration that will be necessary between the compute layer, the data protection activities in the traditional system storage and the backup and recovery systems.*
- *Compatible*—Integration implies compatibility, and compatibility will be best achieved through a narrowing of the number of vendors used to source infrastructure from *and/or* as a result of highly robust scripting from a local DevOps team.

Since the cloud model requires automated provisioning as a result of the self-service approach, storage, virtualization, and backup administrators do not have the

---

* For instance, automated copying of snapshots from primary storage to backup and recovery storage, orchestrated and addressable by the backup software. To be *useful*, such snapshots would need to be entirely integrated with any applications or virtual systems stored on them.

luxury of receiving service tickets for configuring either the primary service or the associated data protection. Instead, their roles shift to a combined function of

- *Policy definition*—Creating the core policies and workflows associated with service-catalog-defined data protection
- *Service intervention*—Resolving issues that may occur with services

The end goal is that once data protection policies and the workflows required to meet those policies are defined, the management software layer driving the infrastructure should automatically add provisioned storage, virtual machines, and applications to the various workflows and policies without human intervention.

An example policy with associated workflows may resemble that shown in Figure 12.7. By developing the protection policy as a workflow, it becomes very easy to see that the configuration process should be automatable. Rather than the backup administrator needing to launch a console, add the clients, and select groups, schedules, and retention periods, the software management layer should do all this automatically. Where data protection configuration has limits (e.g., the administrator or vendor might state that "the backup software should not have more than 150 client systems executing backups simultaneously"), the management layer should take this into account, adding schedules, groups, and containers as appropriate.

12.6.2 HYBRID CLOUD

Many businesses will be perfectly content with private cloud arrangements only, as these will provide a level of agility, efficiency, and cost accuracy well beyond that experienced in traditional datacenter approaches to infrastructure.

Hybrid cloud comes in for those businesses that require a level of elasticity for compute and storage beyond that which is practical for the business to acquire directly.

Automation however remains critical for the successful functioning of a hybrid cloud—workloads should shift or extend into a public cloud without requiring subscriber intervention. So long as the performance requirements of the subscriber have been met, it should make no difference where the workload is running.*

More so, the data protection policies defined and provisioned for should continue to function under the aegis of the private cloud definition regardless of the location. This *may* result in some modification of the service levels. Recall Table 2.2 ("Sample RTO SLAs for data types based on locality of data"), it was suggested service levels may be altered based on whether data exist within the datacenter, in a hybrid cloud or in a public cloud. For example, the "gold" service level had RTOs of

- Traditional infrastructure[†]—1 hour
- Hybrid infrastructure—4 hours
- Public cloud—8 hours

---

* Other factors, such as regulatory compliance around data locality, will of course play a factor in whether or not a workload is shifted into the public cloud and should be handled by the orchestration management software.
[†] This might equally refer to private cloud.

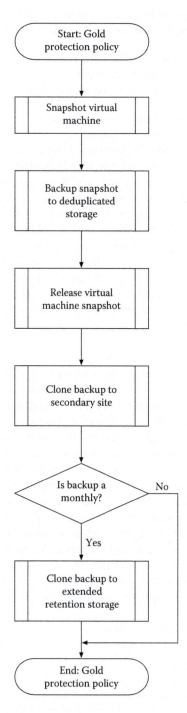

FIGURE 12.7 Example data protection policy with associated workflows.

As part of the provisioning and control mechanisms in a *hybrid* cloud environment, it will typically be possible to place constraints on *where* the service can exist. Mission critical systems with compliance requirements for on-premise data might be functionally locked from ever being migrated to a public cloud service. Less critical infrastructure, or infrastructure that requires the ability to say triple compute resources beyond the capability of the entire private cloud during peak loading might be acknowledged as being a hybrid deployment and therefore delivered *only* with the *hybrid infrastructure* service levels and protection options.

In all cases though, the goal will be to ensure the data protection policies defined by the IT teams and aligned to the provisioned services can be met regardless of whether those services are currently on- or off-premises.

When combined with appropriate development and service provisioning, such flexibility typically grants a business *cloud independence*. By controlling the policies within the private cloud infrastructure, the business can cease to be beholden to variable/limited-liability approaches to data protection offered by public cloud providers and automate any number of data protection deployment operations automatically as workloads are moved into or stretched into public clouds.

Consider the previous workflow for the *Gold* data protection policy from Figure 12.7. Such a workflow can be mapped as equally to a private cloud environment as it can be to a public cloud environment if we make use of in-cloud IaaS backup services. A service might start in the private cloud and receive its snapshots, backup and backup cloning operations serviced from infrastructure in the business datacenter. Over time if the service requirements change, the workload might be shifted to the public cloud, but a compatible backup service in a second cloud be used to provide data recovery services. If long-term monthly style compliance backups are still required for the service, that IaaS backup in the second public cloud might subsequently be replicated *back into* the private cloud infrastructure for guaranteed long-term storage.

12.7   EXTENDING DATA PROTECTION INTO THE CLOUD

A topic getting increasing attraction is the option of expanding traditional data protection services into the public cloud as a means of providing minimized costs for longer-term compliance backups or archives. In essence, this takes advantage of the relatively cheap per-GB costs of object-based storage in cloud storage providers, particularly if there are no strong SLAs on access speed and acceptable cost implications based on projected retrieval frequency and amount.

Such a solution might resemble that shown in Figure 12.8.

This has a parallel to current infrastructure approaches to data retention. If we consider a reasonably typical business, it's now quite normal to encounter a design whereby daily, weekly, and even recent monthly backups are stored entirely on disk (more often than not in deduplicated format). All short-term and most medium-term recoveries will be serviced from disk, allowing for fast local retrieval unimpeded by device contention or media recall requirements. Traditionally, the backups requiring *really*-long-term retention (e.g., those to be kept for 7 years for legal reasons or several decades for medical or manufacturing requirements) have been pushed out

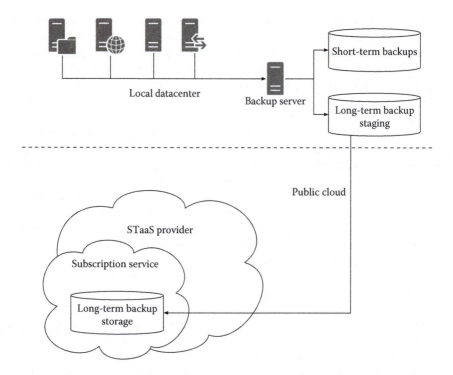

FIGURE 12.8   Utilizing object-based cloud storage to extent data protection services.

to tape, with the tape being stored in a secure, off-site facility. (For redundancy purposes, at least two tape copies would always be generated.)

While tape will continue to exist in many organizations for some time to come (if only to service legacy access requirements), other organizations are seeing cloud object storage as a means of extricating themselves from handling large volumes of physical media, and there are several good reasons to consider this, such as the following:

- *Storage costs*—Off-site tape storage vendors typically charge per unit of media stored, in addition to monthly service fees and/or transport fees. Particularly when in-cloud object storage is written in a deduplicated manner, long-term cloud storage may represent a similar economic scale.
- *Media and equipment costs*—In addition to the actual storage costs, businesses utilizing tape for long-term storage must purchase the tapes that are written to and maintain the tape libraries and devices used to write to those tapes. Off-site tape storage usually features a higher level of media "wastage" than on-site tapes due to the requirement to ship data off-site in a relatively short period of time after it's written. That is, most tape shipped off-site for long-term storage will not have been written to their full capacity.
- *Media testing*—As they are only being infrequently accessed (if at all), it is impossible to tell whether tape has degraded while it is sitting on a shelf in a storage facility. The only way to be sure is to periodically recall media

(or at least batches of media) to confirm the data on it can still be read. This takes time and resources to perform (in addition to incurring recall and new off-site shipping fees*).

- *Media refresh cycles*—A tape written 5 or 10 years prior may not be compatible with tape drives in-use now. A backup requiring long-term retention on tape will need to be periodically recalled and migrated to newer tape as refresh cycles occur. (The alternative, of keeping older tape drives available for recovery purposes, rarely works out either from a reliability or maintenance cost perspective.†)

- *Availability*—While the streaming performance of a tape may arguably be higher than many cloud storage options (particularly based on available bandwidth), if the majority of retrievals are projected to be smaller units of data, this may not be a major impediment to a business, particularly when we consider the ongoing trend of cheaper *and* faster Internet access. A slower retrieval from cloud storage may be mitigated by being able to start the data transfer immediately, rather than issuing a media recall notice, waiting for media to be recalled, waiting for a tape drive to be available, and then initiating the recovery.

- *Discovery*—While there are risks associated with protection data being online,‡ having data online and susceptible to more convenient discovery processes (either for metadata alone or entire content) can potentially save a business a considerable amount of time and money during litigation or compliance verification exercises. Data sitting on tape in off-site storage on the other hand will not be discoverable beyond whatever metadata was recorded at the time the tape was written.

It's worth noting that tape handling, particularly for long-term retention (e.g., 7 years or more), is often poor. It is reasonably common to encounter any or all of the following scenarios in a business using tape for long-term retention:

- Once sent off-site, tapes are never recalled for testing; the only time they are recalled are when they are required for a recovery.
- If a tape fails during a recovery process, even for long-term retention and the secondary copy is used, that secondary copy is not then *re*-copied before sending back off-site.
- When new tape drive technologies are purchased within the organization, tapes in the old format are not converted into the new format.
- When long-term retention tape backups have expired, they are not purged/ destroyed (or reused).
- When new backup products are implemented, tapes in the old format are not converted or otherwise cataloged for easy access.

---

* In reality, few businesses seem to invest the resources into this type of testing, which is a significant oversight that can result in considerable data loss.
† It is actually quite common to encounter businesses still storing tapes of a particular format where they've actually not had *any* tape drives capable of reading them for 5 or more years.
‡ Which, it should be noted, can be mitigated by keeping multiple copies, applying appropriate access controls and even using WORM-style locks.

Failure to do any of these scenarios can result in significant issues in the event of a recovery requirement: a compliance recovery may be requested 6 years after a backup was performed only to have the business discover it doesn't even have a tape drive that can read the data. Or worse, it finds a secondhand tape drive to read the data and that drive *destroys* the tape. And worse again, it turns out the second copy of the long-term data had been lost 4 years prior when an earlier recovery was performed against the same data.

By shifting long-term storage of backups (or archives) from tape to cloud-based storage, businesses can achieve the benefits of disk-based storage for their entire data protection cycle while taking advantage of the economy of scale available to cloud providers or even private object storage. This is especially so if the cost of the long-term retention to the cloud is balanced accurately and fairly against the *true* cost of managing long-term tape retention (regardless of whether the business currently does this or not). It should also be noted that on-premises object storage is a significantly growing area. These provide dense storage (e.g., multiple petabytes in a single rack) utilizing cloud-like access protocols. Such storage can enable a business to use private cloud storage for their long-term retention, eliminating tape and storing larger amounts of data at a lower cost than public cloud providers.

12.8   BACKUP AS A SERVICE

Backup as a Service (BaaS) is a burgeoning service designed to complement business offerings from cloud service providers who target the mid-market and enterprise service space.

BaaS is born of the recognition that many of the SLAs for data retention and systems availability within the cloud space are expressly targeted at limiting the liability of the service provider. While this potentially provides a high level of service uptime for subscribers, it provides little or no self-controlled recovery capabilities for the service subscribers.

By offering a robust BaaS catalog for their subscribers, cloud providers are recognizing that data protection is an important value addition for many businesses, and they discourage subscribers from seeking potentially bandwidth costly inter-cloud backup options such as that shown in Figure 12.4.

It is therefore increasingly common to see cloud providers publish compatible BaaS options for their subscribers. These are often quite economical due to a combination of buying power and strategic relationships with key vendors. (Vendors may even introduce incentives for their own sales teams for pointing businesses at a strategic BaaS provider.)

Businesses looking to use their cloud provider for BaaS functions *might* receive favorable pricing based on multiple services, or if nothing else the convenience of limiting the number of IT utility providers they need to subscribe to. Such services should be carefully examined to ensure the business can confirm adequate separation of primary data and protection data/services for disaster and network failure situations. Additionally, businesses with long-term compliance retention requirements may still need to consider maintaining responsibility for part of their data protection activities based on service catalog options or pricing—or a desire to not be locked down indefinitely to a specific BaaS provider.

Some businesses may move to BaaS regardless of whether they have content in a cloud or not. This may allow them to leverage backup technology they don't want to or otherwise unable to invest in themselves, particularly if backup is seen as a "utility" function beyond the core work requirements of the business. (You might think of this as the next evolution of managed services.) Moving to BaaS is also becoming popular for businesses switching to a maximized OpEx model over CapEx.

12.9 ARCHITECTURAL CONSIDERATIONS FOR CLOUD SERVICE PROVIDERS

For cloud service providers, one of the biggest challenges for data protection services relates to multi-tenancy. While this technically affects a business running a private or hybrid cloud, multi-tenancy considerations to data protection become especially critical for public cloud providers.

It's one thing for instance to be able to offer a service catalog for data protection utilizing an enterprise-class backup and recovery product, but if it isn't architected from the ground up for multi-tenancy (either by the vendor, or by the provider), the potential security implications from information leakage is extreme.

This is essentially no different from standard security considerations in multi-tenanted environments, but data protection by its very nature has potential to expose an *entire* business to information theft or data destruction. Whereas a private or hybrid cloud service provider might be able to leave multi-tenancy considerations as a lower order priority compared to recoverability, it's arguable a public cloud provider must make it the highest priority in design considerations.

This is represented at a high level in Figure 12.9.

At bare minimum a service provider will need to maintain two separate zones within their networking infrastructure; the private or internal zone will be entirely invisible and inaccessible to any cloud tenants. There will additionally be a shared zone that contains systems and infrastructure providing services to tenants. There will likely be a significant networking gap (either physical or firewalled) between the shared services zone and the private service provider infrastructure. (For instance, jump boxes may be required to reach from the private to shared services zone, with no connections permitted from the shared services zone into the private zone.)

While each tenant zone will be able to connect to the shared services zone, security will need to be established to ensure that no tenant can "peer over the fence" at another tenant.

Returning to our example of backup and recovery software, information leakage might happen in one of two different ways if not controlled:

1. *Visibility*—If a tenant can "view" monitoring information or reports that reveals hostnames or operational status* of other tenant zones or the shared services zone, this information might be used as part of social engineering or even to provide information usable in a direct hack attempt.

---

* We could refer to this as *metadata* leakage.

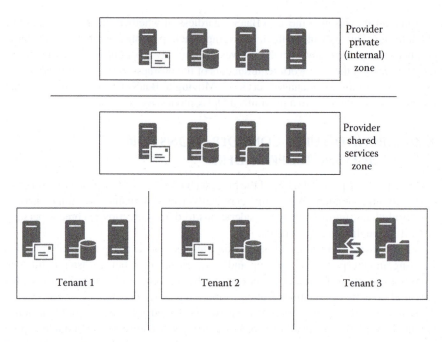

FIGURE 12.9 Zone view of cloud services.

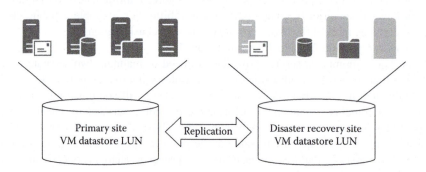

FIGURE 12.10 Basic view of virtual machines on shared storage.

2. *Access*—Allowing one tenant to recover data backed up by another tenant
   would make irrelevant any security steps taken against *primary* tenant data
   and zones.

Multi-tenancy considerations will apply to more than just the risk of data leakage
however. They will also directly impact the efficiency and cost-effectiveness of the
services offered by the cloud provider. For example, consider the implications of
multi-tenancy on system or service replication. Figure 12.10 shows a very basic view
of virtual machines and their associated storage systems.

From a standard storage consideration, it would not matter whether the virtual hosts sitting on a LUN presented for virtualization storage belong to a single

TABLE 12.3

Example Service Catalog Offerings for Data Protection and Availability

	Bronze	Silver	Gold
Failure protection	In the event of storage failure, system will be restarted with no more than 24 hours data loss.	In the event of storage failure, system will be restarted on alternate storage in the same datacenter with no more than 15 minutes data loss.	In the event of storage failure, system will be automatically transitioned to alternate storage in the datacenter with no interruption to services or data loss.
Availability	System will not automatically transition to an alternate datacenter in the event of site failure. System will remain unavailable until hosting site is operational again.	System will automatically transition to alternate datacenter in the event of a site failure. System will reboot and up to 30 minutes of data loss may occur.	System will automatically transition to alternate datacenter in the event of a site failure without interruption or data loss.

tenant or a mix of tenants. However, depending on the service levels offered by the cloud provider to tenants for data protection and recoverability, the layout of virtual machines and storage will be significant.

Consider for instance a basic service catalog for data protection and availability* as shown in Table 12.3.

Each of these service offerings requires distinctly different storage and availability options:

- Bronze
  - *Failure protection*: Snapshot replication performed on a 24-hour basis
  - *Availability*: None
- Silver
  - *Failure protection*: Asynchronous in-datacenter replication with a maximum 15-minute lag
  - *Availability*: Cross-site asynchronous replication with a maximum 30-minute lag
- Gold
  - *Failure protection*: Synchronously mirrored storage systems continuously available and managed as a single unit to the virtualization layer
  - *Availability*: Metro or similar synchronous system mirroring

Such a disparate service catalog requires the service provider to ensure systems are provisioned on storage that matches the offerings the customer has chosen. At the physical storage layer this might require three distinctly different storage systems, or a management layer on top of fewer storage systems that allows for a high level

---

* Backup and recovery services that might be offered are not shown for brevity.

of granularity and control over provisioning and protection systems. Consider for instance that each of the protection and availability models will have both a cost to customer *and* a provisioning cost to the cloud services provider. Even if the services can be managed such that say, a bronze-level customer can have data or systems residing on gold-level infrastructure but only get the *appearance* of bronze-level service, this will have a negative impact on the cost model for the services provider, since bronze-level pricing will undoubtedly be developed against being delivered from bronze-level infrastructure.

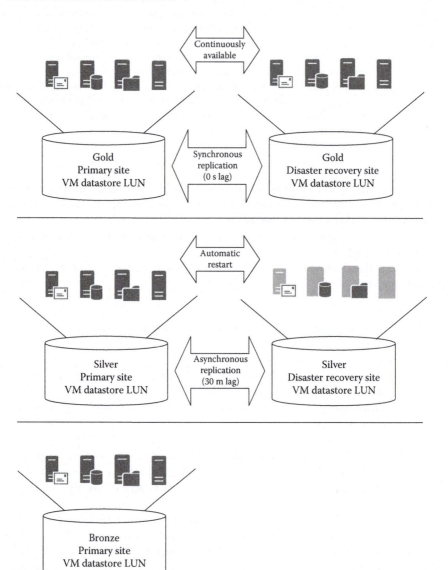

FIGURE 12.11   Service provisioning based on service catalog options.

Thus, our service and storage model at a high level view instead of resembling that shown in Figure 12.10 might instead more resemble a view such as that shown in Figure 12.11.

While initially this model may require additional provisioning cost for the service provider, the end result in a more tightly controlled cost model that allows for appropriate allocation of tenant subscription options to the most efficient and appropriate infrastructure.

12.10 SUMMARY

Despite the relative popularity of cloud in the IT operations for many businesses, this new OpEx/Utility model for infrastructure and IT services is still very much in its infancy. There is undoubtedly considerable scope for businesses to achieve agility and cost control orders of magnitude more impressive than available with traditional approaches to infrastructure management, but it can come at a savage cost if not approached carefully. Cloud services are akin to the "Wild West." There's a fortune to be had, but it's not without risks and challenges. A business that moves workloads into that space without taking adequate steps to protect their data may find themselves in a precarious, if not critical condition.

For service providers themselves, the multi-tenancy nature of cloud adds a considerable layer of complexity in managing and delivering efficient, secure, and cost-effective data protection options to subscribers. Immature service providers that don't sufficiently plan ahead and reconcile service catalogs to infrastructure capability may find their offerings unprofitable at best, and at worst, decidedly insecure for themselves and their tenants.

It should not be seen as doom and gloom—but it is absolutely essential that any business contemplating placing workloads or data into cloud (regardless of whether that's private, hybrid, or public) will need to plan, implement, and maintain the entire process around guaranteed data protection.

13 Deduplication

13.1 INTRODUCTION TO DEDUPLICATION

Deduplication, particularly within backup and recovery environments, has very much become a mainstream technology. As the name suggests, deduplication is oriented toward eliminating duplicate data, thereby reducing the footprint occupied by data storage systems. Deduplication greatly relies on the access speed of the disk in order to deliver operational efficiency. Since duplicate data may occur across a large number of data sets spaced over a considerable amount of time, reconstructing ("rehydrating") those data in a usable time frame relies on high-speed random access unavailable in tape.

Deduplication is a logical extension of two existing technologies—single-instance storage (used quite successfully in systems such as archival products and many mail servers in order to reduce storage requirements) and traditional file/data compression technology.

To understand deduplication, consider a corporate presentation consisting of 10 slides that are initially developed by Lynne before being distributed to Darren, Laura, and Peter for feedback. Darren makes changes to diagrams in four of the slides. Laura adds two new slides, while Peter removes one and adds one. This would resemble Figure 13.1.

In each case, the percentage variances between the original slide pack and the three copies are reasonably minor. If each file was stored in its entirety, there'd be a total of 42 slides across the 4 files.

If, however, we deduplicated at the *slide* level, linking identical slides back to the slides in the original file, we might see a space saving, which is shown in Figure 13.2.

In total, the slide-level deduplication yields a considerable reduction in the amount of storage required, bringing it down from 42 to 17—a saving of more than 2:1. This occupied space reduction is the benefit of deduplication, but it happens at a more fundamental level in the storage environment than at the slide or page level of documents.

Before we can understand the benefits and impacts of data deduplication in data protection, we first need to drill down a little deeper on how it typically works in real-world scenarios.

13.1.1 INLINE VERSUS POSTPROCESSING

There are two broad processing *times* for deduplication, *inline* and *postprocessing*. These refer to *when* the deduplication activity took place. Inline deduplication is the most efficient, but comes at the expense of a higher CPU and memory load during data ingestion. In this method, as data is received by the deduplication storage system, it's immediately segmented, processed for duplicate data, usually compressed, and then written to the storage system in deduplicated format—it is never written in the original, nondeduplicated format. Such storage systems deliver optimal

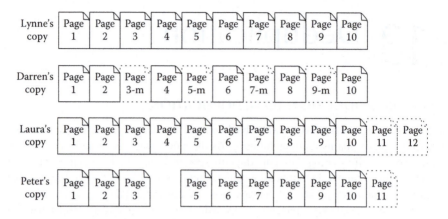

FIGURE 13.1 Document changes prior to consideration of deduplication.

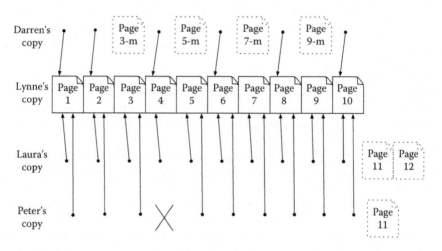

FIGURE 13.2 Slide pack after the application of deduplication.

deduplication, but it's critical for RAM to be large enough to hold as much (if not all) of the hashing tables used to compare checksums for deduplication analysis.* (The purpose of the checksums will be explained in Section 13.1.2.)

Postprocessing deduplication works quite differently to inline processing. For postprocessing, the storage is effectively broken into two discrete segments: a landing/staging area and a deduplication area. Data is initially ingested in its original format and is written to the landing area unmodified. At a later point in time (usually at most once a day due to the performance impact), the storage system sweeps the landing area and performs deduplication processing against all the data in it. As data is processed in the landing area, relevant pointers and unique data is added

<hr />

* Larger deduplication appliances capable of addressing a petabyte or more of actual physical storage may come with upward of 384–512 GB of RAM.

to the deduplication pool, and the processed data removed from the landing area. All this is *supposedly* transparent to the systems using the storage. We say "supposedly" because unless large blackout windows are observed where the system is not used, or solid-state storage is used, the additional IO load from such an intensive operation almost invariably has a noticeable impact on the system performance.

For the most part, inline deduplication represents a considerably more efficient processing time than postprocessing, particularly when we consider the sorts of disks often used in deduplication for data protection storage: SATA and NL-SAS.* While highly efficient at delivering dense storage, neither NL-SAS nor SATA don't exactly win speed races, and depending on the purpose of the deduplication storage, a landing zone may get tens or even hundreds of terabytes added to it each day for processing. As mentioned previously, this usually makes the deduplication processing *very* IO bound, which in turn becomes very difficult to optimize for performance without adding many spindles, or using faster drives.

There are also some storage arrays that support a hybrid model of inline *and* postprocessing, whereby the normal approach is to perform inline processing, but in situations where the incoming IO load is extreme, they fall back to postprocessing. An alternative is deduplication storage that has a nondeduplication tier attached to it to handle data that doesn't deduplicate well—that is, a conventional storage region that is never reviewed for deduplicatability.

13.1.2 Variable versus Fixed Block Size Deduplication

Moving beyond inline deduplication, postprocessing or even hybrid models, the analysis mechanisms tend to be either variable- or fixed-block segmentation processing. (A third theoretical model, file-level deduplication, yields minimal benefits in the real world and is not typically considered.)

Regardless of whether we use fixed- or variable-block deduplication, the overall analysis works in the following way:

- Segment data into blocks
- For each data block:
  - Calculate the checksum of the block.
  - Compare the checksum calculated against the hash/database of previously stored blocks.
  - If the block is unique:
    - Compress the data (for some systems).
    - Store the block and the new checksum.
  - If the block is not unique:
    - Store a pointer to the block and discard the duplicate data.

The data stream being processed is therefore stored as a series of pointers to blocks within the deduplication storage, and those pointers will be to either newly stored unique data or existing data. It then becomes the responsibility of the data

---

* NL-SAS refers to "near line serial attached SCSI," an evolution of SCSI that allows SATA drives to be connected into storage arrays more efficiently.

deduplication storage system to ensure no common data is deleted before *all* references to it are deleted and equally to clean up that orphaned data that is no longer referenced by anything. (That processing is typically referred to as *garbage collection*.) This data stream segment processing is shown in Figure 13.3.

Fixed-block segmentation, as you might imagine from the name, is where all data being processed is split into segments of exactly the same size, regardless of the type of the data or the amount of it. Spreadsheets, documents, presentations, databases, multimedia files, or virtual machine images are all split into the same

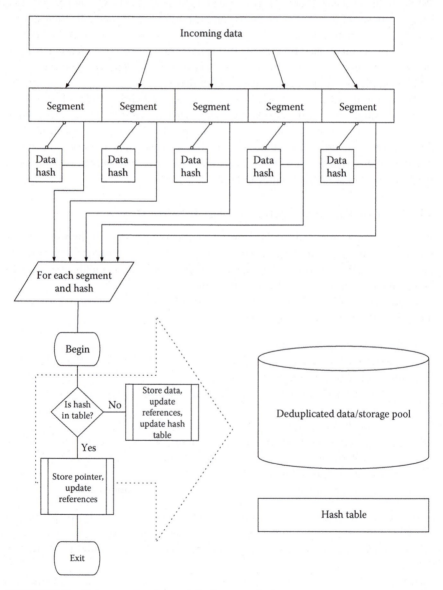

FIGURE 13.3 Data segmentation and checksum analysis.

size blocks, and segmentation processing (as described previously) is done against each of these blocks.

While fixed-block segmentation allows for fast *segmentation* of data being processed, it's not necessarily optimal for *any* of the data being processed. A larger block size may yield better deduplication statistics for databases or virtual machine images, but may result in almost no analysis of smaller files such as word processing files and spreadsheets. Additionally, small *inserts* of data into blocks that have otherwise previously been backed up can result in a somewhat inefficient subsequent backup due to changed block boundaries.

For variable block segmentation, the deduplication system will perform a preliminary analysis on the data to determine its type, and subsequently pick a segment size likely to yield the best deduplication results. Word processing documents and spreadsheets might be allocated a much smaller block size than the incoming data stream from, say, a database. Consider again the data-insertion point made earlier: in variable block-sized deduplication, the system can logically isolate the new data into relatively small blocks, keeping overall deduplication at a much higher level.

Generally speaking, variable block-based deduplication may require slightly more processing time for preliminary data segmentation but can yield more optimized deduplication, particularly when the data being received for deduplication is a broad mix, or data that is still under active use and is regularly modified.

13.1.3 SOURCE VERSUS TARGET DEDUPLICATION

Particularly when we consider deduplication systems for backup and recovery, another factor for consideration is whether deduplication happens at the *source*, *target*, or even a mixed model. This refers to which machine or system is responsible for performing some or all of the deduplication function. Since this is largely applicable only in backup and recovery environments, it will be covered in greater detail later in this chapter.

13.1.4 DEDUPLICATION POOL SIZE

The size of the deduplication pool directly impacts the overall level of benefit one gets from deduplication. The larger the comparison base of data for deduplication, the more likely duplicate content will be found and data reduction will be achieved.

While this seems to create an obvious need for deduplication pool size to be kept as large as possible, the pool size can vary wildly between the implementations performed by various vendors in the marketplace. Leading technologies will typically perform deduplication across an entire storage array, where *all* data ingested for deduplication is typically compared and evaluated. Less-effective implementations may limit deduplication storage pools to arbitrary sizes (e.g., 64 or 128 TB), or individual shelves of disk drives, incoming data types or collections of stream counts, or even something as basic as individual virtual tapes or clusters of virtual tapes within a virtual tape library.

The simplest lesson here is that the effectiveness of deduplication and return on investment from it will be limited by the size of the deduplication comparison pool, so this should be as large as possible.

13.2   WHAT DOES AND DOESN'T DEDUPLICATE?

Not all data is created equally, and the less equal data is, the less likely will it yield
to deduplication techniques. Deduplication ultimately depends on finding common
data patterns that are identical—regardless of whether that's within the same files
or across an entire data stream. Multimedia files (image, audio, or photos) tend to
deduplicate poorly for instance due to space-efficient encoding algorithms used to
save these files.

There are two other very good examples of data that typically yields little to no
deduplication—compressed files and encrypted files. Considering compressed files
first, think about what compression does—it eliminates duplicate data. Therefore,
if you compress a file and it drops from 1 GB to 200 MB, deduplication on the
remaining 200 MB will yield no savings. Similarly, the best encryption techniques
work by removing patterns that might yield an attacker a vector to decrypt the data.
For example, the very basic Caesar ("ROT13") cipher, where letters have their position rotated by 13 characters in the alphabet, can be trivially compromised by a
frequency analysis of letters. While "e" is the most common letter in the English
language, with the ROT13 cipher applied, "r" will become the most common letter
in English language text. To avoid such compromises, modern encryption techniques
highly *randomize* the data and usually even compress it before encryption to further
confuse attempted analysis by ensuring pre- and postencrypted data are of different
sizes. In such situations, encrypted data sent to a deduplication system will typically
be stored with no space saving at all.

While this may not seem much of an issue for, say, a single file, such scenarios are
not typically encountered in isolation. Databases configured to generate compressed/
encrypted backups each day would make a substantially undesirable impact on deduplication storage.

Of course, compressed and encrypted data are just two examples of where deduplication will struggle. Other areas include video and audio files, and even photos.
For instance, remembering the prior point about multimedia files, a medical diag-
nostics company that generates and stores magnetic resonance images (MRIs) and
ultrasounds would find deduplication a poor choice, either for primary storage or
backup and recovery storage.

Depending on the use case for the deduplication, some savings can still be
achieved in backing up data that doesn't readily deduplicate. In particular, a 100 GB
file that doesn't deduplicate sent to deduplication storage as part of a one-off backup
obviously won't yield any real savings—the same file copied during the *second*
backup cycle will deduplicate against the first, and so on. While this is still less
than ideal, it does help to demonstrate the intended workload of the deduplication
storage, which can impact what sort of level of deduplication is achieved against it
over time. This variance can usually be considered in terms of *recent* deduplication versus *global* deduplication. The 100 GB file when first backed up would get a
very poor recent deduplication statistic (say, 1.01:1), but cumulatively over a series
of weeks if the data truly is static, it could yield much better global deduplication
statistics. Returning to our previous MRI example, we can see that while the initial backup will yield little to no deduplication, subsequent backups of the same

unchanging data should deduplicate well. (However, this arguably points to a better strategy of writing such data to highly protected archive storage instead and excluding it from backup cycles.)

Clearly then the deduplicatability of data within an environment will depend on multiple overlapping factors. For this reason, most vendors and integrators will be eager to perform deduplication assessments against intended workloads. This can avoid the dissatisfaction of spending potentially large amounts of money on deduplication only to find a reduction of just say, 1.5–1.

13.3   COST CONSIDERATIONS

Comparing X TB of deduplication storage to X TB of conventional storage is not in any way a meaningful process. It is, to use the vernacular, comparing apples to oranges.

When comparing costs for these two storage types, there should be an estimate (based on a deduplication assessment) of what sort of deduplication ratios are likely to be achieved given the real data in the environment. Thus, if a deduplication system of 50 TB has been priced and will cost $X, it should *not* be compared to 50 TB of conventional storage (which would likely cost considerably lesser than $X). Instead, if an assessment yields an understanding that the 50 TB of deduplication storage will *actually* store 500 TB of data, then that cost should be compared against 500 TB (±10%) of the conventional storage. This is a fundamental mistake often made when comparing costs of deduplicated versus conventional storage.

Further, and particularly when dealing with more than just a few TB of deduplication storage, the other obvious cost consideration that will need to be applied will be power, cooling, and the physical footprint of the unit. For example, considering just the physical footprint, consider a deduplication system offering 50 TB of raw storage. To reach this using, say, 4 TB hard drives, this would potentially require

- 13 drives (12.5) for the raw storage, *or*
- 15 drives for RAID-6 across the entire drive set, *or*
- 16 drives for RAID-6 across the entire drive set *and* a hot spare, *or*
- 2 × (9 drives in RAID-6) + 2 hot spares, yielding 20 drives.

While the first option is sheer foolishness, any of the other options would be possible depending on the potential use of the storage and the acceptable performance impact of rebuild time.

If we assume that this will successfully store up to 500 TB of data prior to deduplication, we'd compare the drive footprint not against a 50 TB conventional array, but a 500 TB conventional array.

Even without any RAID or redundancy, 500 TB of conventional storage will immediately require 125 hard drives. If we use sets of 9 drives in RAID-6, with just 2 global hot spares, there'd be 17.8 RAID groups in the storage pool—so 18 × 9 drives plus another 2 hot spares—162 drives in total.

This is where the real comparison starts for deduplicated versus nondeduplicated storage: Using 15-drive shelves, it's entirely plausible to fit 20 drives in 6 rack units (RU) of occupied space. Assuming a similar density for the conventional storage you'd instead require 33RU for conventional storage—almost an entire full-height rack (42RU). By the time you add the storage controller/head, the deduplication storage might be sitting comfortably in 8RU, but the conventional storage will have filled an entire rack or maybe even overflowed into a second rack.

When companies with datacenters employ people to ruthlessly monitor the number of rack squares occupied in the datacenter, as well as the cooling costs and power requirements for the datacenter, you can immediately understand why this footprint reduction is so desired—particularly as data continues to explosively grow in many organizations.

13.4 DEDUPLICATION CONSIDERATIONS FOR DATA PROTECTION IN PRIMARY STORAGE

When considering deduplication for primary storage, the key considerations typically fall into one of the two following categories:

1. Reliability
2. Performance

While we should *always* be concerned about the reliability of a primary storage system, the risk of individual component failure causing a more serious data disruption does indisputably increase when deduplication is in place, as evidenced by the cautionary statement, "Don't put all your eggs in the one basket." (In this sense, consider deduplicated storage to be a bit like fruit juice concentrate: the loss of 1 L of regular fruit juice means just 1 L of juice lost; the loss of 1 L of fruit juice concentrate might result in 10 or 20 L of reconstituted juice being lost.)

In a similar vein to how current snapshot techniques just capture the *changed* blocks between the original and a snapshot, deduplication can be considered to be extremely dense storage. Reverting to our introductory example of a 50 TB deduplication storage providing 500 TB of actual capacity based on a 10:1 reduction ratio, the loss of even 1 GB of data will have a considerably more devastating impact. A single 1 GB "chunk" on the deduplication store may be referred to dozens or even hundreds of times,* and so if (somehow) that chunk of deduplicated storage were to be either unexpectedly deleted or corrupted, it would have a much higher impact on the failure of a single LUN providing storage for a single host or virtualization server.

While deduplication storage systems will typically "lock away" any conventional back-end operating system access, it's equally the case that most vendors will have the means of circumventing these lock-outs for critical intervention. Such back-door access methods to a core operating system rarely remain secret, so in some cases at least it's entirely conceivable a disgruntled employee with administrator access to

---

* Consider, for instance, primary flash-based deduplication storage for virtual machines or virtual desktops. If the operating system between all virtual machines is the same, and there are hundreds of virtual machines on the deduplication storage, there will be very densely utilized deduplication blocks relating to the operating systems regardless of any other common data.

deduplication storage could cause considerable corruption. Of course, that's not the only possible scenario; human error generally can still play a factor—deleting the wrong pool of deduplication storage could have a catastrophic impact compared to a standard LUN deletion, and firmware or controller corruption errors while largely a thing of the past are not as yet unheard of.

The result of course is that deduplication storage must be rigorously protected— considerably more so than conventional production storage. Returning to the egg metaphor: if you're putting all your eggs in one basket, you really need to make sure it's a top quality, incredibly strong basket that has exceptional security.

Performance plays a factor at all times, but we'll consider the cost of *rehydrating* data. This refers to reconstructing the original data out of deduplicated storage. A 100 GB virtual machine image may have deduplicated down to 12 GB of storage, but if we need to replicate that virtual machine image, will the replication be done against the original data or the deduplicated data? Deduplication is *not* an industry standard. Each vendor will implement deduplication differently, so the only way to perform fully deduplicated replication is to use deduplication storage systems from the *same* vendor for both source and target.* When we consider the need to rigorously protect deduplication storage, this will create a fundamental requirement to replicate, which means the previous example of a 50 TB deduplication storage system will in all but the most specific of examples usually end up being 2 × 50 TB deduplication systems with replication. Otherwise, regardless of whether conventional storage is selected for the replication target *or* another vendor deduplication storage system is selected as a replication target, the data replicated between the sites will be fully rehydrated as part of the process.

The other protection-related performance consideration for deduplication in primary storage relates to what is commonly referred to as garbage collection. The nature of deduplication is that data deleted from an individual host accessing the deduplication storage cannot be immediately deleted from the deduplication storage. Regardless of whether the deduplication storage pool is global, compartmentalized to multiple systems, or even evaluated only against a single accessing system, a single file on a host will not in any way be guaranteed to have a 1:1 correlation to a single chunk or block of data on the deduplication system. Therefore, when a system that is using deduplication storage *deletes* content, this will typically trigger only a pointer erasure on the storage. The deduplication storage will report that the data is deleted, but processing the deletion beyond a simple pointer removal may not occur for hours if not days.

Garbage collection therefore is the process whereby deduplication storage will complete a number of cleanup steps, typically including at least the following:

- Removing chunks of data that are unique and not referred to by *any* pointers on the storage system
- Performing consistency checks against the data that remains

---

* Depending on the maturity of the storage vendor, your mileage may still vary considerably even with a common storage vendor.

Depending on the type of system and how it's used, additional checks relating to aging of time-locked data, rebalancing of stored data across drives, maintenance of hash tables, cross-referencing of checksum hash tables against stored data, and even moving infrequently used data to alternate storage tiers may all be performed during garbage collection activities.

These activities, as you may well imagine, can potentially be IO and/or CPU/RAM intensive on the deduplication storage. To mitigate or even avoid this, deduplication storage systems may have one or more of the following garbage collection control algorithms assigned:

1. *Garbage collect only runs during certain windows*—In this scenario, a specific window (time of day, day of week, or even both) might be assigned to garbage collection tasks. If the tasks do not complete within this time, they may be either aborted without finalized processing taking place or aborted at the point they reached and continued the next day.
2. *Garbage collect aborts if system load grows too high*—In this scenario, garbage collection will be scheduled to run at a time when it is expected system load will be low enough that it will not be impacted by collection. If the system load grows too high, the garbage collection might be aborted, and an alert generated.
3. *Garbage collect has a performance ceiling assigned to it*—In this scenario, the garbage collection will be configured such that it cannot exceed a particular percentage of system resources (e.g., 40%), and its progress slowed or shaped accordingly. This works in much the same way that many RAID systems allow for performance inhibitors to be placed on RAID reconstruction.

Garbage collection is an essential task in deduplication storage—if it's not performed routinely enough, the utilized target storage may grow until it becomes full. This can even become a vicious cycle—garbage collection aborted because it takes too long to run and will only *increase* the amount of storage to be considered on the next garbage collection run. For this reason, it's not unheard of to encounter organizations that have mismanaged their deduplication storage *and* their garbage collection cycles and ended up in a position where they've had to suspend use of the deduplication system for *days* to allow complete garbage collection operations to take place.

13.5 DEDUPLICATION CONSIDERATIONS FOR DATA PROTECTION IN BACKUP AND RECOVERY SYSTEMS

13.5.1 THE CASE FOR DEDUPLICATION

While deduplication storage systems are growing in popularity for primary storage (particularly all-flash arrays), they've usually offered some of the highest cost savings and efficiency gains in backup and recovery environments.

Consider a typical backup and recovery environment circa 2001: this was the period where tape libraries still ruled the earth. Much like their dinosaur ancestors, mammoth tape libraries were potentially huge beasts occupying a large datacenter footprint. Robot heads would swing to and fro at times seemingly constantly to feed tapes into tape drives, and operators would approach tape exchange ports with sometimes buckets full of fresh tapes or to take away the accumulated media from the previous night.

Despite their speed and capacity, tapes have largely fallen out of favor as a direct backup target for many organizations for several reasons, notably as follows:

- Contention
    - *Media*: Tapes are physical items occupying physical space, and a tape drive cannot use more than one tape at a single time. Thus, the ability to facilitate a recovery request is directly impacted by the number of free tape drives available to load tapes.
    - *Host*: Massive data growth within organizations has often led to large pools of data being concentrated in particular locations, and sending all this data across busy LAN links may not always be an option (particularly in pre-10Gbit ethernet environments); tape drives shared via fiber-channel among multiple hosts can still only be accessed by a single host at any one time, and the overall environment reliability can be greatly impacted in such environments.
- *Access (seek) time*: No matter how fast tape gets, it will remain considerably slower than disk for the initial access time, not to mention any data seek operations. The amount of time it takes to start reading from a tape will typically be measured in the tens of seconds assuming that the tape has to be loaded and then a seek operation performed; for disk, the time will be at most usually a few milliseconds.
- *Service times*: Tape or tape drive failures are notorious for causing lengthy timeout delays in environments. A malfunctioning tape may take half an hour or more to successfully timeout, re-spool, and eject from a tape drive, and during that time, the drive (and backup/recovery bandwidth) will remain unavailable to the backup and recovery system. In an environment with *shared* tape access between multiple hosts via, say, fiber channel, a single tape drive fault may impact multiple hosts and even primary production hosts, necessitating reboots or lengthy pauses on backup/recovery functionality.
- *Sequential access*: The sequential access nature of tape leaves it limited in its usefulness that it's highly efficient for high-speed writes and reads of large amounts of data is indisputable, but for newer enterprise backup techniques such as instantly accessing and booting a virtual machine from protection storage, this is no longer sufficient.
- *Streaming speed*: While it's indisputable that tape *can* be of high speed, that speed suffers a sharp drop-off when the incoming data speed drops; this is nonlinear based on tape drives having minimum or step-based ideal speeds.

A tape drive capable of writing at, say, 160 MB/s may not seamlessly accommodate an incoming data stream of 100 MB/s, and instead may need to step down to just 80 MB/s, and so on.

- *Cost of operators*: Like it or not, we live in a time where cost efficiency is a golden goose for most organizations and shareholders. Employees cost a business more than just their salaries, so it's often quite cost-prohibitive to achieve true lights-out operations with tape libraries. As soon as someone needs to load or unload media, that becomes an ongoing cost to the business.
- *Reliability*: Tapes are by their very nature relatively fragile—if not in use then in transport and storage. Like disk drives, tapes may not readily survive being dropped, but unlike disk drives, tapes are also more likely to be physically transported. During the transport, tapes are more likely to be exposed to environmental changes (e.g., temperature and humidity) that may impact the physical reliability. Finally, tapes are actually only one-half of the equation—tape drives are equally highly mechanical devices, and a single malfunctioning tape drive may cause damage to multiple tapes.

Except in the largest of "big data" situations, tape therefore has been relegated in most organizations to one of the following functions:

- Cheap off-siting
- Cheap archive
- Cheap expansion

(It should be noted in each situation you could increasingly replace *cheap* with "*cheap*," as it becomes more a reflection of perception than actuality.)

As disk decreased in price, tape started to be eclipsed. The starting point was using disk storage as staging or landing areas for backup. This was "B2D2T"—backup to disk (transfer) to tape. A business might deploy a 5 TB LUN of SATA disk where all overnight backups would be written. During the day, the backups would be staged out to tape for longer-term storage and the disk space freed up for the next night's backup (where required). Over time, it became obvious that recoveries requested from data still on disk could typically be facilitated much faster, but it was still acknowledged that buying sufficient disk to house even a relatively small backup cycle (say, a weekly full and subsequent incrementals) could be cost prohibitive.

It was here that deduplication entered into its own. With deduplication applied, that 5 TB-landing zone could suddenly hold 20, 30, or 50 TB of backups, and it became *considerably* more useful.

Data growth has not necessarily been accompanied by data uniqueness. With virtualization in the mid-range now practically the norm, *data* often includes the operating system and application imagines installed on hosts. In particular, the use of traditional backup agents installed within virtualized guests has continued to decline with increased functionality for virtual image backups. (This will be covered in detail in Chapter 14.)

More generally, however, consider typical backup lifecycles. An organization might use the following schedules for backup:

- Daily
  - Full backup on either a Friday evening, Saturday, or Sunday
  - Incremental backups for the rest of the days in the week
  - These backups would be retained for 5 weeks
- Monthly
  - Full backup once a week to be retained for 13 months
- Yearly
  - Full backup once or twice a year to be retained for 7–10 years

While the nature of an incremental backup is "that which has changed," it's fair to say the majority of the data in each of the full backups in a cycle such as that mentioned earlier will remain relatively static for *most* systems. A database for instance may experience 5% growth month on month, but much of the content *in* the database, once ingested, will remain the same. This could equally be said of most file servers as well.

Assume then a 4 TB file server where on a month-to-month basis, there is only a 5% change in data content. On the cycle mentioned earlier, there'll be, say, 17 full backups of the system performed every year—the 12 monthly backups, 1–2 yearly backups, and 5 weekly backups.*

If this system were being backed up to either tape or conventional disk, it would require 68 TB of storage. (A 2% daily change† would add another 2.4 TB of storage requirements—so just for a year's worth of backups, 70.4 TB of storage would be used to protect just 4 TB.)

Deduplication, however, would yield a considerably more economical result. A basic analysis would suggest even with a 5% month-on-month change that the full backups might conceivably achieve ratios of, say,

- 4 TB for first full
- (5% of 4 TB) × 16 additional fulls

This would yield 7.2 TB of occupied actual storage. While the incrementals aren't counted in that, that's outweighed by the rather obvious point that there's been no deduplication applied to the first full backup, either. If that achieved even a 4:1 deduplication ratio (which is reasonably conservative for fileserver data), then instead of 68 TB used for conventional storage to hold the full backups from 4 TB, we might actually squeak in at under lesser than 2 TB:

- 1 TB occupied space for first full backup
- 5% of 1 TB × 16 additional fulls

---

* A typical backup strategy will see the weekly full skipped when it's time to run a monthly full, and the monthly/weekly full skipped when it's time to run a yearly full.

† A 2% daily change and a 5% month-on-month change can readily be reconciled by remembering files or data may be repeatedly revised as they are worked on.

There is a substantially reduced data footprint using deduplication; in this example we can see 4 TB being protected in just 2 TB of occupied space versus 68 TB using nondeduplicating storage. Even if we add a second deduplication system for replication between sites, we still yield a considerably better storage efficiency than conventional storage would.

The benefits of deduplication continue to grow (unless a particularly limited version of deduplication is used): most deduplication will have a broader analysis pool than the individual systems being backed up. So cumulatively, the deduplication benefits will considerably scale. It is not unusual, for instance, for organizations to deploy even relatively small deduplication systems with the intent of keeping 6–10 weeks of data online only to discover savings that allow for 6–9 *months* of data being kept online.

These types of savings and efficiencies have seen a very high adoption rate of deduplication in the otherwise reasonably conservative technical field of backup and recovery. The NetWorker Information Hub,* for instance, conducts a yearly survey of how and where organizations are using EMC NetWorker® within their environment and since 2010 has been asking respondents for information on their deduplication take-up:

- 2010—32% respondents using deduplication
- 2011—36% respondents using deduplication
- 2012—63% respondents using deduplication
- 2013—73% respondents using deduplication
- 2014—78% respondents using deduplication

In just a relatively few short years, deduplication has gone from practically bleeding edge to mainstream. While this represents only a single product, it's particularly worth considering that natively NetWorker does *not* natively perform deduplication: instead, it leverages external deduplication technology via specific integration points, and therefore businesses using NetWorker *and* deduplication have made a purposeful choice (rather than it just being a default feature).

Deduplication neatly solves (for many businesses and data types) one of the biggest core problems with backup and recovery—handling explosive data growth and retention requirements.

In short, for a great many businesses, it's no longer a question of *why are you using deduplication* but rather, *why aren't you using deduplication?*

13.5.2 Revisiting Source versus Target Deduplication

Source versus *target* deduplication was briefly mentioned in the introduction to deduplication. This refers to *where* some or all of the processing for deduplication occurs. To understand the implications, we'll consider a backup and recovery system with three hosts using deduplication storage as the destination for backups.

For a target-based deduplication system, this will mean each time any of the hosts need to backup, they transfer their data in their original format to the deduplication

---

* https://nsrd.info/blog. This site is published and maintained by the author, Preston de Guise.

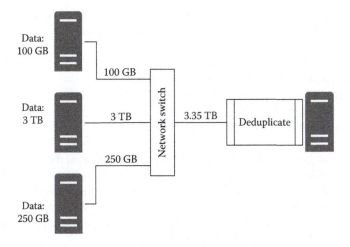

FIGURE 13.4   Representation of target-based deduplication data flow.

storage system. The deduplication system then deduplicates the data (either inline, or as part of postprocessing activities), thus performing all the "heavy lifting" for the deduplication. This is shown in Figure 13.4.

For deduplication occurring at the source, plug-ins or software of some variety will be installed on each of the hosts to be backed up, and these plug-ins will integrate with the backup process. While an individual host will not have a full understanding of all the deduplicated data stored on a deduplication system, it will be able to *at least* perform the basic block segmentation and communicate with the deduplication storage to determine whether or not individual segments need to be stored on the target or simply associated with the backup based on the hashing/checksums performed against the segments. The data that *is* sent across the network may then have further deduplication operations performed on it once received, depending on the system. Some backup and recovery deduplication systems will actually store local copies of the individual host's hashing/segment checksum information to further optimize the backup process. This can make a tangible improvement on backup efficiency. Assume a deduplication system checksums all data segments using a 30 byte checksum. If no local hash table is maintained, *all* checksums must be sent to the deduplication appliance. Assuming 100 GB of data on the source side and the data is segmented on average into 16 KB blocks, we could calculate the checksum data size as follows:

- 100 GB is 104,857,600 KB.
- This would generate 6,533,600 × 16 KB segments.
- Checksums for 6,533,600 segments would occupy 196,608,000 bytes at 30-byte checksums per segment.
- Total checksum data would be 187.5 MB.

Now, assume local hash tables were used and only 5% of the data on the system had changed (5 GB). Therefore, only checksums for approximately 5 GB of data would need to be sent to the deduplication system for global deduplication analysis. We could calculate the checksum data size for this as follows:

- 5 GB is 5,242,880 KB.
- This would generate 327,680 × 16 KB segments.
- Checksums for 327,680 segments would occupy 9,830,400 bytes at 30 byte checksums per segment.
- Total checksum data would be 9.375 MB.

Using source-based hash tables for initial segment analysis, the amount of checksum data sent between the source and the deduplication appliance has decreased by *more than* an order of magnitude in our earlier example. Such savings can represent a considerable efficiency increase over WAN or even 1 Gbit link speeds and have been known to eliminate the need for businesses to deploy separated, high-speed backup networks in LAN backup scenarios.

A conceptual diagram of source-based deduplication is shown in Figure 13.5.

A key advantage of source-based deduplication is it can lead to significantly smaller amounts of data being sent across the network during a backup operation, albeit with a trade-off that the CPU and memory load on the host sending the data is sometimes significantly higher than a standard transfer. Some deduplication systems may offset this by using an *incrementals forever* approach; rather than periodically reprocessing *all* the data on a backup client, sufficient backup metadata will be maintained to only ever necessitate the processing of new or changed data. This means only the first backup will represent a significantly higher potential load on the backup clients—all subsequent backups, while still involving higher CPU load,

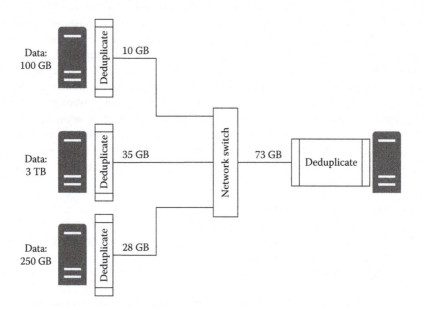

FIGURE 13.5   Source-based deduplication data flow.

will run for a significantly shorter period of time. When we consider the CPU load associated with sustained data transfer over the network for a full, nondeduplicated backup, the net impact not only is considerably smaller but also lasts a considerably shorter period of time.

There is additionally a hybrid approach to source/target deduplication processing, whereby both the individual hosts backing up *and* the backup destination will support deduplication. This serves to significantly scale out deduplication operations: systems that do *not* support deduplication (e.g., NAS hosts being backed up via NDMP) can still send data in a standard format across the deduplication system for processing, but more conventional operating systems where agents can be installed can perform a subset of deduplication tasks in coordination with the deduplication system, in order to still reduce the amount of data being sent across the network.

13.5.3 ADVANCED DEDUPLICATION FEATURES

By its very nature, deduplication is not the type of operation that can be performed by a "dumb" appliance. Regardless of whether the operation is performed inline or via postprocessing, deduplication requires intense data analysis. As such, deduplication systems have the potential to provide more than just a "big bucket" of storage: they can provide a very intelligent big bucket.

This intelligent operation is beginning to unfold in numerous additional integration points. Some deduplication appliances for instance offer *virtual synthetic full backups*. We may recall that a synthetic full backup is one where the backup and recovery software processes previously completed full and incremental backups, combining them into a new full backup without any processing being performed on the actual backup client. The term *virtual synthetic full* therefore refers to the virtual construction of a synthetic full backup.

Synthetic full backups offer at least one, if not two, distinct advantages depending on the environment:

- For larger systems where a standard full backup will take too much time or create too much a processing load on the client, the processing is off-loaded to the backup server (or another nominated host).
- For remote systems where a standard full backup will take too long to traverse the network, a full backup can still be periodically generated without needing to send all the data to the backup environment again.

In either case, the actual processing load for the synthetic full falls to the backup environment—typically the backup server. Depending on the size or number of data sets to be evaluated, this can considerably impact the performance of a backup server, particularly if a large number of systems are configured for synthetic full backups.

Virtual synthetic full backups therefore take advantage of the intelligence of the deduplication system and its inherent use of pointers to reference data. After all, a full backup on a deduplication system is merely a collection pointers referring to actual unique data objects required to reconstruct the data. Rather than requiring rehydration of data to construct a synthetic full backup, a deduplication system supporting virtual synthetic fulls can merely construct a new reference set of data pointers equivalent to a full backup from the full and incremental backups previously stored. This not only removes the synthetic full processing time from the backup server but also can substantially reduce the entire processing time for the activity. Constructing a new full backup from 1 × 4 TB backup and 30 × 100 GB backups (in the case of monthly fulls with daily incrementals) may require up to 15 TB or more of backup data sets to be processed to create a new, say, 4.5 TB full backup. Collating and collecting a new series of pointers referring to data already on disk without needing to actually *read* the data, on the other hand, might be an order of magnitude faster.

Deduplication systems that tightly integrate with backup products for generating *registered* backup copies can represent a considerable time saving. Consider in Section 13.4, where one of the topics discussed was replication. This similarly plays a role in backup and recovery use of the technology. When the backup system itself is deduplication-capable,* one would expect that two systems deployed in different sites would be able to replicate deduplicated backups between each other, thereby eliminating the requirement to rehydrate data or send data between sites if it is already present at the target.

Not all backup and recovery systems are natively deduplication systems as well, and it's equally common to see backup systems deployed using deduplication appliances as targets. In this case, even if identical or otherwise compatible deduplication systems are used at the primary and secondary backup sites, efficient replication of deduplicated data may not be guaranteed. In particular, one of the following scenarios will take place:

1. The backup replication will be initiated and executed entirely at the backup server level, resulting in a complete rehydration of data from the source for transmission to the target, with deduplication taking place at the target again.
2. The backup replication will be initiated and executed entirely at the deduplication appliance level, without any reference to or awareness of the processing by the backup system. Thus, the replicated data will be "unknown" to the backup system and may even cause issues if it becomes unexpectedly available to it.
3. The backup system will integrate with the deduplication system such that the backup system will *instruct* the deduplication system to replicate the data. The data will be replicated in deduplicated format, but the backup system will register the replicated data as an independent copy.

In the first option, the downside is a rather serious one: whatever the *original* size of the backup is, it will be the same amount of data that will be replicated. What's more, the data will be read from the source deduplication system, rehydrated for

---

* That is, the backup system is itself a deduplication system.

transit, sent across a link potentially slower than the normal LAN speed, and then deduplicated for storage on the target system.

The second option may reduce the data being replicated between sites, but at a cost: the backup system will be unaware of the replicated data. This in itself will yield two different scenarios: either that data will need to be cataloged prior to its use or it will appear *entirely* identical to the backup system, making it critical for the backup administrator to prevent the data being simultaneously available at both sites. (For instance, consider replicated virtual tape media: backup products do not typically accept the notion of the same *tape* being in two different tape libraries, virtual or otherwise.) Thus, the saving in data replication time might be entirely undone by the additional management overhead of either cataloging data the backup system should already be aware of, or solving errors created by identical data appearing in multiple locations.

Backup-integrated replication, however, represents the Goldilocks scenario—the data is replicated in its deduplicated format, without any rehydration or reconstruction having taken place, *and* the backup system is fully aware of and able to use the backup copy.

Other advanced functionality available in deduplication systems will be covered in Chapter 14. It's important to note this is still very much a young and evolving field: storage and data protection vendors are increasingly keen to increase the return on investment on backup and recovery systems, and the way to do this is to increase their utility. What was once a huge bucket where backups went to but were infrequently retrieved from* is losing what limited appeal it did have. Intelligent storage systems integrated tightly into the backup and recovery system are allowing backup to evolve from *merely* a corporate insurance system to something more practically useful on a day-to-day basis.

13.6 SUMMARY

Deduplication has now become a mainstay feature in data protection systems for many companies, and is starting to see wider adoption in primary storage systems as a means of mitigating storage costs either via reducing the amount of enterprise flash required or via automatically reducing the storage footprint required for infrequently accessed data.

Deduplication has the potential to introduce considerable savings and benefits to organizations when deployed correctly but does require careful architectural considerations to match functionality to business needs, ensure data deduplicatability, and anticipate maintenance windows associated with deduplication. The most critical consideration, as we've mentioned before, is the impact of data rehydration. A WAN-based source-side deduplication backup solution may very well meet or exceed *all* SLAs for backup *and* replication, but at recovery time still need to send data from the backup system to the recovering client in rehydrated format, thereby failing to meet the most critical SLA—recoverability. Of course, a conventional backup system will struggle on recovery (as well as the backup and replication SLAs), but this does serve

---

* One customer ironically acknowledged this by deploying a backup server they named *sump.*

to highlight despite its utility, deduplication is not a silver bullet that obviates the need for appropriate data protection architecture.

Companies that fail to plan deduplication appropriately will not achieve the high benefits already secured by so many businesses that have already successfully deployed this technology.

14 Protecting Virtual Infrastructure

14.1 INTRODUCTION

Virtualization has become absolute mainstream in most organizations. What was once the preserve of mainframe environments only has become so pervasive that a *lack* of virtualization is more likely to elicit surprise than the implementation thereof.

Virtualization tackles key IT problems for many businesses, including but not limited to

- Deployment speed
- Hardware compatibility
- Manageability
- Cost efficiency
- Power efficiency
- System reliability
- High availability

Ironically, as previously dedicated workloads have been consolidated onto virtual infrastructure and allowed for innovative solutions to the issues mentioned earlier, it introduced a mixed bag of benefits and challenges in the data protection space. These are best addressed by tackling each relevant data protection activity in its own right.

14.2 SNAPSHOTS

Our earlier chapter dedicated to snapshots introduced many of the considerations, advantages, and disadvantages that come from using snapshot technology within data protection, and those carry through to the use of snapshots within virtual infrastructure.

Snapshots play such a large part in virtual infrastructure protection that you could arguably say a full machine snapshot is the holy grail of system administration. While volume management systems (e.g., Veritas Volume Manager, Logical Volume Manager [LVM], Microsoft VSS) have offered snapshot capabilities for some time, and snapshots are also readily available at the SAN and NAS level, these have usually had one substantial frustration: being divorced from the operational or configured state of the host they're associated with.

Consider for instance a Linux host using LVM: At any point a system administrator could issue a snapshot command against individual filesystems on the host,

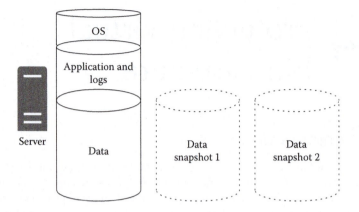

FIGURE 14.1   Traditional snapshots.

thereby creating a point in time copy of filesystem state. Yet it is rare for all content of a system to be on a single filesystem, so administrators taking a snapshot of just the data region on a server might offer protection for it, but at a cost of consistency when compared to other filesystems if it is to be rolled back.

Figure 14.1 shows this scenario: a host might have three distinct filesystems, one for the operating system, one for the data region, and one for the application/log region. In this example, we have two different snapshots taken of the "Data" filesystem. At any point the system administrator might choose to roll back to either of those snapshots and it would be perfectly valid to do so—but application logs and operating system logs stored on the other filesystems will no longer be consistent with the state of the data region. So while protection had been provided for the data region, it hadn't necessarily been provided in a sufficiently consistent way.

One obvious solution to this would be to simultaneously create a snapshot of all three filesystems—operating system, application/log, and data. Thus, the overall state of the system could be rolled back at any point. However, not all operating systems support running on filesystems that can be snapped for the OS or boot region, and since the OS must be running to support a snapshot being taken, the overall state of the host might be a little unreliable if snapshots are rolled back.

Equally, LUN level snapshots executed at a storage layer might not offer application consistent states and at best offer crash-consistent protection.

Virtualization therefore can allow for considerably easier whole-system snapshot scenarios, as shown in Figure 14.2. In such a situation, so long as all the storage devices on the virtual machine can have a snapshot taken, the snapshot becomes a purely binary operation. In particular if the virtual machine has been shut down before the snapshot has been taken, then even if it is rolled back to a particular snapshot, it should be entirely consistent on restart.

This introduces considerable efficiency improvements for many organizations: reliable and cross-filesystem consistent snapshots can be taken for an entire virtual

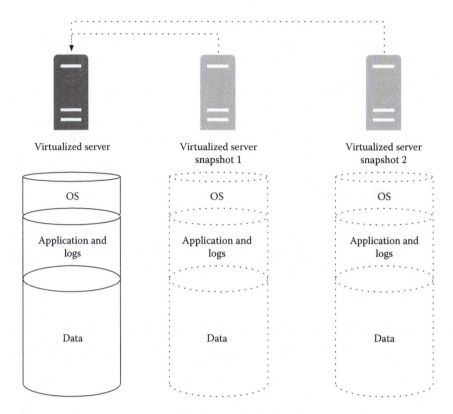

FIGURE 14.2 Snapshots in a virtualized environment.

machine practically at the click of a button before a critical maintenance activity is attempted. This applies not only to production servers but also development, lab, or training servers. (For instance, it is quite common to see virtual machine snapshots used in training environments to allow a baseline setup of a virtual machine to be reset at the conclusion of training.)

Even if a virtual machine has not been shut down before snapshot, the snapshot remains considerably more useful than a conventional per-filesystem snapshot or per-LUN snapshot, particularly when coupled with modern backup techniques. This is something we'll go into greater detail in the backup topic later in this chapter.

It is however important to note that *some* storage presented to virtual hosts may not be susceptible for snapshot operations. For instance, virtualization environments usually offer some form of *independent* and *raw* disks. An independent disk is one that is explicitly excluded from any snapshot operations taken. This might be for performance reasons or because snapshots aren't supported for the type of data to be housed on that disk. Equally, a raw disk is one where storage is presented directly to the virtual host without any virtualization layer involved, and is typically done so for specific performance requirements.

The use of such storage with virtual machines (regardless of the nomenclature of any particular virtualization system) can represent a considerable roadblock for administrators, given either of the following:

- Prevent a virtual machine from being snapshot at all, reducing the data protection options available.
- Silently skip the disks that *can't* be snapshot during a snapshot operation, allowing for the creation of a snapshot as inconsistent as if it had been done at the operating system layer in a traditional approach.

14.3 REPLICATION

Traditionally, there have been two reasons why clustering has been used within IT—for performance scaling and for high availability. While both remain valid considerations, virtual machine replication has significantly reduced the need for many organizations to consider clustering at the operating system level for high availability.

Virtual machine replication can take place in one of two different ways. The first way, shown in Figure 14.3, sees replication being handled solely within the virtualization system between two locations, which we'll refer to as the production and disaster recovery sites. In this scenario, the virtualization hypervisor(s) involved in presenting virtual machines handle the continuous or checkpoint-based replication of a virtual machine from one site to the other, updating blocks within virtual machine image files as appropriate. While an advantage of this is that replication happens at a layer quite close to the virtual machines, it can create a higher workload on the virtualization hypervisors as they manage both standard virtualization tasks *and* data replication, particularly as the number of virtual machines to be replicated between sites grows.

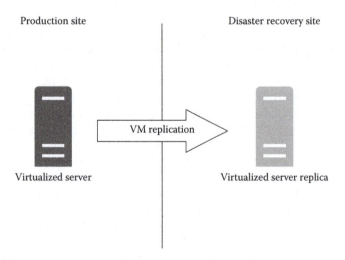

FIGURE 14.3 Virtualization layer replication.

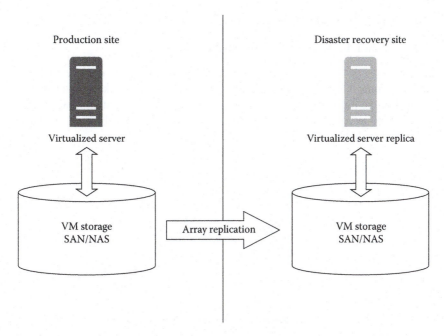

FIGURE 14.4   Array-based replication of virtual machines.

Alternately, as shown in Figure 14.4, virtual machine replication may be handled at the storage array level. In this scenario, LUNs presented to virtualization systems at the production site are replicated to an alternate site via the storage systems, thereby offloading the data processing requirement of replication between sites. This comes at the potential cost of replicating entire LUNs, and so requires careful planning between virtualization and storage administrators to ensure there is no mixing of virtual machines that require replication and virtual machines that don't require replication on the same LUNs.

The benefit this technique brings is to off-load the replication functionality from the hypervisors, and can scale better as the number of systems to be replicated increase. To be safely performed however it needs storage arrays and hypervisors to "aware" of each other's functionality.

Of course, replication is not a perfect replacement for clustering. A key feature of clustering n systems is to allow some number m to fail (where $m < n$) without impeding the delivery of services. Virtual machine replication will replicate all aspects of a virtual machine—corrupt and noncorrupt (or, at least, to specific replication checkpoints). Therefore, virtual machine replication isn't a like-for-like replacement of clustering, but more a means of rapidly standing up a disaster recovery instance of a machine after site loss (regardless of whether that's permanent or transient). Organizations can either choose to wear this risk or deploy forms of Continuous Data Protection (CDP) where the virtual machines are replicated with periodic checkpoints. Thus, if a virtual machine becomes corrupt, the replica of the virtual machine from, say, 60 minutes ago, prior to the corruption having occurred, can be activated at the alternate site (or even the local site).

14.4 BACKUP AND RECOVERY

14.4.1 IMAGE-LEVEL VERSUS IN-GUEST BACKUP

There are two distinctly different techniques virtual machines may be backed up: guest and image. Guest-based backup sees a traditional backup agent or client installed in the individual virtual machines, and the backup system treats each virtual machine as a standard client. This is often considered to be a *legacy* backup option, and is shown in Figure 14.5.

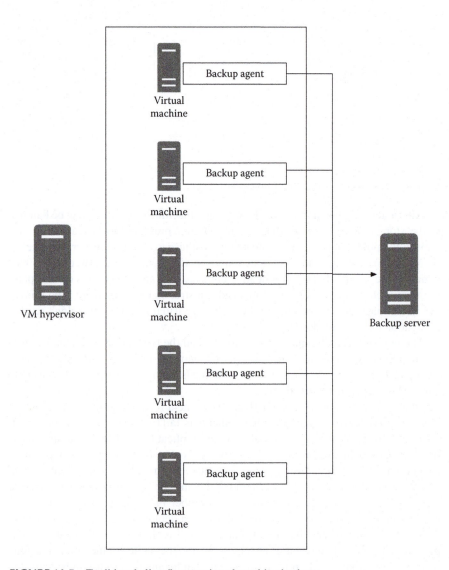

FIGURE 14.5 Traditional client/legacy virtual machine backups.

This backup technique allows for maximum granularity of control over the backup process. Backup systems supporting fine-grained control over what files or data on a client are or are not backed up will perform no differently with client software installed within a virtual machine as they would within a physical host. When virtualization was still within its infancy, this was definitely the preferred backup option. However, as virtualization has expanded and subsumed an extremely high percentage of the IT infrastructure within most businesses, this method has not scaled. To understand the *why* of this, we need to come back to one of the fundamental gains of virtualization: better resource utilization. As CPU speed and memory capacity has increased, virtualization has offered considerable cost savings by recognizing that many systems run at much lower resource utilizations than the hardware offers. A DNS server, for instance, provisioned on a dual core system with even just a modest 4 GB of RAM and dual-core CPUs, may on average never consume more than 10% of those resources. Virtualization offers a neat way around that—multiple guest systems running on a single piece of hardware with the hypervisor directing cooperative use of system resources.

This works neatly until you encounter individual systems that are resource hogs. High performance systems (be they raw compute, data manipulation or databases) can still be found deployed on physical hardware not only to provide dedicated resources, but also to ensure those high demand hosts don't strip resources from other virtualized systems that are resident on the same hypervisors.*

To put it mildly, backup software—particularly *enterprise* backup software—is always designed to be a resource hog. The entire purpose of enterprise backup software is to generate a protected copy of data as quickly as possible (or likewise, recover from that copy as quickly as possible). It is not uncommon to see poorly designed backup environments using in-guest agents to saturate many, if not all, resources within hypervisors: storage IO, network bandwidth, and CPU utilization. This of course violates a fundamental requirement of a backup and recovery system: to not unduly interfere with core operations in order to perform data protection.

Reducing load on hypervisors during backup operations is challenging when using traditional agent software installed within the individual guest operating systems. A backup administrator might carefully assemble backup policies, grouping virtual machines in such a way as to prevent any one hypervisor from becoming overloaded during the backup process, but if either virtualization administrators or the virtualization management software can migrate virtual machines between hypervisors, this work could be undone at any point. Further, since in-guest backup processes will align to standard backup processes, standard operating system backup challenges

---

* Most virtualization systems allow for resource limiting in terms of CPU and RAM, which covers initial allocation (e.g., 2 CPUs) and maximum slices of CPU time (e.g., no more than 6000 MHz), both for individual virtual machines and *pools* of particular virtual machines. However, resource limitations work only so long as you have no systems that require *maximum* resources.

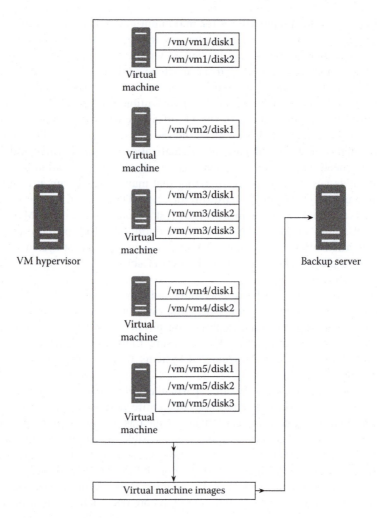

FIGURE 14.6   Image-level backup of virtual machines.

will remain—for instance, virtual clients with dense filesystems will still take longer to backup than desirable.

Gaining considerable popularity and sophistication, the second backup method for virtual machines is an *image*-level backup, as depicted in Figure 14.6. This relies on the obvious fact that each virtual machine is actually at some level a distinct collection of data files. For the purposes of simplification in Figure 14.6 only the "virtual disks" have been cited, but accompanying the virtual disks for virtual machines will typically be a number of other small files representing the current configuration and other state files.*

---

* You will recall in Chapter 11 we discussed block-based backups. Image-level backups of virtual machines closely mirror the advantages of block-based backups.

There are several distinct advantages of image-level backups. These include the following:

- When integrated with snapshots, they allow for a reasonably consistent backup.
- They do not suffer *dense filesystem* issues an in-guest backup process would.
- They can be executed in a more controlled manner to reduce hypervisor and virtual environment loading.

A typical concern with image-level backups of virtual machines is the fact that very little data within the virtual machine may change between backups, yet the virtual machine image file to be backed up may be quite large. Consider a "full Saturday, incrementals Sunday–Friday" backup schedule: if that schedule were applied to an in-guest traditional operating system agent, then only the files *in* the virtual machine that have changed will need to be backed up. On the other hand, given virtual machine disks are usually represented by flat, large files within the hypervisor, an incremental backup is effectively meaningless at a hypervisor file level.

One way of resolving this is sometimes referred to as *changed block tracking*. Rather than actually backing up the entire virtual machine disk file from the hypervisor, the backup product queries the hypervisor to find what *blocks* within the file have changed and only backs up those blocks.

The other key method to mitigate this problem is via a previously discussed topic—deduplication. Consider a virtual machine that has 50 GB of space allocated on the hypervisor for its virtual disks. A full backup will by necessity be of the entire 50 GB, but once deduplication comes into play, this will very likely be substantially reduced in size.* Subsequent backups (either as incrementals or fulls) will continue to make use of this functionality. Indeed, it is not unusual to see 20, 30, or 50:1 deduplication ratios achieved over repeated backups of virtual machines. However, image-level backups to conventional, nondeduplicating storage might be seen as extremely wasteful, consuming large amounts of space.

In short, organizations do not need to fear image-level backups of virtual machines as being a space hog so long as the appropriate infrastructure and technology is used.

There are several different methods an image-level backup can be accommodated, and most backup products will support more than one method. In the simplest scenario, agent software might be installed on the individual hypervisors, in much the same way that agent software can be installed on any physical host. However, this typically relies on the hypervisor running a complete operating system. So-called bare-metal hypervisors that maintain at most a minimal operating system, used *just* to provide the virtualization services, are typically not compatible with agent installation.

Moving beyond in-hypervisor agents, other image-level backup techniques rely on establishing either SAN- or LAN-based communications with the hypervisor. LAN-based methods are the simplest—the backup server or a proxy for the server communicates with the hypervisor and the files associated with the storage and configuration of each nominated virtual machine are transferred over the network to a backup target.

---

* Even more so, if virtual machines have been deployed with thick provisioning enabled (where the entire size of a virtual drive is allocated on creation), this may mean they contain a large amount of empty space.

While straightforward, this *does* mean the entire content of each virtual machine is transmitted across the network, which will very likely introduce LAN saturation, and definitely impact the performance of the virtualization environment. Also, unless some form of encryption is used, the data flow may be considered unsafe.* Adding encryption either requires IP encryption routers or for the hypervisor to handle the encryption, which may introduce sufficient CPU load as to negate any real benefits of moving away from guest-based traditional backups.

SAN-based backups can actually be executed in one of two separate ways. If a physical backup proxy is used, the SAN (or NAS)-based LUNs/filesystems that present storage to the virtualization hypervisors are simultaneously mapped (usually read only) to the proxy, an example of which is shown in Figure 14.7. This allows the proxy to independently access the virtual machine data and facilitate the transfer to a backup target without any actual CPU, network or memory load being placed on the hypervisor. Indeed, image-level SAN backups can (depending on the backup technology) be conducted via a physical *or* virtual proxy. For physical proxies, the SAN LUNs are presented as standard LUNs, potentially indistinguishable from a raw LUN being provisioned for storage. While this requires careful consideration to avoid data loss situations,* it also has the potential to offer very high performance.

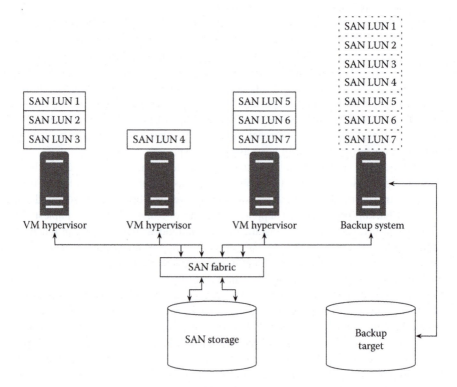

FIGURE 14.7   Physical SAN-based access to virtual machine LUNs for backup.

---

* Though admittedly no more so than any other LAN-based backup process.

However, SAN access from physical proxies is losing popularity in the market, and some vendors such as VMware are dropping support for this access method in newer releases of their hypervisor technology.

A virtual proxy on the other hand will reside on a hypervisor as a guest machine, and that hypervisor will have SAN/LUN level access to all the storage areas hosting virtual machines that are to be backed up. Hypervisor servers such as VMware ESX/vSphere allow for a "hotadd" operation to be performed, where shared data stores hosting virtual machines are presented to the virtualized backup proxy. An example of this is shown in Figure 14.8.

While such a technique reincorporates some of the backup workload within the virtualized infrastructure, it remains a viable option due to the reduction in physical hardware requirements (particularly if it also utilizes source-side deduplication).

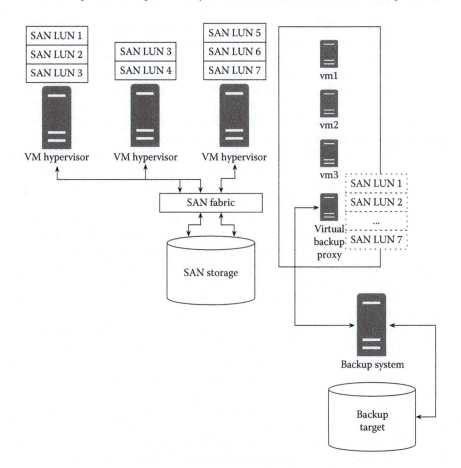

FIGURE 14.8   Virtualized image-based SAN level backup.

---

* Certain operating systems, if not prepared for the contingency of being presented LUNs they do not have read/write or exclusive access to, may in fact write header or disk partition information to new LUNs as they are presented—a particularly disastrous situation.

A physical image-level backup proxy is likely to require dedicated fiber-channel HBAs, NICs, and so on—then, to add redundancy so that backups may continue in the event of a hardware failure, a *second* proxy should also be deployed. By keeping the proxies within the virtual infrastructure, all the (virtual) hardware they will require is already provided by the hypervisors, and they may be cloned, protected by replication or otherwise redeployed rapidly in the event of an OS failure. This, of course, requires a certain level of redundancy within the virtual infrastructure so as to avoid a situation where too much infrastructure and configuration must be rebuilt prior to being able to re-deploy a virtual image backup/recovery node *before* being able to commence the recovery of individual virtual machines.

14.4.2 VIRTUALIZED DATABASE BACKUPS

It's worth noting the techniques described in the previous section primarily refer to decision points relating to virtualized systems that *do not* include database applications (e.g., Oracle, Microsoft SQL Server, Microsoft Exchange Server).

While image-level backups of virtualized systems are becoming increasingly popular, increased in-guest complexity, typically through the introduction of a database, reduces the likelihood of the method being appropriate. The "holy grail" for backup systems covering virtualized infrastructure is to perform an image-level backup of an entire database server and do a recovery of a single table within the database from within that backup. As discussed in Chapter 10, snapshots come in two broad categories: *crash consistent* and *application consistent*. This becomes particularly important when we consider virtual machine backups where a database or database-like application resides within the virtual machine. A *crash consistent* backup will allow the operating system to be restored successfully, as if it had suffered an unexpected power loss. However, without particularly tight integration between the hypervisor, backup software, database, and/or virtual machine tools, backups may not be *application consistent*. Without application level consistency, a snapshot style image-level backup of a virtual machine hosting a database may be recoverable, but not restorable within the application, leading to a corrupted database after recovery.

The evolving functionality here to develop true application consistent backup options for databases and complex applications definitely falls into a *watch this space* category. Data protection vendors are increasingly working closely with application providers and are focused on providing this functionality (if not already providing some of it), but it's still early days.

Until this is fully available, we need a *dual architecture* approach to backups of virtualized environments. Image-level backup may very well be used for a large number of virtual machines, but in-guest client software and database agents may be deployed in virtual machines to ensure databases are suitably recoverable.

14.4.3 RECOVERY OPTIONS

If a virtual machine has been backed up via an in-guest agent (the same way a standard physical server of the same operating system type would be), the recovery options available will be exactly those available to the physical version of the host. In short, this means file-level recovery will be the primary recovery method. Some operating systems and products will feature "bare metal recovery" (BMR) options, which allows for a machine to be quickly restored from either a boot-CD or something similar, and such options *may* be supported for virtualized hosts as well. In particular, where BMR supports booting from a device that can be virtualized (CD, USB), there's a good chance such functions will be supported in a virtual environment as well, *if* you want to go to that trouble. (Normally switching to image-level backup provides a better BMR option, however.)

When virtual machines have been backed up from their hypervisors at the image level, there are two potential recovery options typically available—image and (sometimes) file.

Image-level recovery is the restoration of the entire virtual machine by recovering its container files (e.g., virtual disks and configuration). This might be done "in place" (overwriting the current instance of the virtual machine) or it might be done to either another hypervisor entirely, or it might simply be done by creating another virtual machine with a new name (e.g., "cerberus" might be recovered on January 21, 2016, as "cerberus-20160121").

Image-level recovery of virtual machines can be particularly efficient when there are a large number of files in the virtual machine, and are perhaps the most efficient form of BMR attainable. After all, instead of building a new host (virtual or physical), booting from a "recovery" system and then performing the recovery, an image-level recovery simply brings back the entire machine in one step from the chosen backup.

Some of the more common traps and challenges associated with image-level backup however include the following:

- Not efficient when the actual items required for recovery are small (e.g., recovering a 40 GB virtual machine in order to extract 3 × 100 KB files).
- The virtual machine will typically be restored with *exactly* the same configuration. If the virtual machine is recovered as a copy and powered up, it may try to take the same IP address and offer the same services, causing a service disruption or perhaps even data corruption.

With this in mind, more advanced recovery options are becoming more prevalent whereby image-level backup is performed but file-level recovery is an option. This typically requires tighter integration between the backup product and the hypervisor, but provides "the best of both worlds," where backups are fast, and both types of recovery (file and image) are readily available. Another option available in some products is utilization of changed block tracking to speed up the recovery. With this option, the same changed block tracking system used for speeding up backups is leveraged to allow for high speed in-place recovery of virtual machine images: only those blocks that changed between the backup and the current virtual machine state are retrieved from protection storage. For instance, if a 500 GB virtual machine received operating system patches overnight that failed to apply correctly and began crashing on reboot, it's entirely conceivable that the changes between backups had been 1% or less. At 1% change, just 5 GB of data might need to be recovered in order to complete a *full* image-level recovery of the virtual machine.

As mentioned earlier, database recoveries from image-level backups are still uncommon. However, even virtual systems with databases running might still receive some form of image-level backup in conjunction with agent-based database backups. This can allow for the rapid restoration of the database server from an image-level backup after a disaster, with the database to be recovered following this via the standard agent-based approach. This is typically tackled in one of two different ways:

1. Periodic (e.g., monthly) image-level backups, with daily in-guest filesystem backups (perhaps on a weekly full/daily incremental approach) *and* daily database backups via the in-guest agent
2. Daily image-level backup with daily database backup via the in-guest agent

In the former approach, it may even be deemed acceptable to leave the database running during the monthly image-level backup in order to avoid an outage, and deal with the subsequent inconsistent database state as part of the database recovery process.* To avoid considerable "wasted" backups, the latter approach more assumes the database disks are sufficiently independent of the core operating system/application drives for the virtual machine that they can be somehow skipped during the image-level backup process.

A new form of recovery technique becoming available to virtual machines is perhaps best described as "instant access." This requires considerable integration between the hypervisor technology, backup product and backup target, but allows for extreme flexibility. In this approach, an image-level backup of a virtual machine may be presented back to the hypervisor for copying or power-on without actually having been recovered. That is, the backup target is presented as a data storage area to the hypervisor, and making use of virtual machine snapshot technology, can be powered up and even written to without actually overwriting the backup. (Such a technique entirely depends on the backup target storage being random access—disk rather than tape.)

While as of the time of writing this is still only offered by a small handful of product combinations, the utility of it will likely result in similar offerings across most of the industry.

14.4.4 Virtualizing the Backup Infrastructure

Typically, enterprise backup infrastructure is divided into several different host types:

- *Clients*—The actual servers for the business that are protected by the backup solution
- *Server*—The "master" server that coordinates, controls, and indexes all backups performed, liaising between all the other hosts in the environment

---

* So long as such an approach is fully supported by the database vendor *and* has been thoroughly tested.

- *Media server/storage node/slave server*—These hosts are responsible for handling the transport of data from the clients to the backup targets. The backup server may itself be capable of performing this functionality, though in larger environments that might be kept at a minimum to allow the backup server to run as a "director" for the backup process
- *Management server*—The host that is used to manage the entire environment. (This is effectively dedicated to communicating with the end-administrator GUI functions.) While the management services *might* run on the backup server itself (particularly in smaller environments), in order to allow scaling, it's reasonably common to see larger environments off-load the management services to another host

When the primary backup target was tape, virtualization of the backup infrastructure was practically insane. Tape is an anathema to virtualization systems, and those virtualization systems that do allow for connection of physical tape to virtual hosts usually place a significant number of caveats on that connection, usually at the point of the hosting hypervisor. (Despite what its name might suggest, even presenting virtual tape to virtual backup servers is fraught with challenges.)

As the use of tape as a primary backup target has fallen for many organizations, the potential to virtualize the backup environment has likewise grown. The backup transport server (which we'll call the storage node from now on) has traditionally needed to be a particularly powerful host within the environment to handle the high speed throughput requirements for getting data from host A to target B. However, intelligent, random-access backup targets in the form of deduplication arrays have reduced the performance requirements for the storage node—environments will find the role of the storage node reduced to a "target facilitator" whereby it arranges access to a particular area on the backup target filesystem to individual clients, then the clients themselves stream the data directly.

There are now eminently practical reasons for the complete or near-complete virtualization of backup infrastructure. As environments scale and deploy larger numbers of hypervisors to handle thousands of virtual machines (or more), the infrastructure requirements for even dedicated hypervisors to host backup host infrastructure represents a minimal cost increase. Where once there had been legitimate fears that backup infrastructure would swamp the performance of hypervisors and impede primary production systems, or that hypervisors would be unable to provide the performance requirements for the backup environment, load balancing, resource provisioning, limiting, and guaranteeing have developed considerably, allowing for a safe mixing of primary production systems and backup/recovery systems within the overall virtualized infrastructure.

Most importantly of all we return to a fundamental architectural requirement of any backup infrastructure: the backup infrastructure itself must be adequately protected and sufficiently redundant to ensure it doesn't represent a single point of failure for the environment it's deployed to protect. The virtualization techniques and options that allow for advanced data protection for primary production systems are equally applicable to backup and recovery systems themselves. This allows for backup servers (and accompanying hosts) to be readily failed over between sites in the same way regular virtual machines are, increasing the availability of the backup and recovery environment. A fully virtualized backup environment with replicated protection storage could conceivably failover between datacenters in mere minutes.

Such decisions fall squarely into a *risk versus cost* evaluation. In order to safely guarantee continuity of the underlying virtual infrastructure so that backup and recovery systems can (almost) always be readily available, an organization needs to deploy clustered hypervisors with clustered management systems on replicated storage. Anything *less* than this and there is too much risk of a catastrophic failure of the virtual infrastructure requiring substantial rebuild *prior* to building replacement virtual backup infrastructure *prior* to commencing actual systems recovery. However, for those organizations that are large enough to have a mature, highly redundant virtualization and storage infrastructure, such redundancy will already be built into the base environment, and so adding the backup infrastructure into that protection regime will be entirely logical.

14.5 SUMMARY

The layers of integration points virtualization offers a business for data protection are considerable and can reap deliver substantial rewards. With options to seamlessly snapshot entire hosts, organizations can easily back out of changes or provide added protection prior to upgrades. Those same snapshots also become essential during virtual machine backup and recovery operations, allowing for nondisruptive image-level backup of virtual machines.

Virtual machine replication allows for a new form of high availability, delivering failover previously impossible without clustering. Indeed, when *combined* with clustering for particularly sensitive systems, replication allows businesses to reach high-9's availability with far less investment than ever before. Essentially, what was once the sorts of availability only available to multinationals just a decade ago has become the sort of thing even a small or medium enterprise can achieve with relatively minimal effort.

15 Big Data

15.1 INTRODUCTION

"Space," it says, "is big. Really big. You just won't believe how vastly, hugely, mind-bogglingly big it is. I mean, you may think it's a long way down the road to the chemist, but that's just peanuts to space. Listen …"

—Douglas Adams (*The Hitch Hikers Guide to the Galaxy*, Pan Books, 1979)

With relatively little modification, one might adapt the iconic description of *Space* found in *The Hitch Hikers Guide to the Galaxy* to *Big Data*.

The etymology of the term "big data" is not readily agreed upon, particularly in terms of when it was first used. While its popularity has been growing steadily since the mid-2000s, many researchers suggest that it had been bandied about as early as the mid-1990s.*

If big data represents a headache for conventional storage and compute administrators, that's arguably just the tip of the iceberg compared with the challenges faced by those responsible for ensuring said data is adequately protected.

Big data is often characterized by the "3 Vs":

- *Volume*: More data than can be handled by infrastructure for *conventional* data
- *Velocity*: Usually being generated or requiring interception at high speed
- *Variety*: Largely unstructured, coming from a multitude of sources whose data types have little if no relationship to one another

The *closest* analogy to big data is *data warehousing*. While data warehousing is typically an activity associated with enterprise relational databases and therefore operations and analytics on highly structured data, big data applies order *at the time of analysis* to a view of unstructured data (in addition to dealing with structured data). The value derived from dealing with large amounts of unstructured data is in allowing a freer exploration of the data. Structured systems and databases work by applying the schema or layout of the data on write; big data analysis is so often involved in applying an arbitrary schema to the data as it is being read or processed.

In order to be usefully processed, big data is typically analyzed in a massively parallelized environment. A traditional high-performance relational database environment might feature two or more database servers in an all-active cluster, multiple application servers, and perhaps even separate web front ends and administration servers. This allows for the data to be consolidated on potentially just a

---

* "The origins of 'big data': An etymological detective story," Steve Lohr, *New York Times*, February 1, 2013, http://bits.blogs.nytimes.com/2013/02/01/the-origins-of-big-data-an-etymological-detective-story.

few LUNs of high-performance SAN storage. A big data analytics service, on the other hand, might feature hundreds or more computational nodes, all working on discrete sections of data.

For a long time, CPU manufacturers were focused on one primary concern: making the chips faster and faster: 1, 2, 3 GHz—the goal at each iteration was to make a CPU able to perform more calculations in the same period of time. Yet as the number of disparate operations we needed to do *at the same time* also increased, the net benefits of increasing CPU speed dropped off sharply. If operating systems and applications were designed accordingly, a 4-CPU system running at a lower speed per CPU almost always outperformed a single CPU system with a clock speed higher than the combined 4-CPU system, except in very specific single-threaded circumstances. High-performance computing (HPC) leveraged this by having multiple systems each with multiple CPUs. Over time, CPUs went multicore—effectively providing multiple CPUs on a single die. Instead of trying to develop a 10 GHz CPU, it was easier to develop multicore CPUs running at lower speed. (Thus, today we find ourselves having four and even eight core CPUs even in smart phones.)

The problem of scaling *up* was fixed by scaling *out*. It was also fixed as a *software* function. The "brute force" approach to software performance is to assume evermore powerful systems for single-threaded problem solving. The smart way of solving performance issues in software is to break the problem up and execute as many parallel streams as there are processors to handle the data.

Figure 15.1 shows how data analytics might work in a conventional environment. The key issue for the conventional approach is a poorly scaling analysis time. A user will come up with an idea of a query or function to perform against the data, which will then be handed over to the database server. The database server will perform the querying process against the *entire* selected data set (narrowing it down as the query parameters permit) and will eventually provide the answer to the user.

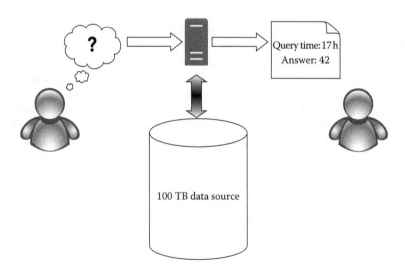

Query time: 17 h
Answer: 42

100 TB data source

FIGURE 15.1   Data analytics in a traditional environment.

If a data set is only small, this processing approach is not normally an issue; however, it becomes time-exhaustive as the amount of data to analyze increases. Logically, this makes sense—if an operation takes 10 seconds to perform against 1,000 complex rows of data for a server, then performing it against 1,000,000 rows of data may very well take 10,000 seconds (approximately 2.8 hours) to complete. As the data continues to increase, the chance of having sufficient memory to hold all data in RAM for the analysis degrades, so the time taken will not even be a linear increase. If each row of data occupies, say, 100 KB, then 1000 rows of data will require approximately 97.7 MB of RAM. And 1,000,000 rows will require 97,656.25 MB or 95 GB of RAM. Eventually, if RAM is exhausted, virtual memory (i.e., swap files) may be leveraged by the operating system, substantially degrading performance.

Traditionally, such performance limits were resolved by buying or building larger and larger servers with more RAM, more CPU, and putting the data to be analyzed on high-performance storage—what we would call *scale-up*. This however has substantial limitations both in terms of maximum size/performance *and* the cost associated with achieving such a server. While it's possible to configure servers with multiple processors, each with 10 or more cores and even terabytes of memory, there will always be practical or fiscal limits to how far a system can be scaled.

To get around those issues, big data approaches the problem from a *scale-out* perspective. Rather than purchase larger, more powerful, and undoubtedly more expensive stand-alone servers to process the data, big data processing splits the data into much smaller data sets to allow smaller, cheaper servers to digest it and perform processing against it. This might resemble a configuration such as that shown in Figure 15.2.

In such a scenario, the user will develop a query that is sent to the management node of the big data environment. The management node will then coordinate with a potentially large number of nodes, handing each node a small segment of the overall data set. The individual nodes work on their segments of data only, handing the results back to the management node when complete. Once all data sets have

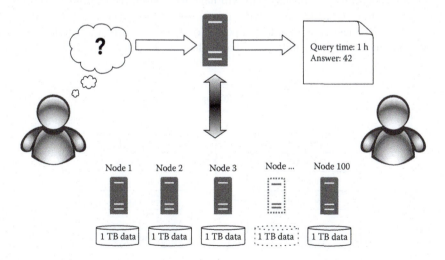

FIGURE 15.2 A big data approach to data analytics.

been analyzed, the management node collates the results and provides them to the end user. By attacking the analysis in such a distributed fashion, it can be sped up by sometimes orders of magnitude compared to a conventional approach. In essence, big data is about finding new methods other than the classic brute-force approach to data analysis: rather than a few extremely powerful servers trying to crunch through a massive data set, a large number of *adequately* powerful low-end systems each crunch through a comparatively very small data set.

15.2 PROTECTING WITHIN THE BIG DATA ENVIRONMENT

For data protection in a big data environment, the central design requirement will usually come down to whether the "big data" itself needs to be protected or whether it's the *results* that need to be protected. For instance, consider a big data environment populated from a series of other data sources (e.g., web traffic log files, databases, and production filesystems). If each of *those* systems has comprehensive data protection deployed against them, the big data system can conceivably be repopulated in the event of a failure from the original locations—and presumably will be periodically refreshed as well. In these cases, it's usually the results generated by the big data system that need to be protected, and these will typically be orders of magnitude smaller than the actual system itself. So long as those results are written or copied to systems with standard data protection, this may be sufficient.

That being said, there will usually be a degree of primary copy protection used on any data set. For example, the Hadoop Distributed File System (HDFS) achieves storage resiliency by replicating data across multiple hosts. Such filesystems might eschew RAID as the base level of protection by guaranteeing n copies of a file, distributed among multiple nodes in the system. (HDFS, for instance, defaults to three copies of the data.) Conceptually, this n-way replication might resemble the layout shown in Figure 15.3.

Each node in the big data system will have its own independent filesystem, but to the end user or the accessing APIs this is usually presented as a single logical filesystem. As files are written to or updated on the system, multiple nodes receive and store the content so that the loss of a single node does not cause data loss. Since

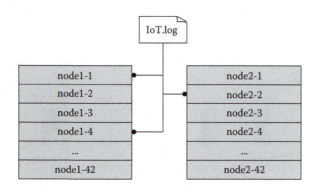

FIGURE 15.3 The n-way replication in a distributed filesystem.

big data systems are usually built on the basis of large scale, distributed filesystems can also be node/locality aware—multiple copies of a file may be stored in nodes in the same rack, with an additional copy stored in a node in a physically separate rack.

Such options usually require functionality to rebalance in the event of node failure and to generally avoid "hot spots" of data in the distributed filesystem. Distributed filesystems can still benefit from RAID storage however—read performance can be boosted coming from multiple drives, and administrators might prefer RAID rebuild times within individual nodes rather than having entire node rebalancing operations occur in response to a single disk failure.* In fact, some scale-out NAS systems feature compatibility with big data filesystems such as HDFS, allowing HDFS nodes to make use of the scale-out NAS as their actual data storage platform without the need for the multi-copy replication previously mentioned. This can drive greater storage efficiency while also giving access to the rich data services offered by NAS systems. (New storage systems with higher tiers of performance beyond regular SSD—in the *tens* of millions of IOPS[†]—have the potential to increase RAID adoption in performance-sensitive big data environments.)

Additional levels of protection can usually be provided in big data processing environments via intercluster replication. A business seeking to achieve a degree of data protection for their big data environment will deploy more than one big data processing cluster and use replication. If the primary or master cluster goes down, the cluster acting as a replication target is able to continue to provide operations against a copy of the data. (Big data intercluster replication is often asynchronous however due to the potential for large volumes of data to be flowing into it at high speed—the copy residing in the target cluster may lag behind the content of the source or "master" cluster.)

While cluster replication provides protection against cluster failure, it does not necessarily provide protection against more specific data loss—particularly if the filesystem being used across the cluster doesn't implement versioning. An option growing in popularity for big data pools is to be able to trigger an export or a copy of the cluster to an *unrelated* storage system—such as scale-out NAS. This allows large conventional storage systems to be used to provide the services *not* provided by the big data systems—such as days, weeks, or even *months* of snapshots, with replication and even options, where necessary to back up the data to disk-based protection storage. This can result in a configuration similar to that shown in Figure 15.4.

An added advantage of this type of solution is in having a copy of the data residing on a *different* platform to the original big data system itself, which can suit businesses seeking to limit the potential for data loss originating from a catastrophic platform failure. While this is usually considered to be unlikely, having entirely different systems providing varied layers of protection substantially reduces the risk of cascading failures in a data loss situation. Alternately, big data systems making use

---

* Bearing in mind a RAID reconstruction will affect only one node in the cluster; node rebalancing may affect a large number of nodes in the cluster.

† Speed that will undoubtedly continue to scale with performance increases in solid state and memory-like storage.

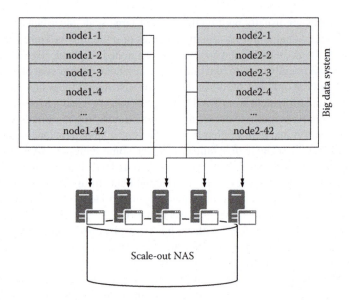

FIGURE 15.4   Big data replicating to scale-out NAS.

of scale-out NAS as their primary storage platform can actually leave most of these data management functions to the NAS system. Snapshots, replication, and even backup if required can be handled as part of standard NAS data services, allowing the big data environment to focus on analytics.

As the use of integrated data protection appliances (IDPAs) grows within traditional backup environments, these become an alternate option for the protection of big data systems. Designed from the ground up as a specialized protection storage system capable of ingesting and deduplicating large quantities of data as quickly and efficiently as possible, they allow for the transfer of big data content into *true* protection storage. While a traditional copy to or between NAS storage requires a 1:1 copy between data in the big data pool and the target system, copying to an IDPA can potentially leverage source-side or distributed deduplication processing, substantially reducing the actual scale of the data that needs to be copied. Such a mechanism might leverage a *client package* integrated with the export options in the big data system or present the IDPA via a specialized filesystem mount that has deduplication assistance drivers built in. In either case, the net result can be to apply traditional deduplication reductions as the data is being read from each node, executing a massively parallel deduplication transfer. In the same spirit of reducing the impact of a backup operation on production infrastructure, this could be integrated into a cluster replication target in a big data system, such as in Figure 15.5. Such a configuration allows the primary cluster to continue operations without any additional workload impact while backups are taking place.

Consider the advantage of deduplication integrated into a big data cluster protection scheme. If we assume 100 nodes each with a local storage capacity of 8 TB at 85% utilization, each node has 6.8 TB of stored data. Assuming three-way replication of content (e.g., in the HDFS default configuration), each node theoretically has

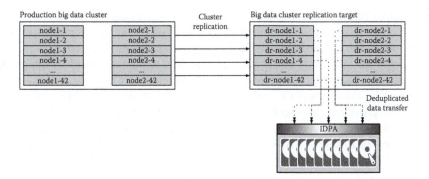

FIGURE 15.5   Big data protection via clustering and backup to IDPA.

around 2.27 TB of data that would need to be copied in an export or backup operation (227 TB in total). Even if we assume a lower overall deduplication ratio due to a mix of structured and unstructured data, and inclusion of some data that doesn't deduplicate well, we might be able to achieve an average deduplication ratio of, say, 4:1 on the first transfer. Assuming an even spread across all the nodes, this would require a first backup transfer of approximately 580 GB per node, occupying approximately 57 TB on the IDPA at the end of the backup (56.75 TB to be precise). Also, 100 nodes of 8 TB at 85% utilization equates to 680 TB of used space *including* three-way replication; considering only unique content, this might be 227 TB—so rather than copying 227 TB to a NAS system, the solution could be to write effectively just 57 TB to a deduplication platform.

If we consider a 20% growth rate between backups, a 20:1 deduplication ratio against previously backed up data, and an ongoing 4:1 deduplication ratio against *new* data, this could result in ongoing backup sizes as outlined in Table 15.1.

TABLE 15.1
Cumulative Deduplicated Protection on Big Data Pool

Backup Instance	Source Size (TB)	Backup Size (TB)	Total Target Consumed (TB)
1	227	56.75	56.75
2	272.4	22.7	79.45
3	326.88	27.24	106.69
4	392.26	32.69	139.38
5	470.71	39.23	178.6
6	564.85	47.07	225.67
7	677.82	56.48	282.16
8	813.38	67.78	349.94
9	976.06	81.34	431.28
10	1171.27	97.61	528.89
11	1405.52	117.13	646.01
12	1686.63	140.55	786.56

(Of course, this assumes commonality between existing backups and new data, but this is quite possible if the deduplication system is also being used for backups from other production systems that the big data system sources its data from.)

Ideally, the number of actual backups that need to be maintained for a big data system should actually be minimal. This is where we turn to a logical separation between the *data in* and the *information out*. Such backups should be seen as a means of providing short-term levels of operational *or* disaster recovery, not long-term compliance data protection. For the most part, it's the information that comes *out* of big data analysis that will potentially require long-term compliance protection, *not* the data that goes into it.

15.3   BIG DATA THAT ISN'T BIG DATA

In the previous discussion, we've mainly focused on the now traditional definition of big data—large sets of data combining unstructured and structured data for (primarily) the purposes of analytics, decision support, and mass number crunching (or some variant thereof).

Yet there's another type of data that is big but not necessarily thought of as "big data"—truly huge, usually tightly centralized *conventional* data sets that strain data protection resources. For instance, consider scale-out NAS systems that can grow to tens or more petabytes. Even assuming a consistent 30 TB/hour transfer rate, a conventional *backup* of a 10 PB NAS would take over 14 days to complete. Such systems might be used as general data repositories in very large businesses, or they might be used for specialist purposes: animation studios, special effects companies, TV channels, medical imaging systems, and so on. As our ability to generate larger and more complex data sets grows, so too will these large data sets grow.

Such data sets often require protection mechanisms outside the norm, and more often than not have to more closely leverage the *same* technology as the primary copy for the secondary copy: that is, replication to another system. For instance, a 10 PB NAS might have regular snapshots taken and also be replicated to a second, perhaps even larger NAS.

Such snapshot and replication protection techniques might see a limited number of short-term snapshots maintained (e.g., 72 × hourly snapshots), followed by retention of less periodic snapshots—4 × weekly snapshots, 12 × monthly snapshots, and so on. This has the potential to introduce two specific risks into a system:

1. *Performance impact*: Depending on the storage technology used and the number of changes made on a system, long-term retention of a potentially large number of snapshots can degrade performance. This requires careful architectural planning to ensure it will not jeopardize system functionality.
2. *Single-platform protection*: Despite there being snapshots and replication, the entire operational protection is provided by the same platform. Since the typical deployment method requires storage arrays from the same vendor as source and target (unless storage virtualization is layered on top), a firmware or software problem—or a deliberate targeted hack—could

conceivably result in catastrophic data loss. Even if storage virtualization is being used, we would still consider all protection being sourced from the same platform.

Even in environments with massive amounts of data, it is usually desirable to find a strategy able to incorporate at least one layer of protection from a different platform or data protection tier. Further, with so few businesses practicing comprehensive data lifecycle management and archiving, long-term compliance retention creates an almost inevitable need for additional steps even in this model.

This usually results in configuring the snapshots and replication options to meet *all* anticipated operational recovery requirements and leveraging backup and recovery systems—not for any SLA-related recovery, but solely for the purposes of satisfying long-term compliance retention. For instance, using our previous example of a 10 PB NAS server, rather than attempt a single, 14-day backup at 30 TB/hour, we might instead break the data set into a series of 10 × 1 PB regions and conduct *rolling* backups over the course of an entire month. Assuming an ongoing backup speed of 30 TB/hour, each 1 PB region could be backed up in a little over 34 hours. This would give time for a new backup to be started every 2 days and still have a complete backup executed every month of the content of the NAS system.

Data protection solutions at scale require meticulous planning and evaluation of *all* options and their flexibility, not to mention a more creative approach to meeting business requirements.

15.4 USING DATA PROTECTION STORAGE FOR A BIG DATA ENVIRONMENT

A common challenge faced by many organizations making use of big data processing systems is the logistics in populating and refreshing data from a multitude of disparate systems. Advanced analytics and decision support systems, for instance, usually need to leverage data from a large variety of sources within the organization, including everything from unstructured file data, sensor and telemetry content, large log files, production databases, data warehouses, and an almost unlimited number of other enterprise components.

Except in very rare circumstances, data is not static, nor is the data held in analytics systems static. Data that has been populated for processing in a big data system will need to be periodically refreshed in order to ensure up-to-date information and trends are being gleaned. This regular refreshing allows businesses to do any of the following (and practically anything else):

- Leverage rapidly changing market conditions to their advantage.
- Offer customers the most likely to succeed bargains based on current buying habits.
- Detect fraudulent activity in near real time.

If we think of all of the systems within an environment that might need to have data pulled from them to refresh a big data analytics environment, we might see a small example in Figure 15.6.

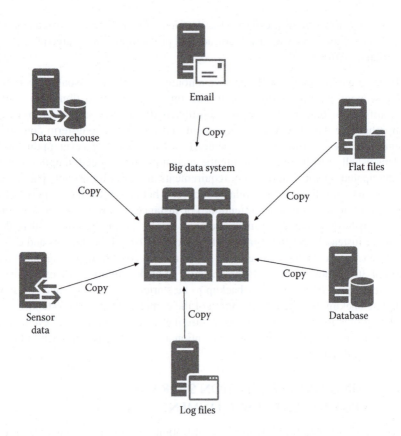

FIGURE 15.6   Repopulating a big data system from the original sources.

While this guarantees access to the most recent data, which sometimes may be an absolute necessity, it can quickly become a logistical nightmare, particularly in larger enterprises. Exporting data from primary production systems *during* production operational hours could have a negative impact on either the performance of the production system or its network link. Application, database, and infrastructure teams directly responsible for production systems may have a plethora of other duties that create delays for copying the required data for the big data teams and change freeze windows (sometimes lasting weeks) for some organizations may directly prohibit new data refreshes from occurring. In larger organizations where requests have to be filed through ticketing systems and routed through to various groups, the administrative overheads of repopulating big data systems might in fact reduce that frequency to the point where its potential benefits to the organization are impacted.

Yet if we think about it, this is not the *only* place this data might be found within an organization, and we can take a lesson from database administrators to understand how else these systems might be repopulated.

For as long as there have been databases used in production, there have been development/test databases, and database administrators have needed to periodically refresh these development/test systems from production data. Database administrators who are particularly mindful of potential impact on production systems created by copy operations have traditionally used database copies residing in backup and recovery storage in order to source a recent version of the production database.

Big data terminology often revolves around water: we refer to big data *pools* or *lakes*. Using that terminology, we might consider data protection for big data to be symbolic of *wells*. Thus, big data protection storage allows us to plumb the protection well.

With the rise of high-speed, random access centralized protection storage systems, businesses seeking to increase the return on their data protection investment can sidestep many of the challenges of repopulating big data/data analytics systems. By retrieving copies from protection storage rather than the original primary systems, the process can be performed without involving primary production administration and infrastructure teams *and* without risk of performance impact to those same systems. This results in a refresh flow similar to that shown in Figure 15.7.

In Figure 15.7, we note the various data sources used by the big data system all require backups (in this case to an IDPA). Since the data required by the big

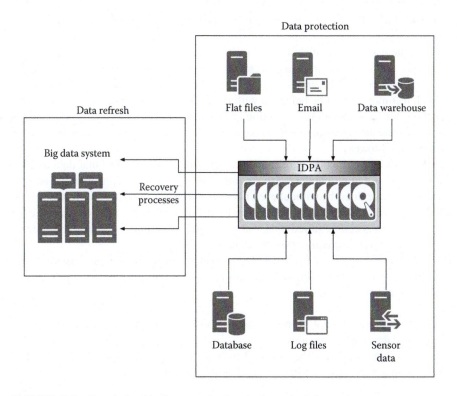

FIGURE 15.7   Populating big data repositories via data protection sources.

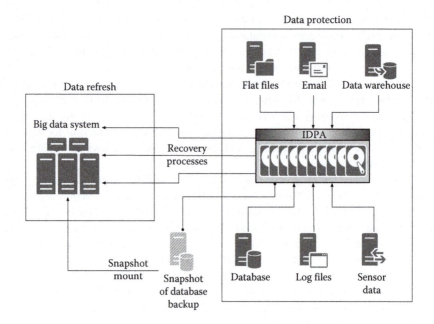

FIGURE 15.8   Using data protection copies as online sources in big data systems.

data system resides on disk and is easily accessible without impact to production systems, the big data teams can refresh *their* systems quickly and efficiently, regardless of what constraints are in place on the primary production teams and systems. (Such techniques must be balanced with the restore speeds available from data protection storage—though the reduction or elimination of primary systems impact by sourcing the data elsewhere may make a recovery more palatable than a direct copy even if it is slower.)

Depending on the mechanism used to actually protect the original data and the format it is stored in, big data systems might even refer to the copy residing on protection storage directly, without even needing to recover the data, and would resemble an access flow such as that shown in Figure 15.8. This has all the advantages of being able to access required data without impacting primary copies *and* reducing the storage footprint required for big data processing.

Of course, snapshots from the data owner on primary storage systems could equally be presented to a big data system for access, but this will inevitably have at least one of two consequences:

1. It has the potential to impact the performance or capacity of the primary storage snapshot regions.
2. In doing so, it has the potential to impact the performance of the actual primary data owner—the original application and so on.

In both cases, sourcing data from actual protection storage mitigates this risk while still providing easy access to the required data. As per copying content from data protection sources, accessing snapshot data directly from data protection sources will depend on the performance characteristics of such storage, and this will likely see higher utility in data protection storage able to at least leverage flash tiers or caches.

Another potential advantage of leveraging data protection sources in a big data system via snapshots such as in Figure 15.8 is the option to leverage *earlier* data for combined or comparative analysis. If a big data cluster has been periodically backed up to an IDPA, those backups might be presented as new source data. Assume, for instance, a big data system is backed up to an IDPA once a month, with a 12-month retention on the data. However, to avoid capacity issues within the big data system, data older than 6 months is routinely purged. If the data backed up to the IDPA can be presented via snapshots and network mappings *back* to the big data environment, calculations and comparisons can be run between, say, the data currently in the system and the data held 6 or 12 months ago. As an example, if financial models are being constantly updated and refined, it would allow a business to re-execute those models against old data to see how accurate they are—how closely the results resemble current known details. This process of plumbing the data protection well can conceivably be leveraged for a number of historical, comparative, and innovative analysis techniques, and may enable data scientists and big data analysts to provide new insights and strategic advantages to a business.

15.5 SUMMARY

In many ways, the problems presented by big data are not necessarily new, but rather are scaled-up variations of existing challenges faced in data protection over the decades. A common problem in IT and computer science as a whole has been that as resources—storage, memory, and computing speeds—have increased, the desire to spend time *optimizing* the use of those resources has declined. Operating systems and applications have grown considerably in functionality, but bloat creeps in as the computers running those applications and operating systems become more powerful. Likewise, data lifecycle management is often seen as a costly and time-consuming process compared to just purchasing and provisioning more storage. Just as big data demonstrates there is a practical limit to how much you can scale *up* the performance of an individual system for data set analysis, big data also demonstrates that there are limits in scaling for conventional data protection approaches as well. The solution is no longer to throw more capacity or higher-speed networks at the problem and hope it goes away, but to leverage technology more efficiently and perhaps more creatively in order to provide a functional level of protection.

Big data also highlights the importance of choosing *what* data to protect: do you need to protect the source data or just the results? For some environments, you still need to protect the *data*, but for others a more sensible and cost-effective approach may be to protect the *information* generated from the data.

This is still a very new and emerging field, and will continue to present challenges to data protection for some time to come. Yet, data protection potentially offers improvements and scalability to big data environments that might be otherwise difficult to achieve: centralized refresh processes, additional pools of data, and deeper historical analysis.

16 Data Storage Protection

16.1 INTRODUCTION

No discussion about data protection would be complete without a review of the most pervasive form of data protection in use within any datacenter—at rest data storage protection. The most common type of this style of protection is of course the redundant array of independent disks (RAID). RAID in particular has become so commonplace that unlike almost all other forms of data protection, it's *assumed* to be present. Data storage protection (regardless of what form it takes) is designed to act as the first line of defense against individual hard drive failure (or any similarly used storage technology, such as solid-state disks).

The undoubted king of data storage protection is RAID, though over time as drive sizes have increased the *form* in which RAID is used has altered considerably. What was appropriate for hard drives of 1, 100 or even 500 GB has had to evolve as hard drives increase beyond the 4 TB size range. Each form of data storage protection has its own benefits *and* its own potential downfalls, especially with increased storage capacities and businesses needing to offer 24 × 7 services with high-performance characteristics.

16.2 TRADITIONAL RAID

The December 1987 paper "A case for redundant arrays of inexpensive disks (RAID)"* written by David Patterson, Garth Gibson, and Randy Katz, outlined some of the fundamental principles of RAID that have remained with us over almost 30 years. While the acronym has changed (from "inexpensive" to "independent"), the core concepts have remained at times remarkably similar.

In addition to the potential for higher reliability, RAID was also developed as a mechanism to offer improved storage performance, particularly compared to monolithic disks developed for mainframe computers at the time. This dual promise—of performance and higher reliability—practically created the data storage industry. The précis to the original paper was quite prophetic:

> Increasing performance of CPUs and memories will be squandered if not matched by a similar performance increase in I/O.[†]

There are a number of different RAID levels that we'll discuss. By itself, RAID-0 offers no protection—it simply stripes data across all drives included in the RAID

---

* University of California, Berkeley, Technical Report No. USB/CSD-87-391, https://www.eecs.berkeley.edu/Pubs/TechRpts/1987/5853.html.
[†] Ibid.

set to maximize performance, so we will ignore it until we come to nested RAID levels. We will also ignore RAID levels 2 and 3, which are uncommon to the point of no longer being used.

In all cases, RAID works by *virtualizing* the combined hard drives (regardless of the way in which they are combined) and presenting the virtualized storage as a single drive to a host.

During the discussion on RAID, keep in mind that RAID serves *only* as data storage protection—it is not a means of protecting against corruption, loss of availability, user error, or deliberate data erasure. The rest of data protection exists for those purposes.

16.2.1 RAID-1

RAID-1, otherwise known as mirroring, is where two hard drives are kept 100% in sync with one another. A representation of RAID-1 is shown in Figure 16.1.

A RAID-1 configuration allows the data to remain accessible and intact in the event of a failure of a single drive. During normal operations (when both drives are present and functional), write operations are doubled as the write must be committed to both physical drives before it is acknowledged back to the host. This is generally described as being the *RAID write penalty*, something that all RAID types other than RAID-0 will suffer in some form or another.

Depending on the RAID implementation, read operations can be staggered across *both* drives, resulting in higher performance than reading from a single drive.

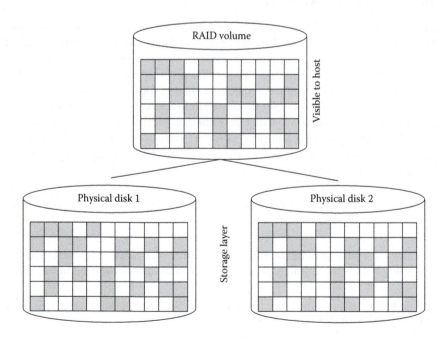

FIGURE 16.1 Logical representation of a RAID-1 volume.

(Some cheaper, consumer-oriented RAID-1 implementations might instead preferentially source all reads from a single disk, which will yield no performance benefit over a non-RAID configuration.)

From a capacity perspective, RAID-1 *halves* the physical capacity used to provide data storage. If 2 × 6 TB hard drives are used in a RAID-1 mirror, the operating system will only be presented with 6 TB of raw capacity.*

Note that RAID sets will usually be constructed by using drives, all of the same size, to maximize capacity utilization. Consider, for instance, mirroring a 6 TB drive with a 2 TB drive. In such a case, the only way to provide data protection is to limit the 6 TB drive to 2 TB maximum utilization so that anything written to the 4 TB drive can *also* be written to the 2 TB drive. For the purposes of the standard RAID levels, we will assume in all cases that all the drives in the RAID set are of the same size. (Later in this chapter, we'll discuss other RAID approaches that can mix drive sizes.)

RAID-1, or variants of it (RAID-1+0 and RAID-0+1, which we'll discuss later), is often used in provisioning storage for mission critical high-performance systems, with a primary reason being the minimized write penalty. Particularly for systems that have a requirement for a high number of IOPS with very little latency, RAID-1 and its variants typically offer the best mix of performance and protection, albeit at a price.

16.2.2   RAID-5

RAID-5 attempts to balance data protection with provided capacity by using the notion of *parity*. The minimum number of drives required for a RAID-5 configuration is 3, but for any n drives in a RAID-5 configuration, the total capacity provided will be $(n - 1) \times C$, where C is the *smallest* capacity drive in the RAID set. Thus, 3 × 2 TB drives will yield a 4 TB capacity after data protection, 9 × 2 TB drives will yield a 16 TB capacity after data protection, and so on. A logical representation of a three-disk RAID-5 configuration is shown in Figure 16.2.

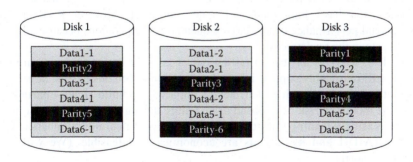

FIGURE 16.2   Logical representation of a three-disk RAID-5 configuration.

---

* For the purposes of simplicity, we will refer to all measurements in TB rather than differentiating between TB and TiB and we will talk in raw capacity rather than expected capacity following formatting, filesystem overheads, etc.

RAID-5 volumes are divided into a series of *stripes*. For a RAID-5 configuration featuring n drives, the incoming data is divided into $n - 1$ segments, and the nth segment of the stripe is constructed by a parity calculation (usually an XOR process against all the data segments). The n segments are written as a stripe across all drives in the configuration. Mostly for reasons of performance, stripes are not of bytes but of blocks. (Stripe *size* refers to the size of the data segment written to *each* drive in a RAID configuration.)

RAID-5 volumes can withstand the failure of a single drive; whenever data is to be read, *either* the complete data set will be able to be read or $n - 2$ data segments plus a parity segment will be read, with a data reconstruction calculation performed against the parity segment and retrieved data to construct the entire data set.*

While RAID-5 can yield a higher capacity while still providing protection from a single disk failure when compared to RAID-1, this does not come at a cost. In any situation that data is updated on a RAID-5 volume, we must read all the data in each affected stripe *and* calculate a new parity before writing the actual updated data to the disks. Thus, an update to any data in an existing stripe becomes the following sequence of activities:

1. Read all the old data.
2. Read the prior parity value.
3. Calculate the new parity.
4. Write the updated/new data.
5. Write the recalculated parity.

Steps 1, 2, 4, and 5 in this list all represent distinct IO operations that must be performed as part of the single operation. For this reason, RAID-5 is considered to have a write penalty of four—each logical write requires four distinct IO operations to service the request.

Based on the write penalty, RAID-5 is often considered to be unsuitable for any workload that has a high number of writes; conversely, however, RAID-5 yields exceptional performance during large sequential read operations because all drives participate in the read process.

Of late, RAID-5 has begun falling out of favor in enterprise configurations. While still reasonably popular in small- to medium-sized businesses, larger drive capacities have had such a detrimental impact on rebuild times—particularly with the increased risk of a second drive failure during rebuild—that enterprises are increasingly leaning toward RAID-6 for larger logical unit numbers (LUNs) where RAID-1 and its variants are economically unfeasible. (We will cover RAID-6 shortly.)

---

* The parity and data reconstruction calculations are beyond the scope of this chapter.

16.2.3   RAID-4

RAID-4 is similar to the behavior of RAID-5, except that the parity disk is dedicated—that is, parity is not striped across all drives in the system. In the event of a single disk failing, data can be read back in one of the two ways:

1. If the parity disk failed, data can be read "as normal" from the original striped data.
2. If one of the disks in the data set failed, the data can be read by reading the remaining segments of the stripes from the working disks *and* the parity details and then subsequently combining the data and the parity information to reconstruct the missing data.

Figure 16.3 shows a logical representation of a three-disk RAID-4 configuration. Note that one disk is dedicated to parity.

RAID-4 is usually avoided for most situations as the dedicated parity disk will experience higher wear than the other drives in the configuration. Like RAID-5, RAID-4 will have a write penalty of four and feature the following sequence of activities whenever any data in an existing stripe is updated:

1. Read all the old data.
2. Read the prior parity value.
3. Calculate the new parity.
4. Write the updated/new data.
5. Write the recalculated parity.

In a situation where, say, 4 KB of data is updated and the stripe width is 128 KB, there is a reasonably high degree of probability that the updated data will be confined to a single stripe (as opposed to spanning two stripes). In this situation, only two drives will need to have new writes performed to them—the one holding the data to be updated and the one holding the parity data. For a RAID-5 configuration, the disk the parity data belongs to varies per set of stripes; for RAID-4, however,

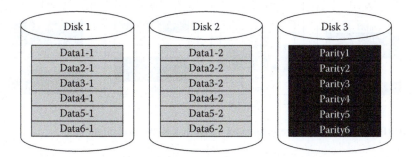

FIGURE 16.3   Logical representation of a three-disk RAID-4 configuration.

the parity stripes are on a dedicated disk, meaning this disk will *always* be written to whenever new data is added or updated. In environments featuring large numbers of writes and particularly large numbers of *updates*, this can lead to the parity disk wearing out much sooner than the other disks in the RAID set.*

(It should be noted that there is also a RAID-3 architecture, which is quite similar to RAID-4, except parity and striping is performed at a byte level. RAID-3 is rarely used any longer.)

16.2.4 RAID-6

RAID-6 extends the basic principle of RAID-5 by adding a *second* parity stripe. This means the minimum number of disks in a RAID-6 configuration is *4* (though this minimum is rarely used in practice). Figure 16.4 gives an example of a logical representation of a four-disk RAID-6 configuration.

The advantage of RAID-6 is it offers dual-drive redundancy; up to two drives in a RAID-6 set can fail before data integrity is compromised. This however does mean losing the capacity of two drives to data integrity. Thus, a 4 × 4 TB RAID-6 set will yield only 8 TB of raw data space. For such a small number of drives, this yields no greater protection than a 2 × RAID-1 configuration, but it is rare to see a four-drive RAID-6 set. Instead, RAID-6 yields itself to larger drive numbers—it is not unusual, for instance, to see an entire 15-drive shelf configured in RAID-6. Thus, 15 × 4 TB drives in RAID-6 will yield 13 × 4 TB or 52 TB of raw data space with 8 TB of parity protection.

While giving a higher degree of fault tolerance, RAID-6 increases the write penalty from 4 to 6. While there are a variety of algorithms used for RAID-6 parity, the reason the write penalty increases to 6 is that the two parity calculations are executed against *different* data. Thus, an additional data read, parity calculation, and data write are performed on top of the previously listed IO steps for RAID-5.

Like RAID-5, RAID-6 is suited for scenarios where there is a preponderance of reads over writes, though it should be noted in both cases that the write penalty is

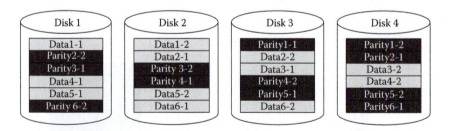

FIGURE 16.4   Logical representation of a four-disk RAID-6 configuration.

---

* Some storage systems will attempt to mitigate this by having large NVRAM caches of parity information to stagger writes to the parity drives or even use mirrored parity drives to mitigate the impact of a parity disk failing. It is usually only with these types of techniques that RAID-4 is considered enterprise suitable.

only experienced when data is being *updated*. Thus, if writes are primarily the result of new data being written (or entire stripes being overwritten), the penalty can be mitigated. This often makes RAID-6 also ideal for *protection storage* and *integrated data protection* appliances.

16.3   NESTED RAID

Nested RAID refers to two RAID levels combined for greater performance, storage efficiency, or protection. These are normally named in their nesting order (innermost to outermost), and some of the more common options are

- RAID 0 + 1
- RAID 1 + 0
- RAID 5 + 0

(It is not uncommon to see the "+" removed in the names, shrinking them to 01, 10, and 50, respectively.)

In Figure 16.5, we can see a logical representation of a RAID-0+1 or RAID-01 configuration.

RAID-0 + 1 sees two sets of striped disks mirrored together. Each pair of RAID-0 stripes offers performance, but no data protection. Data protection is instead achieved by mirroring the two RAID-0 sets. This requires a minimum of four drives and will yield the capacity of half of the drives in the overall presented volume. That is, using 4 × 4 TB volumes will result in 2 × 8 TB stripes, mirrored, with a total data capacity of 8 TB. A RAID-0 + 1 configuration can tolerate either the loss of a single drive in RAID-0 pair or the loss of the path to an entire RAID-0 pair.

RAID-1 + 0 is the logical reverse of RAID-0 + 1. Two RAID-1 pairs are assembled, and then a RAID-0 stripe is created using both RAID-1 pairs. This is shown in Figure 16.6. Like its RAID-0+1 cousin, RAID-1 + 0 will offer half the capacity of the drives in the overall RAID set. RAID-1 + 0 can tolerate the loss of a disk in *each* of the RAID-1 pairs but, unlike RAID-0 + 1, cannot tolerate the loss of the path to one of the RAID-1 pairs.

RAID-5 + 0 is similar to RAID-1 + 0 except two pairs of RAID-5 sets are striped together, as shown in Figure 16.7. RAID-5 + 0 can withstand the loss of one disk in each RAID-5 pair before data integrity is compromised (though it cannot lose access

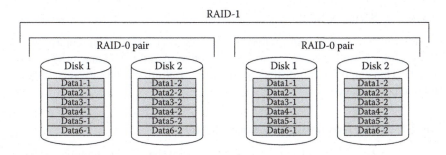

FIGURE 16.5   RAID-0+1 configuration.

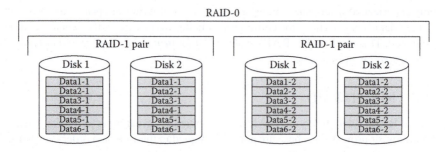

FIGURE 16.6   RAID-1+0 configuration.

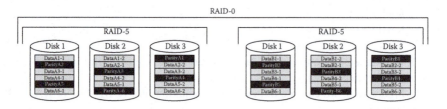

FIGURE 16.7   RAID-5+0 configuration.

to the path for either of the RAID-5 sets that data is striped across). If *n* disks are used in *each* RAID-5 set, the total capacity of the RAID-5+0 configuration will be $2n − 2$. Thus, a RAID-5+0 configuration consisting of RAID-0 striping across $4 × 4$ TB drives in RAID-5 configuration will result in 24 TB of raw data capacity presented to an accessing host.

These are just three of the variants available for nested RAID. (For instance, RAID-5+1 might be used in some instances, particularly when continuously available paired storage arrays are used.) In some cases, nested RAID will result in higher performance; in others, it will result in higher performance *and* higher storage capacity, but such levels should be chosen with careful consideration to the broader storage environment. (Both RAID-1+0 and RAID-5+0, for instance, can offer high-performance improvements, but neither can protect against the loss of connectivity to one stripe in the RAID-0 overlay.)

16.4   SUBDRIVE RAID

RAID is not necessarily *only* performed at a whole-drive level. Some enterprise storage systems as well as more feature-rich consumer-based RAID may offer subdrive RAID. This can offer two distinct advantages—optimized capacity versatility and rebuild performance.

16.4.1   CAPACITY-OPTIMIZED SUBDRIVE RAID

Normally when we consider standard RAID, one of the core expectations is that all drives in a RAID LUN are of the same size; otherwise, there will be capacity wastage.

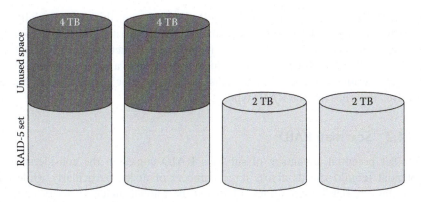

FIGURE 16.8 Conventional RAID-5 configuration with mismatched drive sizes.

Consider, for instance, a RAID-5 set consisting of four drives where two drives are 4 TB and two drives are 2 TB in size. In a standard RAID-5 set, this would result in each drive being configured as a 2 TB drive within the RAID set, leaving 2 TB unused and inaccessible in each of the 2 × 4 TB drives. This would resemble a configuration similar to that shown in Figure 16.8.

Subdrive RAID overcomes this by offering RAID at a level lower than individual drives. This might result in a configuration whereby RAID-5 is performed against the 2 × 2 TB drives *and* the first 2 TB of each of the 4 TB drives, and then RAID-1 is performed against the remaining 2 × 2 TB of each of the 4 TB drives, as shown in Figure 16.9.

This is a particularly common approach in "intelligent" personal/SOHO RAID storage systems and can be sometimes referred to as "hybrid RAID" due to the mixing of RAID types within individual drives. In such configurations, the total protected storage may be offered as a single volume with the user effectively oblivious to the actual RAID levels being used within the configuration.

It should be noted that if the individual RAID types created in a subdrive configuration *are* presented as separate volumes (in the example in Figure 16.9, this would

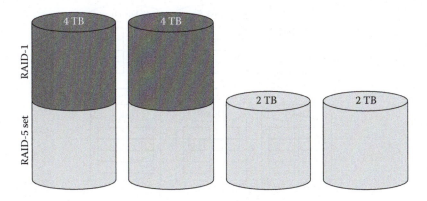

FIGURE 16.9 Subdrive RAID configuration with differing drive sizes.

mean a 2 TB RAID-1 volume and a 6 TB RAID-5 volume), this can potentially lead to performance issues. Not only is there the potential for writes to be sent to the same physical drives concurrently, but the different write characteristics of RAID-1 and RAID-5 will add to the performance impact beyond just a simple scenario of two programs writing to the same physical disk at the same time, given the IO operations involved in writes in *each* RAID type.

16.4.2 SCATTERED RAID

Another potential advantage of subdrive RAID comes in the consideration of potential rebuild speeds across large numbers of disks, particularly while still servicing regular IO operations. (This can be known under a variety of terms including scattered and mesh.) This supposes RAID content has been scattered across a potentially large number of drives. For instance, a RAID-1 configuration might utilize dozens or even *hundreds* of drives, where each data block is mirrored between a *different* pair of drives. In the event of a single drive failing, content can be copied back from multiple drives simultaneously and (more importantly) *to* multiple drives simultaneously. Instead of rebuilding the previous RAID-block pairs, all the participating drives will receive new writes to spare space in order to allow a faster rebuild time.

Consider, for instance, the scattered subdrive RAID configuration shown in Figure 16.10. In this, just four RAID-1 block pairs are shown for simplicity. In a normal RAID-1 configuration, if one of the drives in the RAID-1 pair failed, the surviving RAID-1 pair member will need to be read end to end to copy the contents

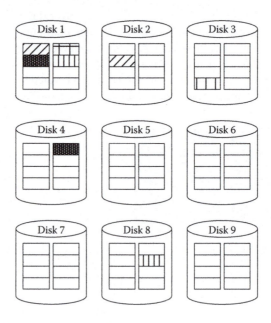

FIGURE 16.10   Scattered subdrive RAID.

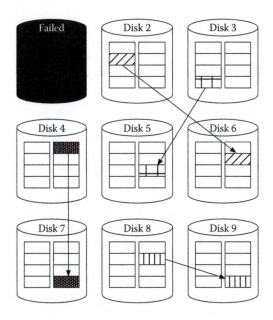

FIGURE 16.11   Scattered RAID rebuild process.

to another drive in order to reestablish full data protection. This scattered RAID rebuild might resemble that shown in Figure 16.11.

As can be seen in Figure 16.11, each surviving RAID block can be copied to a *different* drive in the overall availability set, which will substantially parallelize the rebuild process. Instead of a single end-to-end read of one disk accompanied by a single end-to-end write of another disk, all disks in the overall protection set are simultaneously used to read the unprotected data and write it to spare drives or drives with spare storage in the set.

It should be noted, however, that this comes with a data protection cost: if during the rebuild process *any* of drives 2–9 fail, the entire data set being rebuilt will effectively be lost. Thus, this subdrive RAID approach can lead to highly efficient rebuild times, but the failure tolerance of the RAID level remains the same across all the potential drives in the configuration. Usually in this situation, vendors will argue that because the rebuild time is so fast (compared to a traditional rebuild) the risks of this happening are very low, and there is certainly merit to this argument. Alternatives may see more than two copies of data being stored across the protection set or smaller protection sets than the total number of drives deployed to minimize the risk of overall data contamination via cascading failures. (That is, an array with 500 drives might be logically broken up into 10 × 50 sets. We would typically expect this type of breakdown to create hard limits on the expansion granularity for a system.)

Scattered RAID can be a highly effective solution in all-flash storage systems (i.e., solid-state storage devices) as the space can be more effectively utilized. While a conventional disk solution might need to optimize the data copy process to ensure that no disk being read from is also being written to (or at least minimize the number of disks requiring both), the performance impact of concurrent reads and writes on solid-state storage is so negligible that it usually doesn't warrant consideration by comparison. Additionally, particularly when using enterprise-grade flash,* the risks of multiple units failing at the same time are substantially reduced compared to conventional hard drives with many parts moving at extremely high speeds.

16.5 OBJECT-LEVEL PROTECTION

Object-based storage, often assumed to be a feature only of cloud storage systems, is an alternative to traditional filesystem-based storage approaches. In fact, object storage had been particularly popular in archive systems for years before cloud storage became available and continues to serve in this function in many solutions. While filesystems are based on potentially deeply nested directories and any number of files in any or all of those directories, object storage is usually based on an exceptionally wide namespace where each object (discrete unit of data) contains within its own metadata the globally unique identifier (GUID) that allows it to be individually addressed and referenced, regardless of what end storage system the object is actually located on. While files *may* be encapsulated as objects in object-based storage systems, it should not be assumed there is a 1:1 correlation between objects and files. Object storage systems can be used for practically any type of data, and an object may equally represent a BLOB,† database, or tuple. Ultimately, the nature of the object is determined by the accessing application.

A single object storage system may be scattered across a massive number of consumer storage systems, bespoke storage arrays, commercial and enterprise storage systems, and anything in between. A key differentiation, however, between object storage systems and enterprise storage systems is *where* data resiliency lays. Enterprise storage systems are typically designed to provide all the resilience within their systems—RAID, snapshots, replication, and so on. Object storage systems are usually designed to provide a particular base level of resiliency (as will be discussed shortly), with additional layers of resiliency usually being an accessing application function. Thus, you will be more likely to see object storage systems focused on commodity or near-commodity hardware rather than being underpinned by classic enterprise storage systems.

Regardless of their type, each component in an object storage system is typically considered to be a node (though the nomenclature is still evolving)—and objects will be distributed across multiple nodes. All of this complexity is abstracted from the accessing systems that will typically do one of the following, all accompanied by authorized access keys:

1. Present a GUID and request the referenced object.
2. Present an object to be stored and receive a GUID in return.
3. Present the GUID of an object to be deleted.

---

* Enterprise-grade flash/SSD is usually classed as such by having a much higher tolerance against degradation caused by repeated rewrites—instead of tolerances in the thousands, enterprise-grade flash will have tolerances in the tens of thousands and will usually have a much higher "spare" storage to fill in should individual memory cells fail.
† Binary large object.

While not an exhaustive list, this gives a simple overview of the object storage process. Note this level of abstraction is even higher than we would normally see in, say, a classic filesystem. Within a filesystem in order to access an individual piece of data (i.e., a file), you have to know both the filename *and* the complete path to that file. In an object storage system, you provide the GUID only. (Hence, the common consideration of object storage systems of having a *global* namespace—the GUID—is flat and not hierarchical like a filesystem.)

While being useful for a variety of functions and purposes, one particular advantage offered by an object storage system is scale—while we normally consider classic network-attached storage (NAS) file servers as scaling to millions, tens of millions, or possibly even a hundred million files or so, object storage systems are usually premised on being able to address *billions* of objects.

A discussion on the overall nature, benefits, and limitations of object storage is beyond the scope of this book. However, despite the different mechanics of object storage, the fundamental requirement for data storage protection remains the same. Unlike, say, filesystems provided by a NAS server, object storage is *not* typically RAID protected. At the lowest level, the individual disks comprising the object storage pool operate moderately independently, and it is up to the object storage controller layer (which the accessing applications and APIs communicate through) to ensure multiple copies of objects are stored using the appropriate dispersal patterns available. Object storage is typically defined as being protected by erasure coding, either entirely within one location or with geo-distribution. Compared to traditional RAID, erasure coding *can* result in excellent space efficiencies, though this will often depend on architecture of the object storage scheme. (However, remember the rebuild times of RAID systems will grow as the number and size of the drives increase, and while a token or small comparison of RAID vs. object may be more favorable to RAID in terms of storage overhead, as the volume of data grows, the overhead required by RAID will likewise increase as an ever-growing number of LUNs must be presented.)

16.5.1 GEO-DISTRIBUTION

Geo-distribution, as its name suggests, provides protection from object loss by storing multiple copies of the object in geographically disperse locations. Depending on the object storage system, this might only be offered as an option or it may even be considered to be a key functional requirement/capability. In some object storage models, it might be up to accessing applications to ensure they (1) subscribe to geographically disperse object stores and (2) write copies in each location accordingly. In addition to facilitating object *placement*, geo-distributed object storage can also be used for the purposes of data resiliency. (In this scenario, placement refers to scenarios where users may need to access from either a variety of locations or even anywhere in the world. An object datastore with locations in, say, Melbourne, Austin, and Stockholm, will not only provide each object with geographically disperse protection but *may* also allow users to access the object copy that is closest to them via their network access. This is not necessarily guaranteed, however, and is beyond the scope of the data protection considerations we are currently discussing.)

A common consideration in geo-distributed object storage is how quickly objects are consistent across the different locations. If designed with a global namespace, even if an object is not directly present, it should be accessible (admittedly with a "drag" lag) across locations; object storage systems either might have a high degree of consistency across geographic regions or might offer "eventual" consistency.

Regardless of whether object storage is being deployed in a private or hybrid cloud or being accessed through a public cloud, a subscriber will typically have options to choose between geo-distribution of objects or localized storage only. Geo-distribution is typically considered a more expensive option (it will certainly be expensive when subscribed to in a public cloud scenario) but offers greater resiliency. In particular, just like traditional IT environments leverage multiple datacenters to avoid putting all the infrastructure eggs in one basket, geo-distribution for object stores avoids a scenario whereby data becomes inaccessible or even lost in the event of a single datacenter failing.

16.5.2   ERASURE CODING

At its most basic, you might consider erasure coding to be object-level RAID. This is where an incoming object is split into multiple segments (or *symbols*), with additional segments created such that multiple segments can be lost but the original content can be recreated. Each segment and the encoding segments are then distributed among the disks and nodes in the object storage system to avoid a scenario where the loss of a single node results in unrecoverable data.* Logically, this might resemble the process shown in Figure 16.12.

While it would be understandable to assume that RAID could do just as useful a job for object protection, we must remember that object storage is typically grown by *scaling out*. Rather than a traditional scale-up storage model with, say, two controllers and a large amount of back-end storage, object storage is grown by adding more nodes into an object storage cluster. This allows object storage systems to potentially grow into hundreds of petabytes or beyond if necessary without the limitations typically imposed on large RAID systems, both in terms of rebuild

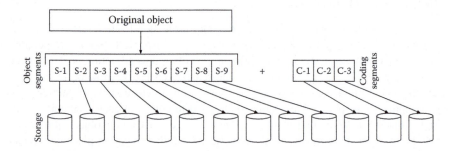

FIGURE 16.12   Erasure coding of objects.

---

* The number of nodes in an environment will affect the level of erasure coding offered. In certain circumstances, particularly when there are a small number of nodes, more than one slice of data may reside on the same node, but the design will ensure data can still be reconstructed or recovered in the event of a single node being lost.

times and the number of drives assigned to a LUN—an essentially foreign concept to object storage. (If objects are being accessed through public cloud, the additional variability, of course, will be network access speeds—i.e., web speed will not be particularly concerned with object storage latencies. While private object storage can be deployed for a greater range of functions, it is not designed to replace, say, tier-1 enterprise storage in terms of raw access speed, however.)

RAID implementations typically will require all disks in the LUN to be controlled by a single storage processor (or a pair in an active/active configuration); the RAID-*like* nature of object-level storage achieves a similar goal but allows every segment to exist on a different addressable node in an object storage cluster. Location-aware encoding mechanisms increase resiliency by ensuring the loss of a single node does not cause data loss, even though a node may have anywhere between a few drives and dozens of drives. (Indeed, with high-density storage shelves becoming increasingly common, 60 or more drives might be provisioned in a single rack mountable node, with all drives and all nodes contributing to the overall storage pool.) This allows for a configuration designed to "scale out," into up to even the exabyte range, while being highly fault tolerant—particularly when geo-distribution of encoded objects is added to the equation. (Unlike many classic enterprise storage systems, geo-distribution does not really refer to "production" and "disaster recovery" sites but may include many sites—3, 4, or more—all participating in the storage pool.)

16.6 SUMMARY

The old mantra "A chain is only as strong as its weakest link" is particularly relevant when we consider at-rest data storage protection. Choosing the *right* data storage protection is the first and most fundamental step on the path toward a full data protection system. By itself it is *not* a data protection solution, but it is extremely rare to find an effective and holistic data protection solution that *doesn't* include at-rest data storage protection.

Each layer of data protection we build into a solution is premised on one simple piece of knowledge: *things* fail. It doesn't matter whether the thing is a storage array, a storage network switch, a filesystem, or an end user making a mistake; *things* fail. A copy-on-write snapshot will not protect against underlying disk failure, and a continuously available system with redundant virtualized arrays is a terrible waste of money if all we need to do is ensure a single disk failure does not result in data loss.

While RAID is practically the standard in data storage protection at the most fundamental layer, as businesses of all sizes move workloads out of traditional storage and into cloud or object storage and we deal with increasingly larger data sets that stretch the capabilities of traditional RAID, we return to this fundamentally *assumed* element of protection and ask the most basic of questions:

1. Can it protect the volume of data I need to store?
2. Is it even there in the first place?

Ultimately, cloud-scale storage capable of addressing billions or more objects has necessitated new massively scalable architectures and will see continued evolution in data storage over the coming decades.

17 Tape

17.1 INTRODUCTION: THE HISTORICAL PRIMACY OF TAPE

There was a time when it was impossible to have a conversation about data protection without tape being a primary focus. Tape has been used in IT practically since its inception, with the UNIVAC 1 using tape for data storage as early as 1951. Tape initially gained ascendency over punched card and became a common storage format for decades until it in turn was supplanted by magnetic disk for primary storage.

As disk systems were developed, the sequential nature of tape forced it into the realms of backup, hierarchical storage management (HSM) and archive. Simply put, tape could not compete effectively with high-speed random access to active data offered by hard disk systems.

Tape had historically offered advantages disk storage struggled to match, including

- Scalable capacity at fixed footprint
- Large capacity at low cost
- High-speed *sequential* read and write capabilities
- Portability

In addition to these, more recently, tape has also been seen as a *green* technology.

Without fail almost every year someone declares tape to be dead. While this isn't necessarily the case, we must also acknowledge that the role tape plays in the modern datacenter has been changing and reducing. This has been caused by disk-based storage systems and, more recently, alternate storage such as cloud. The disruption of tape use cases in the datacenter will continue for some time to come.

In order to appreciate the changing role of tape within data protection, we should first examine the primary use cases it had for the last 20 years.

17.2 HIERARCHICAL STORAGE MANAGEMENT AND ARCHIVE

HSM is a form of storage tiering pioneered in the mainframe realm where data that is less frequently used is moved out to slower and slower storage until eventually due to economies of access, it is removed from disk entirely and placed on tape. To ensure data can still be retrieved when required, "stubs" are left behind at the filesystem or operating system layer so that when a user or process attempts to access a relocated file, it can be identified by the HSM plug-in to the operating system and be retrieved from tape. To the end user, it would be indistinguishable in access method to data still on disk, albeit as a slower-than-usual access.

While HSM and archive are largely synonymous in terms of data movement functionality, the key difference between them is that HSM is usually seen as a process that deals with data that may still be updated even if it has been moved out to slower storage. (Particularly when tape was used for HSM, this would result in the data being moved *back* to a primary storage tier before modification.) Archive has traditionally differed from HSM in that data once moved is likely to be retained largely for legal or compliance reasons and potentially might even be locked, preventing modification. In this, archive was equally suited to tape because of its write-once read-many (WORM) nature. Since tape does not allow for selective data overwrites, once data is written it is not subject to modification and has therefore been easily deemed to be a "golden," inviolate copy—particularly if additional steps are taken to ensure that tape is not erased/ overwritten or otherwise destroyed. Still, the terms have continued to blur, particularly in the non-mainframe IT space.

Typically, HSM and archive systems process files or data based on age and/or access frequency. Particularly when moving data to tape, the goal would always be to ensure that by the time data was relocated from disk to tape, it was old *and* had not been accessed for some time. (In some cases, data might also be moved based on its size and the relative costs of holding it online, regardless of how recently it had been created.)

It was the higher capacity of tape that made it particularly beneficial in archive/ HSM environments—particularly when we consider the purpose was to move data that did not require frequent access. Consider, for instance, LTO Ultrium-1, introduced in 1998 with a capacity of 100 GB. Hard drives, on the other hand, in 1998 had a capacity anywhere between 2.1 and 21 GB. Thus, a single 100 GB cartridge could fit anywhere between 4 and 47 hard drives capacity, a substantial saving for businesses. Even with archival or HSM data written twice (to protect against tape failure), this would still be potentially cheaper than maintaining sufficient hard drives for online storage of all data. Conversely, 100 GB hard drives would not enter commercially availability until approximately 2001.* While each new generation of tape has traditionally started at a high per-unit cost, that cost has inevitably been lower than a comparable capacity in hard drives.

By using even a relatively small tape library for HSM and archive functions, a business could substantially extend its storage capacity at a lower cost and potentially smaller footprint than the disk-only equivalent. Even a basic rack-unit tape changer with, say, 2 tape drives and 20 slots would offer between 2 and 4 TB (depending on compression) of additional capacity to a business using LTO-1 tape, possibly within a size of approximately 8 rack units (RU) high or less. Assuming 19 GB drives were used in 3 RU storage shelves with 15 drives per shelf, 106 drives would be required for 2 TB *without* any RAID considerations—occupying as much as 24 RU in space. (Adding configurations such as RAID-5 14 + 1 would result in an increase to approximately 120 drives, but a similar rack size.)

It should be noted that neither HSM nor archive are technically data protection activities, but rather information life-cycle *management* activities. That being said,

---

* Remember that enterprise storage vendors will usually be slower to support new drive sizes in order to ensure that key requirements such as reliability, stock availability, and maximum compatibility with existing systems have been met. This often means that new hard drive sizes may take some time before they are available in the enterprise storage space.

we reference them here because of their historical impact on tape usage *and* because an effective data protection regime includes policies and processes to delete or otherwise archive data that is no longer required on primary storage, thereby reducing the overall data protection *and* primary storage costs.

17.3 BACKUP AND RECOVERY

If HSM and archive seemed like a good value proposition for tape, it was nothing compared to the use case for backup and recovery. Tape ticked almost every box for backup, but most notably it satisfied three very key requirements:

1. Fast
2. Cheap
3. Removable

The backup industry in the 1980s, 1990s, and early 2000s revolved around tape—so much so that when the de facto industry standard (DLT) struggled to evolve beyond the 35 GB backup cartridge, much of the backup and recovery industry stagnated.* The LTO consortium breathed new life into the backup industry in 1998 with its first release, a 100 GB cartridge, and the industry accelerated from that point.

Despite sometimes popular opinion, tape offered high-speed backups long before disk-based backup. As early as 1997, backup speeds of 1 TB per hour had been attained using tape, and by 2003 speeds of 10 TB per hour had been achieved. When it came to moving large amounts of data as quickly as possible, tape served the industry well for a long period of time, and this must be acknowledged when considering the history of data protection.

Entire backup products were developed with around tape architectures, and it's pertinent to consider several of the key aspects offered by backup vendors to deal with tape-based limitations, since in specific cases tape can still offer a valid use case for backup or backup duplication purposes.

17.3.1 MEDIA SPANNING

Media spanning refers to a single backup needing to spread across more than one tape. This might happen in situations where the tape is smaller than the backup set (e.g., backing up a 10 TB filesystem to a set of 2 TB tapes) or simply in situations where the remaining capacity on a partially used tape is less than the capacity of the data set being backed up.

While most enterprise backup products supported media spanning, some products, particularly open source products, took a long time to offer this support, which would result in backup and system administrators having to manually carve up backup sources to allow them to fit on tapes. Such a process is time consuming and

---

* This is not to suggest DLT was the *only* tape technology at the time. However, it was a critical and highly used technology.

error prone (no matter how carefully done) and would inevitably result in media wastage. By allowing backups to span over as many tapes as required to ensure the data is backed up, enterprise products avoided tape wastage and reduced the potential for human error preventing key data from being backed up.

17.3.2 Rapid Data Access

Rapid data access goes hand in hand with both spanning and backup catalogs. Rapid data access refers to whether the backup product is able to identify (via the catalogs) only those pieces of media that are really needed for a recovery, and within those pieces of media, identify as small a portion of data as possible that must be read in order to facilitate a recovery. For example, consider a situation where a backup spanned four tapes, and a single file needs to be recovered, which so happens to be stored on the third tape. Enterprise backup software will first use the catalog to determine that only the third tape is needed for the recovery and then use high-speed tape "seek" operations to jump to a position relatively close to the data required for recovery. Less sophisticated products might need to load the third tape and read from the start, and even more primitive products without a sophisticated catalog might need to start reading the backup set from the very first tape, throwing away the majority of the data read before finally locating the specific file required.

Backup vendors will typically use file and record markers to target with a high degree of granularity the portion of the tape that needed to be accessed. In this case, "file" refers to approximate area on tape, not "file required for recovery." For instance, regardless of the size of the data being backed up, a backup product might record an end-of-file marker on the tape after, say, every 2 GB of data has been written. If the catalog identifies the data required for recovery is somewhere within the block starting after the 42nd end-of-file marker written to the tape (i.e., somewhere around 86 GB into to the tape), the backup product could load the tape and then issue 42 "forward space file" (FSF) instructions to the tape to do a high-speed fast forward to the starting block of data. Record markers might then be used to provide further granularity in the seek process—for instance, a record marker might be written every 100 MB.

Practically, all tape drives support the following operations:

- *FSF*: seek forward the nominated number of end-of-file markers on the tape
- *Backward space file (BSF)*: seek backward the nominated number of end-of-file markers on the tape
- *Forward space record (FSR)*: seek forward the nominated number of records on a tape
- *Backward space record (BSR)*: seek backward the nominated number of records on a tape

Returning to our example, the backup server's catalog might be able to identify that the required data for recovery is not only in the block of data 42 end-of-file markers through the tape, but within that block starts in the record chunk that is five record markers into the block. This will allow multiple "fast forward" operations to be performed before read operations are initiated, drastically reducing the amount of sequential data reading required to recover the data actually requested by the end user.

Old dog teaches new tricks

It's worth noting backup to disk benefits from similar levels of catalog data. Despite lay opinion, backup to disk doesn't generate mirror copies of filesystems: the eventual file count over successive backups (especially if deduplication is in use) would render the backup filesystem unusable. So backups tend to be written in large, monolithic files (e.g., one file per filesystem backed up). It would likewise be unfeasible (and wasteful) to read the entire monolithic file for a recovery of a single small file, even with disk access speeds. So even in backup to disk environments, catalog data will be maintained to allow quick access to individual files or at least blocks of data in the overall backup file.

17.3.3 MEDIA MULTIPLEXING

Media multiplexing refers to writing multiple backups simultaneously to the same piece of media, and the primary purpose of media multiplexing is to deal with tape streaming performance requirements. While tape drives and tape vendors publish performance guidelines for the speed of their systems (e.g., LTO-1 cited 20 MB/s uncompressed), this performance is entirely dependent on the data flowing from the backup environment to the tape at a *constant* 20 MB/s. The reduction in backup performance was *not* linear in response to degraded backup throughput. The concept of *shoe-shining* is fairly consistent in most tape technologies—this is where the incoming data speed is lower than the ideal streaming speed of the tape drive. A tape drive will write data at the rated speed of the device (e.g., 20 MB/s), but then due to pauses in the data stream relative to the streaming speed is forced to stop, seek back to the end of the previous data stream on tape before it can continue to write (so as to avoid gaps in the media). Thus, it is entirely conceivable that a tape drive that *streams* at 20 MB/s might, with an incoming data speed of just 18 MB/s, instead write as slow as 10 MB/s once shoe-shining comes into play.*

To (partially) work around this, more recent versions of tape technology have included the capability to step down their ideal streaming speed to lower speeds—for example, a drive might be capable of stepping down to 75%, 50%, and 35% of its native streaming speed without needing to shoe-shine.

While the capability to step down streaming speeds helps to smooth performance when writing to tape, it is only a relatively new addition to tape technology, and it still does not provide absolute guarantee against shoe-shining and poor performance when the incoming data stream is slow. The workaround offered by many enterprise backup products is to combine the data streams from several sources into a larger, faster stream going to tape. This is called *multiplexing*.

---

* This isn't to say that 8 MB/s of data would be lost—just the incoming data stream would likewise need to be reduced to keep up with the slower performing tape drive.

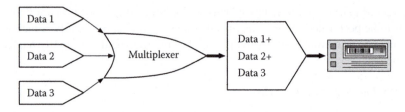

FIGURE 17.1 Conceptual view of multiplexing.

Figure 17.1 provides a high-level conceptual view of multiplexing—rather than individual data streams being sent directly (and 1 by 1) to a tape drive, they are passed through a multiplexer service. The multiplexer service combines the data streams into a single stream that is then sent to the tape drive.

The advantage of multiplexing is that the speed of the backup is no longer directly dependent on the speed of any individual data stream coming from a client—as more data streams are combined, the chances of keeping a tape drive running at full speed are increased. Slowdowns in data streams from an individual client are compensated for within the multiplexer service by allowing additional data from one or more of the other data streams to be incorporated into the multiplexed stream.

(While in theory there is nothing preventing backup stream multiplexing to disk-based backup devices, it is more usually than not the case that when performing backup to disk, enterprise backup technology will instead write each individual stream as its own backup file or set onto the disk—there are no logical advantages in writing a multiplexed stream as a monolithic data set to disk, given disk does not shoe-shine.)

A segment of multiplexed tape (at the logical level) might resemble that shown in Figure 17.2. Consider this multiplexed tape consisting of

A. Host "orilla," filesystem /Users/pmdg
B. Host "mondas," filesystem /home
C. Host "faraway," filesystem C:\

In the example tape segment, we can see that the tape has been written with three-way multiplexing and filled with data segments as they become available from each of backup jobs A, B, and C. Assuming such levels of multiplexing continued throughout the entire tape, it might be assumed that the hosts "mondas" and "faraway," each providing only 3 of the 11 multiplexed segments, might have been slower clients compared to the host "orilla," which provided 5 of the 11 multiplexed segments in the diagram.

Tape-level multiplexing can be absolutely necessary to keep tape drives streaming at optimum speed but, depending on the level of multiplexing and the type of recovery that is required, can have a deleterious effect on the most important component of a backup system—the recovery.

FIGURE 17.2 Multiplexed tape segment.

Consider again the example of our multiplexed tape. Depending on what size each chunk of data is on the tape, individual file recovery may be relatively unaffected by the multiplexing. However, let's examine what would be required to read, say, the entire orilla "/Users/pmdg" filesystem from the tape. Based on the tape segment in Figure 17.2, this would result in the following scenario:

- Read first chunk of A
- Read second chunk of A
- Read over *or* seek past the first chunk of B
- Read the third chunk of A
- Read over *or* seek past the first chunk of C
- Read over *or* seek past the second chunk of C
- Read the fourth chunk of A
- Read over *or* seek past the second chunk of B
- Read over *or* seek past the third chunk of B
- Read the fifth chunk of A

This process would continue until such time as all of the "/Users/pmdg" filesystem for the host "orilla" had been recovered. Depending on the individual chunk sizes and the number of concurrent chunks from backups we're not interested in recovering, the backup software *may* be able to execute an FSR or FSF command to jump areas of the tape that it doesn't need to recover from, but multiplexing is usually performed in reasonably small chunk sizes to reduce the risk of shoe-shining, so potentially a *lot* of redundant data may be read and thrown away by the backup product when doing a complete recovery from a multiplexed tape. The more the tape is multiplexed, the more wasteful this type of recovery becomes.

Optimizing the wrong performance

A company wanting to eliminate shoe-shining and keep tape drives streaming at their maximum rated speed tuned their entire backup environment to generate 64-way multiplexing on all their tape-based backups (the maximum supported by a particular product at the time). This seemed to work fine for backups, but shortly after implementing this change they found themselves having to recover an entire filesystem. With the level of multiplexing on the tape, what should have been a 1- or 2-hour recovery at most stretched to over 8 hours. It's a worthwhile reminder that the fastest backup in the world is pointless if it can't be recovered efficiently and quickly.

17.3.4 Twinning/Automated Replication

Larger backup environments that make use of full silos rather than their smaller tape library counterparts sometimes make use of silo-controlled tape replication.

Silo or tape library?

You'll note we refer to both *silos* and *tape libraries*. While naming conventions between siloes and tape libraries are somewhat vendor dependent, for the purposes of our discussion, we'll refer to a silo as a system that has a separate control host managing partitioning and access control, and more likely to have multiple robotic arms handling tape changing. A tape library, on the other hand, for the purposes of our discussions, is more likely to have a single robot arm handling tape changes and is directly connected to the host(s) using it for backup/recovery purposes. As tape density has increased, this differentiation has blurred, with many tape libraries supporting partitioning.*

While the importance of backup duplication has long been acknowledged, larger businesses have often found it difficult to schedule duplication time when using tape. Silos enable a means of circumventing the time-to-duplicate problem by effectively performing a form of "RAID-1" on tapes—generating *two* identical tapes. The danger of this approach is usually that the backup product will be unaware of the copies and rely entirely on the silo to ensure that the two copies never become simultaneously visible to the product.

Alternatively, some backup products may perform a software version of this replication approach, simultaneously generating backups to two different tapes. While this has the advantage of ensuring the backup product is aware of both copies, it introduces a logical challenge to backup administrators—is a backup considered a failure if just one of the two tapes fails (and therefore just one copy of the backup is generated), or is it considered a failure only if *both* tapes failed?

17.3.5 Library/SAN Sharing

While initially tape libraries were SCSI connected, over time this gave way to fiber-channel connectivity, particularly for larger tape libraries, thus enabling SAN sharing of the library. This allows multiple hosts to be zoned in and connected to the tape library simultaneously.

In Figure 17.3, we show a sample SAN shared tape library. In this configuration, there are a variety of standard network connected backup clients, but additionally the tape library is shared over fiber-channel connectivity to both the backup server and a database server. In this scenario, we would assume the database server contains a large amount of data and either can't be efficiently backed up over standard network connections or mustn't be affected by the network impact of such a backup process.

Typically in this scenario, the backup server will maintain control over the robot head that performs tape change operations. One or more tape drives will be zoned into the backup server, and the remaining tape drives will be zoned into the database server.

This style of configuration is often referred to as offering LAN-free backups—for the database server in this example, the backups do *not* traverse the IP network at all, being sent direct via fiber channel to the tapes within the tape library. (Metadata exchanges between the backup server and database server will still typically occur.) Library sharing can also be accommodated via standard SCSI connections—the backup server will typically have control over the robot head and one or more drives, and the remaining drives will have direct SCSI connections directly with the hosts that need dedicated access.

---

* In the context of tape libraries and siloes, partitioning (or *hardware* partitioning) refers to presenting one physical unit as multiple smaller units; a 10,000 slot silo might be presented as 10 × 1000 slot systems, for instance.

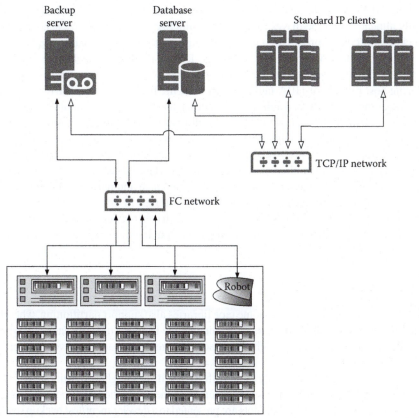

Fiber-channel connected tape library

FIGURE 17.3 Sample SAN shared tape library.

The disadvantage of the basic sharing of tape libraries is *dedicating* tape drives to individual hosts, something overcome with a technique referred to as *dynamic drive sharing* or *SAN drive sharing*, covered in the next topic.

17.3.6 DYNAMIC DRIVE SHARING

Referring to Figure 17.3 again, library sharing is where specific tape drives are dedicated to individual hosts within the backup environment, providing maximum resource availability to those hosts. This comes with the risk those tape drives will sit idle for long periods during the backup window once the individual hosts with access have completed their backups.

To make better use of limited tape drive resources, several enterprise backup products developed a technology referred to as SAN sharing or dynamic drive sharing for fiber-channel connected libraries. In this situation, individual tape drives would no longer be dedicated to specific hosts, but zoned in such a way that multiple hosts could theoretically access the tape drives. (The robot head would remain

controlled by a single host.) The backup server or other nominated host dynamically allocate free tape drives to hosts requiring SAN-level tape drive access during
backup or recovery processes, ensuring resources are spread around as required.

This does not come without challenges. Due to multiple hosts having access to
individual tape drives, it becomes critical to mask SCSI resets (typically triggered
during host reboots or HBA faults). Otherwise, the host *using* a tape drive may find
the tape unexpectedly rewinding and ejecting the tape because another host with
access to the drive happened to reboot. Additionally, since multiple hosts can access
the drives, ensuring a compatible tape block size is used becomes critical, otherwise a tape might be initialized and written to by one host but then loaded *into the
same tape drive* by another host (usually of a different operating system) and be
completely unusable. Generally speaking, maintenance and hardware faults become
considerably more problematic or at least more complex in this style of environment.
(In fact, as solutions go, the SAN sharing of tape drives between multiple hosts often
introduced more problems than it solved into any but the most rigorously maintained
environment.)

17.3.7 LIBRARY PARTITIONING

While mostly a feature of silos, some tape libraries also support partitioning, whereby
the library can appear as multiple independent tape libraries (usually each one with a
smaller configuration) and thereby be presented to multiple backup servers or storage
nodes/media servers.

For instance, a 1000 slot library/silo with 10 tape drives might be partitioned in such
a way that 800 slots and 7 drives are presented to the production environment backup
server and 3 tape drives plus 200 slots are presented to a development/test backup server.
In such a configuration, the host given access to the large library partition would not
have any visibility over the smaller library partition and vice versa—to all intents and
purposes, the individual partitions would be seen as entirely separate libraries.

Key reasons for library partitioning for many enterprises included

- *Security considerations*: DMZ systems might be configured to use their
  own backup server, with internal system backups completely inaccessible
  in another partition.
- *Multiple backup products*: As environments grew and converged, a variety of
  departments using different backup products might pool resources and share a
  single tape library via partitioning. Alternately, a new backup product might be
  deployed, with the old backup product requiring ongoing access to its media.
  As the migration progressed more resources could be allocated to the new
  product, reducing the retired product to minimum access for recoveries only.
- *Mixed library usage*: The workloads of HSM/archive and backup within
  a tape library are not necessarily complementary, so library partitioning
  could be used to ensure that sufficient resources were always available to
  both activities.
- *Mixed media usage*: Particularly when considering older versions, not all
  backup products have been tolerant to multiple media types within a single

tape library. Library partitioning would allow a backup product with such a limitation to access all its media without concern it might try to load, say, an older DLT cartridge into a new LTO tape drive.

For the most part, library partitioning works via the notion of a *control* host for the tape library. When partitioning is performed, no one server using the tape library can have exclusive access to the robot head(s) nor are products designed to service tape load requests for other products (regardless of whether they come from the same vendor or another). In such situations, accessing hosts submit load/unload requests to a library control host, which is the only system with direct access to the robot heads. This host maps the partitioned load/unload request to the physical tape library configuration, performs the operation, and then advises the requesting product that it has been performed.

17.3.8 PHYSICAL MEDIA MANAGEMENT

After a tape has been used comes the task of properly storing it and retrieving it when it needs to be accessed again. Tape media and pools will often be written either for designated on-site or off-site retention—the idea being that a copy of each backup resides somewhere other than the datacenter for the duration of its lifetime, and a copy resides either in or *near* the datacenter (e.g., in the same building) for "rapid" day-to-day operational access.

Multisite businesses may choose to store their off-site copy in alternate datacenters, while other businesses may prefer to use a third-party tape storage and retrieval company. Sending media off-site requires as understanding of the environmental and storage processes, for instance:

- Is the media shipped in sealed boxes or satchels preventing outside humidity or other adverse weather conditions to affect it?
- Is the media tracked individually (e.g., by barcode), or by satchel/box?
- If media is tracked by satchel or box, can it be recalled individually? (If not, it usually requires the business to perform its own mapping between box numbers and contained barcodes/labels.)
- When using a third-party off-site storage provider, is the provider insured, use audited processes, and has appropriate security and document retention credentials?

Since tape media represents a relatively portable copy of production data, strong physical security must be applied to it as well. Businesses with compliance requirements are now required to encrypt data sent to tape and store them securely—either in locked safes or vaults when on-site and not in a library, or with reputable and certified storage companies when off-site.

You can't control the world

You should never keep only one copy of the backup, yet this was quite common in tape-only environments over longer retention periods. For instance, companies might duplicate their short-term retention backups in order to have an on-site and an off-site copy, but the longer-term retention backups—for example, the monthlies—might only have a single copy generated.

To keep only one copy of a backup implies a trust that nothing bad will ever happen when you need to recover the data. A company that followed this policy once found themselves unable to recover urgently needed data from several months prior—not for any reason you might expect, but because the driver for the tape-recall company was in a collision when returning the media, and the tapes required, held in just a simple satchel, were crushed in the resulting collision.

17.4   DECLINE OF TAPE

Tape is still used in many organizations, but many of the use cases, particularly for "average" enterprises, have substantially declined over the past decade or more. In this section, we will discuss where and why tape use cases have been supplanted, and the technology that has replaced them.

While tapes have substantially increased their capacity over the years, so too has their performance, and performance *requirements*. LTO-7, released in 2015, has a native transfer rate of 300 or 750 MB/s based on rated compression ratios. This is like having a jet car on rails: it can go *really* fast, but it can't brake easily nor can it turn left or right. As the performance of tape scales up, the potential advantages offered by its increased capacity are limited by the streaming performance requirements, reducing its practicality for particular workloads or data set sizes.

17.4.1   HSM AND ARCHIVE

Consider a standard tape read operation. It will consist of the following activities:

- Load tape
- Seek to location on tape containing the data required
- Read data required
- Rewind tape
- Eject tape

Each of these activities takes tangible periods of time. Even the fastest tape systems typically require 3–5 seconds to load a tape, and *average* tape systems require quite a few more seconds than that. (For example, one vendor* quotes a 7 second load/unload time for its LTO-4 tape drives, and 17 second load/unload time for its LTO-5 tape drives.)

If we assume even just a 60 second seek time for the required data on tape, 5 seconds to read the data required, and then 65 seconds to rewind from that end position, a single access of HSM/archive LTO-5 tape could take as long as 164 seconds to 2.7 minutes.

It is these slow access times in particular that have vastly reduced the use of tape in HSM/archive situations. As users and organizations have grown to expect fast

---

* http://www.overlandstorage.com/PDFs/LTO_Tape_Media_DS.pdf.

access times, a delay of multiple minutes to retrieve data is more likely to have the access request canceled due to impatience than to actually be completed.

Comparing this to HSM/archive stored on lower-speed large-capacity disks, the worst-case access times are likely to be in seconds rather than minutes, and average requests more likely to still be serviced in times of 5 seconds or less, depending on the size of the data being read.

However, disk introduced another efficiency that tape could not match—single instancing and deduplication. Single instancing refers to saving only one copy of any archived data* and works on a similar principle to deduplication, but typically at the file or object level.

Regardless of whether single instancing or deduplication (or both) are used within an archive system, this dramatically decreases the cost of disk compared to tape for storage. Such techniques allow disk systems to hold considerably more than their "raw" capacity with negligible performance impact for data read situations—especially compared to tape access speeds.

(Deduplication in particular is meaningless if tape is being used as the storage medium—read from deduplicated storage consists of many random IOs to reconstruct the data, and such a read from tape would take too long to be of any practical value for a business. Indeed, products that support writing deduplicated data to tape require a large amount of that data to be "staged" back into disk storage to facilitate data access if requested.)

17.4.2 BACKUP AND RECOVERY

17.4.2.1 Disk-to-Disk-to-Tape

As disk storage became increasingly cheaper, many enterprises started developing disk-to-disk-to-tape backup (D2D2T) solutions. The "disk-to-disk-to-tape" referred to transferring backups from backup client disks to backup server disks and then on to tape. This would allow overnight backups to be written to disk storage on the backup server and/or storage nodes/media servers, and then be "staged" out to tape during the day when backups weren't running.

This had several advantages:

- Tape drive failures would not immediately impact the backup process
- Shoe-shining during the backup process was eliminated
- Transfer to tape could happen faster without shoe-shining by being a single sequential read from disk to SCSI or FC attached tape on the same host
- Recoveries executed from backups still on disk were fast

While initially disk staging areas were often designed to hold only one or two days worth of backups, many enterprises found the benefits of being able to service short-term recovery requests from fast-start storage extremely compelling, particularly as environments grew. As such, companies started looking to increase their

---

* Not including any RAID/storage redundancy.

disk backup environments from relatively small staging areas to larger buckets capable of holding up to and including their smallest backup cycle (e.g., 1 week).

17.4.2.2 Disk-to-Disk-to-Disk

As the recovery utility benefits of keeping backups on disk grew and further influenced backup architecture decisions within organizations, some enterprises began experimenting with completely eliminating tape from their environments, thus disk-to-disk-to-tape became disk-to-disk-to-disk, since the fundamental requirement of ensuring all backups have at least two copies remains regardless of the technology used. (This was sought for reliability as well as cost reduction through elimination of all the manual handling associated with tape.)

Eliminating tape for most organizations is achieved through use of deduplication technology, discussed in detail in Chapter 13. Multiple backups are accommodated on tape by increasing the number of units of media used within the system, but it is not economically feasible to simply continue to write the same data again and again to disk storage, infinitely expanding that disk storage to accommodate the data. That is, disk-to-disk-to-disk requires using disk backup targets intelligently rather than being a like-for-like tape replacement.

As disk targets for backup became more pervasive within businesses, more advanced backup techniques have further driven tape out of backup infrastructure. The SAN infrastructure required to share tape drives out to multiple hosts is expensive and scales poorly, with the number of tape drives always acting as a limiting factor. Intelligent and integrated backup appliances with IP connectivity and client-agents allow for *massively* distributed backup environments, significantly reducing the overall cost of backup services infrastructure by reducing or even entirely eliminating storage nodes/media servers.*

At minimum, enterprises will deploy disk-to-disk-to-disk backup solutions with the express intent of cutting tape out of the backup cycle for all but the longest retention backups. For instance, an organization that performs daily incrementals with weekly and monthly fulls, keeping the daily/weekly backups for 6 weeks and the monthlies for 7 years, will typically design a disk-"only" backup solution to ensure all daily/weekly backups exist *only* on disk, with only the longer-retention monthly backups *eventually* pushed out to tape. For some businesses, even this has not been a sufficient elimination of tape and they have made use of additional deduplication/compression technology in PBBAs/IDPAs to keep all backups, regardless of their retention time, on disk.

17.4.2.3 Disk-to-Disk-to-Cloud

We're increasingly seeing a shift to operational expenditure (OpEx) over capital expenditure (CapEx) spending. "Pay as you go" and "pay for what you use" is

---

* Consider that in either tape-based or dumb-disk-based backup environments, storage nodes/media servers are typically high-end servers designed for pushing large amounts of aggregated data through as fast as possible. Such systems often have multiple CPUs, fast backplanes, expensive IO cards, and multiple high-speed network connections.

dominating in an economic landscape where every department in almost every business is required to minimize the amount spent at any given time. Thus, a single upfront purchase of data protection storage requirements for, say, 3 years may be more difficult to arrange for many businesses (particularly in the commercial rather than the enterprise space) than 36 months of operational expenditure, even if the total operational expenditure exceeds the 3-year capital expenditure.

The shrinking cost of cloud storage and increasing bandwidth of Internet connectivity is providing these businesses a new avenue of eliminating tape from their environments and we are seeing the start of the disk-to-disk-to-cloud backup strategy. These configurations see short-term retention backups kept on local disk, with longer-term retention backups pushed out to low-cost cloud storage, usually with some form of deduplication involved to reduce the overall cloud storage spend. (Such strategies are based on the economics of a limited number of recoveries from long-term backups* and the generally accepted lower SLA for such recoveries.)

17.5 DO UNMANAGED TAPES PROVIDE PROTECTION?

Consider the release dates of common tape formats, as shown in Table 17.1.

If we consider a 7-year retention time in 2016, there is a vast potential for legacy tape formats to still hold data a business is legally required to keep. Counting back from 2016, a business that has updated its tape drives on every new release will have potentially used a large number of tape formats during that time period. Further, tape that is not actively being read is not being checked. While a backup product may very well be maintained for 7, 10, or 15 years or more within an organization, the number of tape formats that could be cycled through during that period may very well be extensive.

True media management is rarely practiced in organizations. Tapes, once generated, are sent off-site and retrieved *if and only if* a request is made to recover data from them. This isn't real media management.

TABLE 17.1
Release Years of Common Tape Formats

	DLT-IV	LTO-1	LTO-2	LTO-3	LTO-4	LTO-5	LTO-6	LTO-7
Year	1994	2000	2003	2005	2007	2010	2013	2015

---

* It is worth noting that as longer-term retention backups become easier and faster to access (something not usually afforded with tape), the chances of more recovery requests being executed against those backups can increase. When calculating the potential costs of retrieval from public cloud, businesses should always assume a higher number of recoveries than might be currently serviced from tape.

For organizations using tape, *true* media management must comprise *at least* the following activities:

- Migrating all data on old format tapes to new format tapes: While LTO-*x* guarantees being able to write LTO-*x-1* and *read* LTO-*x-2*, it doesn't read older formats. Before tape drives that read these old formats are decommissioned, the tapes *must* be migrated.*
- Periodic recall and testing: True purpose-built backup appliances will have a rigorous and ongoing consistency check process, performing regular validation of all data written to them *and* avoiding the chance for filesystem corruption (e.g., by only ever deleting or writing new data, never appending to existing data). Tapes sitting on shelves or in storage are *not* being checked, and so must be periodically tested.
- Safe storage and transport: Tapes are actually somewhat delicate, *and* they're also highly portable. Without correct care and attention:
  - Tapes have been physically stolen or lost
  - Tapes have been stored in environments that don't offer suitable temperature and humidity protection
  - Tapes have been transported so haphazardly as to render them unusable

If a business *is* going to use tape for data protection, it *must* institute a rigorous, comprehensive tape management regime, or else data protection is just a "check in the box"—premised on luck, designed on false economies, and run by laziness.

Unmanaged tapes do not offer real data protection at all.

17.6   FUTURE OF TAPE

Tape is not dead. However, the prevalence of considerably cheaper disk storage at high capacities, highly dense storage efficiencies such as deduplication and the benefit of massively distributed backup systems via IDPAs is increasingly pushing tape out to fringe use cases within data protection.

Two key examples of where tape still has relevance within organizations are

1. *Long-term cold storage*: Agencies and businesses that must maintain geological, mapping, or health image data that is rarely if ever accessed *may* still find the economics of tape appealing.
2. *Deduplicatability of data*: If data being backed up is already compressed, encrypted, or otherwise does not yield itself to deduplication, tape *can* represent a practical and efficient storage mechanism.

That being said, the ongoing evolution and utility benefits of disk storage for extending and enhancing a data protection environment, as well as the falling costs of cloud storage, will likely continue eroding tape use cases. It can certainly be argued, however, that we've well and truly reached the point where tape use in data protection is by exception rather than by rule.

---

* It is not uncommon at all to hear of long-term recovery processes including "buy a second hand tape drive online."

18 Converged Infrastructure

18.1 INTRODUCTION

The traditional approach to datacenter components has developed as a series of silos originating out of the individual groups responsible for service delivery. Network administrators procure and build networks, storage administrators procure and build storage systems, and system administrators procure and build hosts that access the storage and the networks. On top of all of this, application administrators, developers, and database administrators request resources and, once they get them, start doing the activities seen by the business. Outside of this, there can be larger business activities where the company assembles authorized personnel from a variety of areas who go off and procure their entire infrastructure stacks for transformative projects that must eventually be integrated into the broader IT environment.

It's almost the proverbial duck on the pond: it looks graceful and effortless (or unmoving and unhurried in particularly process-laden environments) above the water, but if you check under the waterline there's a lot of activity going on.

If we think of standard change and development processes within most enterprises, the start to finish process of allocating a host for a developer or database administrator can be quite a time-consuming one. First, a request has to be made for an IP address and DNS entry. Then, a request has to be made for the system as well as a storage request for that host. Assuming the host will be a virtual machine, the host has to be provisioned, then the operating system built according to standard processes (unless it's included in the provisioned virtual machine via a template), the storage attached, and so on.

While there are merits to such a formal provisioning process, there are greater merits to being able to step through the process automatically and *quickly*, which is a considerable reason why cloud-based approaches to agility and automation have taken hold in many enterprises.

Converged infrastructure seeks to make this service provisioning and delivery process even faster and easier by tightly coupling network, storage, and compute so their delivery can *all* be automated and available in a self-service manner. This is not, however, something as simple as putting an IP switch, fiber-channel switch, servers, and SAN in the one rack and calling it "converged." An orchestration or management overlay needs to also be present to allow these components to be adroitly handled as a single logical function.

There are in fact two variants of converged infrastructure—converged and *hyper*-converged. While there is still a degree of nebulosity for each term and overlap between the two, one generally accepted differentiation is the level of integration; *converged* is deemed to be loosely coupled components, perhaps even following a reference architecture and allowing a prospective business to achieve a degree of modularity in the component types (e.g., replacing storage systems). *Hyper*converged, on the other hand, is generally accepted to be far more tightly coupled through the entire technology layer, with the supplied system almost immediately ready for deployment from the moment it is installed in racks and powered up in the datacenter. Comparing to traditional approaches of infrastructure within the datacenter, the converged and hyperconverged market is about "buy" rather than "build."

Regardless of whether it is converged or hyperconverged, the business imperative of this type of infrastructure is simple: is it the role of IT staff to build infrastructure from the ground up, or build *services* on infrastructure? The old model—much like the "build your own PC" model—is premised on IT departments having sufficient time and resources and skills to build infrastructure. The new model is premised on IT departments providing rapid service creation and presentation to the business on top of modular, scale-out infrastructure ready for production use almost immediately after delivery.

Some will claim that there is a premium to pay for converged or hyperconverged systems, and indeed a dollar for dollar comparison between the cost of the complete infrastructure in its converged/hyperconverged form and the cost of the individual components may seem to back this claim up. Yet such a simple cost comparison fails to take into account all the intangibles in the entire process. Returning again to our analogy about building a PC versus buying one, think of the time and effort required in that build process: determining what parts are going to be compatible with one another, picking the specific parts for each component, and then assembling the entire unit. Compatibility in this sense doesn't just refer to *physical* compatibility, such as whether CPU X will plug into motherboard Y, but whether all the device drivers provided by all the hardware vendors used will not only be supported by the operating system you want to run, but also interoperate with one another without causing system issues. Conversely, someone buying a brand new PC direct from the manufacturer should be confident that the various device drivers and hardware components *will* be compatible with one another. This is precisely the difference between traditional infrastructure builds and converged or hyperconverged infrastructure—the time taken from the initiation of the project to the point where the equipment is being productively used without fear or concern about compatibility issues. Someone needing to research and buy all the individual PC components and then build the system from the ground up, including OS and application install, will take considerably longer to reach *useful productivity* on the finished system than someone who purchases a complete unit, powers it on, and starts productively using it within, say, 10 minutes.

A complete review of converged infrastructure is outside of the scope of a book about data protection, but as you would well imagine, there *are* data protection implications of utilizing converged infrastructure within a modern IT environment, and this chapter will briefly review those considerations. For the purposes of our discussion, we will consider converged and hyperconverged interchangeably.

18.2   PROTECTING CONVERGED INFRASTRUCTURE SYSTEMS

Converged infrastructure is almost invariably aligned to 100% virtualization—that is, typically all of the business-consumable systems provided by a converged infrastructure environment are virtualized hosts. The nature of converged infrastructure also tends to result in reasonably *dense* virtualized environments in relation to the rack-space occupied by the physical systems.

The data protection considerations for converged infrastructure will be the same as those used for conventional infrastructure. Storage will still need some form of data storage protection, systems requiring high or continuous availability will require protection from storage system failure, and there will still need to be options for data recoverability in the event of loss.

When deploying converged infrastructure, a key question the business must ask is: "does the converged infrastructure come with its own data protection solution?"* If the infrastructure *does* come with its own data protection solution, this yields further questions for the business, notably:

- Is the data protection solution one that allows physical separation of protection data copies and the original data?
- Are the data protection options available in the in-built solution immutable, or can they be grown and/or changed in response to changing business requirements?
- Does the company already have a data protection solution?
    - If so:
        - How will management of the two solutions be handled or merged?
        - How will monitoring, reporting, and trending be achieved across the two solutions?
    - If not:
        - Will the protection solution provided within the converged infrastructure be able to provide data protection services for the rest of the business?

If the converged infrastructure is being procured without a complete data protection stack, then the company has to evaluate how to use or extend its existing data protection services to cover the converged infrastructure.

It's fair to say that none of these are new questions: arguably exactly the same total project-life data protection questions asked of any infrastructure must also be asked of converged infrastructure. The list of considerations for a single server relating *just* to backup and recovery outlined in Section 5.3 applies regardless of whether a single server or a thousand servers are being deployed. Even at its most basic, converged infrastructure will very likely deploy a number of servers capable of running a much larger number of virtual machines, and at the extreme end using rack-scale hyperconverged infrastructure may see the deployment of hundreds or thousands of physical nodes capable of running tens of thousands of virtual machines. Quite simply: converged infrastructure makes the notion of "dumb luck" serving as a data protection design rule impossible.

18.3   WHAT WILL BE PROTECTED? (REDUX)

In Chapter 8, the question "What will be protected?" was posed. It's very easy to become complacent in IT and think of data protection as only needing to be performed against primary data storage components—servers, SAN systems, and NAS

---

* Ideally a true converged infrastructure, and even more so a true *hyper*converged infrastructure, will have a fully integrated and compatible data protection strategy built into it from the ground up.

systems, for example. Yet there is a wealth of other systems within your environment that houses data that should be protected—for example, IP switches, SAN switches, and PABX systems. In converged infrastructure, much of this configuration data is hidden from the individual hosts being presented. A set of hyperconverged nodes, for instance, offering a virtualization environment can host a virtual machine that performs backups of all hosted systems, replicating those backups to an offsite location, but what is protecting the hyperconverged data? Is it sufficient to have a multi-node cluster to protect that data, or does the infrastructure management layer of the system require appropriate levels of data protection to mitigate site loss or extreme corruption situations?

Converged and hyperconverged systems can make deployment and management of data protection systems as easy as they make deployment and management of primary production systems, but data protection considerations must be broader than the virtualized infrastructure provided by the said systems. All data points within the infrastructure should support appropriate levels of dump and restore functionality, or be appropriately protected via clustering (local and multisite) and self-healing/self-building capabilities: IP networking, SAN networking, hypervisor management, and orchestration layer databases.

18.4   CONVERGED STAFF

As mentioned in Section 4.2.4, the increasing complexity involved in ensuring comprehensive data protection policies are developed and implemented creates a need for *infrastructure administrators*.

Converged infrastructure reinforces this need: trying to keep to traditional, formal deployment processes requiring manual requests and manual intervention at every step along the way completely eliminates the advantages of infrastructure convergence. The management and orchestration layer required for true converged infrastructure allows (or, indeed, *requires*) administrators to become policy coordinators and architects, with the infrastructure's control system handling the mundane, day-to-day implementation services.

In traditional IT delivery models, there is a reasonable amount of time assigned to each individual group of administrators (virtual, storage, system, application, and database) to contemplate and perhaps even discuss the data protection requirements for a project or service. With converged infrastructure, there is *no* time during the implementation; the data protection options must be backed into the service catalog offerings or they will not be delivered. Properly implemented, the orchestration layer and self-service portals for converged infrastructure will allow subscribers (e.g., developers or technical project managers) to requisition and receive access to their systems within minutes, with no human intervention on the infrastructure side. Data protection will either be performed automatically based on other selections made by the user (or perhaps even the user's profile) *or* will come from a limited set of options available to the user during service provisioning.

Thus, the importance of having broad infrastructure administrators cannot be overstated when using converged infrastructure. The data protection policies made available must be built alongside the rest of the service catalog and be aligned to business requirements. Only administrators and architects who are across all aspects of the converged infrastructure will be able to ensure the service catalog as implemented will maximize data protection capabilities.

18.5   SUMMARY

Once implemented, there's little difference between the data protection requirements for converged or even hyperconverged infrastructure and classic IT infrastructure. Regardless of whether systems are deployed through automated methods or a more traditional, manual approach, systems must be kept available, data must be replicated, snapshots must be generated, and backup and recovery policies must be configured based on the requirements of the business and the type of data, not the infrastructure being used to host it.

In fact, there are usually only two differences between converged/hyperconverged infrastructure and traditional infrastructure when it comes to data protection: scale and automation. As we saw in Chapter 4, the technology used plays only a small part in the successful delivery of a holistic data protection strategy within a business, and this remains the case with converged infrastructure. If anything, converged and hyperconverged infrastructure serve to demonstrate the criticality of planning, processes, and automation in data protection at scale.

19 Data Protection Service Catalogs

19.1 INTRODUCTION

For a complete understanding of service catalogs, readers are advised to study appropriate disciplines, such as ITIL v3. Completely explaining the entire service catalog approach to business IT systems is beyond the scope of this book, but it is worth understanding some of the critical components of working with service catalogs and data protection.

For many businesses, particularly the small office through to medium enterprise, there has traditionally been a substantial gulf between that which is desirable and that which is achievable for IT systems. This has gradually eroded as virtualization, XaaS, and cloud access have significantly expanded the options available even with relatively limited budgets. Ongoing increases to Internet speeds have and undoubtedly will continue to enable greater options, particularly for those that leverage the cloud.

We would consider most businesses now to be reliant on IT (regardless of what form it takes) for operational success. A pharmaceutical company might consider drug manufacturing to be its key operational requirement, but the IT systems that hold and model research data, that control production lines, and that perform inventory, billing, and stock shipping, not to mention payroll and other personnel functions, are *all* significant contributors to the success (or failure) of the company.

While it's usual to consider the cloud model on the basis of user-driven provisioning and elasticity, additional components that are much desired by businesses include rapid turnaround and well-defined service models. At a broad level and focusing on the consumers of the cloud, we can say that there are two key aspects to cloud-like service delivery:

1. Automation
2. Service catalog

The automation is what allows someone to go to a web portal and request a new database server with a particular amount of storage attached to it. At the back end, the automation leverages virtualization, REST APIs, highly functional command lines, and DevOps-generated code that takes what used to be days or weeks of disparate provisioning and turns around the request within minutes for the user.

The service catalog becomes the curated menu of options for the consumers. As businesses seek cloud-like service levels within their own operations, a service catalog that clearly defines options available to consumers becomes an imperative—not just for the consumers, but for the teams that automate the process from end to end. Thus, as cloud continues to affect the business attitude toward and requirements of IT, so too will the importance of service catalogs in the business/IT relationship continue to grow.

19.2   KEY REQUIREMENTS FOR A SERVICE CATALOG

In order for a service catalog to actually be useful, it has to meet certain essential criteria. Arguably, the most important criteria (particularly when it comes to data protection) are

- Utility
- Measurable
- Achievable
- Distinct
- Costed
- Priced

19.2.1   UTILITY

There is no point providing a service catalog option that serves no meaningful function. Each service catalog option must be matched to either a business requirement (for internal service catalogs) or a saleable service (for XaaS providers). By ensuring all service catalog options have a purpose, we avoid building overly complex and confusing service catalogs.

19.2.2   MEASURABLE

Service catalogs reflect a move toward formalized delivery of IT services, whether they are automated through some DevOps process or merely developed as templates for guaranteed consistency of service. In Chapter 2, we stated:

> If you can't measure something you can't improve it.

Likewise, if you can't measure something, you can't *prove* you're delivering the service the consumer is ordering from you. This can be deemed as critical for any of the following:

- Charging
- Costing
- Continuous improvement
- Monitoring
- Reporting

None of these can be accurately and effectively performed unless the delivery of the service option can be measured.

19.2.3 ACHIEVABLE

Intimately similar to *service-level agreements* (*SLAs*), service catalog options have to be realistically deliverable in terms of the technology, process, automation, and personnel available to the business. Service catalog options should not promise continuously storage availability if the environment can't cater for this; likewise, offering recovery from backup in a disaster to a secondary site in under an hour is meaningless if backups are still performed to tape and it takes 3 hours to ship tapes to the secondary site.

19.2.4 DISTINCT

Each service catalog option that is listed must effectively be unique. Making the same option available at multiple tiers simply confuses consumers, creates expectations of differing services, *and* likely antagonizes consumers if they could have been paying less for the same option.

From a simple design perspective though, having distinct service catalog options fulfills a basic tenet of IT design, that being

> The system should be as simple as possible, and no simpler.

By introducing nonunique service catalog items, we only serve to make the system more complex than it needs to be—this in turn has the potential to affect automation, perceived value, utility, measurability, and deliverability. (This is not to say that all aspects of each service catalog tier should be unique. For example, replication might be offered for multiple service catalog tiers, with differentiating features being synchronous versus asynchronous, or more broadly, the lag time between source and target.)

19.2.5 COSTED

The business should have an understanding of how much it costs to deliver this service item. This applies to both *X*aaS providers and to businesses offering service catalogs for internal consumption. For *X*aaS providers, the reason is obvious: it allows the business to subsequently *price* the option effectively and avoid scenarios where the cost to the business is higher than the price charged to consumers.

Even for businesses offering the service catalog only for internal consumption this is important, as it allows the business to accurately understand the utility cost of the service catalog, and provides a mechanism to prevent internal consumers oversubscribing to the highest service catalog options simply because it's a selectable option. Some service catalog options will effectively *share* resources. It could very well be, for instance, that a backup service has both short-term (30 days) backups and longer-term (say, 2 years) written to the same protection storage. The system, and therefore the delivery costs, might be architected on the basis of 75% of subscribers choosing the 30-day retention model and only 25% of subscribers choosing the 2-year retention model. Understanding the cost to deliver a 30-day versus a 730-day retention allows better management of subscriber options and capacity growth.

19.2.6 Priced

In addition to understanding the cost to the business of delivering each service catalog option, the business should understand the price for subscribing to that service,
particularly since the price inevitably includes meta-costs outside of IT controls,
such as broader staffing considerations, overall business operational costs, etc.

Yet like for the *Costed* option, this applies as equally to the XaaS provider models
as it does businesses offering service catalogs for internal consumption. For the XaaS
model, the rationale is simple: the consumer is the customer, and the customer must
pay to make use of the service.

For internal service catalog deliveries, there are two (potentially overlapping) reasons why a pricing structure might be developed. For businesses that engage in full
cross charging, this might be the mechanism used by the IT department to not only
recoup costs of service delivery but also partially fund research and development, or
new initiatives. For those businesses that do not engage in cross charging, it is likely
the pricing structure will at least match the costing structure to enable per-division or
per-subscriber amortization of service provisioning costs.

19.3   SERVICE CATALOG TIERS AND OPTIONS

Service catalogs tend to be categorized by a few different common naming
approaches. The two most common naming approaches are usually aligned to either
numbered tiers or precious metals. Thus, options might be "tier 1," "tier 2," "tier 3,"
and so on, or "platinum," "gold," "silver," and "bronze." There is no right or wrong
approach, but the naming standard adopted should be kept consistent to maximize
clarity (i.e., you should not have "platinum," "gold," "silver," "bronze," and "tier 5").
Thus, if a business is concerned they'll need more than four tiers of options for any
particular service type, it might be best to avoid using the precious metals naming
approach. For the purposes of our discussion, however, we'll use the precious metals
approach and stick to just three levels—platinum, gold, and silver.

A service catalog for data protection is not necessarily going to be as straightforward as defining options for "platinum," "gold," "silver," and "bronze," however, and
it may not necessarily be the case that all platinum options are created equally, all
gold options are created equally, and so on. A few different scenarios that might be
leveraged in the classification of service catalog options are outlined next.

19.3.1 Service Catalog Based on Application Type

This strategy focuses on data protection options based on application type. The same
service-level name might be defined multiple times depending on what applications
it is available for, and the specifics of what is provided by the service level may
change based on the suitability for the application. An example breakdown based on
this strategy can be found in Table 19.1.

This allows for the presentation of a very simple and straightforward service catalog for data protection, but it does come at the cost of flexibility. What happens, for
instance, if a database needs to be placed on continuously available storage (CAS)
with 24 × 7 synchronous replication, *but* has lower performance requirements out

TABLE 19.1

Data Protection Service Catalog by Application Type

Service Level	Application	Provides
Platinum	Database server	• Continuous storage availability • Synchronous replication of storage systems to secondary and tertiary site • Snapshots taken every 15 minutes • Snapshots replicated to secondary and tertiary sites • Nightly full backups via direct primary storage to protection storage module
Platinum	File server	• Continuous storage availability • Synchronous replication of storage systems to secondary site during business hours; asynchronous replication with a lag of up to 30 minutes permitted outside of business hours • Snapshots taken every 30 minutes under the management of the backup application and replicated automatically to the secondary site • Snapshots "rolled over" into data protection storage as a backup at midday and midnight
Gold	Database server	• Continuous storage availability • Synchronous replication to secondary site during business hours; asynchronous replication with up to a 15 minute lag permitted out of business hours • Hourly snapshots with replication to secondary site, managed by backup application • Nightly full backups to data protection storage via database module provided by backup software
Gold	File server	• Continuous storage availability • Asynchronous replication to secondary site with no more than a 30 minute lag permitted at any point • Hourly snapshots with replication to secondary site, managed by backup application • 10 pm snapshot "rolled over" as the backup into data protection storage each day
Silver	Database server	• Traditional SAN storage • Application journaling and log transport used to keep copy on secondary site up to date asynchronously • Daily snapshots managed by the SAN • Nightly full backups to data protection storage via database module
Silver	File server	• Traditional NAS storage • Six snapshots generated per day (4-hourly) by storage system policies • Nightly NDMP backups to data protection storage

of hours and could instead be backed up via a standard database module? In such a scenario, the platinum database service option would need to be used, and this would automatically use the more costly backup option where data is transferred direct from primary storage to data protection storage.

Another potential challenge created by this option is confusing what level of protection is provided *between* applications. Consider the platinum options, for instance: the platinum database option has synchronous replication to the secondary and tertiary site 24 × 7, whereas the platinum file server option has synchronous replication only to the secondary site, *and* the replication becomes asynchronous out of business hours. While it's perfectly reasonable for a business to require and provide higher service levels for mission-critical databases versus file servers, consumers of the service who use *both* options might more readily confuse the service levels provided based on application type.

19.3.2 SERVICE CATALOG INDEPENDENT OF APPLICATION TYPE

This model offers the same level of protection irrespective of the application or business function calling for the option, and an example can be seen in Table 19.2.

TABLE 19.2

Data Protection Service Catalog Independent of Application Type

Service Level	Provides
Platinum	• Continuously available storage • Synchronous replication between metro-connected datacenters • Asynchronous replication to tertiary disaster recovery datacenter in an alternate city, maximum half-hour lag • Half-hourly snapshots with replication snapshots between sites • Daily backups using the most appropriate high-performance/minimized impact option for the application or data type • Backups automatically replicated to secondary and tertiary site; backups for secondary and tertiary site kept for the same time as the production site copy
Gold	• Continuously available storage • Asynchronous replication between metro-connected datacenters, maximum half-hour lag • Asynchronous replication to tertiary disaster recovery datacenter in an alternate city, maximum 4-hour lag • Backups automatically replicated to secondary and tertiary site; backup copy at secondary site maintained for same length of time as production site copy; backup copy at tertiary site retained for 7 days only
Silver	• RAID-protected SAN or NAS storage depending on the data type (RAID-6 for filesystems, RAID-1/RAID-10 for production databases, RAID-6 for non-production databases) • Log shipping as replication between metro-connected datacenters for databases or asynchronous replication with up to 4 hours lag between metro-connected datacenters for file-based data • Daily backups using the most appropriate option for the application or data type • Backups automatically replicated to disaster recovery site only

---

While this model further simplifies the service catalog and allows subscribers or consumers to more easily choose what they want, it suffers a similar flaw to the previous option—what happens, for instance, if a consumer needs the more advanced storage availability or snapshot options, but doesn't need the more advanced backup options?

19.3.3   SERVICE CATALOG OPTIONS PER DATA PROTECTION ACTIVITY

This model presents more data protection options for the consumer/subscriber, allowing a higher granularity in the options chosen, as shown in Table 19.3.

While this provides maximum granularity, it can lead to "option overload" to a subscriber—that is, it may be seen as being more complex because of the number of options it provides. There are additional considerations that must be taken into account with this type of service catalog however.

First, when each service catalog item refers to a single piece of data protection functionality, it is more easy for there to be options that are the same for different *levels*. For instance, in Table 19.3 the gold data storage option is listed as "not available

TABLE 19.3
Data Protection Service Catalog per Data Protection Activity

Service Level	Applies To	Provides
Platinum	Data storage	Continuously available storage.
Platinum	Replication	Synchronous replication to secondary and tertiary site.
Platinum	Snapshots	Snapshots taken every 15 minutes, snapshots replicated to secondary site. Snapshots retained for 7 days.
Platinum	Backups	Daily backups via primary storage direct to data protection storage *or* backup application managed snapshot rollover (depending on application applicability). Backups automatically replicated to secondary and tertiary site.
Gold	Data storage	*Not available* (*choose platinum or silver*).
Gold	Replication	Asynchronous replication to secondary and tertiary site, maximum 15 minute lag.
Gold	Snapshots	Snapshots taken hourly, snapshots replicated to secondary site. Snapshots retained for 5 days.
Gold	Backups	Daily backups via appropriate module or agent, automatically replicated to secondary and tertiary site.
Silver	Data storage	Standard SAN or NAS depending on application requirements. RAID-6 for file-based data, RAID-1 or RAID-10 for database data.
Silver	Replication	Asynchronous replication to secondary site only, maximum 30 minute lag.
Silver	Snapshots	Snapshots taken once per day, not replicated. Snapshots retained for 30 days.
Silver	Backup	Daily backups via appropriate module or agent, automatically replicated to tertiary site only.

(choose platinum or silver)" for the reason that—comparing to previous service catalog examples given—the gold option may be the *same* as the platinum, in this case
both would refer to CAS.

This can become less of an issue when a data protection service catalog is also
tied to the data storage services as a broader consideration. This might result, for
instance, in offerings of

- Platinum data storage:
  - *Storage tier*: SSD
  - *Storage protection*: continuously available storage
- Gold data storage:
  - Storage tier: 10,000 RPM SAS, hot spot tiering to SSD (max 10%)
  - Storage protection: continuously available storage

Such offerings may be modified according to the expected technical capabilities
of the potential subscriber. For the purposes of clarity, we cite actual storage types
earlier; in an actual service catalog provided to subscribers, this might be simplified
to state "high performance" and "standard performance" for storage speed, and so on.

Our second consideration with this service catalog is offering this level of granularity requires either careful decoupling of dependencies *between* data protection
options *or* logical enforcement of available options to ensure dependencies are
always subscribed to. Consider, for instance, a "platinum" backup option that performs backups direct from the primary storage system to the data protection storage
system; this might be dependent on a type of primary storage system only available to subscribers of the platinum or gold data storage service catalog options. If a
user chooses the platinum backup option but the "silver" data storage option, how
would this be reconciled—would the system prevent the platinum backup option
being available while the silver data storage option was selected, or would the user
be silently "upgraded" (at no extra cost) to the platinum data storage option but not
informed?

19.4   RETENTION MULTIPLIER

For some forms of data protection (e.g., snapshots), it might be acceptable to have
the retention time available to the data protection option locked to the service level
required. For other forms of data protection, a business may find itself having to offer
a variety of retention options for legal or compliance requirements, and this should
be understood when working on data protection service catalogs.

Consider snapshots, for instance: if a platinum service level defines that snapshots
will be taken every 15 minutes, that would result in 96 snapshots being generated per
day. A silver service level might define snapshots being taken every 8 hours, which
would result in three snapshots per day. It might therefore be deemed reasonable to
retain only 3 days of platinum snapshots (a total of 288) while retaining 30 days of
silver snapshots (a total of 90). Given snapshots in particular can have a detrimental
impact on primary storage performance if they're kept too long and the change rate

becomes too high, this might be so architected into the solution that there are no variations available to the consumer.

When it comes to backup, it may not be possible or even appropriate to hard-code the retention time into a policy. Some mission-critical applications may not require long-term retention of backups, while other applications or systems of lower importance may in fact require the longest retention. A mission-critical database, for instance, may have older content automatically copied and/or archived to a data warehouse. As such a relatively short retention period may be acceptable for backups of the mission-critical database itself, while the data warehouse instead might require its less frequent backups (e.g., monthly or yearly) retained for many months, if not years.*

Service providers offering backup and archive as part of an XaaS model may not be unduly concerned with any legal retention requirements. For such providers, there is no duty of care, for instance, to confirm that financial accounting data is retained for 7 years: it becomes the responsibility of the subscriber to the service (i.e., the actual legal owner of the data) to ensure the appropriate retention period is offered or the appropriate steps are taken to export/copy the data periodically to meet compliance retention requirements.

When a service catalog is being offered internally though as part of a hybrid or private cloud model or simply for streamlined service access, the line of responsibility is more difficult to draw. Is it the responsibility of the subscriber who is choosing options from the service catalog to confirm the correct retention requirements, will the business just perform the same type of retention per a traditional backup and recovery/archive model, or will the service catalog have retention offerings based on more easily understood options? (For instance, a subscriber might have to choose between whether the data being stored is financial, legal, life sciences, development, or temporary, and each data type has a back-end association with the most appropriate retention policy.)

Regardless of how it is approached, a business should be prepared to have some flexibility for subscribers regarding retention times applied when providing backup and recovery options in a data protection service catalog.

19.5 INCLUDING SERVICE LEVEL AGREEMENTS IN SERVICE CATALOGS

Up until now, our focus on the service catalog has been on the level of overall protection provided—frequency of snapshots, level of replication, frequency of backups, etc. However, there's another critical aspect to consider in service catalogs—the SLAs associated with them. In fact, the SLAs effectively dominate the options provided in the service catalog; service offerings of synchronous replication imply

---

* As mentioned in Chapter 3, more comprehensive data lifecycle policy should see data deleted if it is no longer required or archived if it has to be retained for an extremely long period of time. However, this is not necessarily well practiced and many businesses will use backup and recovery software to achieve a simulacrum of archive functionality.

a much higher requirement for fault tolerance than, say, asynchronous replication. As we've established throughout this book, a single form of data protection isn't actually enough though—synchronous *or* asynchronous replication will still happily replicate corrupt data, either immediately or with lag. SLAs relating to RPO and RTO in particular will therefore trigger the need to select appropriate forms of data protection at each layer. This might include synchronous replication to allow for automated failover of storage access in the event of an array fault, *and* continuous data protection to allow for application-consistent journaled roll-back in the event of a data corruption incident, *and* of course, traditional backup and recovery as well.

Previously, it was desirable to individually consider the SLAs for every single system or business function deployed and customize each SLA precisely. However, the driving goal for agile and automated deployment of infrastructure and applications creates a compromise—the need for reasonably *generic* but sufficiently appropriate tiers of SLAs—again, tied to the *tiers* of actual service levels offered by the catalog.

As mentioned in Table 2.2, a requirement in the modern IT environment is to ensure SLAs are designed around *where* the service may be provisioned from. In Table 2.2, for instance, a gold RTO/RPO was established as dependent on data locality:

- Traditional/private cloud—1 hour
- Hybrid cloud—4 hours
- Public cloud—8 hours

While enterprises with larger budgets or agile businesses with few critical requirements may be able to accommodate the same SLAs regardless of data locality (the former through using like-for-like or similar-enough infrastructure both on premises and in the cloud for data protection, the latter through simply using the worst-case scenario SLA for *all* SLAs), many businesses will have to codify different SLAs depending on data and compute locality. In actual fact, this is merely an analogous extension to the existing requirements of building SLAs based on actual available budget and resources. (That is, a small business might *wish* to have a RPO and RTO of 5 minutes for all systems, but practically this may be unattainable. The "where is the service?" question is merely another consideration along the same lines.)

In businesses not requiring 24 × 7 services, an additional consideration may need to be made as to whether SLAs for RPO and RTO in particular are the same *inside* operational hours as they are *outside* operational hours. Using a service catalog, the alternate approach however may instead be to limit the highest service levels for rapid RTO and small RPOs to those systems that require 24 × 7 availability or access, though this would still require business agreement.

The business will also need to carefully define in the context of a service catalog whether SLAs or SLOs are being offered. An SLA defines a hard target that *must* be met, usually at risk of either an internal or external fine being imposed. A service-level *objective*, on the other hand, is just that—a desirous option but one that is not necessarily enforced. When a service catalog mixes both SLAs and SLOs, it should be clearly outlined whether an offering is an agreement or an objective, and at no point should SLAs and SLOs be mixed in the *same* option.

19.6   BUILDING A DATA PROTECTION SERVICE CATALOG

Almost every business will have a slightly different attitude toward service catalog options, and those attitudes will be formed on the basis of the business, its customers, its requirements, and its budget. What might barely be deemed a "silver" data protection option for a multinational enterprise could very easily be classified as "platinum" for a small to medium regional business.

Companies that are unfamiliar with building service catalogs should not shy away from adopting them for data protection. Instead, it can serve as an excellent entry point for formalizing options within the broader IT environment starting with an important yet relatively narrow focus (compared to whole of IT). Successfully developing and implementing a service catalog for one IT discipline can help provide incentive for the business to expand the discipline to encompass all IT disciplines. (If approaching service catalogs for the first time, businesses would be well advised working with consulting companies with experience in service catalog architecture and delivery in IT.)

Except in the smallest of businesses, it is rare for service catalogs to be built end to end by a single individual. Usually, it will be a collaborative project involving both IT and broader business staff. IT staff will include architects, subject matter experts, and the manager who will be responsible for the catalog. The number and type of business staff involved will very much depend on the type of organization and may include any combination of

- Legal counsel
- Financial controllers
- Sales managers
- Key business function managers or their representatives
- Project managers

Indeed, the service catalogs should be discussed in a technology-independent fashion between IT and the business; the business should not need to concern itself with the minutiae of the technology characteristics, but be able to describe availability and protection requirements—and receive service catalogs documented—in business-appropriate language: availability as a percentage, data retention requirements, maximum data loss, etc. It's only when we get to the back-end IT service catalog that the technical details of the service catalog offerings *should* be documented.

Traditionally for many companies, storage systems, virtualization systems, and backup and recovery systems often operate on reasonably different refresh cycles. It's not unusual, for instance, to see backup and recovery software and hardware come up for refresh while there are another 2 or 3 years on a storage system contract, or vice versa. Ideally if *all* systems are being refreshed simultaneously, it becomes easier to build a complete service catalog based on the most modern options available, rather than, say, having to part-build the service catalog over a series of system refreshes.*

As mentioned previously, for a service catalog to be useful for an organization, each component must

- Have utility
- Be measurable
- Be achievable
- Be distinct
- Be costed
- Be priced

While the technical details of data protection service catalogs will undoubtedly be populated by IT architects, managers, and specialists, the *requirements* for the service catalog ultimately must be provided by the broader business, and this will undoubtedly require negotiations with IT based on what can actually be provided, in the same way that the business and IT must be able to agree to practical limits and capabilities for simple SLAs. This is regardless of whether the service catalog is being developed for internal consumption or whether it will be offered by a *X*aaS provider. In either case, there's no point in offering service catalog options that aren't aligned to either what the business *needs* or what the business is comfortable *selling*.

There will always be *two* versions of a service catalog—the public or consumer-facing version and the business-internal version of the service catalog. Up until now, the service catalog options we've shown have been more representative of consumer-facing catalogs (though the examples have not included pricing). A full internal version of the service catalog provides a complete map to the business and the IT teams of what must be delivered and how much it will cost.

For instance, if we were to consider the platinum options only in Table 19.3, the *internal* details of those options might include details such as the following:

- Data storage:
  - *Provides* (*utility*): CAS
  - *Measurable*: 100% agreed uptime, storage allocated on CAS arrays only, monitored by storage reporting system
  - *Costed*: $X per GB per month
  - *Priced*: $X + y per GB per month
- Replication:
  - *Provides* (*utility*): synchronous replication to secondary and tertiary site
  - *Measurable*: 100% up-to-date copies at primary, secondary, and tertiary sites, monitored by storage reporting system
  - *Costed*: $X per GB per month
  - *Priced*: $X + y per GB per month

---

* This can be a compelling argument for converged and hyperconverged infrastructure: refresh everything at once, deploy highly integrated options, and develop data protection service offerings taking maximum advantage of the hardware/software convergence.

One other factor for consideration is service catalog *versioning*. Almost everything that goes into a service catalog is subject to change—for example:

- Pricing for systems, power, networking, and staffing will fluctuate based on market conditions, conversion rates, and competition
- New technology and functionality becomes available
- Existing technology exits service life or becomes too expensive to maintain due to age
- Maintenance and support contracts may be altered during update cycles

(In more extreme cases, vendors or service providers might exit the market entirely or cease offering services that particular catalog items are designed around.)

Over time, any of these factors (and a variety of others) may cause the service catalog to be updated. Depending on the nature of the change, consumers may either need to have their service options automatically migrated (e.g., if new storage has been purchased and it has new functionality) or the business may need to maintain delivery capabilities for multiple versions of the service catalog until all consumers of previously available options have changed to other options, ceased using the service entirely, or been migrated following contracted period of access to the older options.

19.7   SUMMARY

While there will often be some similarities between service catalogs from different companies, the process of developing a service catalog for data protection is almost entirely dependent on the specific resources (staffing and technical) available to each business, as well as the intended use (internal or external) of that service catalog.

There is a tendency in many IT departments to resist service catalogs due to their perceived formality and binding nature. Yet by formalizing the offerings available, they actually *free* an IT department to more easily provide, monitor, and maintain a well-defined set of services. Rather than every single service being treated and delivered as a wholly bespoke one, services delivered either automatically or via a set of clear templates speed up both provisioning and service delivery, *and* reduce the risk of human error. In the same way that *most* IT departments, particularly within larger enterprises, will have virtual machine templates for common operating systems, database servers, and particular application servers, a clearly defined and readily repeatable set of templates for all facets of data protection services is worth the effort required to develop in order to improve business functionality.

20 Holistic Data Protection Strategies

20.1 INTRODUCTION

Up until now, we've mostly looked at each type of data protection option or strategy in isolation. While it's important to broadly understand each type of data protection that can be leveraged, implementing a single option is not sufficient for all but the most niche or esoteric of businesses.

As outlined in Section 1.4, data protection isn't just one single activity—it's a mix of proactive and reactive steps that you take—or might take—depending on the type of data you're trying to protect, its level of importance to the business, and your business requirements.

The types of data protection we've discussed thus far have included

- Continuous storage availability
- Replication (including continuous data protection)
- Snapshots
- Backup and recovery
- Data storage protection

It's fair to say that at-rest data storage protection (e.g., RAID, or object storage equivalence) will always feature as part of a complete data storage strategy, enabling data to survive the failure of at least the most fundamental part of the data storage platform, the drives themselves.

In this chapter, we'll provide three examples of multilayered data protection approaches based on particular environments. These are in a definitive set of examples, but they will provide a common baseline to the decision processes and techniques that often go into planning data protection.

20.2 EXAMPLES OF HOLISTIC DATA PROTECTION STRATEGIES

20.2.1 LARGE NAS PROTECTION

One of the best examples of a multilayered data protection approach comes from large NAS storage. These systems have always been large, but with the growth of scale-out storage fueling the prevalence of multi-petabyte systems, the data protection challenges posed by NAS are proving to be a common headache for many organizations.*

---

* While this example focuses on NAS protection, it can be equally applied to SAN systems with the same capabilities.

Filesystem 1   Snapshot FS1-1

Filesystem 2   Snapshot FS2-1

Filesystem 3   Snapshot FS3-1

Filesystem 4   Snapshot FS4-1

FIGURE 20.1   Single level of protection for NAS, taking a snapshot.

One of the simplest types of protection for NAS systems is to take snapshots of each filesystem, such as that shown in Figure 20.1.

Data protection requirements typically center around the requirements of Recovery Time Objective (RTO) and Recovery Point Objective (RPO). Remember that RTO refers to the maximum amount of time it can take to achieve system recovery, and RPO refers to the maximum amount of data loss that can be achieved. Additional considerations depending on the maturity of the business and the field in which it operates will include business continuity (and specifically, disaster recoverability) and legal compliance requirements.

In response to filesystem corruption or data deletion, a single snapshot is likely to achieve excellent RTO, as the snapshot data can be made available almost instantaneously. The RPO however in such a situation is quite variable, depending on when the snapshot is performed. Therefore it's more likely to see multiple snapshots performed for active filesystems over the course of a day, such as that shown in Figure 20.2.

The number of snapshots that can be taken per filesystem is usually independent, so the number of snapshots maintained and the regularity of which they are generated will be entirely dependent on the criticality of the data. Some filesystems might be snapped hourly, others even more frequently. Snapshot retention time becomes an important consideration here—unless data is almost entirely static, snapshots *can't* be kept forever. A typical approach is to have time-tiered snapshots offering different levels of retention based on how long

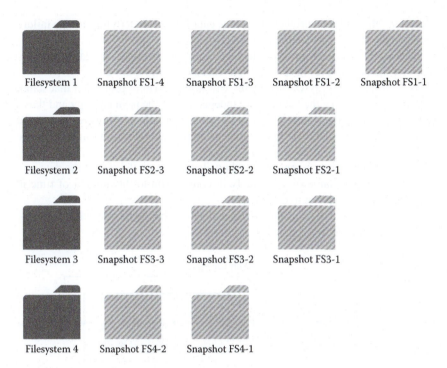

FIGURE 20.2 Taking multiple snapshots of each filesystem.

ago the snapshot was taken. For example, snapshots might be configured with the following frequencies and retention:

- Hourly snapshots maintained for 24 hours
- Daily snapshots maintained for 7 days
- Weekly snapshots maintained for 14 days
- Monthly snapshots maintained for 3 months

Typically in these situations the longer-term retention snapshots are designated instances of the more frequently performed snapshots. For instance, the daily snapshot above might simply be the hourly snapshot taken at 18:00, the weekly snapshot might be the Saturday daily snapshot, and the monthly might be the first weekly snapshot of a given month.

Retaining multiple snapshots allow us to address both typical RTO *and* RPO requirements. In the event of data loss or corruption at the filesystem level, the snapshot remains almost instantly available thanks to the nature of its design, and the frequency of the snapshots will conceivably be orchestrated to meet the RPO requirements of the business for the types and criticality of the data held on each NAS filesystem.

However, by their very nature the most common snapshots (CoFW and RoW) are dependent on the original source of the data they are protecting. While they will provide protection against, say, a file being deleted, or even intentional corruption of a filesystem, they offer no protection against catastrophic underlying storage failure—for example, three disks failing in a RAID-6 LUN.

Alternately at this point, it might be tempting to consider standard backup services for the NAS server instead, such as that shown in Figure 20.3.

Regular backups of NAS filesystems will offer *a* form of protection that standard snapshots can't, in that the backups are independent of the primary copy and thus can be used to recover the primary copy in the event of a failure.* However, they equally present limitations in large data environments unpalatable to most businesses, namely:

- The time taken to complete a backup, depending on the size of the data set, may be quite large (most notably in comparison to the amount of time it takes for a snapshot to execute)
- The time taken to *recover* from a backup may equally be quite large depending on the size of the data set

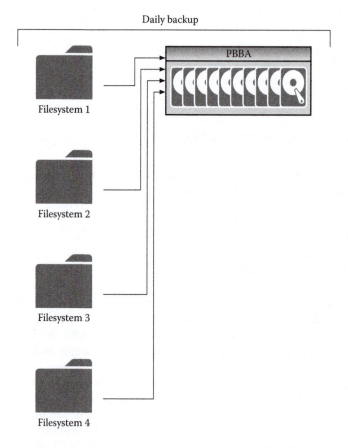

FIGURE 20.3   Daily backups of NAS filesystems.

---

* We would consider this to be "off platform" protection, that is, protection that is completely decoupled from the platform the primary data resides on.

Given the less frequent nature of backups (e.g., once a day), it's more usual to see them used for situations where we have an RPO of more than 24 hours, or purely as a disaster recovery option. If the business has data with an RPO measured in hours or even minutes, traditional backups are unlikely to meet these requirements. Equally, needing to stream back the entire backup (in the case of, say, filesystem corruption) may exceed both the RTO *and* RPO.

Each of these examples has effectively only utilized two layers of data protection— an underlying data storage protection (e.g., a RAID-6 LUN allocated per filesystem) and a single higher level data protection option: snapshots or backups. For smaller organizations, or even larger businesses looking at protection for test/development systems, this *may* be sufficient. However, other businesses will not stop at this point and have additional RPO, RTO, compliance, or business continuity requirements.

A business that has basic requirements toward providing disaster recovery capabilities of their data might look toward layering snapshots *and* backups, such as that shown in Figure 20.4.

In such a configuration, short-term RTO and RPO requirements can be met by hourly snapshots of the individual NAS filesystems; longer-term RPO/RTO

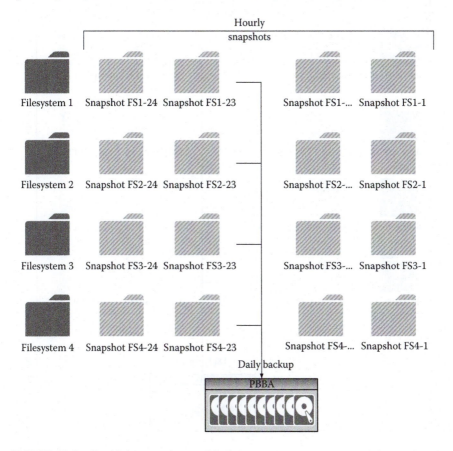

FIGURE 20.4   Combining snapshots and backups.

objectives could conceivably be met by the backup and recovery system, as could disaster recovery capabilities.

We again however return to the specific limitations of each type of data protection here though. Snapshots executed frequently enough will provide excellent RTO and RPO, but are unable to defend against catastrophic storage loss. A backup and recovery system is unlikely to meet stringent RTO and RPO requirements, but offers a layer of protection divorced from the original storage platform and therefore more applicable in a disaster recovery situation.

This three-layer approach to data protection may still not yield sufficient levels of protection for a business depending on its operational needs or regulatory compliance requirements. In particular, so far we've not made any consideration toward the *location* of the data protection. Assuming a business has a requirement to have copies of their data provisioned in a secondary site for disaster recovery requirements, this *might* be met by backing up over a high speed inter-site connection such as dark fiber, effectively yielding a data protection solution such as that shown in Figure 20.5.

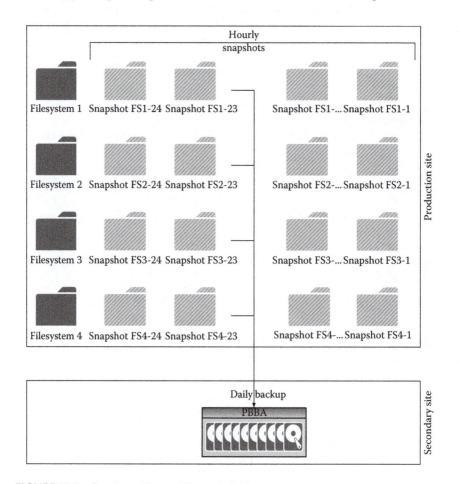

FIGURE 20.5   Local snapshots with remote backups.

By sending backups to a secondary site, a business is able to both provide local short-term RPO and RTO options while still meeting a level of disaster recovery capabilities, and for some businesses or particular types of data even for larger businesses, this may be entirely sufficient for their requirements.

However, there will be some businesses—either bound by tighter RPO and RTO requirements regardless of whether where data is being accessed from or by compliance requirements where such an arrangement is insufficient. (In the event of a disaster, operational service restoration via a traditional recovery may be deemed to be too slow.)

In such a scenario, it may be the case that replication is used—filesystems on the NAS host are replicated to an alternate NAS system in the secondary site, with snapshots similarly replicated—an arrangement that may resemble that shown in Figure 20.6.

In Figure 20.6, we can see a set of filesystems at the production site that have hourly snapshots taken. Additionally, the base filesystems have been replicated to a secondary site, and the snapshots taken hourly at the production site are replicated to the secondary site.

Such a configuration offers higher levels of data protection than previously discussed methods, in that

- Protection against casual data deletion or filesystem corruption provided by local snapshots, meeting tight RPO and RTO requirements
- Protection against catastrophic storage failure with replicated content
- Disaster recovery in the event of primary site loss

This then may seem to be an appropriate multilayered approach for data protection adequate for all businesses, but even at this level it is not necessarily so. There are three other considerations that come into play: decoupled platform, long-term retention, and compliance.

From the platform perspective, consider *all* data protection is being provided by the same technology platform: the NAS system. Even with a replication target in place we have not achieved "off platform" protection, just an additional layer of hardware redundancy. Firmware/OS upgrades causing issues, or deliberate platform targeted malware could still render both the primary and "backup" irreparably damaged.

In an ideal world, no backup would need to be retained for more than, say, a month—or at most, a year; anything requiring longer-term retention would instead be stored in an inviolable archive format. However, data lifecycle management strategies with comprehensive archive policies are still the exception rather than the norm for *all* data within an organization, or indeed even the majority of organizations. Even those organizations that utilize some form of archive usually limit it to specific types of data, such as email only. This then creates a gulf between what is *desirable* and what is *achievable*, and this exposes the limits of snapshot technology: longevity in the face of ongoing data change.

At a point where, say, a monthly copy of the data must be retained for 7 years and archives are not employed, the safe, platform independent option is to incorporate

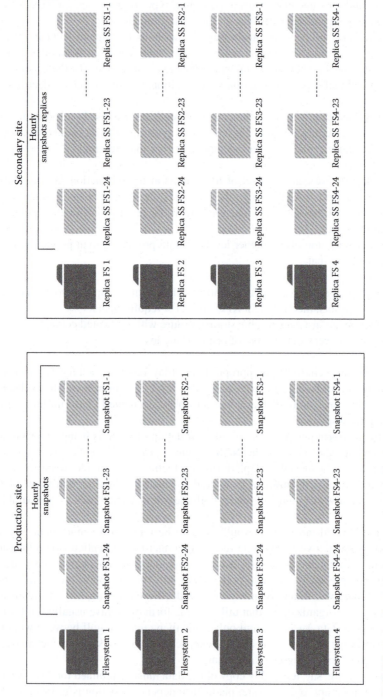

FIGURE 20.6 Combining snapshots and replication.

some form of traditional backup processes as well. However, this can be intelligently leveraged with the snapshot and replication functionality to minimize the frequency at which the backups are executed.

This may result in a configuration similar to that shown in Figure 20.7, whereby

- Hourly snapshots are taken daily and retained for, say, 24 hours
- One hourly snapshot per day is designated the daily snapshot and retained for 30 days
- Filesystems are replicated to a secondary site
- Hourly snapshots are replicated to a secondary site and retained for 24 hours
- Daily snapshots are replicated to a secondary site and retained for 30+ days
- At the end of every month, the last daily snapshot replica of the month is written out to backup storage*

This level of protection meets the same RPO and RTO requirements met by previously discussed options and also provides long-term data protection/retention. This four-layer data protection technique has an added bonus: whereas in a normal data protection environment it's necessary to ensure a backup can complete in no more than 24 hours (and in fact usually its highly desirable for it to complete in a much smaller amount of time), since all the casual, day-to-day data protection *and* typical disaster recovery scenarios are all serviced by snapshots and replicated snapshots, the backups are for long-term compliance only. This makes it entirely conceivable that additional time can be taken for the backups, eliminating or at least reducing the performance requirements that might otherwise be placed on the backup and recovery system to protect the data on the NAS system(s).

(The compliance requirements effectively mirror the long-term retention requirements above, but focus specifically on those businesses where there is a mandated requirement to keep long-term backups: i.e., the law has not necessarily caught up with the technology available, or the simplest and easiest to attain technology has been mandated.)

It should be noted the backup examples in this section have been simplified diagrammatically. As discussed in more detail in Chapter 11, backups should typically be replicated, cloned, or otherwise copied to ensure they are not a single point of failure within a data protection strategy.

20.2.2 VIRTUAL MACHINE PROTECTION

A common example for most businesses now is the multilayered approach required for comprehensive data protection services in virtual machine environments.

Increasingly virtualization represents a significant and mixed workload/footprint within most organizations. Even the smallest of organizations recognize the cost savings by running multiple independent hosts on a limited number of servers.

---

* This long-term retention backup could then be migrated to, say, Cloud object storage for cheap, cold retention.

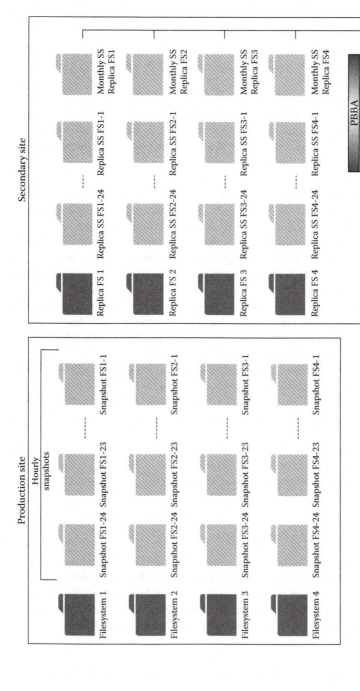

FIGURE 20.7 Combining snapshots, replication, and backup.

This can often lead to a complex mixed workload on these servers; depending on the size or operational requirements of a business, there may be a mix of production and non-production virtual machines running on the same physical servers, and workloads sharing the same physical resources could be file, print, email, terminal services, specific applications, databases, or development platforms—just to name a few.

A holistic approach to virtual machine protection effectively encompasses several (if not all) of the techniques discussed already in Chapter 14, so rather than building a step-by-step sequence as we did for Large NAS protection, we can discuss the complete model from the start.

A high level example of multilayered data protection within a virtualization environment is shown in Figure 20.8, with the numbered segments representing the following activities:

1. Key production systems that are required to be running regardless of whether the environment is running in the production datacenter or the disaster recovery datacenter are kept in sync via cross-site replication. In the event of a disaster, the replicated systems can be automatically started up in the disaster recovery datacenter, typically within a crash-consistent state to a few minutes (depending on the replication speed). This usually requires a "stretched network" or "stretched VLAN" so that the IP addressing scheme at the production site and disaster recovery site match, allowing operations to continue without any client services or DNS details needing to be changed. (Note that non-production systems might *not* be replicated between sites to save on bandwidth and focus business continuity efforts only on those systems that are essential to operations.)

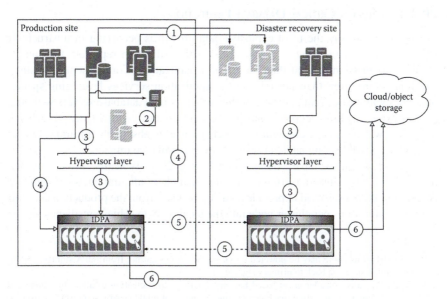

FIGURE 20.8   Multilayered approach to data protection within a virtualization environment.

2. Critical database or application servers have continuous data protection systems deployed against them with application-aware journaling; this provides the facility within the same site to almost instantly roll back a virtual machine to a prior checkpoint in the event of a data corruption issue. The journal system might even be used to trigger an application-consistent clone of the virtual machine for testing purposes.

3. All virtual machines within the environment, regardless of whether they are production or non-production, receive *image* level backups via hypervisor plugins to an Integrated Data Protection Appliance (IDPA), allowing advanced functionality such as "instant access"* and file level recovery.

4. Traditional, agent-based backups are performed for situations where
   a. A database or complex application resides within a virtual machine and requires more than a "crash consistent" image level backup, *and/or*
   b. Long-term retention of the content of the virtual machine is required and archive systems are not in use†

5. All backups of virtual machines are replicated between sites so that the backup system does not become a single point of failure for the environment.

6. Backups that must be retained for long-term purposes are migrated to a cheap storage tier, such as Cloud/Object storage.

The architecture described is not the *only* way to provide a multilayered approach to virtualization systems. Other approaches could more heavily utilize hypervisor-integrated storage snapshot systems, though as per previous discussions of snapshot limitations, this would be limited to short-term retention to avoid performance and/or capacity issues, and the risks associated with having no "off platform" protection.

20.2.3 MISSION CRITICAL DATABASE PROTECTION

While it's fair to say the most explosive data growth is occurring in unstructured data, structured data—that is to say, *databases*—still often represent the sources of the most mission critical data within an organization. Core, essential business functions more often than not rely on the application services leveraging specific databases within the organization. For this reason critical database servers will often have an extremely high degree of data protection associated with them, and such data protection will need to be configured in such a way as to absolutely minimize or even as much as possible completely eliminate any performance impact.

Consider as an example configuration Figure 20.9. Typically, mission critical databases will be clustered affairs, and our example configuration is no different. A cluster of systems is used to provide database services from the production site, with multiple connections per cluster node into the local SAN to achieve resiliency against

---

* Where a virtual machine may be powered up via a read/write snapshot from IDPA storage, without even needing restoration back to primary storage.
† We would typically consider agent-based backups for long-term retention to allow for changes in hypervisor technology or virtual machine container format that might otherwise prevent recovery or use of recovered data after an extended period of time.

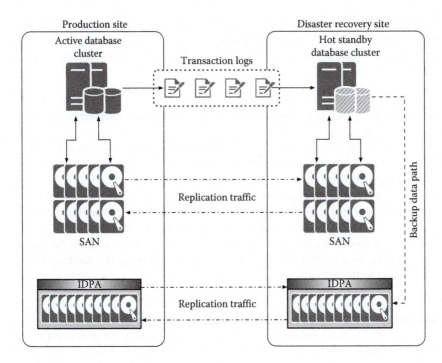

FIGURE 20.9 Database data protection with hot standby database.

path failure. Clusters provide local fault tolerance from individual system failure—one or more individual servers hosting the database can fail without service lost.

Most database servers feature options for enterprise high availability through some form or another of transaction log transfers. In this, a standby database server, either locally or at another site, is kept up to date with changes performed on the primary database by receiving transaction logs from the primary database as they are closed off. These transaction logs are applied automatically to the standby database, keeping it *mostly* in sync with the production copy.

While we have shown SAN replication in the diagram it may not necessarily be active when transaction log shipping is running between the databases, and simply exist in this scenario as an *option* for the database server if required. (For example, SAN level replication might be used to reseed the production site copy for *failback* after a failover has occurred and the production site is ready to take over from the disaster recovery site again.)

To fulfill the previously stated business requirement of minimized performance impact during backup operations, it's quite normal in this type of configuration to have the database backup executed from the disaster recovery site instead—the application of transaction logs from the primary copy is delayed for the time it takes to execute a backup, but this means there is no performance impact on the production database during the backup process. Once the backup has been completed, queued transaction logs on the standby database server are again applied, and in the background the protection storage system on the standby site should replicate a copy of the backup to the production site so the backups as well are protected against site failure.

Such a configuration is not necessarily perfect, however. Database vendors typically charge considerably more for options around standby database servers, which
can materially increase the cost of the solution. There are other potential disadvantages as well, including

- The log holding area on the secondary database server will need to be large
  enough to hold all the transaction logs that will queue up while the backup
  is running
- In the event of a site failover, any performance impact associated with the
  database backup will be experienced while the standby database server is
  acting as the production server
- In normal production site operations, database recoveries from, say, corruption
  may require the recovery from the "primary" backup, accessible only from the
  secondary site. This may cause bandwidth constraints on the recovery
- In a worst-case scenario, it may actually be required to recover the database
  into the secondary database server and then replicating the database back
  across to the production site

(While different database servers will support various rollback options to deal
with corruption, the level of capability available will be platform dependent.)

Figure 20.10 shows an alternate data protection strategy for a mission critical
database system.

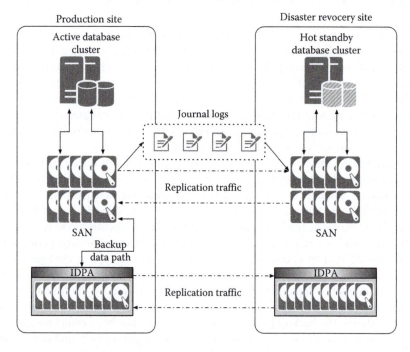

FIGURE 20.10   Mission critical database protection with continuous data protection and
primary storage data protection integration.

The example configuration shown in Figure 20.10 eschews log shipping at the database level and instead integrates application-aware Continuous Data Protection (CDP) working at the storage array level. CDP typically works by intercepting IO operations and maintaining a journal of write operations performed against the LUN. These are collected into logs such that when they are applied to an alternate system, result in an application-consistent copy.

CDP systems can be used not only to provide application-consistent replication to another host, but can also be used for "rewind" operations against the production system being protected by CDP as well. Thus, in the event of logical corruption to the database it becomes possible to recover quickly and easily by stopping the database, rolling back (at the storage layer) the changes that had been performed, and restarting the database.

While CDP offers excellent RPO and RTO, usually businesses build CDP recoverability only around a limited window—for example, 24 or 48 hours. Longer-term recoverability will still require a more traditional backup process where the data is copied to data protection storage. In the scenario in Figure 20.10, we're showing that the backup could be achieved by leveraging integration between the primary storage system and the IDPA. In such a scenario, we typically see a fiber-channel link between the primary storage system and the IDPA, and the backup process works as follows:

- The database server triggers a backup process
- The database goes into hot backup mode
- The primary storage system takes a snapshot of the LUN the database resides on
- The database exits hot backup mode
- The primary storage system transfers the snapshot database LUN to the IDPA

Such a backup process frees the database server itself from the need to participate in the data transfer. A traditional database backup will see the database server *read* the data from the storage system and transfer that data to the protection storage system. The net result is the database server itself is the transfer conduit. By removing the database server from this process, the performance impact on the database is removed,* and by halving the amount of paths the data has to take for protection, we substantially increase the backup performance. This might be further improved by leveraging deduplication to reduce transfer requirements. Alternately, leveraging virtual synthetic operations allows the backup to take place by only transferring changed blocks on the LUN since the last backup, with the IDPA logically synthesizing a new full as a set of pointers from these new blocks and prior backups.

---

* That is, the SAN will undoubtedly support more than one application accessing it concurrently. When we consider performance impact to mission critical systems during backup, that impact is almost invariably as a result of that mission critical system *participating* in the transfer of its data.

20.3 PLANNING HOLISTIC DATA PROTECTION STRATEGIES

In essence, the planning of a comprehensive data protection strategy is one which cannot be performed in isolation. This refers as much to the planning of the individual data protection components for a "silo" of business function as much as the view of *all* data protection components for *all* business functions within an organization. Consider, for instance, our three data protection strategies outlined in previous examples: large NAS, virtual machine, and mission critical database protection. While these might be developed and modified independently based on implementation schedules within an organization, a complete data protection strategy must be built with an understanding of the way in which specific solutions might impact on one another. All three strategies, for instance, rely on cross-site replication of

- Production/mission critical virtual machines
- NAS storage and snapshots
- Backup copies/clones
- Database content

Assuming an organization needed to use both of these data protection techniques, the bandwidth considerations for data protection *can't* be determined in isolation; they will cumulatively consume cross-site bandwidth. If the database protection requires a minimum of 100 MB/s throughput, the virtualization protection requires a minimum of 200 MB/s throughput, and the NAS cross-site protection requires a minimum of 150 MB/s throughput, then a 1 Gbit link is not going to be sufficient*— particularly if that link is also shared for standard operational production communications between sites as well. Whenever deduplication is involved, this becomes even more critical a consideration during recovery operations—a link that may be perfectly sufficient for deduplicated *backup* operations may become saturated dealing with the flow of *rehydrated* data during a recovery.

In Chapter 6, we also spoke of the need to accurately track and analyze data protection capacity—both in terms of storage requirements *and* performance. In particular, in Section 6.3.2 we discussed the value of reporting for trending in predictive planning, and this becomes even more important in an environment using a mix of data protection techniques. While some data protection techniques will exist largely independently of one another,[†] others *may* be dependent. Consider the large NAS protection strategy described previously: since the long-term backups are executed from replicated snapshots, then a failure in the snapshot system will likely cause a cascaded failure into the backup and recovery system. So while multilayered data protection techniques can increase the level and options for data availability and recoverability within an organization, they can introduce additional dependencies that must be understood, tracked, and planned for.

---

* WAN/MAN link compression techniques can *mitigate* bandwidth requirements to a degree by reducing the amount of data that must be transmitted, but they always have their limits.

[†] For instance, the type of RAID storage used by a system *usually* does not impact whether or not it can receive traditional backups.

20.4 SUMMARY

In modern business it's practically unheard of to leverage only a *single* data protection strategy. Before host virtualization it was largely possible to merely loosely coordinate data protection strategies: application administrators might generate their own backups or dumps of databases to spare storage, storage administrators would provide specific RAID protection, and operating system administrators would execute appropriate traditional backups. (As backups grew to be heterogeneous in function, backup administrators became more common to provide a centralized protection option for *all* operating systems within a business.)

Host virtualization and subsequently storage, network, and datacenter virtualization have led to a far more converged level of infrastructure planning (thin provisioning of both storage and virtualization environments, for instance, requires a close working relationship between storage administrators, virtualization administrators, and operating system/application administrators). While businesses may try to keep storage administration, virtualization administration and backup administration as distinct roles, administrators in all three areas must liaise closely and regularly to ensure compatible, holistic data protection strategies are developed and implemented, and these techniques *do not* leave gaps that expose the business to risk. Equally, a holistic approach reduces the number of costly overlapping functions; systems planned in isolation may needlessly duplicate functionality or protection at a direct fiscal cost to the business. Reducing overlap can result in true cost savings. The growing presence of converged infrastructure is demonstrating the need for a new type of administrator: the *infrastructure administrator*, who combines multiple previous siloed roles, and the net benefits are not just for the primary production administration but also the administration of data protection as well. (Arguably, infrastructure administrators add value regardless of whether fully converged infrastructure is used, and in a modern IT environment could be considered essential to developing and maintaining a comprehensive data protection strategy.)

A holistic data protection strategy is no longer something only 24 × 7 and multinational or global businesses require; it is essential for the modern IT environment.

21 Data Recovery

21.1 INTRODUCTION

Despite all the best proactive steps that can be taken toward data protection—any mix of data storage protection, snapshots, RAID, replication, and continuous storage availability—there is always the chance of *some* data loss situation that requires a form of recovery to be performed.

If we consider data protection to be a form of insurance, then data recovery is what occurs when a business needs to make a claim against its data protection policy: something has happened and data must be retrieved.

Just like a regular insurance policy, a data protection "insurance policy" comes with an *excess fee* when it comes to making claims, and just like insurance, the level "excess" to claim against the policy—the cost of the recovery—is usually intimately related to whether sufficient financing and planning was invested in the data protection strategy in the first place.

Although recovery operations themselves are product-centric, some common practices and considerations for recoveries exist regardless of what product or technology is being used. These include

- *System design*—To what level are recovery requirements (and their associated SLAs) a primary consideration when designing a protection system?
- *Best practices*—Procedures and guidelines to follow during recovery and disaster recovery processes.
- Adequacy of recovery testing.

In this chapter, we'll be reviewing various data protection options on the basis of the above key requirements.

21.2 RECOVERY VERSUS SERVICE RESTORATION

One of the most important data recovery considerations is one of the most overlooked—the difference between *data recovery* and *service restoration*. Data recovery merely refers to retrieving data from protection storage, but depending on the nature of the failure, storage, and data, there may be considerably more effort involved in achieving service restoration. At its simplest, this might be as simple as starting application services once a recovery process has been completed, but for more complex workloads, this might involve any or all of the following examples:

- Executing recoveries across multiple systems
- Coordinating service starts or restarts across application and database servers
- Adjusting IP addresses and redirecting DNS
- Notifying users or consumers the service is available again

In Chapter 4, we described the elements of a data protection system, with technology only being one element alongside five others (people, training, testing, service level agreements, processes, and documentation). Similarly, we see other components involved in service restoration beyond just transferring data from one source into another or redirecting where we access data from.

Understanding the service restoration activities and times they will take is critical to correctly determining the real service level objectives that can be offered to the business. For instance, merely estimating that a database can be recovered in 8 hours because the backups can be read from protection storage in 8 hours pays no consideration to any consistency activities that may have to be applied post-recovery,* what services might need to be reset, or what nontechnical post-recovery processes might need to be performed before the business deems the service to be "restored."

21.3 CONTEXT-AWARE RECOVERIES

You may have an excellent painter working on your house: not a drop splashed, not a line of wall missed, and working at a speed that leaves you in awe. But if there's a sudden power surge that leaves half of your house needing to be rewired, would you turn and ask the painter to rewire your house simply because she's the current expert on site?

It's a similar story with data protection. Even with the best backup administrators delivering 100% success rates, is it sensible to have them executing the end-to-end recovery of a complex, mission critical database they're not certified in—just because they're experts at managing the protection infrastructure? In Chapter 11, we mentioned a new form of backup topology—the hybrid approach, with centralized protection storage but the control decentralized and shared between core backup administrators and application administrators. (While referencing backups only, this equally applies to all forms of data protection—just think *storage administrators*† and *application administrators*.) The hybrid approach enables greater flexibility in coordinating *backups*, but more importantly it can allow for a more intelligent and efficient approach to coordinating *recoveries*. The backup administrators are able to coordinate resources at a broader level and assist with recoveries that don't require high degrees of application awareness, without impeding the

---

* Consider again for instance that in databases, the nomenclature *restore* versus *recovery* is used. Restore typically refers to pulling data back from protection storage/backup, but *recovery* refers to actually rolling forward transaction logs and other details to reinstate consistency in the database.
† Or more broadly, *infrastructure* administrators.

efforts of application administrators who also need to get mission critical systems back. You might even say that a key principle of centralized protection storage in a hybrid topology approach is to ensure that backup administrators do not become a recovery bottleneck.

21.4 DESIGNING FOR RECOVERY

No matter how you look at data protection, one of two fundamental approaches must be taken depending on the RPOs of the data or services involved. These are:

- Design for recovery, *or*
- Design to avoid recovery

If a mission critical system within the organization has an RPO of zero, or near enough to, the primary design principle must be to *avoid* recovery at all practical costs. Such systems will leverage continuous storage availability, replication, and snapshots to achieve instantaneous or near-instantaneous restoration in the event of a service outage. While traditional backups may still be used for these systems, they are likely to be used for longer-term data retention requirements or reseeding test/ dev or even big data systems rather than intended for service restoration. Resorting to traditional backup systems for service restoration in these scenarios is a sign of architected or cascaded failure exceeding operational expectations rather than *by-design*.

For systems with less rigorous SLAs relating to RPOs, RTOs, and service outage times, where traditional backup and recovery systems will be part of their operational recovery strategy, a fundamental design principle must be to ensure that data (and services) can be recovered within the required time frames established by the *business*. (IT alone cannot decide RPOs and RTOs.)

> Consider for the moment a backup environment leveraging deduplication. If implemented including source-side deduplication, it can also substantially decrease the amount of data that has to be sent across a network. This has seen an explosion of backup topologies featuring a number of remote office sites backing up to a single central datacenter over relatively small links. For instance, a site with 1000 GB of data that has high commonality to centrally stored data may comfortably backup across a link that has a maximum sustainable throughput of 10 MB/s, or even less. Backing up 1000 GB of data at a continuous rate of 10 MB/s would take 28.4 hours without deduplication, but once the first backup is done* assuming a maximum 5% change rate on any given day and a 5:1 deduplication ratio against that changed data, only 50 GB of data would need to be backed up a day, and only 10 GB of new, unique data would need to be sent across the link per day—less than an hour of backup time.
>
> Consider though: what happens if the remote site experiences a catastrophic failure and *all* that data needs to be streamed back from the central site? Deduplication in

---

* Which if timed correctly given the previously stated commonality of centrally stored data may not need to be a full 1000 GB transfer.

itself doesn't improve recovery performance, and we've already determined that even maxing out the transfer it would take 28.4 hours to send that data *back*. If this is unacceptable, the system must be designed accordingly—such as installation of a smaller deduplication system in the remote office that acts as a local cache and replicates the backups into the central office; in the event of *many* failure situations, the local cache can be used to facilitate recovery at LAN, rather than WAN speeds.*

Recoverability—or avoiding the recovery in the first place depending on the value of the data to be the business—has to be the primary design requirement of any data protection system; while operationally on a day-to-day basis the speed at which the protection is executed is important, ultimately the business will be far more concerned with the time required to achieve service restoration in the event of an issue.

21.5   RECOVERY FACILITATION

21.5.1   AUTOMATED VERSUS MANUAL RECOVERIES

As system automation through portals, Cloud-like automation and auto-healing storage becomes more commonplace, automatic recovery processes are likely to enter the datacenter more pervasively. These will gain popularity in highly available storage, continuous data protection and replication systems in the first pass, allowing intelligent storage systems to automatically achieve system restoration in the event of a storage system failure. This is of course not new: RAID systems in particular have long utilized hot-sparing to commence reconstruction of a volume in the event of a single disk failure *without* administrative intervention. Storage virtualization in particular allows for policies to be established more easily and at a higher configuration level by administrators, leaving an automation and orchestration layer in charge to handle the actual actions. While the IT industry has for the most part moved on by considering Full Time Employee (FTE) requirements per TB or even PB, higher levels of automation for provisioning, management, and restoration *do* allow for sometimes even individual administrators to manage large amounts of storage in the tens of petabytes or higher.

Automated recovery can play a part in good system design for backup and recovery environments as well. Products or orchestration layers that support recovery automation can free up application, system, or backup administrators from required but otherwise tedious regular recovery activities such as

- Reseeding development, test, and QA systems from production backups
- Compliance-required regular testing—A catalog of necessary recovery tests might be built and periodically executed to satisfy legal requirements
- Pre-arranged recovery activities—When a required recovery is known well in advance, building an automated recovery policy to execute the recovery at the required time can free up administrators for other activities

---

* If service levels permit, an alternate recovery strategy may be "build and ship"—conduct the recovery at the backup destination/central site over a high speed LAN link, and transport the recovered server or data back to the site. This is effectively an evolution of Andrew Tanenbaum's statement: "Never underestimate the bandwidth of a station wagon full of tapes hurtling down the highway."

While there will always be scope for manual recoveries, automated recoveries will increase in popularity and use as businesses demand more agility from their data protection products, and third-party orchestration layers become more mature.

21.5.2 WHO PERFORMS THE RECOVERY?

There are usually several factors that determine which role will perform a recovery:

- *Data complexity*—Does it require specialist knowledge to perform a particular recovery? As the data or the services reliant on data become more complex or critical, the chances of the recovery requiring specialist knowledge will also increase. Thus, databases tend to be recovered by database administrators rather than, say, help desk staff.
- *System architecture*—Does the data protection system, and the way in which it has been integrated into the environment support the required or desired roles for recovery? A business for instance might *prefer* all end-user data to be self-service recoverable, but if the environment has been architected to require administrator level privileges for any form of recovery, recoveries are likely to require escalation to the IT department.*
- *Product architecture and security*—Ensuring that data cannot be recovered by the wrong people can become an active consideration; a product that may allow *any* user to perform a recovery sounds like a good idea until we consider the possibility of an office clerk being able to recover, say, the CFO's sensitive budgetary planning data.
- *User education*—How much training is required for a user before he or she can complete a recovery? Ideally if end users are expected to perform recoveries of at least some of their data (e.g., Office documents or email messages), then the functionality should be integrated such that it appears part of the base product itself, and is completely intuitive. (For example, a SaaS backup product may add a "Recover" option to a user's email toolbar, allowing users to perform self-service recovery without needing to understand the complete backup product.)

Particularly in tape-based environments, recovery functionality is often constrained to a very limited number of users—for example, the backup administrators, application and operating system administrators, and a few help desk staff at most. This reduces the chance of the environment being flooded with recovery requests all waiting on tapes requiring recall, or drives to be freed up.

Businesses are increasingly seeing the benefits of allowing (where possible) user-directed self-service recovery thanks to the growth in disk-based protection storage. "Users" in this scenario may not literally mean end users, but providing self-service

---

* Businesses moving to data protection services in the cloud (private, hybrid, or public) will find this consideration particularly critical, as such changes will often impact IT staffing numbers.

recovery access to a broad spectrum of administrators and developers within the organization—application administrators, platform developers, and so on.

True end-user self-service recovery is normally seen as a topic reserved almost entirely for files on home drives, and individual email messages. There will still be times where specific types of data will require administrator intervention for recovery, but with cost-cutting (or at least, *operational efficiencies*) a perpetual consideration for IT departments, allowing users to recover their own basic documents and email can substantially free up IT resources for strategic activities. (It is very likely however that businesses shifting to SaaS applications in the Cloud will discover more regular opportunities to grant access to self-service recoveries.)

Ensuring the systems deployed can be used by the *right* users at the *right* time is an architectural process and educational challenge, and usually encounters the most challenges where a particular level of self-service or recovery functionality is *assumed* rather than fully investigated. Allowing more users to perform recoveries (be they particular application administrators, help desk staff, or even end users) can have anything from a subtle to a profound improvement over operational efficiencies within a business. Depending on the *reason* why a user needs data recovered, the delay taken to formally request a recovery and wait for a limited number of operational staff (usually with other duties) to complete it may slow down business functions or even effectively cost the business money in lost productivity. Understanding the anticipated load and/or costs associated with self-service recoveries—and being able to track them—is important, too. If there is a tangible cost to the business to perform a recovery (e.g., data restoration from Cloud object storage), that cost must be tracked, accounted for, and budgeted the same way as any other.

21.5.3 FREQUENCY OF RECOVERY

The more frequently recoveries are performed, the more the system must be designed to support a high recovery workload. When tape was the primary backup and recovery mechanism for instance, this would often mean architecting backup environments to ensure that a sufficient number of tape drives were *always* available to perform recoveries: a tape library with 10 tape drives might be configured such that 2 drives are permanently configured as "read only," providing greater assurance of their availability to facilitate a recovery.

With disk-based systems being more likely as not to be used as protection storage, the physical limitation between read and write activities found with tape has reduced substantially. However, simply using disk does not create a blank check when it comes to recoveries. Items for consideration include

- Regardless of storage type used:
  - How many concurrent read streams can the protection storage handle without performance degradation?
  - What impact does the network connectivity to protection storage have to single recovery streams *and* concurrent recovery streams?

- Are there "housekeeping" activities that must be performed which would reduce the capacity to service recovery requests?
- If backup data is tiered to slower, longer-term storage (tape or Cloud), is the system designed to ensure the most common recovery requests come from online rather than near-line or off-line storage?
- If data is tiered off to other storage, is it done in such a way as to make access completely transparent to the user?
- If using deduplication storage:
  - If the deduplication is performed as a "post-process" operation:
    - Are there differences between service capability for deduplicated and non-deduplicated backup data?
    - Post-processing is typically IO intensive—what is the typical duration of post-processing based on average data transfer per day and the impact this might have on a recovery if post-processing is *running* while a recovery is performed?
  - Regardless of inline or post-process deduplication:
    - Has adequate consideration been given to the amount of data that might need to be rehydrated during a recovery process and the time this takes to complete? (regardless of how fast a deduplicated backup can complete)

21.5.4 Recentness of Data Protection

Looking at traditional backup and recovery operations in particular, most organizations will want to balance the speed at which a recovery can commence with the recentness of *when* the data was actually backed up in the first place.

For the most part, the more recently something was backed up, the more likely there is of a need to recover—and the faster the recovery should be. For instance, consider an environment with the following basic backups:

- Daily backups retained for 6 weeks
- Monthly backups retained for 13 months
- Yearly backups retained for 7 years.

Leaving aside the merits of considering data management and archive operations instead of using backup for long-term retention, the above sort of backup and retention schedule is reasonably common within a lot of businesses. Also common is the chances that the recoveries *most* frequently requested will be for data backed up in the last 24–72 hours. Therefore, the backup system should be designed in such a way that the data backed up most recently can be recovered fastest: it should be online, the product should support an instant start of a recovery when requested.

In architectures where backup to disk is primarily seen as a staging operation—backups land on disk for a relatively short period of time before being moved to tape—the goal should be to support at least 80%–90% of the most frequently requested recoveries from the disk backups, and those disk backups should be sized accordingly.

Disk used just for staging can be risky

While backup to disk originated as a "staging" area, ongoing use of disk only for staging does introduce risk into the environment. Since the landing area is normally low in capacity compared to the overall environment being protected, data must be moved quickly to create more room for upcoming backups. A failed tape drive (assuming that's where data is being staged *to*) can quickly result in banked up or even aborted backups as the staging area fills. Also, since staging is an IO intensive process and done *outside* the backup window—usually during production hours—it may potentially impede recovery performance, or perhaps even *block* recoveries until the data has been moved.

Environments where *all* backups are stored on disk (usually leveraging deduplication—or more importantly, *inline* deduplication—to minimize footprint) will rarely need to consider this 80% or 90% rule, since data backed up yesterday will be recoverable at the same speed as data backed up 3 months, 12 months, or 5 years ago. (It should be noted that deduplication systems performing *post-processing* deduplication can have entirely different performance characteristics depending on whether data can be recovered from the landing tier or the deduplication tier, *and* if the system is IO bound performing deduplication when a recovery request is made, this can substantially impact recovery performance.)

A new data-tiering option gaining traction is moving longer-term backups to cloud-based object storage, regardless of whether that's public, private, or hybrid cloud.* Cloud object storage *can* represent a much cheaper storage mechanism for cold data that is infrequently accessed than near-line storage,[†] so as an evolution of "disk to disk to tape," "disk to disk to cloud" is entering the data protection field. Cloud object storage typically represents a cheaper storage option at the cost of slower retrieval.[‡] It's entirely reasonable after all for the business to maintain different recovery SLAs for operational or "business as usual" recoveries versus long-term compliance recoveries. While operational recoveries need to be geared for speed, recoveries for compliance reasons are usually allowed to take longer. After all, if a business achieves compliance recovery from backup rather than archive platforms, the total capacity required for long-term retention will usually massively exceed the operational recovery capacity.[§] This requires cheaper storage, and with it, typically slower storage. Thus, in these situations, cloud object storage as a target for long-term data retention required for compliance only is quite a sensible approach.

---

* This tiering option is usually an attractive *additional* use case for businesses looking to deploy their own multipurpose object storage systems.

[†] Though the cost of retrieving bulk data from public cloud storage is not always considered, it can have a substantially deleterious effect on budget if unexpected situations occur. (Cloud tiered storage that can leverage the near-line tier as a cache on long-term recovery requests can be an excellent mitigation technique.)

[‡] Remember in Chapter 11 we also discussed that tape is often not handled correctly when used for long-term retention, improperly skewing price comparisons.

[§] Assume a starting size of 50 TB and no data growth for simplicity. With 4 weeks of daily incremental/weekly full backups and a 3.2% daily change rate, this would generate approximately 240 TB of backups. On the other hand, if 7 years worth of monthly fulls must be retained for compliance reasons, 84 monthlies will generate 4200 TB of backups.

21.6 RECOVERY PROCEDURES AND RECOMMENDATIONS

Most of the recommendations in this section are focused on recovery operations from backup; that being said, many will equally apply to any data recovery operation that requires human intervention, regardless of whether it is performed out of a backup product or some other form of protection such as snapshots, CDP, replication, or continuous storage availability.

The purpose of this topic is to move beyond the simple aspects of what can or can't be done for any individual product and discuss the more challenging topic—what *should* or *should not* be done.

21.6.1 READ THE DOCUMENTATION BEFORE STARTING A RECOVERY

While this might simply be thought of as "be trained in performing recoveries," there is more to it. While vendor supplied documentation will outline the practical steps involved in performing a recovery *from within the product*, as discussed in Section 21.2, there can be more involved in successfully restoring a function or even basic data than just simply following the recovery instructions in a product manual. This means that staff involved in recoveries should have a grasp of the recovery steps well *before* needing to perform a recovery, and there should be run-books or some other form of instructions customized to the business to handle ancillary details associated with the recovery that occur—or require consideration—outside of the backup product. This might include such details as

- What processes or authorities need to be consulted to allow a recovery
- What system activities need to be quiesced (if any) on either the client or the backup server to facilitate the recovery
- What security requirements must be fulfilled to permit the recovery? Sites with more secure access policies may automatically tie system access or even access permissions with change requests
- Organization standards or practices for where files and data should be recovered to, and under the various circumstances deemed most likely to occur (e.g., recovery of use files, user mail boxes, applications, databases)
- How to recall or access backups that are not immediately online, particularly in tape-based environments
- The procedures or processes to follow at the *end* of the recovery, differentiating particularly between what needs to be done at the end of both successful and *unsuccessful* recoveries

Of course, this is just a sample list, and the actual list could vary considerably between businesses of different sizes, industry verticals, or maturity—but it does serve to highlight that company-built procedures for recoveries *should* be the norm, not the exception.

21.6.2 CHOOSING THE CORRECT RECOVERY LOCATION

It goes without saying that if not handled correctly, a recovery could conceivably result in a loss of even more data than being recovered—or a greater outage. One of the worst ways this can happen is to recover data to the wrong location. If a backup system supports directed recoveries, this can aggravate the problem further. As such it is very important to confirm the recovery location before initiating the recovery, and to understand any limitations that exist on where file(s) or data can be recovered to. Examples of recovery locations include

- The original host and original location of the data
- The original host but another location for the data
- An alternate host with the same filesystem location/path
- An alternate host with a different filesystem location/path

Each option has different advantages and disadvantages. For instance, being able to perform a recovery to the original host and location is obviously critical when performing disaster recoveries, but can also be important for recovering critical files or system data that has been accidentally deleted or overwritten, as well as recovering partially deleted directory trees.

Recovering to the original host but a different location is typically a useful function for backup administrators, operators, or help desk staff. This is particularly the case if they perform the recoveries for end users who are unsure as to exactly which file(s) they want recovered. In this case, it is not unusual for an entire directory tree to be recovered to an alternate location, with the user asked to winnow through the recovered tree to locate the required file(s) before deleting the remainder of the (unneeded) recovered data.*

When recovering to an alternate host, recovering to an alternate directory path is often useful but may not always be required. For instance, if an environment features a production and a development system configured exactly the same way, the development system could be refreshed periodically with a copy of the production data via a recovery to the same location on a different host. Equally, when end users make recovery requests and can cite the exact files or location of the files to be recovered, many help desk and operations staff will recover those files back to their local machine and then simply email the files back to the end user.

One recommendation when performing recoveries is that before the final "go" is executed on the recovery, the person performing the recovery should always ask him or herself the following questions:

1. Have the correct file(s)/data been selected?
2. Was the correct host logged into prior to running the recovery command?
3. Has the correct recovery location been selected?
4. Is the recovery going to run to the correct destination host?

This typically amounts to 30 seconds or less of checking, but being in the habit of performing these checks can prevent some of the worst types of recovery mistakes that can be made.

---

* These styles of recovery requests might be dealt with alternately in situations where the backup product or an extension to the backup product handles more complex search options. Presented with an imprecise set of requirements from the end user, an administrator or recovery operator might be able to use a web-like search interface to find all matching data/files and execute the recovery directly from the search interface.

The recovery you don't want

In a former role as both the consulting manager and the backup administrator for a company, a consultant came to me on a Friday afternoon saying he'd patched his Linux laptop but the patching failed. He'd already done some investigation and found that if he rebooted the laptop without recovery, it would likely fail to the point of needing a complete disaster recovery. However, if he could recover the root drive *before* rebooting, it should be OK.

I brought up a terminal window on his system and confirmed a couple of details, but his laptop was experiencing DNS issues, so I quickly ssh'd across to the Solaris backup server to manually tweak some security settings in the backup product to allow connectivity, went back into the command line recovery interface, selected the root filesystem for recovery and hit go. I was keen to get home for the weekend.

The recovery was running for about 5 minutes when someone came in to tell me they couldn't log onto their thin desktop – provided by the Solaris backup server. I glanced at the recovery window and saw it was up to the /dev area* ... and realized I'd never logged out of the Solaris backup server before I started the recovery.

I was recovering a Linux root filesystem *over* a Solaris root filesystem, and it was for the actual backup server itself.

Instead of getting home for a relaxing weekend I spent almost all of the weekend in the office fixing a catastrophic mistake.

Since that weekend I have *never* started a recovery, no matter how trivial, without first asking myself those four questions previously mentioned.

21.6.3   PROVIDE AN ESTIMATE OF HOW LONG THE RECOVERY WILL TAKE

In a help desk environment recovering standard files, this estimate should be provided effectively by the SLAs: a user should know that files will be recovered within 8 hours of the ticket being assigned, or email will be recovered within a day. But for more complex recoveries, for *infrastructure* recoveries where administrators have to get involved, estimates should be provided of how long the recovery is likely to take.

21.6.4   PROVIDE UPDATES DURING RECOVERIES

In addition to providing an estimate of how long a recovery is likely to take, it's important to periodically provide updates on how the recovery is progressing, even if that update is "still recovering, no problems." Consider for instance a recovery that takes 4 hours and fails toward the end.

If no updates are given, the process might look like the following:

- 09:30—Recovery requested.
- 10:00—Recovery initiated, estimate of 4 hours to complete the recovery given.
- 15:00—User pings for an update because more than 4 hours has passed and the data is still not back. Told there was an error and the recovery will be reattempted.

---

* Unix special devices for low-level hardware access, essential for system functionality.

Picture yourself as the end user—this will be a frustrating experience, especially if having to *ask* for an update only to be told the clock is going to be reset. However, consider the following:

- 09:30—Recovery requested.
- 10:00—Recovery initiated, estimate of 4 hours to complete the recovery given.
- 12:00—Update indicating the recovery is proceeding OK is given.
- 13:30—Recovery fails. Update given to users saying the recovery will have to be restarted using the off-site copy, and this will take 8 hours to complete.
- 14:00—Users informed the recovery from the off-site copy has been initiated, with a new ETA for the recovery completion being start of business the next morning.

The personnel performing the recoveries are not the only ones under pressure—in some senses the users requesting or *requiring* the data to be recovered are more impacted. As such, keeping them informed of progress is a small but psychologically important task, and can have an excellent impact on business/IT relations.

Avoid shrapnel recoveries

In a former role as a junior system administrator there was one user who would become so panicked at the thought of data loss that he incessantly pestered the team any time he asked for a recovery. He'd be told how long the recovery would take to complete, but would then proceed to contact the team every 5 minutes, or come in and badger the person performing the recovery, even threatening formal complaints if it weren't recovered "soon."

When we realized his problem was more the "unknown" and started providing regular updates during recoveries, he stopped trying to micromanage the process.

21.6.5   DON'T ASSUME A RECOVERY CAN BE DONE IF IT HASN'T BEEN TESTED

A backup product should be reliable enough that you do not need to execute tests against 100% of the data being protected on 100% of the systems being protected to guarantee recoveries will work.

However, whenever a *new* system or a *new* application or a *new* set of backup requirements come into the environment, those systems, applications, or backup requirements should be thoroughly tested before entering production usage.

Or to put it another way: a business that introduces changes, new types of data or new applications without appropriate change control and data protection testing is inviting disaster.

21.6.6   RUN RECOVERIES FROM SESSIONS THAT CAN BE DISCONNECTED FROM/RECONNECTED TO

It's the nature of recoveries to take a variable amount of time to complete depending on the amount of data or the complexity of the systems involved. It's frustrating enough having a recovery fail due to a hardware or media failure, but it is particularly time-wasting and frustrating to have a recovery fail simply because the connection was lost between the recovery interface and the backup server. Equally, it's frustrating to be forced to remain in the office until a recovery completes because it's been initiated from a session that can't be disconnected from without interruption.*

21.6.7 KNOW THE POST-RECOVERY CONFIGURATION CHANGES

This should be covered from Section 21.6.1—once the data recovery is complete, there may be post-recovery configuration steps that are required (or even more recoveries) in order to achieve system restoration. The person performing the recovery should *always* be aware of what these steps are—or who to notify so that these steps can be performed.

21.6.8 REMEMBER QUANTUM PHYSICS

Monitoring can be useful, but excessive monitoring can result in skewed results if the act of monitoring impacts the performance. Therefore, the level of monitoring should be carefully chosen when performing recoveries. For example, if recovering a few hundred files there may be little impact in seeing a file-by-file listing of what has been recovered. However, if recovering a million files, the display of each filename may become a limiting factor in the ability to obtain accurate updates of *where* the recovery is up to.

A watched recovery never completes?

When running a disaster recovery once on a Solaris server via a 9600 baud console, the recovery appeared to take 6 hours to complete. But when the recovery finally "finished" and the server could be accessed again, it was observed the recovery had actually completed in 4 hours—it had simply taken another 2 hours to finish displaying all the files that had been recovered, one at a time.

Recoveries always need to be monitored (if for no other reason to report their completion), but can be frequently monitored through less intrusive mechanisms (even at a loss of some granularity) to see where the recovery is up to. For instance, rather than seeing a file-by-file listing for a large filesystem, periodically checking the *size* of the recovered filesystem, or the amount of data reported as recovered by the backup product may provide a sufficient update on the recovery progress.

21.6.9 BE PATIENT

Almost everyone would have been told when growing up that "patience is a virtue," usually in response to wanting something faster, sooner, or better. As computers, storage, and data transfer speeds continue to increase patience is sometimes forgotten. This comes down to a "brute force" approach to solving problems—if it isn't fast

---

* Backup servers increasingly have GUIs that allow the decoupling of selecting and initiating a recovery from the control of the recovery. But not all recoveries necessarily have to use such GUIs. CLIs and recoveries initiated on the recovery client may not feature such decoupling.

enough, don't optimize, just throw more memory/CPU/spindles at the problem and hope that it goes away. Yet, big data tells us there is a point at which adding more speed to a single system becomes either impractical or pointless: sometimes problems have to be optimized, and in fact, sometimes you still just have to wait. This can be particularly true when performing a recovery.

While systems should be designed to ensure recoveries can complete within the required SLAs, there's always a limit to miracles. Recovering 100 GB of data over a link with a maximum usable throughput of 10 MB/s will take at least 2.84 hours no matter how urgently the data is to be recovered. Sometimes aborting a recovery to diagnose why it's "going slow" might result in no performance improvement *and* needing to restart the recovery from scratch. In short: when performing a recovery, there will always be an upper limit on how fast it can be completed, and you should either know or be able to work that out at least approximately.

21.6.10 DOCUMENT THE CURRENT STATUS OF THE RECOVERY

Some recovery scenarios can't be completed in a single work-shift. Particularly in major disaster recovery situations, entire storage systems might need to be rebuilt or re-provisioned, virtual infrastructure may need to be stood up, and *then* a recovery might still need to be performed. A single person may not be able to perform the entire end-to-end recovery, and therefore anyone working on a recovery should be certain to document progress—and any issues encountered to date—so that in the event of someone else having to take over, they have a good understanding of the current progress that has been made.

21.6.11 NOTE ERRORS, AND WHAT LED TO THEM

Particularly for mature or compliance-regulated businesses, a Root Cause Analysis (RCA) may be required after a recovery. Alternately, smaller businesses may not need to perform RCAs, but should regardless be desirous of making each recovery a more stream-lined and simple process.

Either way, if errors are encountered during a recovery, they should be noted, their solution (or workaround) also noted, and this should be documented for the organization. If the errors result in the need for support cases with a vendor, those support case IDs and end solutions should also be noted.

21.6.12 DON'T ASSUME THE RECOVERY IS AN EXAM

A certification exam usually consists of being locked in a room without any internet access, notes, or communication, and the student is asked to solve a series of problems from memory. This isn't really a real-world situation; it usually demonstrates rote memorization and some problem solving capacity, but it isn't reflective of how we solve problems when we're faced with them in normal situations. During a recovery situation therefore, always remember to leverage any information or access to support that exists, whenever it is needed. Obstinacy does not guarantee results in most cases, nor does getting flustered to the point of not evaluating other options.

It's not uncommon to see people struggling with recoveries for an extended period of time without checking documentation, searching the internet, or contacting vendor support. What starts off as a small problem when there is plenty of time to spare in the recovery window can end up becoming a critical problem when the recovery window has almost expired. Therefore, why exacerbate the problem by treating it like an exam?

21.6.13 ENSURE THE RECOVERY IS PERFORMED BY THOSE TRAINED TO DO IT

Unless recoveries are designed to be entirely self-service via a cloud-like XaaS portal, they should by and large be performed by the *intended* user who has had the *intended* amount of training. While this means an end user might recover their email directly from their email tool by clicking a "Recover" tab (particularly in a SaaS environment), it's equally the case that as the complexity of the recovery increases, the training of the person performing the recovery should also be increased. This is something we've already touched on in Section 21.3—databases and complex applications in particular should be performed by their subject matter experts, not just someone with limited experience in the backup product and no experience in the application.

A corollary to this is to ensure that staff *are* adequately trained, regardless of whether that's formal or informal training. It is still common to encounter managers who are reluctant to train their staff in the administration and operation of low-level infrastructure such as storage and data protection.

21.6.14 WRITE A POST-RECOVERY REPORT

This speaks to maturity and formalization within the environment; application, business function, and system recoveries are *serious* business, and should be documented accordingly. As mentioned earlier, this may be through a RCA, but it may be as simple as an email summary sent to management and the appropriate teams to inform them what was done, what issues were encountered, what lessons were learnt, and, equally importantly, what *worked* properly. (Environments that keep track of support cases or trouble tickets will likely see this report generated as part of ticket closure.)

21.6.15 UPDATE INCORRECT INSTRUCTIONS

Documentation is not always updated with the same frequency as changes are made within an environment, however much we'd like them to be in lock-step. Operating systems might be upgraded, backup agents might be upgraded, even applications might be upgraded, and the documentation might be left the same as it was originally written.

So if a recovery is being performed and the steps required to complete the recovery differ with what has been documented, the changes and the circumstances that lead to those changes should be included in the documentation. Note that it's preferable to expand documentation with additional use cases rather than simply assuming the scenario encountered is the *only* possible scenario that might be encountered. For instance, while some steps might be determined to be redundant for a particular operating system and database, they may still be essential for an earlier version of either, and such versions may either still be in use or have compliance backups that *might* (1 day) need to be recovered from.

21.6.16 CONSIDERATIONS SPECIFIC TO TAPE

While tape is decreasing in use, it still appears in a variety of environments and there are some considerations that are particularly focused on tape:

- *Acclimatize off-site recovery media*—Tapes are particularly sensitive to changes in humidity and temperature. If tapes are either stored or transported in such a way that their temperature or humidity is different from the computer room in which they'll be used, they should be given up to 24 hours to acclimatize to the new temperature and humidity before being loaded into a drive.* Failing to do this in particularly humid environments can result in tapes being destroyed on access.
- *Always write-protect tape before starting a recovery*—A customer summed this up perfectly over a decade ago: "if you have to touch a tape, write-protect it." Their policy was a simple one: when removing tapes from their tape library, operators were required to enable the write-protect tab. The write-protect tab would *always* be left in the read-only mode *unless* operators received a specific request to reload the tape *for recycling*.
- *Patience particularly applies to tape*—Earlier we said you should be patient during recoveries. This particularly applies to tape-based recoveries. Tape loads, unloads, deposit and withdraw operations all take a particular amount of time and can't be rushed. If your environment still uses tape, you should be particularly cognizant of the amount of time each of these operations take.
- *Recall all media required before starting a recovery*—If you need to perform a recovery that uses media currently stored off-site, make sure you request *all* required volumes in one go. Even if some of the media required is already on-site, do your best to avoid a situation where the recovery is "hung" waiting for media to come back from an off-site location.
- *If media errors occur, retry elsewhere*—If a tape fails in a particular drive, the error may be with the tape, or it may be with the drive. If the tape gets "chewed up" another copy of the data will be required to recover from, and as much as possible this should be loaded into *another* tape drive to attempt the recovery from in case the fault is with the tape drive rather than the tape.
- *Preserve the number of copies of backups*—The same number of copies of a backup should exist at the end of a recovery that existed at the start. If a tape fails during the recovery process and the clone/duplicate tape needs to be used for recovery, then at the end of the recovery a *new* copy should be generated to ensure there are still two copies of the data available.*

---

* A customer operating in Darwin, Australia, less than 1500 km from the equator, would store their "local" tapes in a safe approximately 200 m from their computer room. Even at this short a distance, transporting them from the safe to the computer room would leave the tapes needing acclimatization before being used in a tape drive.

- *Send off-site media back off-site*—If media is recalled from off-site for a recovery, it should be sent back off-site at the end of the recovery, unless it is going to be reused within 24 hours. The media was sent off-site for a reason: for disaster protection. Keeping the media on-site, presumably having *all* copies of the backup on-site, introduces risk to the business.

21.7 DISASTER RECOVERY CONSIDERATIONS

Everything previously mentioned for recoveries will equally apply to disaster recoveries, but there are a few additional recommendations and best practices to apply during a disaster recovery situation as well.

21.7.1 Maintenance Backups

Wherever possible, *before* major maintenance tasks are performed, backups should take place. System patches, core driver changes, major application upgrades, and a plethora of other maintenance operations can cause significant damage if they go awry. Having a backup which is as up to date as possible to recover from can substantially reduce recovery time and amount of data loss in the event of a significant failure.[†] Note that depending on the type of system maintenance being performed, other forms of online data protection such as snapshots may be more desirable before maintenance operations.

Equally, if a major system change is performed (e.g., the operating system is upgraded, or the database is upgraded triggering a data format change), performing a new full backup of the system as soon as possible is equally important. This can dramatically reduce recovery complexity, or even prevent recovery failure, in the event of a failure happening a short period after major system changes.

21.7.2 Avoid Upgrades

Disaster recoveries are not the time or place to perform additional upgrades or changes to the system. The goal should be to get the system back *as it was* and introduce no further complexity into the process. Indeed, businesses with mature IT processes (e.g., following ITIL) will expressly forbid changes being performed during disaster recovery situations.

21.7.3 Read the Documentation before Backups Are Performed

Disaster recovery can be a complex task, and may require preparatory steps to be performed as part of the backup process. A "disaster recovery guide" for instance

---

* This is another common example of where best practice tape management is not always performed, and can contribute to complete data loss situations if the same data is requested at a later point in time.
† This can be even more critical in virtualized environments. If a product can leverage changed block tracking for *restores* as well as backups, a virtual machine might be recoverable in minutes or less after a failed maintenance cycle.

may not only provide steps for performing a disaster recovery, but details of procedures to enact during backups, such as

- Operating system databases requiring scripted exports
- Operating system or application files that are not backed up by default
- Key files that may not be accessible when in use

All of this information should be known and understood during the backup and, indeed, should be understood as part of the system *architecture* process.

21.7.4   Disaster Recoveries Must Be Run by Administrators

Although standard recoveries can often be handed over to help desk staff or even end users, disaster recovery operations should be considered essential activities of the appropriate administrators relating to the applications, systems, and infrastructure that has failed. (See again Section 21.3.)

21.7.5   Use Compatible Infrastructure

If recovering physical systems this usually means recovering to the *same* physical systems—the same CPUs, the same adapters, and so on. However, this is not always the case—some backup products support "Physical To Virtual" (PTV) recoveries where a previously physical system is converted into a virtual machine as part of the recovery process. (This may even allow conversion during the recovery between supported hypervisor types.) While PTV recoveries may seem contrary to the previous recommendation to "avoid upgrades," they should be deemed acceptable when (1) required *and* (2) supported by the backup product.

Regardless of whether the recovery is a physical or virtual one, other considerations include

- Ensuring the same system resources are allocated (CPU, memory, etc.)
- Ensuring the same (or sufficient) storage is allocated
- Ensuring shared infrastructure is not impacted by the recovery—for instance, if a heavy workload virtual server is recovered onto a hypervisor already at its operational limit, this could cause larger problems for the environment

21.7.6   Know the System Dependencies

This combines the need for context aware recoveries, a requirement to understand the difference between data recovery and system restoration *and* the importance of system dependency maps and/or tables, as outlined in Section 4.4.2.2. A system map is critical in disaster recovery situations to ensure that systems are processed in the correct order to ensure business functions are restored as efficiently and quickly as possible. Knowing the system dependencies allows the coordination of multisystem and multifunction recoveries with the appropriate prioritization given to resources and systems.

21.7.7   KEEP ACCURATE SYSTEM DOCUMENTATION

This can be reduced to two factors:

1. Deployment of a data protection system should not be seen as an excuse to avoid documenting required system components (e.g., licensing, application configuration).
2. A data protection product can only protect what it is designed to protect—for instance, a backup product can't reconstruct LUNs at the storage level.*

System documentation deemed essential to ensuring overall environment recoverability should be stored both on-site and off-site in a suitably secured location.† Similarly, essential passwords and licenses should be appropriately protected so they are available in a disaster, using corporate and/or regulatory security standards.

21.7.8   DO YOU KNOW WHERE YOUR LICENSES ARE AT 1 AM?

Although hinted at in the above point, this deserves special mention: there is more to a disaster recovery than just restoring data. Indeed, if handled correctly, the data restoration component should be the most straight-forward and least-interactive part of the entire process.

The best-laid disaster recovery plans can come unstuck for the simplest of reasons. What if the data protection software or system won't install or activate required functionality without the licenses? Always ensure the disaster recovery documentation includes *complete* details of all the licenses used by the data protection systems so they can be manually re-keyed or copied/pasted if required.

21.7.9   DISASTER RECOVERY EXERCISES

Disaster recovery exercises are a vital business activity that should be regularly performed to check the health of the data protection environment. There are several approaches to disaster recovery exercises:

- *Simulated disaster*—A "what if" scenario is posed and the appropriate staff and teams are assembled to map out what would be done to restore business operations.
- *Readiness tests*—Disaster recovery systems are isolated and their production components (e.g., databases) are started on them to confirm either disaster recovery procedures or functional readiness.
- *System failover*—Individual hosts or storage systems are failed over from one site to another.

---

* This is often seen as another advantage of converged or hyperconverged infrastructure and the software defined datacenter. Virtualized and systems running on hyper converged infrastructure becomes highly mobile and allows infrastructure administrators to execute end-to-end protection processes without regard to the underlying physical infrastructure.

† Remember this documentation is a blueprint to overall environment recovery and practically offers the keys for the environment to an attacker if stolen.

- *Business function failover*—An entire business function (e.g., invoicing, online shopping/eCommerce) is failed over from one datacenter to another and used in production for a nominated period of time.
- *Operational failover*—The entire operations are failed over from one data-center to another and used *as production* for a nominated period of time.

In actual fact, *all* exercises above have their own use within the business. Simulated disasters are an excellent form of planning, readiness tests can be used to validate documented procedures, and each of system, business function, and operational failover actually help the business *prove* that it can successfully migrate functional-ity from one datacenter to another. Further, each of those exercises (system, business function, operational) provide proof of something equally important: that the disas-ter recovery environment can in fact run production operations. Many businesses—particularly in the mid-market to low-end enterprise space—will populate their disaster recovery site with equipment that has been phased *out* of their production sites. As production sites grow, this can result in situations where the disaster recov-ery site may not actually have sufficient compute or storage resources to *run* produc-tion. While optimally this should be avoided at an architectural level or discovered at a monitoring level, it is still better to determine it during a disaster recovery exercise when the production site still remains than in a true disaster recovery situation.

For organizations needing to provide compliance-style proof of their disaster recovery readiness, engaging external auditors may be a mandatory function of disaster recovery exercises. For smaller organizations and businesses that are not in heavily regulated industry verticals, external auditors may not be required, but periodic engagement of subject matter experts to supervise and monitor (to "ride shotgun," as it were) the disaster recovery exercise can be essential in providing feedback on the likely reliability and accuracy of the procedures.

21.8   PROTECTING THE PROTECTION ENVIRONMENT

For the most part our discussions have been around the protection of primary data—regardless of whether that's applications, business systems, or core data. Yet, there's another type of data and system within an environment that needs protecting—the protection environment itself. A common mistake is to consider protection systems to be nonproduction. While they aren't *primary production* in the same way that a database server hosting a mission critical system is, they are true "secondary" production systems in that their availability and reliability is critical to overall infra-structure and systems availability and recoverability within the environment.

Or to put it another way: your protection environment should never represent a single point of failure within the environment.*

Consider storage replication—this is dependent not only on the availability of the target storage system, but also the link between the two storage systems. A busi-ness that seeks to provide synchronous or even small-granularity asynchronous rep-lication between storage systems hosting business critical functions will find that

---

* And if somehow it is, it should only be after the business has signed off against the risk.

replication interrupted immediately if the replication link disappears. Thus, a single link between sites may very well represent a single point of failure in data protection to the business. (Indeed, this is one of the most common failure points that businesses will seek to design around.) Having standby links or active/active links that allow data protection replication to survive the failure of a single communications channel isn't about "gold plating" the environment, but about ensuring adequate protection can be provided even in the event of a single failure.

Similarly, when we think of backup and recovery systems, those systems need to include a high degree of redundancy to ensure a cascading failure (e.g., a primary system failure and a protection system failure) does not prevent data recoverability. This includes options such as

- Ensuring disk-based protection storage uses RAID to survive the failure of one or more disks—protection data loss should not occur as a result of disk failure
- Ensuring deduplication protection storage has self-checking and self-healing mechanisms beyond simple RAID*
- Ensuring backups of production systems are duplicated to another storage system (be it protection storage, Cloud, or tape) at another location
- Ensuring the configuration and metadata associated with the backup system—or indeed any protection system—is replicated and recoverable in the event of the protection system itself failing and is retained for the same life span of the protection data being generated

One item often not considered when protecting the protection environment itself is log files—these should be protected (via backup or whatever mechanism is appropriate) for the length of time the data they are protecting is being retained for. The reason is simple: there is a considerable difference between being able to say a failure has occurred and being able to report *why* the failure occurred. Regardless of whether it's snapshots being retained for a fortnight, backups being retained for 7 years, or archives being retained for 70 years, the logging information associated with the protection (or archive) operation performed should be retained for *at least* as long as the data itself is being retained for. This enables far more comprehensive analysis at any point in the retention period if an attempt is made to retrieve the data and it fails. Current logs will allow analysis as to whether the failure has occurred as a result of the retrieval operation, but historical log analysis may allow an administrator or technician to determine if the protection was ever properly performed in the first place. While ideally such failures *should* be captured at the time of the event, short-term log retention against long-term data retention is a reckless space saving approach that blinkers a business during root cause analysis and diagnosis functions.

---

* Self-checking and self-healing storage beyond plain RAID—for example, regular checksum validation and options around storage evacuation are critical in deduplication systems. While traditional tape-based backups or even regular disk-based backups can potentially survive the loss of a single backup or a single piece of media, deduplication is space efficient by having multiple copies reference and leverage the *same* stored data, almost in a similar way to snapshots. Without additional checking and healing capabilities a business may be exposing itself to unacceptable risk.

21.9   HISTORICAL CONSIDERATIONS AND DATA MIGRATION

When considering data protection, backups in particular represent what is often referred to as a *sticky product* within an organization. While organizations may readily switch between network, compute or even storage vendors with relative ease, organizations with long-term retention requirements often find themselves considerably averse to changing backup products.

In an ideal world, this actually shouldn't be the case. As discussed in Chapter 3, a mature and comprehensive data life-cycle management policy includes an emphasis on both deletion and archiving to reduce the amount of primary data that requires protection (and the amount of backup data generated) *and* the longevity of the retention required for backups in particular. Figure 3.2 in particular highlighted a high level but more mature approach to data life cycle, being

- Create
- Use, then
  - Delete *or*
  - Archive and maintain/use
    - Then delete

(Ideally, backups should only be required of the data that is being actively used, with archives using their own storage protection and retention locking.)

"Delete" is often a dirty word in business when it comes to data, with "archive" not far behind it, and as the amount of data within a business grows, the entrenched aversion to implementing a holistic data life-cycle management policy also grows. The net result is we are left with a less than ideal requirement to maintain long-term compliance retention via backups.

This long-term retention requirement imposes long-term management overheads on backups that are not dealt with as well as we would normally like to see. Backups requiring 7-year retention and written 5 years ago may be written on incompatible media formats *and* by a different product to what is in use in the business today.

As discussed in Chapter 12, and touched upon again in Section 21.5.4, true media management (including periodic recall and testing, media migration and format migration) is not practiced by many of the organizations relying on tape for long-term retention. Using either disk- or Cloud-based formats for long-term retention can alleviate the migration process by reducing the media handling required for migration, reducing the risk of media failure being noticed only during migration, *and* allowing more efficient migration methods.

While backups can usually be migrated relatively easily between different formats using the *same* backup product (e.g., moving from LTO-6 to Cloud object storage), the migration *between* backup products is usually more challenging. A "classic" approach is to maintain the last used copy of the previous backup product and sufficient infrastructure to allow it to recover data, but this is fraught with risk—usually part of the migration strategy is to stop paying for support and maintenance on the disused product, but if a recovery encounters issues at a later date then time and materials or "best effort" support may be prohibitively expensive, if available at all. Since backup products typically don't read each other's formats, the other migration options tend to be either a whole-scale recovery and re-backup of previously backed up material or the use of one of a small number of third-party utilities that can read and selectively convert between different backup products.*

21.10   ISOLATED RECOVERY SITES

Gone are the days where hacking is primarily seen as a function of corporate espionage. Organized crime and other aggressive malicious hackers are increasingly using tools such as *ransomware* to extort large amounts of sums from individuals *and* businesses. Ransomware might be a payload on top of a normal virus or Trojan which not only infects systems, but it *encrypts* systems and refuses to handover the decryption keys until a verified payment is made by the user.

Such an attack on a consumer is bad enough—particularly given end consumers typically have a lackadaisical approach to data protection. Reports of consumers either losing all their data—sometimes years of photos and documents—or being forced to pay hundreds or thousands of dollars to get access to their own data again are becoming an almost daily occurrence.

Imagine uncontrolled ransomware infecting a corporate fileserver, potentially *petabytes* of data becoming encrypted. Imagine organized crime deliberately infiltrating via social engineering and other discovery processes an organization enough to not only get ransomware encrypting data, but *also* deleting backups, forcing the payment of millions or more for data access. This is no longer science fiction; it is inevitable. The systematic deletion of backups prior to erasing primary storage data has, in fact, already happened to multiple companies.

This is leading to a new strategy in data protection—Isolated Recovery Sites (IRS). These are "dark" sites that business critical data is written to, typically via protection storage, and architected in such a way that compliance-compatible locking is used to *enforce* data retention and security. This may mean for instance that backups are replicated from the primary or secondary datacenter during a limited window (e.g., the network may only be opened between sites for 4 hours a day), *and* the protection storage is operated in a WORM format—data once written may not be overwritten, changed, or even deleted until the expiration date has passed. Thus, in the event of a significant and destructive intrusion into the IT environment causing complete data loss, the company can resort to a "read only" copy. While such environments may represent a significant spend, the alternative—particularly for businesses seen as key targets of organized crime—of paying orders of magnitude more to gain access to data encrypted by malware is increasingly making the notion of an IRS a *must-have* rather than a *nice-to-have* for major enterprises. Such replication is usually configured as a "pull" replication from the IRS during periodic network connectivity. Most critically, the primary backup system will not be aware of the tertiary, IRS copy. Thus, even if the primary backup environment is compromised, it will not lead to the compromise of the IRS copy.

---

* It should be noted that such third-party recovery/conversion options are actually *disallowed* as part of the end-user license agreement by some backup products, presumably as an attempt to discourage businesses from moving away.

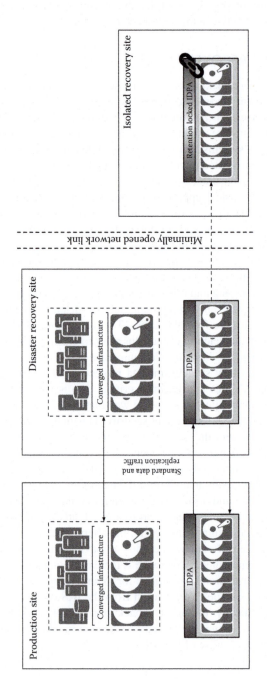

FIGURE 21.1 Isolated Recovery Site in comparison to production and DR sites.

IRS work best and are architected best in situations where

- A minimum number of storage, infrastructure, and data protection vendors are used
- Converged or even hyperconverged infrastructure is used
- Centralized data protection storage is used
- Data protection techniques are standardized throughout the business
- The system is well documented with excellent processes
- Recovery roles are well understood

While an IRS can be built and maintained with *none* of the above, each of the above can significantly speed recovery time should the site ever be needed, and can make the ongoing maintenance of the IRS considerably simpler. Critical, of course, is the ability to define "retention locks" against data protection storage that are vendor and compliance certified so that even if a rogue attacker *does* get electronic access to the system, they have insufficient capabilities on their own to cause data deletion or corruption.

It should be noted that an IRS is *not* a disaster recovery site. The typical production/disaster recovery site relationship still exists and remains the same. In Figure 21.1 we can see a basic high level diagram of the relationship between the three sites. For the purposes of simplicity, automated control and test systems residing in the IRS environment have not been shown in the diagram. Control systems will initiate network links and drop them after a predetermined amount of time has elapsed and instruct test systems to validate data. Test systems should be configured within the IRS environment to automatically recover data (including any backup server disaster recovery functions) and verify the integrity of that data. This serves to (a) constantly confirm that recovery in the event of a catastrophic data encryption/deletion is possible and (b) potentially even detect such an event as it is taking place, particularly if it is being executed slowly.

An IRS is not constructed for regular disaster recovery situations—site loss or site destruction—but for one particular scenario, site *erasure*. It assumes the production and/or disaster recovery sites still exist, and still have the equipment required to run the business, *but* have had systems or storage compromised to the point where a large amount of data has either been erased, or *must* be erased in order to restore operational integrity. Thus the primary infrastructure at the IRS will be whatever retention locked protection storage is required to act as a source for recovery in an erasure emergency, *not* traditional disaster recovery infrastructure including compute, network, and primary storage.

21.11 SUMMARY

Data protection is more than just a *proactive* process. A multitude of steps can be taken to avoid the need to recover data, and in cases where mission critical systems must be available 24 × 7 it's a practical imperative that data *recovery* from backup is never required. Systems with no countenance for data loss and a requirement for instantaneous or near-instantaneous service restoration will require advanced data protection techniques to allow for continuous replication, continuous journaling, continuous availability and the ability to roll-back to a prior data point orders of magnitude faster than recovery from a backup or perhaps even recovery from a snapshot.

Yet for most businesses, regardless of their size or their complexity, recovery from backups *is* a typical business process. For smaller businesses this could be an optional recovery technique for almost all systems, and for larger businesses it will apply to a subset of systems for which mission critical 24 × 7 availability is not required. (Providing "platinum" service levels for *all* systems, even development and test, or noncritical business functions is too costly in an IT world dependent on shrinking budgets and is something few if any Chief Information Officers or company boards would agree to.)

For the foreseeable future, traditional backup systems remain a cornerstone of a data protection environment, and likewise, traditional *recovery* processes remain a cornerstone of a data protection environment.

22 Choosing Protection Infrastructure

22.1 INTRODUCTION

As we've established in previous chapters, data protection is rarely, if ever, a one-size-fits-all approach. It's remarkably rare to encounter an individual business where a single data protection product meets all the operational and recoverability requirements. Indeed, as soon as fundamental data storage protection techniques (such as RAID) are considered as part of a holistic data protection approach, a single-product approach is extremely unlikely.

When planning a data protection infrastructure, a simple rule is offered:

> There are old protection environments, and there are bold protection environments, but there are no old, bold protection environments.

Or to put it another way: leading edge is fine for a data protection environment, but bleeding edge could very well cause more trouble than it solves. Always tread carefully when developing a data protection strategy.

22.2 IT'S NEVER ABOUT THE TECHNOLOGY

As we established in Chapter 4, there are multiple components to a data protection *system* for your environment. Reiterating, these are

- People
- Processes and documentation
- Training
- Service level agreements
- Testing
- Technology

Technology comprises just *one-sixth* of a data protection system. The remaining components—people, processes and documentation, training, service level agreements, and testing—are independent of the technology used, and no technology, no matter how awe inspiringly complete or comprehensive will provide an adequate data protection strategy if the business does not invest in the other five-sixths of the equation.

It's important when reviewing this chapter to keep that equation in mind: one-sixth technology, five-sixths the rest. If unsure, you may wish to take a step back to Chapter 4 and review before continuing this chapter. The simple message is this: investing in the best technology will achieve nothing if the business does not properly *realize* that investment by working through the non-technology components of a data protection strategy.

22.3   IT'S ALWAYS ABOUT THE TECHNOLOGY

Conversely, choosing a data protection system for your environment is *all* about the technology. It doesn't matter how good the people, processes and documentation, training, service level agreements, and testing are if the *wrong* technology is chosen. If the technology deployed is not fit for purpose, is not compatible with business objectives and requirements, and unable to meet operational needs, then the data protection system will be premised on luck and good fortune rather than an accurate and compatible architecture.

Infrastructure choices (regardless of how agile the business is) can be quickly made but *unmaking* them either takes time, costs money, or both. While this is readily understood for *physical*, on-premise infrastructure, the implications in a more abstract and nebulous Cloud-based infrastructure are much less appreciated.

Case in point

Businesses looking for a "quick win" in a Cloud strategy to satisfy senior executive requirements are frequently looking at moving elements of data protection or data management (i.e., backup or archive) to the Cloud, without a realistic consideration of the potential costs therein. A per month fee of 3c per GB may seem phenomenally cheap compared to purchasing and maintaining centralized backup data storage, but many businesses dive into such arrangements without considering ramifications of needing to perform large-scale data retrievals, or even the costs of returning *all* the data to an on-premises solution. Cloud-based data storage is usually cheap to ingest and cheap to store, but expensive or slow (or both) to retrieve data from.

Some Cloud object storage facilities aimed at archival storage charge seemingly infinitesimal fees for holding the data, but impose serious practical limits on the amount of data that can be retrieved per month without paying hefty egress fees.

In 2016 a widely distributed Medium article* for instance demonstrated this risk, even at a personal level: a user who wanted to do a bulk retrieval from Amazon Glacier ended up paying $2.50 per GB for the retrieval. (Consider extrapolating these sorts of fees out to a company that needs to retrieve 10 TB of archive urgently and had to pay that premium—$25,600.)

This is not to say Cloud object storage *shouldn't* be part of the strategy for a business, but it does serve to remind that there's no such thing as a free lunch: no matter what infrastructure is used, switching will always incur a cost of some sort, and therefore it's imperative to choose wisely and accurately.

22.4   COVERAGE

22.4.1   VALUE PRODUCTS THAT VALUE PROTECTION

In the realm of data protection, it seems odd to suggest the need to value products that actually *value* protection, but there can sometimes be a vast gulf between the

---

* "How I ended up paying $150 for a single 60 GB download from Amazon Glacier," Marko Karppinen, https://medium.com/@karppinen/how-i-ended-up-paying-150-for-a-single-60gb-download-from-amazon-glacier-6cb77b288c3e.

operational integrity and reliability of differing data protection products. Sometimes this can be based on product maturity—a v1 product may offer nowhere near the features of a v9 product, but product version numbers are insufficient in themselves to really differentiate degrees of protection. Instead, for each type of data protection being sought, you need to evaluate how true the product is to the data protection you want. Consider for instance the following examples:

- *RAID systems*: There are a variety of high equality consumer grade NAS and DAS RAID systems on the market, and there are equally a large number of "cheap and cheerful" products supposedly in the same market space but usually half to a quarter of the price. Most of the "cheap and cheerful" style consumer products work excellently so long as you're only after RAID-0 for performance. They tend to be far less reliable, and far more likely to struggle or fail under load when using them for actual protection-based RAID, particularly of the parity variety.
- *Backup and recovery*: Some backup and recovery products *still* fail to implement dependency tracking, allowing the product to automatically delete backups outside of a retention window that backups *inside* a retention window rely on for full system recovery.
- *Replication*: A journaling replication system offering bandwidth compression but unable to support cluster mode for the replication appliances (virtual or physical) introduces what many architects would consider to be an unacceptable single point of failure within the data protection framework. If intra-site storage replication can be brought down by a *single* appliance failure at either end, the SLAs offered to the business must be reconsidered.
- *Protection storage*: Deduplicated protection storage that offers no data integrity services beyond standard RAID parity is a risky proposal. Deduplication minimizes the number of data copies (compared to, say, tape), and therefore requires a higher degree of data integrity enforcement than merely protecting against hard drive failure.

A simple rule to follow when evaluating components of a data protection strategy is that no component should introduce a single point of failure. This can be achieved either through the type of product deployed *or* the architecture of the implementation (e.g., ensuring backups are copied to alternate media).

In a marketplace filled with startup companies offering new techniques for data protection we return to the adage "there are old protection environments, and there are bold protection environments, but there are no old, bold protection environments"—a startup may seemingly offer a cheaper or more innovative solution, but will the startup still exist in 1, 2, or 3 years? This is not to disparage startups—by their nature they tend to be industry disruptors, but particularly in data protection startups exemplify "caveat emptor"—*let the buyer beware*.

22.4.2 VALUE FRAMEWORKS OVER MONOLITHS

Essentially, we should seek products that offer extensibility and customization. A monolithic product focuses on doing everything the designers anticipated or planned for a user to be able to do, but nothing else. A framework product should of course be able to do everything the designers anticipated, but adds a layer of customization and extension. In essence, a monolithic product requires the business to adapt its processes and workflows to suit the limitations of the product, whereas a framework allows the product to be adapted to suit the processes of the business.

It would seem for the most part that framework products have won in enterprise IT. Prospective buyers increasingly look for features such as a rich command line interface or a REST API to allow integration in alternate management, automation and orchestration tools. Indeed, a framework approach to products is practically essential to deliver an *X*aaS style offering to the business. It should be noted that while REST APIs are favored with almost religious fervor among DevOps and *X*aaS service development teams, a rich CLI can offer equal levels of customizability if the tools being used to access it are flexible enough.

22.4.3 Don't Assume

It should be common sense, and it should go without saying, but perhaps the most *common* mistake made when planning data protection infrastructure is to *assume* functionality instead of *confirming* it.

At each step in the data protection journey your business should be acting on informed and researched understanding of products rather than assumed knowledge. This applies to the entire data protection spectrum—for example:

- Knowing what operating systems are supported by continuously available storage platforms
- Determining databases supported by backup and recovery systems
- Understanding application support for CDP-based replication systems
- Confirming storage snapshot support options for virtualization systems

It should actually be a reasonably trivial task for a business to articulate the various operating systems, applications, and databases currently in use as well as any planned upgrades or changes as part of a requirements list. This might be as simple as a table of requirements, such as that shown in Table 22.1.

TABLE 22.1
Example List of Feature Support Requirements

Feature	Version in Use	In Planning
Microsoft Windows	2008 R2	2012 R2
Solaris	V10	V11
Oracle	11gR2	12c
Linux	SLES 11	RHEL 7
SQL Server	2008	2014
IP Networking	Cisco 10 Gbit	N/A
FC Networking	Brocade 8 Gbit	Brocade 16 Gbit
Virtualization	VMware vSphere v5.1	VMware vSphere v6

While business requirements change over time based on a variety of factors, products providing business-critical functions that will rely on an intended data protection service should be particularly probed for current and future compatibility, as well as intended future support.

22.4.4 Functionality Checklist

When planning new protection infrastructure, it's equally important to build a checklist of required product functionality and confirm products supply it. This goes beyond confirming support for in-use products within the business—it's about making sure the product more broadly performs and provides what the business needs.

Table 22.2 provides an example subset of criteria that might be used to evaluate backup and recovery software. In terms of typical tenders, this might be considered to be a baseline for the *functional requirements* list for a product.

Don't lock yourself in

When calling for a list of requirements (even mandatory ones), be sure to allow for alternative options for non-compliant answers.

For instance, even something as simple as "does your product support incremental backups?" is no longer as straight forward as you might imagine. Some advanced deduplication products actually execute a *full* backup every time, at the cost (time and resources) of an incremental backup, thereby eliminating the need for incremental or differential backups. (This is not so much a "synthetic full" in the classic sense, but an automatically synthesized full, generated at the time of the backup, via pointers.)

In short: Don't eliminate a product from consideration because it provides an architecture not catered for in your questions.

22.4.5 Data Protection is an Internal Function Too

As mentioned previously, data protection is a multi-layered activity, but one of those layers is sensible systems design, architecture *and upgrades* within a business environment. Businesses fret regularly about whether or not an operating system or database no longer supported by the *manufacturer* will be supported by a data protection vendor.

Case in point

Even as late as 2016 it has been highly common to encounter businesses looking for, and evaluating data protection requirements against operating systems such as Windows 2003 and even Windows 2000. Microsoft ceased supporting Windows 2000 in 2010, and ceased supporting Windows 2003 in 2015.

Continuing to provide business functions on products that are no longer supported by their actual manufacturer is reckless, perhaps even outright foolish, and there's usually very little excuse. (It's practically unheard of for a vendor to drop support for a product without providing ample warning, and product support timelines are usually published well in advance.) In almost all cases this situation happens when a business-critical function is developed around a specific operating system, and budget is not allocated to keep the function modernized. There is nothing sensible about such decisions.

TABLE 22.2

Example List (Subset) of Criteria a Company Might Use to Evaluate Backup and Recovery Software

Functionality	Mandatory or Optional	Compliant	Alternative
Control and management			
Centralized	M		
Hybrid	O		
Supports remote administration	M		
Supports centralized administration of multiple servers if required	M		
Supports REST API	O		
Supports CLI	M		
Backup levels			
Full	M		
Incremental	M		
Differential	O		
Synthetic Full	O		
Filesystem backup types			
Online	M		
Online with filesystem snapshot	M		
Online block-based backups	O		
Retention strategy			
Automatic dependency tracking	M		
Media pool support			
Data separation for different locations	M		
Data separation for different retention	M		
Arbitrary data separation	M		
Virtualization support[a]			
Hypervisor image level backup	M		
In-guest agent level support	M		
File level recovery from image level backup	M		
Database recovery from image level backup	O		
Power on guest from protection storage	O		
Change block tracking support for backup	M		
Change block tracking support for recovery	M		
Cloud support			
Backup to Cloud Object Storage	O		
Duplicate to the Cloud Object Storage	O		
Deduplication support			
Source (client) deduplication	M		
Target deduplication	O		
Deduplication embedded in database agent	M		

[a] It should be noted given the number of hypervisors now on the market it would be extremely prudent for a business to break out this section for each type of hypervisor in use within IT infrastructure to avoid serious misunderstandings.

In short: businesses worried about protection support for an operating system, application, or database that's no longer maintained by its manufacturer should be more concerned with their internal processes and budgets for upgrades and changes.

22.4.6 Minimize Vendors, Not Products

Given all the different data protection options you may need to consider, product minimization is desirable, but there will always be a lower limit on the number of products you need. (There's not a single backup product on the market for instance that can also double as continuously available storage.) Since there will always be a certain minimum number of products involved in a data protection strategy, minimization is more something that can be achieved through reducing the number of vendors involved. This allows more strategic relationships to be built between enterprises and their vendors, with increased synergies at different layers of the data protection stack. For instance, if multiple storage vendors provide systems that *all* meet the requirements, but one comes from the same vendor as the backup and recovery software being used, there may be enhanced integration points achievable by picking the same storage vendor as the backup vendor. A 2014 survey* conducted against 3300 businesses worldwide determined the actual total IT budget spent on data protection differed based on the number of data protection vendors employed by the business:

- One vendor—7.04% of IT budget
- Two vendors—7.32% of IT budget
- Three or more vendors—8.91%

Additionally, the number of disruptions experienced by the businesses seemed to correlate to the number of data protection vendors used by the company, notably:

- Companies experiencing data loss events:
  - 24%—One data protection vendor
  - 33%—Two data protection vendors
  - 38%—Three data protection vendors
- Companies experiencing unplanned systems outages:
  - 42%—One data protection vendor
  - 52%—Two data protection vendors
  - 54%—Three or more data protection vendors

While individual company experiences will vary, there is logic in achieving enhanced reliability through deploying integrated stacks of products rather than disparate collections. In no way does this *eliminate* data protection issues, but it can help to minimize them.

---

* EMC Global Data Protection Index, conducted by Independent Research and Analysis firm, Vanson Bourne in 2014, http://www.emc.com/collateral/presentation/emc-dpi-key-findings-global.pdf.

22.4.7 Understand the Costs

There's a wide variety of costs associated with data protection strategies. As mentioned earlier, switching products or strategies is rarely going to be both cheap and easy. This means it's important to understand the various costs associated with new data protection environments, *and* equally to understand the costs associated with a *current* data protection environment.

If a cost comparison is to be made it should be against both the direct and indirect costs. This includes staffing-associated costs—not just the number of staff required to run a particular service, but also such areas as the training and certification requirements (time and fiscal).

Equally it's important to compare "apples with apples," so to speak. Building a flat rate comparison of cost-per-GB for, say, 100 TB of deduplication storage and 100 TB of standard storage requires understanding of the storage efficiencies achieved via deduplication. (A 100 TB deduplication appliance achieving, say, 8:1 deduplication should be compared to 800 TB of standard storage, not 100 TB of standard storage.*) Likewise, comparing any form of disk protection storage against tape protection storage needs to include details such as

- Energy requirements for both the disk system and the tape libraries
- Per-tile occupancy costs of equipment in a computer room
- Tape handling fees, including
  - Removing from site
  - Returning to site
  - Storage off-site
  - FTE costs associated with media migration
  - FTE costs associated with media checking
- Tape duplication times
- Disk storage replication times, bandwidth requirements, and costs

The high level costs are usually easy to account for, but as the saying goes—the devil is in the details. Cost comparisons can be tedious, but are truly essential to perform an accurate and complete comparison between different data protection technologies and products.

22.5 SUMMARY

Given the disparate components, data protection is usually mixed over multiple purchase cycles—for example, alternate storage refreshes and backup/recovery refreshes. (Converting to converged infrastructure can substantially simplify planning around data protection, but this is still a relatively new approach for many businesses.)

Further, with growing Cloud (private, hybrid, or public) adoption in many organizations, the borders of data protection for a business are constantly changing.

---

* Additionally, the bandwidth cost for network replication for a non-deduplicated solution versus a deduplication solution should also factor into the cost comparison.

Few if any businesses are truly unique—for instance, almost every business picking a new data protection product will seek references based on other companies in the same industry vertical. The best approaches therefore in considering data protection infrastructure can be summed up as follows:

- Don't make assumptions
- Don't forget the non-technical aspects of a data protection solution
- Do your homework on functional requirements
- Understand the costs, both initially and forward looking
- Make strategic as well as operational decisions
- Be prepared to evaluate strategic or architectural recommendations that don't immediately conform to your idea of a "perfect" strategy (i.e., be prepared to think outside the box).

23 The Impact of Flash on Data Protection

The first hard drive system was announced in 1956. The IBM 350 disk system had fifty 24-inch platters and a total capacity of 3.75 MB, and it spun at a speed of 1200 RPM.

To date, the highest performance hard drives operate spin at 15,000 RPM—a net increase of 13,800 RPM in 60 years. Over the years, various performance improvements have been made to boost hard drive performance—RAID/striping, caches, improved interfaces, and of course higher rotation speeds. But the actual performance differences between the very first hard drives and the current top of the line hard drives are negligible when we consider the improvements in CPU and memory performance during that same time.

If we consider the transfer rates achievable with hard drives, even 15,000 RPM drives offer sustained transfer rates only of somewhere between 167 MB/s and 258 MB/s.

Particularly in enterprise use, a performance characteristic we often focus on with storage is the IOPS—the number of Input/Output operations Per Second the drive can process. A 7200 RPM SATA drive—of the variety commonly used in end-user computers—will provide somewhere between 75 and 100 IOPS, while those high performance 15,000 RPM SAS drives are considered to offer anywhere between 175 and 210 IOPS—which is frequently averaged to around the 190–192 IOPS mark.

Using traditional hard drives, the accepted way to achieve a high number of IOPS was to combine a high number of hard drives working together. This not uncommonly led to storage configurations that were massively over-populated in terms of *capacity* in order to provide sufficient IOPS for the performance requirements of the application.

Conversely, when solid state drives started entering the market around 2008, they were already featuring performance ratios of 5000+ IOPS, and commercially available *consumer* SSDs are now routinely capable of delivering 50,000–100,000 IOPS per device.* Sustained read and write speeds of 500 MB/s is quite common even just on a SATA-3 interface. PCIe-based flash storage increases these performance options even further, leading us to a point where in 2016 dense flash memory storage *systems* are capable of delivering sustained performance in the order of 10,000,000 IOPS.

In the same way that tape ruled backup for so long because the dollar per GB ratio was so much in its favor, traditional hard drives have up until this point in time outstripped the capacity of their higher performance SSD cousins, and been the mainstream of primary storage systems.

---

* Of course, the actual number of IOPS delivered by a stand-alone consumer SSD will depend on overall system performance.

It is no longer the case that SSDs can't match traditional hard drives for capacity—current traditional hard drives peak at the 8–10 TB size, while SSDs are already available at 15 TB+ and storage manufacturers expect this capacity/density to continue to increase for some time.

While a 10 or 15 TB SSD will cost substantially more than an 8 or 10 TB hard drive, the performance differences between the two cannot be overstated. There is however a means of increasing the cost benefits of SSD at higher capacity, one which is becoming increasingly common in "flash only" dedicated primary storage systems: deduplication.

As discussed in previous chapters, deduplication works by squeezing out commonality between data, reducing the total storage footprint. Depending on that data commonality, deduplication ratios can become quite high—for instance, consider 100 × Windows Virtual Machines, each built from a standard template and each sized for 100 GB. At the point where these systems are deployed, they are practically byte-for-byte copies of one another, with only some registry details and basic configuration settings differing. Stored with thick provisioning (i.e., all the required capacity allocated up-front), 100 × 100 GB virtual machines would occupy 10,000 GB of storage—9.76 TB. With global deduplication on the storage array though, that number shrinks dramatically. Assuming the deployed base image achieves even just a mediocre 2:1 deduplication ratio,* you might be mistaken for thinking this would result in storage requirements of 4.88 TB. Remember though each of those virtual machines will deduplicate against each other, and the commonality there will be extremely high in a just-deployed scenario. In fact there might be as much as 99.5% commonality between the virtual machine images; even if the first virtual machine stores in only 50 GB of data, each subsequent virtual machine may require as little as 0.5 GB of additional primary storage initially. The total occupied size then after deduplication for 100 × 100 GB virtual machines would be 99.5 GB. (In fact, this sort of storage has proven to be a common workload for all-flash storage—virtual desktop infrastructure.) Of course, post-deployment they will end up being a potentially large amount of drift between virtual machines as they are used for different functions. In fact, it is usual to see primary storage systems using deduplication sized for a lower level of deduplication than we might see in say, protection storage appliances, due to the different operational workloads and reduced number of identical/near identical copies.

As all-flash storage becomes increasingly available and leverages deduplication to reach price-parity (or even be cheaper) than traditional disk-based storage systems, we will see a number of shifting dynamics in data protection.

There are several key examples of where flash—and particularly deduplicated flash storage systems—will have marked impacts on data protection: snapshots, replication, continuous data protection, and backup/recovery.

Consider first snapshot technology. In Chapter 10, we described a variety of snapshot techniques, such as Copy on First Write (CoFW), Copy on First Access (CoFA),

---

* Very unlikely if the virtual machines have been thickly provisioned and are mostly empty. In such a situation the first round deduplication might be 10:1 or higher, but we have used 2:1 for simplicity and account for a worst case scenario on the first set of data.

and Redirect on Write (RoW). Each of these snapshot techniques has particular performance implications—CoFW, for instance, is typically geared toward low-write situations, since any write performed against the original filesystem or LUN while the snapshot is active triggers three high level IO operations—a read of the original data, a write of the original data to the snapshot storage pool, and then a write of the new data to the original location.*

In the case of either maintaining active snapshots *or* releasing aged snapshots, there is some form of performance overhead involved, however small. On traditional spinning disk, even a small performance impact for a single snapshot can magnify quickly if a storage system is managing *hundreds* or more snapshots. While some of those performance impacts may logically still exist in an all-flash system, the level of impact given the IO performance of all-flash systems will drop substantially. This will allow more snapshots to be kept without fear of maintenance tasks eating into system performance, and the increased number of IO operations required for writes while snapshots are active (e.g., for CoFW) will not be felt when the overall storage operates orders of magnitude faster than traditional disk systems. Indeed, well-designed systems optimized for flash will likely eschew traditional snapshot options such as CoFW and instead use dynamic pointer tables, allowing ease of access to any snapshot with little or even no performance impact. With deduplication applied to the snapshot storage pool as well, the cost of capacity for maintaining more snapshots will also be reduced.

Likewise, replication should see benefits in an all-flash deduplicated storage environment. As we have observed over the past decade or more with deduplication in backup environments, replicating the deduplicated data substantially reduces the overall bandwidth requirements. One TB of data deduplicated down to 100 GB will require far less bandwidth to replicate than 1 TB of data in its original form. Coupled with falling bandwidth costs, this will result in companies being able to replicate more of their data, granting higher availability and fault tolerance for more systems and business functions.

Continuous Data Protection—journaled replication of data—could enter new realms of utility in all-flash storage systems. With the journals held on flash, and snapshots allowing for access to the journaled data at any time-stamp, some systems may be switched away from backup and recovery for short-term retention, relying almost entirely on CDP. (This of course would be dependent on ensuring the CDP copy is sufficiently "off platform" to provide protection against a failure in the primary storage system.)

It is in backup and recovery systems that we will see perhaps the biggest *challenges* from flash storage. The transfer speed from flash storage—even factoring rehydrating the data for a read operation—substantially outstrips that of a normal read from hard drive–based storage. Flash storage will likely drive much higher adoption of source (or at least distributed) deduplication technology—it will be imperative to keep pushing down the network capacity required for backup data transfer, otherwise backing up all-flash hosted data will be a tedious and slow process.

---

* Note that *doesn't* include updating pointers for the snapshot or any underlying multi-IO operations required by RAID systems, particularly in sub-block updates.

Inline, distributed and source deduplication will hold at bay for a while the need to shift to all-flash data protection storage for PBBAs and IDPAs, but just as tape eventually was supplanted by disk, we may too see disk supplanted by flash in data protection storage to drive the next generation of performance gains.

Flash storage was initially introduced into primary storage via tiering—as data was more frequently accessed it would be promoted up from traditional disk storage onto flash storage to speed up operations against it, and the reverse would occur when the data was no longer being frequently accessed. This seems a logical place for flash to be introduced into data protection storage as well. This will allow for more secondary use cases for data protection storage, increasing its utility to businesses. Backups of key databases might be pushed into flash storage for high speed access in big data systems, and large data sets being accessed interactively (e.g., virtual machine "instant access" functions) might see the deduplicated data copied up into the flash tier at the start of the request, allowing for higher speed random access to the data.

Will data protection storage eventually go "all-flash" too? This will potentially be a longer-term game for data protection: since data protection is already leveraging deduplication, and doing so to logically store potentially hundreds or thousands of similar copies of data, switching to all-flash *now* given the economics of high density flash storage doesn't make sense. If the economics of flash storage drops such that the per-GB cost of flash and traditional hard drive storage *without deduplication* reaches parity, this would become the tipping point to seeing all-flash data protection storage going main-stream. Until that point, flash tiers in data protection storage seem to be a more logical technology trend.

There is no doubt that flash storage will alter the dynamics of data protection activities—CDP, snapshots, and replication in particular will all benefit. While there will be some challenges faced by backup and recovery services when dealing with all-flash data, new use cases for data protection storage being introduced into the business with flash tiers, delivering additional benefits, will drive down the perceived cost of data protection storage.

24 In Closing

Our species has lived through a variety of ages: we speak of the stone age, the bronze age, and the iron age, and each were named after the most prevalently used or important material. Depending on your culture or geographic background, other "ages" are somewhat fluid and may have more elements (e.g., European culture is usually classified as having had a medieval age as well). More recently at around the turn of the eighteenth century, the leap into the Industrial age happened.

If we're to name ages based on the most prevalently used resource, we're now in the early days of an *information age*. This makes data protection a critical activity for any organization: infrastructure can be rebuilt, replaced, or superseded; staff are replaceable and customers come and go, but the real value of a business is its data. (Look at what happens when a business collapses: any infrastructure is sold off at rock bottom prices, employees leave, and the real horse trading happens over the intellectual property—the *information* of the business.)

A cynic might suggest that the most prevalently used resource now is *money*, but since we're long past counting money in terms of bars of gold bullion stored in a vault, you might equally say that money, too, is merely information.

The core reason for data protection has remained the same for the entire history of the IT industry: bad things happen. Yet in itself this fundamental reason is no longer the *only* driving force behind innovation in data protection. Data protection may be a form of an insurance policy, but businesses seeking to creatively leverage their IT investments and wanting to drive through cost optimization are increasingly looking at data protection as a mechanism to achieve those goals. Thus, data protection is also becoming an *enabler* for new processes around data movement and data processing.

Despite the seeming panacea of the Cloud, we're learning that it doesn't matter *where* your data is, there's still a high degree of certainty that you have to be actively involved *at some level* in its protection. In the most extreme "as a service" models this will simply mean ensuring you choose the correct protection policy, but for most businesses it will require more involvement for some time to come.

Data protection is not a one-size-fits-all strategy, and it's a topic still continuing to evolve. Options now common were practically unheard of a decade ago, and there is little doubt a peek 10 years into the future would reveal a significantly different landscape again.

A progressive and adaptable data protection environment will be layered, use appropriate tools, enable automation and orchestration, and will integrate at the most important layer: reporting and monitoring, such as that shown in Figure 24.1. Ideally, as business requirements change with the system being built as a framework, appropriate products to provide protection should be slotted into the protection layer, and products no longer required should be retired—without disruption to the business or the business functions. The monitoring/reporting and orchestration/automation layers should be the visible aspects of data protection and resemble the proverbial duck on a pond.

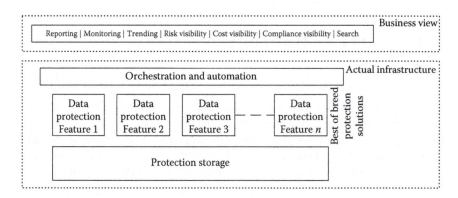

FIGURE 24.1 A holistic view of a data protection environment.

Truly effective data protection comes from a holistic approach considering the entire data lifecycle and all required SLAs. Data protection is not RAID, is not erasure coding, and nor is it continuous availability, replication, snapshots, or backups—it is *all* of them, combined in a considered and measured approach to meet *all* the requirements of the business. Indeed, with growing adoption of flash/solid state storage we're seeing new opportunities and challenges for data protection. *Challenges*, because on top of cloud, big data, virtualization and convergence, data protection now needs to keep up with storage systems that are leaping ahead in performance, disrupting a rather long status quo. *Opportunities* because low latencies and the phenomenal access speeds of flash will enable more agile approaches to data protection to emerge—as well as secondary use cases to data residing on protection storage.

A modern approach to data protection requires optimized, appropriate, and integrated technology, but that's only one part to the equation. Virtualization, converged infrastructure, and the Cloud are all driving us toward having *infrastructure administrators* who are able to work up the entire infrastructure stack. Big data is driving businesses to find more efficient approaches to moving around and safe-guarding data. Through it all, the price of information—the *value* to the business—is going up and up, making the role of a data protection advocate critical to business success.

An agile, integrated approach to data protection based on frameworks and extensibility is no longer a luxury, but a necessity.

Appendix A

GLOSSARY OF TERMS AND ACRONYMS

Term	Description
CapEx	**Capital Expenditure**. Upfront infrastructure or component investment typically performed on a longer-term budgetary cycle (e.g., 1–3 years).
Cascading Failure	A series of two or more failures that exceed the architected protection limits and cause a data loss scenario. For instance, having the second drive in a mirror fail while the first is being replaced from a previous failure would be an example of a cascading failure.
CDP	**Continuous Data Protection**. Refers to a form of replication that occurs concurrently with the actual write stream to a storage target. A write interceptor or splitter is inserted into the data path and writes that are intended for the target storage system are also committed to an alternate storage system. CDP may be either synchronous (requiring write-acknowledgment from both the primary and secondary destination before the acknowledgement is sent back to system that issued the write) or asynchronous (where write-acknowledgment to only the primary destination is required before the acknowledgment is sent back to the system that issued the write; the write to the secondary target can be buffered and issued within specific timeframes based on link speed and/or configured timers.
CLI	**Command Line Interface**. Utilities and options that can be executed on a command line (e.g., Windows prompt or PowerShell, Unix shell/terminal).
DevOps	**Development and Operations**. Software development activities designed primarily for automating IT services within an organization. It requires a high level of integration between the developers and the rest of the IT staff (particularly infrastructure staff), and use of deeply functional APIs provided by vendors of the infrastructure used. DevOps originated from Agile development methods that emphasize regular incremental release cycles with continuous feedback and improvement rather than large multi-month or multi-year blocks of development.
IOPS	**Input/Output Operations Per Second**. A common mechanism for reporting the average number of read/write operations a storage system can perform. This can be highly variably depending on the storage system and workload, so key metrics usually include *sustained* and *peak*. While there are other factors, in very broad terms the more IOPS a storage system can deliver, the faster any storage related processing *can* be.

(Continued)

Term	Description
LUN	**Logical Unit Number**. A logical addressable piece of storage presented to an operating system, typically from a SAN. While originally LUN was intended to refer merely to the specific SCSI address for a storage target, it is typically now used to refer to a logical disk presented by a SAN.
NAS	**Network Attached Storage**. Similar in concept to a SAN, with many of the same advanced data protection options and management that is independent of the accessing systems, NAS is focused on *file*-based storage rather than block-based storage.
OpEx	**Operational Expenditure**. Short-cycle running costs, such as energy, backup media (when tapes are used), and more recently, unit costs for Cloud computing, typically incurred on a monthly basis.
Parity	A mechanism used to achieve redundancy within storage systems; parity is calculated from the actual data, and both the data and parity are written. Typically associated with RAID.
RAID	**Redundant Array of Independent Disks**. A mechanism to protect data stored on disks (hard drives or SSD) such that the data can still be read even if one or more drives fail. The number of drives required, the number of drives that can simultaneously fail, and IO penalties depend entirely on the RAID level chosen. RAID is covered in detail in Chapter 16, Data Storage Protection.
REST API	**REpresentational STate API**. A programming interface that allows stateless interaction between the system being accessed and the application accessing it. This is favored by DevOps and agile development, particularly in infrastructure environments, as it allows a high degree of scaling and extensibility.
Retention (Governance) Lock	The option to write data in such a way that it cannot be deleted or modified until a retention time specified at write has passed, or a two-step delete has been issued: the command by a data administrator and the authorization by a security administrator. The two scenarios are both covered by various government regulatory definitions. In some instances, full retention-based locking may be required, and in others the 2-role delete featuring a security officer may be permitted.
ROI	**Return On Investment**. Specific benefits (both tangible/measurable and intangible) achieved as a result of implementing a particular process, operational change, or portion of infrastructure.
RPO	**Recovery Point Objective**. Refers to the amount of data that can be lost, e.g., an RPO of 1 hour indicates that at most 1 hour of data can be lost when performing a recovery from the most recent backup or data protection activity.
RTO	**Recovery Time Objective**. The maximum amount of time it can take to perform the nominated recovery. This will vary by organization as to whether the RTO countdown starts from when the request is made or from when the recovery actually starts.

(Continued)

Term	Description
SAS	**Serial Attached SCSI**
	The original form of the SCSI interface (see SCSI, further below) was *parallel*, meaning multiple devices could be connected together in a chain. SAS was developed as a variation of SATA, allowing each drive in an enclosure to be directly connected to a storage backplane, rather than in sequence.
SATA	**Serial ATA,** or **Serial AT Attachment**
	A commodity/consumer grade storage attachment mechanism common in desktop and laptop PCs and some lower cost storage systems aimed at mid-market and small office/home office. SATA was the extension to the classic "IDE" connection mechanism offering considerably higher throughput partly by having each drive connected directly to the backplane of the computer.
SCSI	**Small Computer Systems Interface.**
	A common connectivity protocol (and sometimes physical interface) typically used for communication between compute resources and storage systems.
SAN	**Storage Area Network**.
	A disk array that presents logical block storage assembled from a potential large number of physical devices to a number of hosts. SANs will typically feature advanced data protection in addition to a variety of RAID levels, all of which can be managed independently of a host that has mapped access to the storage.
SLA	**Service Level Agreement**.
	A contract between two parties for the meeting of specific operational targets. In backup and recovery, for instance, SLAs are typically expressed in terms of backup times, failure rates, and RPOs/RTOs.
SLO	**Service Level Objective**.
	An understanding of preferred operational targets that may not necessarily have contractual obligations.
SSD	**Solid State Disk.**
	Flash or memory-based storage technology (as opposed to traditional "spinning disk").
WORM	**Write Once, Read Many**.
	Traditionally representative of tape, WORM refers to applying compliance grade retention locks on data once it has been written, guaranteeing against modification or deletion prior to a specific time frame set by the storage, legal, or compliance requirements of the business.
ZLO	**Zero Loss Objective.**
	A term sometimes applied to systems that have an availability requirement of 100%.

Index